THIS
WORLD,
OTHER
WORLDS

This World, Other Worlds

Sickness, Suicide, Death, and the Afterlife among the Vaqueiros de Alzada of Spain

MARÍA CÁTEDRA

TRANSLATED BY
William A. Christian, Jr.

THE UNIVERSITY OF CHICAGO PRESS
Chicago and London

MARÍA CÁTEDRA teaches anthropology at the Universidad Complutense de Madrid. In 1992 she was the Edward Laroque Tinker Visiting Professor
in the Department of Anthropology at the University of Chicago.

The University of Chicago Press, Chicago 60637
The University of Chicago Press, Ltd., London
© 1992 by The University of Chicago
All rights reserved. Published 1992
Printed in the United States of America
00 99 98 97 96 95 94 93 92   5 4 3 2 1
ISBN (cloth): 0-226-09715-3
ISBN (paper): 0-226-09716-1

This translation is based on a revised version of *La muerte y otros mundos*,
published in 1988 by Ediciones Jucar, Madrid.

Library of Congress Cataloging-in-Publication Data

Cátedra Tomás, María.
  [Muerte y otros mundos. English]
  This world, other worlds : sickness, suicide, death, and the
afterlife among the Vaqueiros de Alzada of Spain / María Cátedra ;
translated by William A. Christian, Jr.
     p.   cm.
  Translation of: La muerte y otros mundos. 1988.
  Includes bibliographical references and index.
  1. Funeral rites and ceremonies—Spain—Asturias. 2. Cowboys—
Spain—Asturias. 3. Death—Religious aspects. 4. Death—Folklore.
5. Folk medicine—Spain—Asturias. 6. Asturias (Spain)—Social life
and customs. I. Title.
GT3262.A84C3813   1992
393'.08'8636—dc20   92-21044
                                                              CIP

⊗ The paper used in this publication meets the minimum requirements of the
American National Standard for Information Sciences—Permanence of Paper
for Printed Library Materials, ANSI Z39.48-1984.

TO BILL, SUSAN, AND JIM
COLLEAGUES AND, NONETHELESS, FRIENDS.

CONTENTS

CONTENTS

ILLUSTRATIONS

ACKNOWLEDGMENTS

The study of death is neither easy research nor a "cold" theme. This human situation is difficult and complex, extreme and radical like no other. It conceals solidarity. I received help, understanding, and intellectual stimulus from various persons and institutions. Among the latter, I must single out the Fundación Juan March. This foundation supported my work when I needed it most, generously financing part of my first stay with the Vaqueiros, my graduate work in the United States, and part of my thesis tuition. Among persons, Carmelo Lisón first taught me social anthropology, directed my first Ph.D. thesis from Madrid University, and patiently read most of what I wrote at the beginning of my professional life.

This book is a shortened version of my doctoral thesis for the University of Pennsylvania. I spent three years in the anthropology department there, an excellent place for scholarship. My two tutors, Ward H. Goodenough and Ruben E. Reina, have been extremely gracious and helpful in many ways. I thank Goodenough for much of my theoretical preparation, for helping me to shape the idea of the work and plan the research, and for his careful editing of the manuscript. I thank Reina especially for his knowledge of the Hispanic world. Professors William Davenport and Edward F. Foulks provided valuable criticisms and suggestions. I also benefited from contact with Professors Bernard Wailes, Igor Kopytoff, Brian Spooner, Anthony Wallace, Dell Hymes, and the late Erwin Goffman. Ray L. Birdwhistell suggested the topic of the thesis to me when we were talking about Spaniards, life, and death.

On my return to Spain I joined the department of anthropology at the Universidad Complutense de Madrid, where I have learned much from my colleagues Teresa San Roman (for her work with Gypsies), Blanca Asensi (for her help with early drafts), and Enrique Luque (for his sensitive—and sometimes ironic—criticism and suggestions about the manuscript). José L. Garcia, Ramón Valdés, and Luis Fernandez-Galiano also read the manuscript in its entirety, providing helpful insights. The first two are research fellows in neighboring areas of Asturias. The last two were part of a jury that granted part of this work the first prize of the Premio Nacional de Investigación "Marqués de Lozoya" del Ministerio de Cultura in 1986. I shared portions of the work with Claudine Fabre-Vassas and Daniel Fabre in Toulouse, Joan Frigolé in Cataluña, Marcial Gondar in Galicia, Julian Pitt-Rivers, Stanley Brandes, Renate L. Fernandes, José A. Nieto, and Alberto Cardín. Other fellows at the Facultad de Ciencias Políticas y Sociología read and advised in different ways: Eduardo Crespo, Jesús Leal, Felipe Reyero, Txema Uribe, and Blanca Olías. The Hon. L. W. Bonbrake M.P., and Joseba Zulaika were very sympathetic and discerning critics. My gratitude includes Joan Prat, one of the oldest and most faithful and affectionate readers of my work, and Les Freeman, a new reader but just as helpful and effective. I also thank the careful reading and valuable suggestions of an anonymous reviewer, and David Brent, editor at the University of Chicago Press, for his patience and his interest in the manuscript. The book and its translation have been much improved by the painstaking copyediting of Ellen Feldman.

Listening to the Vaqueiros speak about death and life was an unforgettable experience. The centrality of their ideas and sentiments in my work is obvious. I will not mention any of them by name, but I would like to say that after so many years I cannot forget them, dead or alive. To my Vaqueiro and *aldeano* friends, I express my heartfelt gratitude for the patience and affection they offered. Although they did not totally understand my work, they confided in me, took me into their houses, taught me their culture, and most important, gave me their love. That the feeling was mutual I hope will be evident from the work that follows.

Finally, I was fortunate to share the friendship and ideas of three American anthropologists who were working or had worked on neighboring areas, Cantabria and other districts of Asturias: William A. Christian, Jr., Susan Tax Freeman, and James W. Fernandez. Their work, which focuses respectively on religion, marginal groups and cultural metaphors, served as a model of thinking and research; as friends they boosted my spirits when I was down. Bill Christian has translated this work, in a way enriching it by his editing and his suggestions. I thank him for his stimulation and his patience, and for the time he spent doing the translation at the expense of his own fascinating research. All of them have been very generous with their care, time and efforts with this work and, perhaps more convinced of its worth than I, have pushed for its publication in English. I dedicate it to them for the pleasure afforded me by their personal and professional cross-cultural friendship.

ACKNOWLEDGMENTS

INTRODUCTION

In 1971, while I was doing fieldwork among the Vaqueiros in the far north of Spain, I followed in great detail a suicide in a hamlet up the mountains from where I was staying. I was working at that time on my dissertation for the Universidad Complutense de Madrid on the way of life (not the way of death) of this group of cattle-raising people. The suicide interested me at once, and not only because of its inherent drama, for I quickly realized that the people there did not consider suicide a strange, inconceivable, or isolated event but something traditional and familiar. They had a name for suicide by hanging, *el cordelín* [the little cord], and compared this suicide in some detail with several others in the area. Furthermore, I was pointed to a study by a judge who, in the course of his profession, had noticed the high frequency of suicide in the Vaqueiro region (Soto Vázquez 1965).

I registered this event in my field notes, and it stuck in my memory until several years later when, having completed my graduate work at the University of Pennsylvania, I decided to return to the same group to study the process of death. This book, then, is an ethnographic account of the cultural construction of death, sickness, suicide, burial, and afterlife of the Vaqueiros de Alzada, a marginated transhumant people of the mountains of Asturias. My focus on death and not just on suicide is part of my theoretical framework. I believe that the contrast between suicide and natural death is relevant to understand both. Suicide as a subject has been treated primarily in isolation. I believe it should be studied within its wider context, a context that considers suicide not only as a form of death, but also includes the complex ritual of sickness and the passage to the other world. These apparently disparate phenomena are intricately interwoven. I hope this work will help understand suicide not as a pathology but as something culturally constructed, part of the system of local beliefs.

I approach the experience and interpretation of death among the Vaqueiros from a cultural rather than a social or psychological perspective. As a cultural account, the book focuses particularly on the cosmology implicit in death. My principal argument is that death is a process much broader and longer than has been supposed. For the Vaqueiros, death begins while one is still alive, and life con-

1

tinues after death. The passage to another world involves an intricate and complex set of symbols and sentiments.

THE PROBLEM

As I said, it was a suicide that led me to study death as a cultural process. Let me begin by looking briefly at the ways suicide has been studied. There are two basic approaches, sociological and psychopathological, and the classic proponents of these approaches have been Durkheim and Freud (Durkheim 1951 [1897]; Freud 1959a [1917], 1959b [1917]). Sociologists used official statistics as their basic data; psychologists used case histories. In general, both have studied suicide in Western societies. Sociologists after Durkheim have emphasized status, status integration, status change, aggression, social structure and ecology as independent variables (J. D. Douglas 1968, 1973). Psychological theories are divided into psychoanalytic and nonpsychoanalytic explanations, but both, by definition, search for the "cause" of suicide in the individual, not in the society (Jackson 1957). Most recent theories tend to involve a synthesis of sociological and psychological approaches. Thus sociologists now recognize the limitations of official statistics and advocate a more direct and richer method, like case histories and interviews with the family of the deceased (J. D. Douglas 1973, 163ff.; Breed 1963). On the other hand, psychologists have abandoned their clinical emphasis on suicide and its internal drama as a product of an idiosyncratic individual and mind.[1]

There is a third level, which has been neglected: the *cultural* aspect of suicide. Perhaps the best exponent of this approach is Maurice Halbwachs in his work, *Les Causes du suicide* (1930). What Halbwachs calls ways of life today could be translated as "culture," in the sense of shared and transmitted meanings (J. D. Douglas 1973, 128). Few anthropologists have dealt with suicide in different cultures, and only a handful have followed Halbwachs's cultural emphasis (Devereux 1931; Bohannan 1967; Iga 1961; Zilboorg 1936; Balikci 1960; La Fontaine 1975). Suicide has strong negative moral connotations in most Western cultures, a fact that may have impeded anthropologists from considering it objectively as a cultural phenomenon. By the same token, psychologists and sociologists have been the scholars most interested in suicide, but their final agenda is its prevention. The cultural anthropologist who chooses to study suicide must explore the nature of the morality attached to it rather than take it for granted.

The high frequency of suicide and the honor associated with the act among the upper classes of ancient Rome, the tradition of

2   INTRODUCTION

suicide in Japan, the importance of death by suicide in the European Romantic movement, among Scandinavians, and in Eskimo culture would suggest that the individual often reflects the attitudes of the culture at large with respect to suicide, death, and the afterlife.

Finally, the study of suicide has placed much emphasis on the act of self-destruction, very little on the meaning of death. While suicide is an individual and social act, as a form of death it is a cultural act as well. J. D. Douglas states this point of view and lays out part of the program for this study when he writes:

> When some "ronin" of Japan or some Asian Buddhists perform actions which lead to what American or European doctors classify as death, we must recognize that this is a classification by Western doctors, not by the actors involved. Their linguistic expressions for such actions may be totally different from the ones Western observers use and certainly might mean totally different things to the actors and the significant observers of these actions within their own cultures. Anthropologists and sociologists have decided that one cannot very well understand the kinship system of other peoples except in terms of their own language. How, then, can one conceivably understand something so immensely more complex as "death" in any terms other those of the actors involved? And, though the differences in meaning might not be as great within one general cultural tradition, still, does it not seem plausible to expect that there are some systematic differences of meaning involved in the uses of the term "death" between one nation and another or between one subculture and another? It is certainly my contention here that this is the case and that no great advantages can be made in the study of suicide until the researchers determine what these differences in the meaning of death are and how they influence the actions of individuals. (J. D. Douglas 1973, 182)

Every known culture has provided people with some answers to the meaning of death through religion, philosophy, and political ideology. The very fact of death is usually a socially significant event. However, very few studies have been made of it.[2] This is particularly true for anthropology. Death occurs as frequently as birth and more frequently than marriage, but these topics have a copious bibliography in comparison with the neglected last rite of passage. It seems that death has been a taboo, one that anthropologists, so interested in the taboos of others, have failed to detect in themselves (Gorer 1965). This taboo may be related to the notion of "privacy," a notion so venerated in the Anglo-Saxon world that it leads to a "natural reluctance to intrude in people's lives at a time of anguish" (Rosenblatt et al. 1976). When death is studied, it is held at a distance like something alien. P. Palgi and H. Abramovitch find that "when reading anthropological literature . . . one is left with the impression of coolness and remoteness. The focus is on the bereaved and on the corpse but never on the dying" (1984, 385). J. Fabian touched on the same idea in 1973 when he noted that research has centered on "how others die."

Some anthropologists have studied death as a heuristic device to get at other matters like societal institutions or aspects of social life. Thus W. A. Douglass describes the social structure of a Spanish Basque community through its funerary ritual (1969); J. Goody studies the system of inheritance and transmission of roles and rights in conjunction with mortuary institutions among the Lo-Dagaa and the LoWilii in Western Africa (1962); and G. Gorer utilizes death to investigate grief and mourning in a sample of the population of the British Isles (1965). These three works, representative of their approach to death, were written with diverse methods and aims. They emphasize social, economic, and psychological interests and approaches respectively, but all are centered more directly on "customs" and mortuary practice than on the person who is dying. As a general rule, the monographs begin with a corpse.

Douglass and Goody tend to emphasize the ritual and ceremonial apparatus of the people they study at the expense of their system of ideas, beliefs, values, sentiments, and attitudes. Such an emphasis is typical of the more sociological studies and the structural-functionalist tradition.[3] It is my contention that ritual and ceremonial behavior are important for understanding the ideological system, but that ideology can also help us to understand behavior. Anthropologists have the tools needed to pay attention to the conceptual aspects of culture and ideology in relation to death. They can draw out not only the obligations that death imposes upon society, but also a people's everyday understandings of a death that is inevitable for all. It is quite obvious that we learn how to live but not quite so obvious that we learn how to die. We have cultural norms for the way, form, time, and meaning of dying as well as a system of values and options for death.[4]

Palgi and Abramovitch have shown that "few areas of contemporary anthropological inquiry are still so dominated by *fin de siècle* thinking as in the study of death and mortuary ritual" (1984, 326), referring to the work of R. Hertz and A. Van Gennep. Both showed that death is not an instant event but rather a long process in which a transition to a different state of being occurs. Hertz pointed out that death as a social process begins with the funerary ritual (1960 [1907–9], 48). Van Gennep dealt with death as a rite of passage (1960 [1909], 11), a powerful and useful metaphor that has endured since the beginning of the century. For both authors, physical death is the beginning of an ongoing process. However, both fix the boundaries of death in a conservative way. They point out death a posteriori, but they fail to detect death a priori, the continuity of death in life, as in sickness, which is a part of the process of dying. Like suicide, sickness is another pathway to death, usually the most common one.[5] Perhaps this limited focus is due to the strong tendency to consider death as the removal of a social person from society, and thereby reduce the problem of death for society (Humphreys and King 1981).

T. Parsons (1963) has pointed out how in American society, death has been divorced from its long and complex relation with suffering because of technological advances. With a few exceptions—one is a paper by W. Goodenough (1975)[6]—anthropologists have not studied this relation thoroughly, although their methods (long stays in the fields) are appropriate to the task. Death can be viewed as a continuum whose center is the physical death itself. If either end of the continuum is studied in isolation—illness (the "before" of death) or the funeral (the "after" of death)—one loses perspective on the event as a process.

While few anthropologists have studied the "before" of death, its "after" was the focus of attention of early anthropologists (like Frazer 1913–24 and 1933–36, and Bendann 1930), especially in regard to three broad topics: cults of the dead, ancestor worship, and ideas on the afterlife and immortality. B. Malinowski (1954 [1925]), A. R. Radcliffe-Brown (1948), D. G. Mandelbaum (1965), W. L. Warner (1959), M. Gluckman (1937), G. Wilson (1935), C. Geertz (1960), and G. Lienhardt (1962) have followed this approach.[7] More recent work, including two excellent books published in 1982, L. M. Danforth's monograph on rural Greece and M. Bloch and J. Parry's collection have the same emphasis on after death.[8]

Probably for that reason, and because in anthropology one focuses on "how others die," the aftermath of death has been considered a basic part of religion. But I do not agree with this assessment. The theme of death is a clear instance of the scholarly problem of boundaries and demarcations of subjects of study. To search for the meaning of death in strictly religious terms is like considering the meaning of life the same way. Although the religious meaning attributed to death is important, so are the physical or social environment, the ethos, worldview, morality, and ideology.[9] Here again the problem of "how others think" arises. Paradoxically, when we study suicide or death in modern society, we tend to center on human and profane questions; when we study death in "primitive" societies, we focus on supernatural beliefs. In other words, the way that death is studied, the selection of the kind of data and the approaches used, affects the interpretation and definition of the phenomenon.

Anthropologists have written about the ideology of so-called primitive people as though it were a part of religion, because it is couched in what Western culture regards as supernatural terms. Indeed, religion has served as a kind of catchall category that includes every sort of phenomenon about which the anthropologist feels intellectually uneasy. This has distorted our understanding of religion, done inadequate justice to ideology, and perhaps unnecessarily reified notions of mental structures or compartments. In my view, this excessive use of the category "religion" reflects a certain ethnocentrism.

The Vaqueiros are officially a Catholic people, and they bury their dead with much the same ritual one would find anywhere else in Spain. In recent years especially, the Catholic Church has tended to accentuate uniformity in ritual and to suppress differences. However, the Vaqueiros are a marginated group not only ecologically and socially but religiously as well. The only time a priest normally enters Vaqueiro territory is when a death occurs. But it is precisely in death that Vaqueiros most clearly express their differences from conventional Catholicism. We will see what the similarities and the differences are between the official sphere and the local one.

The Catholic Church has institutionalized the problem of salvation in the context of the relation between the individual and the priest. Because of their marginal position, Vaqueiros participate very little in this relation and receive very few of the priest's services. They also lack knowledge of the corpus of doctrine a Catholic must know in order to achieve salvation in accordance with official norms. But the Vaqueiros have a rich ritual life of their own. Because they are outside religious control the Church exercises, Vaqueiros differ substantially from the Basques that Douglass describes.

> Basques are thoroughly Roman Catholic and manifest
> unquestioning adherence to Catholic doctrine. In the rural
> areas the local priest *is* the Church, and his interpretation of
> religion *is* the doctrine. The Basque clergy has traditionally
> emphasized a fundamentalist brand of religion. Sermons
> abound with fire and brimstone. The members of the congre-

INTRODUCTION

gation are warned to subordinate worldly pursuits and pleasures to a concern with their fate in the afterlife. Consequently, the Basque considers his death to be the most important event in his life cycle. What is more, it is not to be feared, since the purpose of life is preparation for death. (Douglass 1969, 209–10)[10]

Vaqueiros confront death under quite different conditions. I have tried to study death in Vaqueiro culture with warmth, close up, in a way in which the data does not lose its immediacy. To this end I use quotations extensively. They are essential to the thickness of the interpretation and provide a better understanding of the Vaqueiro point of view. Let us see who these people are and participate as much as we can in their experience.

THE PEOPLE

The Vaqueiros de Alzada live in the western part of Asturias, in the north of Spain near Galicia. The province comprises a band of land between the Cantabrian Mountains and the sea (see fig. 1). The *concejos*, or townships, that form the home base of the Vaqueiros (Luarca, Tineo, and Cangas de Narcea) are in the area more or less bounded by the Nalón and Navia Rivers (see fig. 2).[11] The number of Vaqueiros has been calculated to be about fifteen thousand, although estimates range as low as 6,448 (Soto Vázquez 1965, 174–75; Feo Parrondo 1980).

In this zone, the Vaqueiros are those people who live in the *brañas*, small hamlets on the crests and slopes of the mountains. Those who live in the same zone, but in the valleys or the flatter and more fertile areas, are not held to be Vaqueiros, but are called *aldeanos* or *xaldos*. For the sake of simplicity, in this study I will use the term Vaqueiro to refer to those who live in the *brañas*, but, as one will see from the quotations, it is a term that outsiders use for these people. It is used only infrequently by the people themselves. The Vaqueiros are dedicated almost exclusively to the raising of cattle. Some of them still practice an age-old system of transhumance in which the family group and their animals move up to the high pastures during much of the year. These places, known as *puertos* or *alzadas*, have provided Vaqueiros with the second half of their name, because they *alzar* [go up] or change their residence periodically. Their neighbors in the home zone, the *aldeanos*, are sedentary farmers, although they, too, have cows.

It is difficult to fit the Vaqueiros into a simple category of European cultural ecology. Geographically they occupy one of the marginal highlands of the Atlantic Fringe (Arensberg 1963; Kenny

Asturias

FIGURE 1 MAP OF SPAIN

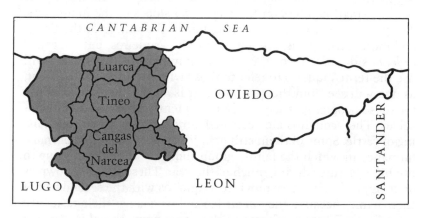

Vaqueiro Townships

FIGURE 2 MAP OF ASTURIAS

1963), but they are also utilizers of the final thrust of the circum-Alpine unit that R. K. Burns widened timidly to include the Pyrenees (Burns 1963). The form of transhumance practiced by the Vaqueiros, for example, is very similar to the old (now nonexistent) family-pastoral pattern of the Alps (Honigmann 1964; Burns 1963, 139). In any case, a parish, the normal administrative unit of the area, includes two kinds of ecological niches: the mountainous zone, with semidispersed and pastoral settlements (the *braña*), and the flat land of the valleys, whose inhabitants are concentrated in small agricultural villages.

The Vaqueiros de Alzada have a long past about which little is known. Although they owe the name Vaqueiros to the practice of cattle pastoralism, today the name evokes the idea of a caste or race, not a profession. The Vaqueiros traditionally have been stigmatized by their sedentary neighbors, who consider them an ethnic group different from the rest of the population. Some writers, regional and national, have classed the Vaqueiros as one of the "accursed races," one of the marginal groups of Spain, like the Chuetas of Mallorca, the Agotes of Navarra, the Pasiegos of Santander, the Maragatos of León, and the gypsies of the entire peninsula.

There are no specific references to the transhumance of Vaqueiros or their existence as a group until 1433, when the accounts of the Count de Luna list sums paid to Vaqueiros who had gone to Laciana, in the south of the province, from the coastal region (Uría Riu 1976, 123).[12] Fifty years later, in 1485, two documents of the Catholic monarchs provide evidence that the Vaqueiros considered themselves a group and constituted a *pueblo*. The first document is a complaint Vaqueiros filed because of attacks against them and their cattle, in which they ask for protection; the second is an order sent to the *corregidor* of the principality and its *justicia* that they be protected.

Later documents confirm the situation described in these earliest ones. Some have to do with payment of rent for pastures, generally in kind—cheese, butter, wax, and so on—and others involve complaints and lawsuits for various grievances and taxes the Vaqueiros considered excessive. It seems that although the Vaqueiros paid for the use of pastureland, in times of drought the *aldeanos* who owned the land tried to keep the Vaqueiros out because they needed the pasture themselves. To support their claims, the *aldeanos* referred to themselves as *vecinos* [residents], with rights deriving from obligations like the taxes they paid to the *concejo*, as opposed to the Vaqueiros, who were only *half*-residents because they spent half the year in one township, the other half somewhere else, and attempted to avoid the taxes in both places.

Vaqueiros do seem to have used the concept of half-residency to suit their convenience. In 1523, several Vaqueiros from the township of Valdés (now called Luarca) complained to the authorities that the township had charged them taxes as if they were residents when they were really "outsiders and itinerants." The *aldeanos* subsequently cited this itinerancy to keep the Vaqueiros from using township pastures and to discriminate against them in other contexts. In 1776, in a lawsuit concerning the parish of La Espina in the township of Salas, a group of Vaqueiros de Alzada sued the *aldeanos* in relation to seating and other honors in the church, which they had been denied. One of the plaintiffs denied he was a Vaqueiro on ecological grounds: he did not move, but rather maintained a fixed residence, tilled his fields, and paid his tithes and other taxes like any other full resident (Acevedo y Huelves 1915, 83, 131).

The discrimination against Vaqueiros took different forms. The most notorious was the separation of Vaqueiros from *aldeanos* in the local churches, by placing either a physical barrier or marker like a pole or beam on the floor across which "Vaqueiros will not pass to hear mass." In some places Vaqueiros were obligated to enter the church by a door, known as *la puerta falsa*, different from the main entrance used by the *aldeanos*.[13] These customs (which originally may have been related to social class, since according to the historian J. Uría Riu, certain noble Vaqueiros had preferential seating) seem to have gotten worse in the eighteenth century. At that time, in at least one parish, it was forbidden to give communion to Vaqueiros except at the door of the church in any circumstance. Discrimination in church seating and ceremonies also occurred with regard to burial sites. Those Vaqueiros buried inside were buried the farthest away from the altar; in cemeteries they were given the least prestigious plots, worse even than those of paupers from the *aldeas*. Their funerals were stigmatized by the use of the "bad" crucifixes and the least honorific ceremonies. And Vaqueiros were denied the right to carry banners of images in religious ceremonies.

This discrimination against Vaqueiros in churches may have originated in the obligation of all parishioners to pay tithes, for the transhumant life-style of the Vaqueiros made it easier for them to avoid paying than for the resident *aldeanos*. In addition to these material reasons for discrimination against Vaqueiros by parish priests, the Vaqueiros were often not model Catholics. Their transhumant way of life and the isolation of the *brañas* meant that their religious conduct and their level of catechization was, to say the least, deficient. An eighteenth-century memoir for the Synodal Constitutions of Oviedo points out that the Vaqueiros "are more concerned with providing earthly fodder to their animals than in receiving spiritual fodder for their souls" and recommends that they not be allowed to serve as third-person witnesses in lawsuits "because they would come to them almost in the same circumstances as in the Indies," that is, with little regard for a sacred oath.

The Vaqueiros encountered similar problems with town governments when they attempted to avoid the payment of local taxes. In several townships they were forced to remain in their *brañas* and forbidden to make their seasonal migration. In a 1536 suit, the Vaqueiros appealed these laws, claiming that as poor persons they were forced by necessity to move with their families, cattle, and households whereas the rich could afford to be sedentary and send a hired hand with the cattle to the summer pasture. In their suit they pointed out that they paid their full share of town taxes. On other occasions they were forced to move, forced even to take the doors off their barns so that the *aldeanos* could use the hay and pastureland that they had vacated. Another legal problem was caused by the Vaqueiros' avoidance of military service, since many of them were not on the rolls in any place at all. In 1752, a royal resolution sought to put an end to this situation, which nonetheless continued well into the nineteenth century. To cite another kind of civil discrimination, in 1718 Vaqueiros were not allowed to vote or run for local office, even if they paid local taxes.

In addition to this religious and civil discrimination, the Vaqueiros experienced everyday social discrimination at the hands of the *aldeanos* wherever the two groups came into contact: bars and taverns, dances, fiestas, and churches. The Vaqueiros held their own dances or fiestas and religious holidays; they were not welcome at those of the *aldeanos*. Many of the fights and confrontations between the two groups, until very recently, took place on the dance floor. With this virtual prohibition on mixing in the main arena of local courtship, it is no surprise that for centuries Vaqueiros of necessity have been endogamous. In bars, Vaqueiro men were served with containers made of horn while *aldeanos* were served with glasses.[14] And the church, too, frequented especially by women and children, has been the site of many fights and incidents, usually when Vaqueiros attempted to cross the demarcation line and occupy the preferred seating. Such incidents often would occur during Vaqueiro funerals.

The backdrop and justification for all this discrimination has been the theory that Vaqueiros have a different origin than their neighbors, the *aldeanos*. In addition to documenting certain local traditions, over the last two centuries scholars from the region and the nation have attempted to prove these origins "scientifically," or have created others through conjecture and dubious historical research. Most of the work on the Vaqueiros' origins shows the persistence of theories and intellectual fashion with little or no historical justification (Cátedra 1986b, 1984).

I have stated elsewhere my thoughts on the margination of the Vaqueiros, which I will summarize here only briefly (Cátedra 1976b).[15] I consider the racial ideology about supposed ethnic origins to be a cultural-historical myth. Both local groups have their own myths about the origins of the *braña* dwellers. The *aldeanos* insist on the idea of a race, in particular the Moorish race, manipulating the historic symbols of the region for their own purposes. Vaqueiros, on the other hand, seek to explain their origins by traditions related to their way of life and ecology, traditions that also take the form of myths but have a different content than those of their neighbors. Apart from the idea of race or origin, the sentiments expressed by members of both groups contain a set of attitudes and concrete experiences that forms the base of the myth and sustains it. Although the external signs of discrimination against the Vaqueiros have disappeared, each group still considers itself very different from the other, and one still can sense tension and antagonism between them. One must ask, then, what does being a Vaqueiro mean? Or, conversely, under what circumstances does Vaqueiro identity become diluted or disappear? These circumstances are quite precise: when the Vaqueiro is rich, lives in the city, attends church frequently, and knows enough church doctrine; or does not speak in dialect, and has a good education, has friendships with *aldeanos* and bears him- or herself correctly in their presence, etc. If we take the obverse of these conditions, we have the essence of being a Vaqueiro. One might argue that these values are subjective and relative, but so is the racial ideology that sustains them. Nevertheless, there are also some more objective criteria. Vaqueiros and *aldeanos* cannot communicate to a significant degree because they speak differently, both literally and metaphorically. They use different dialects and raise different topics for conversation. Furthermore, they *do* different things as transhumant pastoralists and as farmers. And they even eat different things. While ways of speaking, working, and eating constitute important differences between these two groups, there are other things, like ways of thinking, that are even more critical.

The question "What is it to be a Vaqueiro?" is not and has never been as important as "What *was* a Vaqueiro?"—that is, what was the origin of these people, their mythic history, and the race from which they came? The evidence of the present is used primarily as clues to the past. All historical evidence leads us to believe that it is the way of life the Vaqueiros lead, now as in the past, and the difference between this way of life and that of their neighbors, that explains why there should need to be a myth in the first place. In the literary ramblings, the pseudohistorical divagations, and in the local oral tradition itself there is much that is revealing about Spanish intransigence, a regional chauvinism and a local ethnocentrism when faced with a diverse ways of life and thinking. It is no coincidence that the "Moorish race" theory should be the one most favored as the origin of the Vaqueiros, given a war of eight hundred years in the peninsula and the Vaqueiros' presence in the region where that war began. Spaniards maintained their sensitivity toward the idea of race in the centuries after the reconquest through a preoccupation with purity or cleanliness of lineage [limpieza de sangre]. This preoccupation may also be seen after 1492 in the new fervor regarding the theory of the purity of Mary, the Immaculate Conception.[16] In any case, the formation of these ethnic categories and the emphasis on purity is fundamental to Spanish history, and molds religion, culture, and even scientific thinking.

Each house in the braña has its own space and functions as an independent territorial unit. The larger shelter contains the living quarters, the attic, and the stables in a single building. At one side is a hayloft; sometimes there are storehouses for corn, gorse, and firewood. The stables are the most important part of the house— the part that receives the most care, is the most modern, and has first priority. The living quarters are built above the stables as a function of how much space is taken up by the cows.[17]

Agricultural activity varies from braña to braña. Vaqueiros mainly cultivate corn, but raise clover, alfalfa, rye, potatoes, and a small garden as well. The brañas where the people are transhumant, for instance, reduce cropping to a minimum while sedentary Vaqueiros plant more. Both transhumant and sedentary Vaqueiros, however, devote most of their attention in the summer to their prados, or meadows, which constitute the majority of braña land. The braña crops, with the exception of a very small proportion destined for the household, are grown for the animals. In addition to cows, the Vaqueiros have pigs and mules or horses. Until a few years ago, the braña children used to tend flocks of sheep in the surrounding monte. Most houses maintain two pigs, which supply an important part of the protein in the Vaqueiro diet. The Vaqueiros eat hens on important occasions and eat eggs daily. They use mules as a means of transport and also to help cultivate of the fields. All of these animals are useful but not absolutely essential to life in the *braña*.

This is not true of the cow. As one Vaqueiro says, "A noble cow, you love it like a person. Because we here, without cattle, are nothing. Here there is nothing else. The cows provide food and four *pesetas* for shoes and clothes." Vaqueiro households maintain six or eight cows and a number of calves. They may also have a bull or a couple of oxen, although this is not typical. The number of cows a house will have depends on how much land they have. It is often necessary for a house to buy cornmeal or feed to maintain its herd. The traditional *braña* animal is the "red" cow, a tough, strong animal adapted to the environment. These cows graze in the meadows all year round, even in the cold. If necessary, they can spend long stretches in the *monte* during the summer. The red cow also is put to work. It gives little milk compared with other breeds, but its milk is high in fat content and ideal for nourishing calves. The main purpose of the cattle in the *braña* is to produce the calves that the Vaqueiros sell for meat. The owner accompanies the calves and cows to be sold to the cattle fairs. The most important are the district fairs, which take place once a year in the larger *aldeas*. There are also monthly fairs in the smaller towns, which serve as commercial centers.

The Vaqueiros' dependence on their cows results in their transhumance. The earliest descriptions of Vaqueiros have them going up to the high pastures near the León border from Saint Michael's Day in the spring (May 18) to Saint Michael's Day in the fall (September 29). This massive, long-distance transhumance has long since been eliminated. Indeed today the majority of the Vaqueiros are sedentary, live year-round in the *brañas*, and till their fields. Virtually all Vaqueiros remember and once made an intermediate-distance transhumant migration in the summer, known as the *puerto de Cangas*, although none make it now.[18] During these migrations, the cattle roamed the pastureland of the mountains freely day and night; and one of the Vaqueiros, called "the *vaqueiro*," was delegated to tend them. He would stay in a small hut that served as both dwelling and stables, and he would care for his own animals, those of his relatives, and those of anyone else who hired his services.

The short-distance transhumance still practiced today is known as "two hearths" or "two lives." In the small zone I studied, more than three hundred persons practice it.[19] In this system there are more frequent trips (eight moves), more transhumants from each house, and more moving of persons, goods, and cattle back and forth between the winter *braña* and the *braña de alzada*, middle-altitude pastureland in the interior of the province. The difference in altitude between winter and summer quarters is about five hundred meters, and the trip can take anywhere from three to eight hours. This contrasts with the *puerto de Cangas*, where the difference in altitude with the winter *braña* was about one thousand meters and the trip took two days. Unlike the *vaqueiros* of the *puerto de Cangas*, those of the *alzadas* care only for their own cattle. A winter *braña* may be totally transhumant or only partially so; in some winter *brañas*, only one or two houses are transhumant while the rest are sedentary.

This "two hearth" system provides a balanced way to exploit two altitude zones alternately and intermittently for raising cattle. The cattle are nourished with the hay reserves and the growth of the meadows and wild pasture in both zones. Moves between *brañas* are timed to take maximum advantage of the climatic differences between the two zones and to diminish the risk of damaging the meadows by overgrazing. In times of drought, the *braña de alzada* pastures remain green because of their altitude, and in the winter *braña*, the transhumants have protection from snow and bad weather. The Vaqueiros refer to these transhumant trips as *pasear el carro*, because carts [*carros*] are used to move between the two *brañas*.

When I spoke of the location of the "house" in the *braña* I was not referring merely to the building. For Vaqueiros the idea of *casa* is much more expansive: it includes the land that pertains to the house (in fields, meadows, and *monte*), animals, persons, absent family members, and even the dead.[20] In spite of the fact that houses may differ considerably in number of inhabitants, for social purposes the house, not the family or the *vecino*, is the critical social unit in the *braña*. Even in cases where the dwellings of both the winter *braña* and *alzada* are occupied year-round, they are considered one house. All socially significant activity is house-marked, as it were. People are not known by their given name but rather by that of the house.

Normally the house is inherited by only one of its members, in theory the *mayorazo*, or eldest son, of the owner of the house. In practice, the owner, *el amo*, can choose any of his sons or daughters as heir. When the heir is married, he or she is said to be "married in the house" while siblings are said to be "married outside the house." The inheritance system, known as the *manda*, consists in ceding to the favored heir as much as two-thirds of the house and the right to have an equal share of the remaining third. Many wills state clearly that this final third, the *legítima*, must be paid or received only in money, and always at the convenience of the heir.[21] This assures that the house will not be divided but will be handed down intact from generation to generation. There is a strong moral value attached to the integrity of the house, rooted in a sound ecological, economic base. As Vaqueiros will tell you, "Even though it all goes to one person, it's not very much. One lives badly off it, everyone [siblings] together couldn't live off it at all. Here there would only be hunger and a lot of people." For there is little slack here. The house is a family enterprise that can support a limited number of persons, generally the *amo* and his spouse, the heir and his spouse, and the children of the younger couple. The farm work and the pastoral work are distributed proportionally among all persons, creating an equilibrium that would be destroyed if the house were divided. That is why the heir's siblings must choose between remaining single and working for the heir in the house, or leaving the house, whether to get married to some other heir or to work "out in the world," either in Spanish cities or in other countries.

There are two ways to cede an inheritance. The most common method is by will. The *amo* draws up a will before a notary public, favoring one of his sons or daughters. Such a will can be changed any time before the *amo*'s death. The chosen heir is obligated to (1) care for parents and "all the old people of the house" (uncles, servants) until they die, attending them in their illnesses and old age; (2) allow unmarried siblings to remain in the house until they marry or leave of their own accord; (3) work in the house under the orders of the *amo*, without salary or personal funds, until the *amo* dies or is physically incapacitated. It is common for the parents to "help" the heir in choosing a spouse, with an eye to the dowry that will come to the house. The other method of inheritance is by deed, which is not a provisional agreement but an irrevocable transaction. In practice, through fake sales, the house can be transferred almost entirely to the heir before the *amo* dies.

It is hard to say just where the zone under study begins and ends. I have studied the parish of Naraval, together with another, Villatresmil, which I used for contrast. But in practice, the zone I studied was larger and more varied. It did not correspond to any religious or administrative territory because it took its shape from the natural activities of the Vaqueiros (see fig. 3).

The parish of Naraval belongs to Tineo, but it has a stronger relation with the township of Luarca. Boundaries virtually disappear in certain contexts since, for example, all of the social and commercial life of Naraval is closely related to Luarca, which is

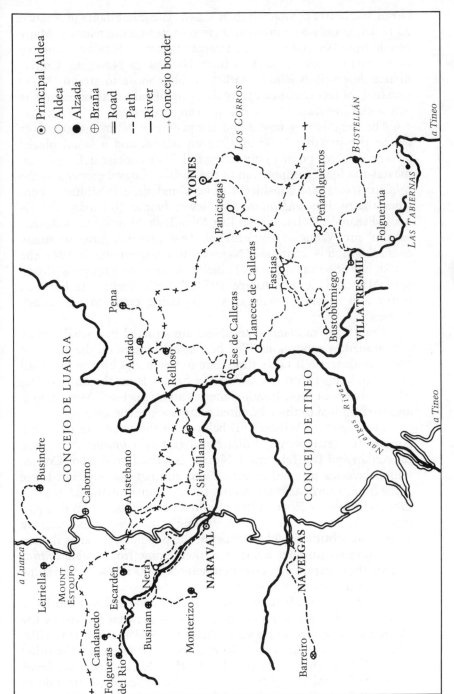

MAP 3   STUDIED ZONE

Principal Aldea
Aldea
Alzada
Braña
Road
Path
River
Concejo border

CONCEJO DE LUARCA

CONCEJO DE TINEO

a Luarca
Leiriella
Busindre
MOUNT ESTOUPO
Caborno
Candanedo
Folgueras del Rio
Escardén
Nerá
Businan
Aristebano
Monterizo
Silvallana
NARAVAL
Barreiro
NAVELGAS
Navelgas River
Pena
Adrado
Relloso
Ese de Calleras
Llaneces de Calleras
Paniciegas
Los Corros
AYONES
Fastias
Bustoburniego
Peñafolgueiros
VILLATRESMIL
Folgueirúa
Bustellán
Las Tabiernas
a Tineo
a Tineo

closer and better connected than Tineo. The inhabitants of Naraval go to Tineo only for administrative or bureaucratic reasons. Many people from Naraval go to the Luarca market on Sundays; other go to a market four kilometers from Naraval in Navelgas. Convenience determines which market people choose to attend. A few hundred meters distance can make a significant differences in the way social interactions and relations are structured.

The neighboring towns and the people of Naraval themselves define the parish as "Naraval, seven *brañas* and a small place" ["*Naraval, siete brañas y un tchugar*"]. This concise definition indicates the local composition of the parish; Naraval proper and the *tchugar* (Nera) are considered *aldeas*, and their inhabitants consider themselves *aldeanos*. The seven *brañas* (Businán, Candanedo, Escardén, Folgueras del Rio, Silvallana, Monterizo, and Aristébano) are Vaqueiro settlements. Few parishes have so many *brañas*, which is what made Naraval interesting to me. In 1971, the parish had 568 inhabitants (225 *aldeanos* and 343 Vaqueiros) (Instituto Nacional de Estadística 1973).[22] Each *braña* has between thirty and seventy inhabitants comprising eight to one dozen houses.

The *aldeas* of Naraval and Nera are situated in a small valley surrounded by mountains. The *brañas* are located on the slopes of these mountains. It takes time (one to two hours by foot on small paths) and effort to reach any of the *brañas* from the *aldeas*. The *aldeas* are about three hundred meters above sea level. Most *brañas* are two hundred to three hundred meters above the *aldeas*.

The parish of Villatresmil belongs to the township of Tineo. Among its settlements, Villatresmil has two *brañas de alzada* (Bustellán and Las Tabiernas). Nearby is a third *braña*, Los Corrus, which belongs to another parish and another *concejo*. But these three *brañas* form a single habitat for the transhumants. A total of fifty-eight houses (about three hundred persons) make up this particular transhumant population.[23] Some come from *brañas* that are mainly transhumant, where most of the population makes the annual move to summer quarters. Others come from stable *brañas* and are the exception among their neighbors, as is also true of some *brañas* of the parish of Naraval.[24]

The spacing in altitude between *aldeas* and *brañas* is similar to that in Naraval, although the contrast is somewhat blurred by the existence of intermediate small hamlets. The main *aldea*, Villatresmil (188 inhabitants) is 510 meters above sea level; the other *aldea*, Bustoburniego (82 people), is 450 meters above sea level. Two small hamlets, Folgueirua and Pelafolgueiros (thirty houses between the two),[25] stand seven hundred to eight hundred meters

INTRODUCTION

above sea level, and the two *brañas de alzada*, Bustellán and Las Tabiernas, are at 870 and 920 meters respectively. Given their altitude and location, the snow makes access to these *brañas* very difficult in the winter, and they are virtually uninhabited for much of the year.

Just as the people of Naraval have their commercial center in Luarca, so those of Villatresmil have theirs in Tineo. Both towns have medical specialists, morticians, notaries, banks, and shops. The main *aldea* of each parish also includes the church and the cemetery. The priest generally lives in the main *aldea*, as does the doctor (when there is one). There are also small shops or *chigres*, a combination of bar and general store. These *aldeas* also have a public telephone service and are served by the main local roads.

Up in the *brañas* these services are nonexistent. They not only lack churches, but do not even have the little chapels that dot much of rural northern Spain. The very few that exist in the *brañas* have been put up only recently, and for external reasons (by a rich family or by government authorities to celebrate a fiesta for tourists). By contrast, the small *aldeas*, which are often as small or smaller than the *brañas*, generally have their own chapel, which is the focus of a local fiesta. There is usually no telephone service in the *brañas*; in some *brañas* there is still no electricity or running water. In 1970, toilets and sewers were practically unheard of in the *brañas*. There was just one car in the whole parish of Naraval.

All manner of improvements and "advances" reach the *aldeas* before they reach the *brañas*—schools, for example. There has been a rural school in Naraval since the eighteenth century (Madoz, 1845); in 1906 there was a government schoolmaster there, and an inhabitant of Nera had endowed the school with a monthly income. But the only two schools in the *brañas*, in Businán and Folgueras, were not founded until 1936 and 1942, respectively.

THE VAQUEIROS AND I

I began this study of the Vaqueiros in the first days of October 1970. I would like to evoke here the atmosphere in which my fieldwork took place, the successive roles I held in the eyes of the people of the *brañas*, the kind of relationships we had, and how I went about my work.

During my Christmas vacation in 1969, I had gone to Asturias to explore the possibility of fieldwork, choosing the province mainly because no other anthropologist had worked there. On this trip I ended up in the parish of Naraval for serendipitous reasons (I got a ride there). In a tavern in the *aldea*, I met a pair of Vaqueiros who told me with irony and resentment of the *aldeanos'* long-time discrimination against their group. Although I previously had read about the Vaqueiros, it was my presence at an interchange of veiled reproaches and mordant insinuations between the two Vaqueiro men and some *aldeano* men in the tavern that quickened my interest in the subject. Over the course of several weeks I continued my trip through an ample zone in the western part of Asturias, using the *correos* [mail buses], talking with the other passengers, and learning the basics about the country.

When I began my fieldwork several months later, after a couple of days in the *aldeas*, my first problem was how to find a welcome in the *brañas*. The *aldeanos* lost no time in informing me about the (alleged) suspiciousness of the Vaqueiros, and the difficulty some journalists had encountered in gathering information in the *brañas*, taking pictures of the people, or even talking with them. A pair of *aldeanos* found the solution: perhaps I could give classes, or in local terms, *poner escuela*, for a couple of weeks for the *braña* children since the teacher had not arrived. These *aldeanos* quickly made contact with the *braña* mothers, and two or three days later I found myself on my way up to a *braña* with a group a women who insisted on carrying my luggage. For three weeks I assigned arithmetic exercises, corrected dictations, and gave classes in geography during the mornings in a school that served three *brañas*, about thirty children in all. I spent the afternoons talking to the people of the *braña* where I lived.

While I was getting to know the people, they were getting to know me. During the first days, very respectful of local custom, I did not smoke in public, not having seen any women do so. I would take advange of school recess to close the door and light a cigarette. After three days, the man of the house where I was staying offered me a smoke. When I turned him down in surprise, he said, "Go ahead, light up, woman. The boys have already told us you like to." The entire *braña* knew my secret, which, they assured me, was very common among the old women who had emigrated to South America and returned. These women wrapped their own cigarettes.

My new "profession" lasted exactly three weeks until, to my great relief, the real teacher turned up. When I refused pay, my students' parents began to invite me, one after another, to eat in their houses. Since at this time each house was performing the annual pig slaughter, I had a chance to meet many relatives from other *brañas*, to whom I had to try and explain what I was doing.

My first nickname was "the teacher [*maestrina*] who set up school." Later, after months had gone by and I no longer taught, I was given other titles: "the photographer," "the mountain climber" (because of my frequent comings and goings), and finally, "María, *la de la tesis*," although no one really knew what a thesis was. Other less complimentary nicknames, like "Franco's spy" and "the tax woman," fortunately were short-lived names given me by outsiders. Today the people call me what they would call any Vaqueiro in my situation, "María *la madrileña* [the woman from Madrid]. " I am glad of my first nickname, because it enabled me to circulate with ease in the Vaqueiro area. My first trip to the mountain pastures or *alzada* was on horseback in the company of the mother of one of my students. It was a weekend trip she made expressly for me. The Vaqueiros themselves suggested relatives with whom I could stay. In spite of their worries over the lack of comforts in their houses for someone accustomed to city life, the Vaqueiros admitted me with generosity into their homes and their lives.

From the very beginning of my fieldwork, I tape-recorded my conversations. For my informants, my tape recorder became part of me. At first the existence of the "apparatus," as they called it, was part wonder and part suspect. Many had never seen one before and were fascinated to hear their own voices, but all worried about what I would do with the tapes. I am bound to say that certain journalists and amateur folklorists were the cause of some of the Vaqueiros' reticence. Such persons would climb up to the *brañas* for a few hours in search of exotic material, which they subsequently would use sarcastically or thoughtlessly in the media. At times material was taped, interviews made, or photographs taken without the participants' awareness or permission, then played back, shown, or reported on radio or television, citing names, as examples of "superstitious beliefs" and irrationality.

I tried to solve the problem by explaining what I would do with the tapes: I would use them to record correctly what people told me, since my memory was not good enough and I could not take notes quickly enough. I assured them, as was the case, that as soon as I transcribed the tapes I erased them. One event helped people to accept my integrity in regard to the "apparatus." In the second *braña* I visited, people asked me to play back what the people of the first *braña* had told me, especially some songs sung by a group of men. At first I was going to do it, but then I instinctively refused because I did not have the first people's permission, in spite of the others' insistence and the possibility of seeming rude or discourteous. The best argument I found was that "surely you would not like it if I played back what you said in other places." My stand was quickly known in the first *braña* and commented on with approval. At times when I was talking with someone, someone else would remark ironically, "You're going to end up on the radio." He or she would be told, "No, she does it so she can write it down. The people from X wanted to hear what we said, and she wouldn't let them." These attitudes should explain why I have preferred to leave my informants anonymous in this study.

Over time I became used to using the tape recorder and making transcriptions, by far the most tedious work. I would ask permission to use the machine at the beginning of the conversation, warning my informants that their voices would be recorded and that if they wanted to say something off the record they should warn me so I could turn the recorder off. This occurred on very few occasions. I never hid the recorder and never turned it on without permission. Generally there would be a very short period, ten minutes at most, when people replied in monosyllables or in a very controlled way, but soon they would forget the recorder was there. Further conversations would be more relaxed, and some persons, when they had something important to say, would make sure the recorder was on.

These interviews took place in varied settings. Most took place in warm kitchens while women prepared meals, or after the meals during spinning sessions. Others were taped in fields while watching cows at pasture. Such tapes would be punctuated with short interruptions of "OO-O, Asturiana!" calling a cow, with cowbells as background music. (In the houses it would be children playing or the sound of a bubbling pot). Other tapes were made walking on mountain paths, or even while cows were being milked in the stable. Some conversations were one to one; others were collective. The first were more intimate and personal; the latter had the advantage that people would correct each other, stimulate each other's memories, and bring up new facts.

I transcribed the conversations almost immediately so I could check information, follow up on subjects I had not noticed in the conversation, or deepen my understanding of other subjects of which I was unaware. As I said, this was the hardest work, done in long stretches of the night or taking advantage of the times my conversants were working. Over time I became relatively quick at it. The conditions under which I did my transcribing were not always optimal. Sometimes I used an oil lamp, taking advantage of the small warmth of the flame, or I transcribed wrapped up in bed, for I had no table in the cold winter nights. At first I let the conversations go where they would, although I doubtless showed more interest in some matters than others. But little by little, as I became more familiar with the culture, I began to control the interviews, focusing on specifics and checking with others as to the general applicability of those specifics. I have not included in this study information about which I could not obtain a general consensus, although at times people would complain about how boring I was when I would pose to someone else a question that they had previously answered.

Choosing informants at first posed some problems. In some *brañas* there are certain individuals who specialize in receiving outsiders and entertaining them with conversation. The journalists or amateur folklorists I mentioned normally would talk to these people, who generally would have a very limited repertoire of information: songs, local verses, the customs of the old-time Vaqueiro weddings, and a couple of rituals supposedly performed in the past. Some of these persons, after going through this repertoire, turned out to be excellent helpers, after their initial shock that my questions did not fit the normal pattern. In other cases I amiably declined their help, after it was clear that it was hard for them to break out of accepted wisdoms or when they would insist that "this is what is really interesting." But generally my informants were anonymous men and women who were not, as it were, "in the business." Some of them understood my work well enough so that over time they began to distinguish me from other outsiders with comments like, "No, I've already heard you're not interested in stuff like songs and Vaqueiro weddings. What you want to know is how we live." I think they saw me as someone with a lot of curiosity, sticking my nose into everything, but as someone they could trust with sensitive and confidential details about Vaqueiro life.

While at work I maintained intense relations with the people of the *brañas*, living in their houses, eating with them, accompanying women to the pastures, men to the cattle fairs, and attending virtually all the fiestas and markets in the region. I tried not to miss the birth of a single calf or the formal visit to new mothers or bereaved families. I bought a small car after a few months, and a Vaqueiro baby was almost born in it on the way to a hospital because of what seemed to be a dangerous labor. Because of the car, I was also delegated to make emergency runs to call the doctor or the veterinarian in other emergencies. In the houses I tried to help out by keeping an eye on infants as I was copying my tapes and help, however minimally, hauling corn, scything grass for the cows (to the hilarity of my Vaqueiro friends), or milking enough to feed "the cat of the house." The *aldeanos* would gently make fun of me when I came down to the *aldeas* in wooden shoes, calling me "*Vaqueirina.*" This epithet pleased the Vaqueiros immensely. As I had during my first visit, I witnessed some of the oblique confrontations, friction, and misunderstanding between Vaqueiros and *aldeanos*, and I tried to remain neutral, but it was not always easy.

I was also, at times, very lonely, discouraged, or sad. And my Vaqueiro and *aldeano* friends understood, respected, and helped me through these spells with their affection and confidence. I treasure their friendship for its naturalness and because it was built from a mutual attempt to communicate across the barriers of different values and cultural presuppositions.

My first spell of life in the *brañas* lasted eleven months between October 1970 and April 1972, interspersed with time in Madrid where I presented my *Tesis de Licenciatura* (1971) and *Doctorado* (1972).[26] During this period I acquired a basic, essential knowledge of the people and their culture, focusing on Vaqueiro ecology, transhumance, modes of life, and especially on their marginality. In August 1972, I began graduate work in anthropology at the University of Pennsylvania, remaining in contact with Vaqueiro friends through a correspondence in which they told me about upcoming harvests, the births of calves, and the deaths of neighbors.

My previous fieldwork enriched the more theoretical preparation of classwork. Indeed, as I said before, the subject of the present research had as its antecedent the suicide of a Vaqueiro man in the *braña* where I lived. Cultural contrasts and differences have traditionally motivated anthropological attention, and I was no exception. Just as Vaqueiro attitudes toward suicide were different from what I knew, so were American attitudes toward death. I especially remember my visit to an intriguing, beautiful house—a funeral home—near the university campus, which I passed every day; and the pleasant and unreal ambiance (for me) of some American cemeteries, kinds of parks where children played and couples strolled. Some reading on the subject[27] and conversation with American friends confirmed my sense that Americans departed from this world in a different way, and increased my interest in the difficult subject of the last rite of passage.

Although I had not planned to do more fieldwork among the Vaqueiros, I changed my mind when I decided to study the cultural process of death. Given the nature of the subject, so intimate and sensitive in some of its forms, I knew it would be difficult to study among people I did not know well. The work, as I planned it, would be complex enough without having to take the time to know and be known in a new kind of place. Also, I would be doing something quite different than what I had done before. In late 1974, I made a three-month trip to Asturias to gather preliminary material on the

INTRODUCTION

subject. I drew up my thesis proposal in April 1975. I was in the *brañas* in May and June, and sporadically thereafter, as my teaching obligations in Madrid allowed.

In this latter period of fieldwork I concentrated on information about illness, local categories of death like natural death and suicide, and everything having to do with the afterlife. During a total of seven months of intensive fieldwork, I talked to Vaqueiros about these matters, attended funerals and anniversaries, visited the sick, gave my condolences, and participated in wakes. On a couple of occasions I even helped to shrive the dead and prepare the body. Although I spoke with persons of all ages (my youngest informant was a five-year-old girl who told me about the death of calves and her grandfather), I paid particular attention to the elderly because of their sensitivity and attention to the matter. People approved of my work, as they saw that my visits entertained the very aged, and the old folks themselves, often bedridden, saw they were helping me. A typical comment of a passerby when seeing me talking with an elderly man in a field would be, "Courting, eh?" In general, Vaqueiros were very patient with my newfound interest, and no one rejected the subject outright, although it was not unusual for someone to say, "María, why don't you study weddings, which are happier?"

Unless otherwise cited, all information in this study comes from my own observations and tape-recorded interviews. In all, I gathered in two thousand crowded pages transcriptions of 128 conversations with about one hundred persons, more than seventy of whom I know well and have spoken with on several occasions. This material is the product of about 250 hours of conversations, none less than an hour in length and few more than three hours, with one or more persons. More than half of this material is devoted exclusively to the subject matter of this book; the rest contains abundant references to it and other closely related aspects of Vaqueiro culture.

Throughout the study I have used generous quotations from these conversations. The organization and analysis of the taped material has cost me considerable time and effort, not only in terms of checking facts and the generality of attitudes, but also in evaluating its meaning within the cultural system. I have tried to let the material direct me to its structure rather than forcing it to fit into my structures. I am not sure whether I have succeeded in giving way completely, nor do I maintain any pretense of objectivity beyond the normal limits. But I believe this is a good way to present the ethnographic material for a number of reasons.

First, I am interested not only in the behavior of the Vaqueiros in regard to death, but also in their ideology, and a good way to get at what people have in their heads is to listen to what they say. As this study will show, I do not deny the importance of behavior. But instead of describing in my own words what people do, I prefer to let the actors speak for themselves, describing not only their significant acts but also their feelings, thoughts, and evaluations of their acts. Only when their judgments conflict with my own observations have I attempted to intervene, pointing out the discrepancy and explaining it when possible. This stance is not new. At the beginnings of anthropology in America, Boas insisted that ethnographic material be gathered in native tongues, and emphasized the literal transcription of texts and primary sources. Even when these texts reflect purely personal and idiosyncratic formulations, such formulations reflect cultural ways of perceiving and feeling. As Monica Wilson wrote regarding Nyakyusa symbols, "It was at least a Nyakyusa subconscious, and the interpretation in terms of their culture" (M. Wilson 1957).[28]

The abundance and primary character of my interview material permits further analysis by other scholars. For this reason, I have tried to separate as much as possible the ethnographic information in its contexts, which I offer in the first part of every chapter, from my own analysis at the end of the chapter, even when this separation may disrupt a description or make certain repetitions necessary. A third advantage is the artistic and poetic nature of the direct quotes, which I hope will come through despite the inevitable loss in translation. The grace, ingeniousness, and freshness of the local speech serve as counterpoint and contrast to the colder, academic ethnographic descriptions. Vaqueiros, at times, can capture imaginatively in a few phrases what a scholar would take pages to explain. I feel that evoking the emotional impact, the feelings, the humor, and the existential poetry of the "other" people is just as important in fieldwork as collecting objective data and studying the formal aspects of the culture. Monographs do not usually treat these feelings and attitudes, although they are essential aspects of human communication, the study of which is one of the objectives of our discipline.

Apart from the content of this study, I am concerned about how to present ethnographic evidence. The use of tape-recorded material is by no means new, but perhaps my analysis depends more heavily upon it than is often the case. Although this work was designed in 1975 and carried out between 1975 and 1984, the form in which it is organized, and the kind of sources and how they are used, reflect more recent trends of ethnographic writing and the theoretical focus on communication between cultures that experimental ethnography supposes.[29]

I see at least three reasons for this interest in the local voice. In the first place, it is probable that the emphasis on behavior rather than on words had to do with the degree to which the ethnographer failed to master the language. Perhaps the native rather than the foreign anthropologist will place a greater emphasis on language. It would be interesting to find out whether this is true and to determine how much the old emphasis on formal, exterior, or "visible" aspects of a culture (performances, ritual behavior, customs, and social structure) was not an issue of making a virtue of necessity, given the difficulty of communicating native epistemology, sensibility, and aesthetics when one does not handle the idiom adequately. Ethnography, like translation, becomes a kind of provisional way to confront the otherness of languages, cultures, and societies. In order to translate, one first must understand; at times, neither is easy. Translation in cultural interpretation requires a negotiation of concepts between ethnographer and informants, and then between ethnographer and readers. Understanding itself requires a negotiation of presuppositions, signifieds, and contexts. That is why many modern experimental ethnographies try to include as faithfully as possible the experience of fieldwork, making explicit these kinds of dialogues or negotiations. In the case of native ethnographers, the risk is that they may be under the illusion that there is no translation going on, in which case they are actually involved in a monologue and do not know it.

As Rabinow (1977) has indicated, fieldwork is a cultural activity: the information sought is cultural, and the manner of understanding and interpreting the world is also a cultural process. But he also points out that the informants themselves provide us with information that is mediated by history and culture. The ways of presenting evidence, too, are influenced by a tradition of cultural expression. It has been pointed out that in the culture of Spain, "the poetic—verbal play of various kinds and the indirect language of metaphoric and metonymic allusion—arises with great facility in rural areas." (Fernández 1976, 140).[30] No doubt this trait affected my interest in conveying not only the information but also the form of the Vaqueiros' expression. Among the themes experimental ethnography raises is an attention to kinds of ethnographic writing differing from the Anglo-Saxon tradition. It is evident that when one takes native culture and discourse into account on its own terms, the next logical step is a respect for native intellectual traditions.

Third, it is probable that the human factor plays a decisive role in ethnographic studies. Attention to local discourse probably has to do with one's sense of security in oneself, which one transmits in one's interaction with others. There are persons very convinced of their own perceptions who seem quite sure of their interpretations. I do not have that certainty, and I prefer, if possible, to offer both discourses, mine and those of my informants. In any case, I do not believe that one discourse can or should be substituted for the other. The risk in offering "native voices" yet one more time is the illusion of dialogue, a dubious idea inasmuch as in reality it is the ethnographer who decides which voices to listen to and on what topics. The ethnographer, in the end, continues to hold the pen and retain authority (Geertz 1984).

Another personal and professional trait is "a high tolerance for unending ambiguity" (Kaplan 1984)—a recognition that meaning is contingent on its context, that ethnographic material is elusive and often neither simple nor clear. This trait goes with an attention to detail and moment, and tends to point up complexity and ambiguity.

In any case, my decision to use of extensive direct quotes is the best I could find to transmit the most vital and valuable understandings. I hope that the form and the content help the reader to enter the here-and-now world and the other worlds of the Vaqueiros, and to get a feeling for their culture.

PART ONE

THE PATH
TO DEATH

1
Sickness and the
Vaqueiro Cosmology

In this chapter I will analyze the most common way to death: illness, which is a complex concept for the Vaqueiros. Among the
local theories about the causes of illness are environmental causes,
which arise from contact with the Vaqueiros' habitat; physical
causes, which show the configuration of the human body as a system; and social causes, produced by the interaction within and outside of the group that the Vaqueiros characterize as envy. Healers
work within this cultural model of sickness and serve as intermediaries between different spheres dealing with physical, social and
moral problems. By discussing sickness, I hope to make evident Vaqueiro cosmology.

CAUSES OF ILLNESS:
THE NATURAL ENVIRONMENT AND ANIMALS

In the mental universe of the Vaqueiros, the concepts of health and
sickness are frequently associated with a symbolic dichotomy of
blessed and accursed, the *bendito* and the *maldito*. I will try to
show how, according to the local definitions, different aspects of
the environment—time and space, cyclical changes, animals,
plants, and even human beings—are classified in one of these two
categories.[1]

One of the variety of meanings of the categories blessed/ac-
cursed is derived from the act of blessing or cursing performed or
approved by three kinds of beings: supernaturals, priests, and laypersons. According to local tradition, the Virgin Mary and Baby Je-

sus intervene directly in blessing or cursing certain plants or animals. The action occurs in a mythical time in which these divine beings visit the earth and are helped or impeded by various plants or animals. This help or injury may be purely accidental and may involve a mere touch. Such are the reasons given for why holly [xardon] and the mule are blessed and accursed respectively.

The holly was blessed by the Virgin one day when she hid on Mount Calvary because the Jews were after her; she had the baby in her arms, and she crouched down beneath [the holly] and they didn't see her.

The holly is blessed because the handkerchief of the Virgin was caught on it.

The mule is an accursed animal because it does not have offspring. The mule is accursed, too, because it ate the hay [in the manger] of Jesus.

In addition to these mythical blessings, the divinities continue to bless different objects through contact with religious images in churches and shrines. The best-known shrine in the region is that of the Virgen del Acebo, the Virgin of the Holly Tree.[2] All who go to the shrine touch to the image objects like clothes, berets, handkerchiefs, bread, ribbons, medals, religious pictures, and scapulars. Many Vaqueiros bring cowbells and the metal medallions they hang from cow collars. All of these objects are considered blessed once they have touched the image and protect those who use them.

Before we had the custom of putting something blessed on the kids when we took them out. Look, one time I went out with one of mine to the doctor, and he was a very handsome child. And when we went by X, G said: "I can't believe, E, that you are taking this baby out without something blessed. Don't you have a medal or something?" "No, I don't have anything." "Well, don't let this child out of the house again without something blessed." They say nothing will happen to them [children] if they wear something blessed.

The holy place as well as the image is blessed and a source of blessing. Vaqueiros bring candles, holy water, and incense from churches and shrines to their houses. The level of blessedness conferred depends on the fame of the church or shrine as well as the day on which one obtains the objects. Thus the candles of El Acebo are much prized, especially those lit at the shrine on the day of the feast of the Virgin; so are those from any other church that have been lit on Maundy Thursday. Candles, holy water, and incense are used as a prophylaxis against different ills.

We ought to keep a bottle of holy water in each house. It's good to sprinkle through the house, and good to give a few little drops in the feed of the cattle, in the trough, in the flour, or whatever, so nothing will happen to them.

And incense is very good, is blessed, when you ask the priest for a little bit, which he might not even charge you for, and carrying it this way, in one's clothes, it's blessed so that envy doesn't get to you.

It's customary to light these candles and go down to the stable and make on them [the cows] this cross [with the candle]. And some people let [the wax] drip all over their bodies. I did it a lot when the cows went to the high pasture. Grandmother always said, "It's time to go put holy wax on the cows in the stable."

Like the image and the holy place, the priest can also impart blessings. The priest blesses the plants the Vaqueiros take to church on Palm Sunday, bay leaves in particular. The priest's power of blessing extends beyond the church, for candles lit in his presence also become holy. People light candles when the priest comes to the *braña* to visit the dying. These candles and the bay leaves also have ritual uses.

Bay leaves are blessed; they are taken to church Palm Sunday and get blessed. When it thunders they burn a few leaves so it will pass.

It was customary to go from all the houses with a candle when [the priest] came to confess somebody. And later the priest would leave and everybody went home. Everybody brought a candle, and this was the candle they used to make a cross on the haunches of the cows.

Laypersons also bless their cows and themselves daily with a holy gesture—the sign of the cross—when leaving the stable or the house. This ritual also is thought to prevent possible misfortunes.

I usually make the crosses and cross myself each time I go out with the cattle, each time I yoke them up.

And each time we leave on a trip we have to make the sign of the cross, cross ourselves, and then the Virgin accompanies us and nobody envies us.

In addition to the cross, Vaqueiros count on prayer as an efficient instrument for blessing. While the blessed objects considered so far have a protective power that is diffuse, pronouncing a prayer or formula, together with other practices, is used to heal a group of specific illnesses. This form of curing is locally referred to as "praying the words" ["*rezar las palabras*"] or "curing by word" ["*curar de palabra*"]. The causes of the sickness cured by words are accursed animals. The first group of accursed animals is known as "animals of sickness." These are "animals that drag themselves along, ferocious, because they are revolting and poisonous." This category includes mainly reptiles (snakes, asps, lizards) and other creatures like mice, spiders, toads, and stellions (a kind of lizard). In addition to attacking one directly, any of these animals may produce two diseases with similar symptoms and treatments: *las espinas* and *el cosiyo*. *Las espinas* [thorns, bones] can be contracted anywhere, although they are frequently associated with work in the pastures and fields. They cause an infection in certain parts of the body, generally the hands. The origin of *las espinas* is always contagion from one of the accursed animals, whether by mere contact, with the venom people believe that they release, or by contact with their skeleton or *aresta*.

If you have an infection of a finger when you're in the fields, like when you get stuck with a thorn or a nettle, and it has been infected because a lizard or a toad passed over it, then your finger will swell up, get inflamed.

Las espinas is a wound you get from a thorn and get infested [sic]. From a toad or a snake. If you try and kill one and you are touched by the urine they have inside or some liquid they squirt, that is where the poison comes from, they say.

Las arestas they call it. When you stick yourself with something that is infested or poisoned. They say that toad dies and dries up and then what's left is the skeleton, and you may come in contact with it.

El cosiyo appears to be a more extensive infection than *las espinas*. It, too, appears on the hands and other parts of the body. To cure both sicknesses, one needs ashes and the following prayer, which enumerates the accursed animals that could have caused the sickness:

Espina del espinar	Thorn from the briarpath
Cosiyo del cosiyar	*cosiyo* from the *cosiyar,*
¿Qué viniste aquí a buscar?	What have you come here for?
Comer y tchamber ceniza del tchar	To eat and lick ash from the hearth

THE PATH TO DEATH

Carne humana no te la quieren dar.	Human flesh they don't want to give you.
Si sos de culebra, veite a la cueva.	If you are from the snake, go to the cave.
Si sos de tchagartón, veite al tcherón.	If from the big lizard, go to the rocks.
Si sos de lagarta, veite a la tcharta.	If from the lizard, go to the puddle.
Si sos de sapo, veite al furaco.	If from the toad, go to the hole.
Si sos de ratón, veite al balchón.	If from the mouse, go to the thicket.
Si sos de araña, veite a la paña.	If from the spider, go to the cliff[?].
Y si sos de sapaguera, metete na tchera.	If from the stellion, get back in the sand.

The cure is completed by rubbing the infection with ashes and making the sign of the cross over it and over oneself. This prayer provides a way for people to come to an understanding with the sickness symbolized by the accursed animals. The poem contains dialogue with sickness (or evil) in the abstract, the *espina* or *cosiyo*, offering it a compensation, ash, instead of human flesh. Then the specific evil, the animal, is ordered to leave the human being and go back to its place in nature. Although the words are considered ritualistic and some of them are difficult to understand, the ones that are clear indicate the normal habitats of these animals—caves, holes, rocks, and so on. Such places are underground, hidden and wild; cultivated land is supposed to be free of these pests,[3] and so, even more, is the human being. The intrusive nature of the *espina* and the animals is made explicit in the second line, "What have you come here for?" and in the subsequent orders "go" and "get back." In the structure of the prayer the following dichotomies appear:

Ash :	Human flesh ::
Pets:	Human being ::
Cave, rocks, puddle, hole . . . :	Here (hearth , house)

The hearth is the focal point of the house, the place most representative of the human being, the most intimate cultural nexus, while the other places (cave, rocks, etc.) are hideouts underground, wild habitat. The animals cause sickness when humans encounter them in the cultivated land in the course of their work, and their evil effects carry over into the house. The prayer attempts to restore health by constraining the animals to return to their proper place. It deals with the confusion and the interference of wildness from below the earth in the human cultural sphere. Because it assumes that this intromission leads to illness, the requisite separation of the two worlds is thought to restore health. The clear separation of categories impedes the disorder caused by the sickness. The basic movement that appears in the prayer of the *espina* could be depicted as follows:

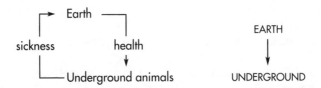

But if dialogue fails, much more severe measures must be taken. This is frequently the case with the snake. Of all the animals named, it is the one that most frequently attacks humans and domestic animals. The snake turns up suddenly in different places and at different times: when the cut grass is drying in the meadows, in the hay stored in the loft, in the stable with the cows, and in the foundations of the house. When a person or cow is bitten by a snake, one must follow a ritual that includes the recitation of a prayer as well as a number of specific actions. The "prayer of the snake" describes an authentic ritual combat between one blessed animal, the hart or deer, and one accursed animal, the snake or serpent.[4]

Entre la cervatina de Dios	Between God's deer
y la serpiente maldita	and the cursed serpent
hicieron una apuesta;	a bet was made;
la primera que se vistiera,	the first to get dressed,
la primera que se calzara,	the first with shoes on,
la primera que subiera allí arriba	the first to get up there
la su cornatina tocaba.	and sound its horn.
La cervatina de Dios, como era bendita,	The deer of God, since it was blessed,
fue la primera que se vistió,	was the first to dress
la primera que se calzó,	the first with shoes on
la primera que subió allí arriba	the first to get up there
y su cornatina tocó.	and sound its horn.

THE PATH TO DEATH

Y *la serpiente maldita*
metiose por debaxo de tronco
    carronco
y fue a salir a debaxo de raiz
fresno feliz.
¡Séquele la boca como seca la
    estopa!
¡Séquele la babai como seca la
    pai!
¡Séquele el corazón como seca
    el carbón!
	And the cursed serpent
	went down under the gnarled
	    tree trunk
	and went out under the root,
	happy ash tree.
	May his mouth dry up like
	    tinder!
	May his spit dry up like straw!
	
	May his heart dry up like
	    charcoal!

In the ritual formula, the animals compete in a series of tests: dressing, putting on shoes, climbing a height, and sounding a horn.[5] Of these tests, the first two and the last one are obviously anthropomorphic. The third test is quite easy for the deer, an animal that runs and lives in the mountains, but quite inappropriate for the snake, an animal that crawls and lives underground. Thus the bet is won in advance, and the deer wins by going *up high*, the place closest to God; the serpent loses and therefore has to hide itself *down low*, by the roots inside the earth, which is where it should be. The final analogies indicate not only the ingredients of the therapy—tinder, straw, and charcoal—but also the destruction of the animal beginning with the mouth (the organ that made the wound, the spit), then the poisonous substance, and finally the heart.

Good and evil, health and sickness, are symbolized not only by blessed and accursed animals but also by the spatial values of up and down. Sickness is a test that can be won or lost; in the ritual contest there can be no truce and no carelessness. The prayer thus has a dual purpose: in the first part the two animals are placed in their respective habitats, one above and one below that of humans, reestablishing the order of the universe of which the sick person is a part. But it also attempts, with the final analogy, to destroy the origin of the sickness in the hope that by dealing with its cause, one deals with the effect. The resulting diagram of the prayer of the snake offers a more complete cosmology than that of the *espina:*

Animal of heights	MOUNTAIN
↑	↑
Human being ⊰	EARTH ⊰
↓	↓
Animal of roots	UNDERGROUND

This ritual contest involves the interference of an accursed animal in the human habitat, an animal that has left its proper place in the bowels of the earth. But unlike the previous prayer, this one does not give the accursed animal orders but works by analogy, a more subtle but equally effective form of pressure. The serpent loses the contest and the deer wins, health triumphing over disease. In any case, the result means a balanced separation of both animals from the human being. Ordering the universe, maintaining the sharp differentiation of categories, is the way to overcome disease.

The movement and urgency that pervade the ritual formula (the bet is won by speed) also indicate the conduct to be followed in the application of the cure. People say:

> If [the snake] bites you, you have to hurry; you have to rub it well with nine rye straws, nine pieces of charcoal from the fire, and, of course, if there is tinder like there used to be. . . yes, it was also good. And say the prayer. And then, in the fields there are thistles; well, it's good to rub it well with them. I cured one of my boys, and one bit me, too, near the house. I was spreading out grass by hand and felt it bite me, a deep bite. "Ay, the snake bit me!" I went down to the house, running to treat it, and the bite was getting bluish, and I began to rub it with thistles; I prayed the words, and rubbed it with all those things, and it got better.

As one can see, the Vaqueiro tries at all costs and by all available means to overcome the evil—dialogue, trickery, threats, and so on. Although any strategem is valid in the face of illness, the Vaqueiro cannot trust in victory. Illness may be cured in some cases, but there are other cases in which death is considered inevitable. This is particularly true of illnesses caused by the lizard, which is considered the most dangerous animal of all. Wisdom, knowledge, and even supernatural assistance cannot prevail against this animal. While its *espinas* may be cured with the prayer cited above, its bite is considered fatal almost immediately ["*mordedura de tchagartón, ni cura ni confesión*"]. Yet I know of only one case, somewhat legendary, of the bite of this animal leading to death, the case of a young Vaqueiro girl.[6]

> All [of the accursed animals] are bad, but the worst is the lizard; there is no cure for it. A sister of the father of C of G died from a lizard bite. They were coming down through R meadow in the grass and a lizard bit her. And she died at once. They said she went all green. The lizard is very, very bad.

THE PATH TO DEATH

It is no accident that the lizard attacked the girl, for it is thought to prefer to attack women.[7] It is said it "is more friendly with men than with women," whom it is thought to attack sexually.

No, the lizard is bad; it's worse than accursed; it's much more dangerous because it disappears. But it's revolting with women; they say it chases a lot of women and jumps up . . . up there, and whips around and sticks in its tail, they say, but that's never happened here. [They say] it goes much more after women, and when she isn't well a lot more.

The confusion between the society of humans and nature reaches its maximum level with the figure of the lizard. This most accursed animal is responsible for violating women, with the aggravating factor of doing it during their menstrual periods. Vaqueiros prohibit all sexual activity during menstruation, so it is no surprise that if the violation of this taboo is thought to bring on various terrible diseases,[8] an accursed animal can lead to the death of a woman. There can be no other outcome when one of the most terrible animals interferes in one of the most intimate human activities, of creating an aberrant, unorthodox sexual couple.

The "animals of sickness" are not the only ones that are accursed. There is another such group composed of the eagle, the fox, the wolf, and the bear. Here the dichotomy blessed/accursed divides those animals useful and productive for humans from those that are ferocious and harmful, those that cause trouble to Vaqueiros, their property, and their domestic animals.

There may be many blessed animals, but the only ones you know well are the ox, the cow . . . I think that all the ones you eat must be blessed. Well, the deer, the dove, too. And the swallow . . .

But *hombre*, those wild beasts, revolting, how can they not be accursed? Any animal that doesn't help you, that is not domestic, is accursed; we curse it. That is what is accursed, any animal that you don't have; because a domestic animal that you keep in your house for your benefit, so you can use it, why would you curse it?

Among the blessed animals named there are two distinct categories. Domestic animals, primarily oxen and cows, comprise the first category.[9] This group of animals has a set of wild opposites, the animals that attack them, especially wolves. Domestic animals cohabit with humans in the same house; their enemies dwell in the wilds, occasionally making incursions into cultivated land and houses to commit their crimes. So the opposition here occurs on the same level:

EARTH —— Domestic animals ⟷ Savage beasts

The other category of blessed animals includes the deer, the dove, the swallow, and the bee (whose honey is blessed and serves as medicine). It is thought that some of these animals enter the category of blessed because they were supposed to have helped Christ, Mary, and other saints, but most frequently these creatures are associated by the fact that they "don't do any harm." I will refer in some detail to the swallow below.

> We hold the swallows to be blessed because they live in the stables of the cows, and they say it is a very bad sign to knock down their nests because they say they are blessed. And the swallow doesn't do any harm at all to the farmers. They say that it is a beast that brings much luck to the house where it nests.

Swallows' nests are thought to protect the building on which they are located from lightning. This is no small service, as lightning is known to destroy stables by fire and kill the animals inside. The "bad sign" has come to mean that if a swallow is killed, a cow will die.

The swallow and the cow are thought to share some common features. For example, people believe that the swallows, moved by the pain of Christ, used their beaks to pull out Christ's thorns when he was on the cross. At his death they went into mourning, hence their black plumage.[10] The swallows still maintain their relationship with God today. They take water to God between the clouds, winter in holy places, and are compared to the Virgin, who is said to be their godmother.[11] This same intimacy and familiarity obtains for cows in their relation to humans; I have written elsewhere of their mutual dependence (Cátedra 1981). Swallows are blessed because they pertain to the sky and come in close contact with supernatural beings. They come down to earth, make their nests in stables, and protect the cows. Cows also have served as ritual intermediaries between humans and divinity, but inversely: in the face of danger or tragedy, they have been the traditional offering humans make to the holy images of the area, particularly to the Virgin of El Acebo. The possibility of a symbolic substitution of both animals—"if a swallow is killed a cow dies"—shows that the swallow, in addition to being God's messenger, is also "God's little cow." Animals are signs not only for social distinctions,[12] but also for metaphysical distinctions. In other words, the cow is the animal of humanity as the swallow is the animal of divinity. These animals have become symbolic representatives of the divinity, carriers of luck, and benefactors of humanity. By contrast, their accursed opposites, the animals of the underground that cause misfortune and sickness, are symbols of evil. The opposition between them can be seen in the Vaqueiro house. The swallow nests in the eaves while the pests find refuge in the foundations of the house.

In this context, the ability to move upward may be understood as an essential characteristic of blessed animals. Several of these animals—the swallow, the bee—can fly, establishing communication between heaven and earth; others, like the deer, climb and inhabit the heights, the zone closest to the sky. The following diagram represents this movement.

        Animals that fly

The structures and diagrams I have outlined so far clearly delimit and assign values to the three levels of the Vaqueiro universe: sky, earth, and underground. However, the eagle confuses these categories. The eagle is an accursed animal but is also an animal of the heights. Danger also comes down from the sky, as when the eagle carries off hens and sheep. The ritual formula for this creature is as follows:

Santa Bárbara bendita	Blessed Saint Barbara,
que en el cielo estás escrita,	who is written in heaven
en el valle las arenas,	in the sand in the valley,
en el cielo las estrellas.	in the stars in the sky.
Pousa la prenda que llevas,	Put down the object you take away,
que ni es tuya ni es mia	which is neither yours nor mine
sí es del dueño que la cría.	but which belongs to the owner who is raising it.
"¿Quién es el dueño que la crió?"	"Who is the owner that raised it?"

According to scholars who have written about this prayer, the first line originally read *"aguila maldita,"* then became *"aguila bendita."* [13] The incongruence of this semantic change is said to be due to "routine" that changed the more archaic version. The replacement of *aguila* with *Santa Bárbara* in the version I recorded would be a further step in this change. Following the same reasoning, one may suppose a confusion arose between the prayer of the eagle and that of the *truena* [thunder], which is used to send away the storms that can do so much harm to Vaqueiro property. The prayer of the thunder follows:

Santa Bárbara bendita,	Blessed Saint Barbara,
que en el cielo estás escrita	who is written in heaven/sky
con papel y agua bendita	with paper and holy water
en el ara de la cruz	on the altar stone of the cross
para siempre, amén Jesús.	forever, amen Jesus.

But perhaps these are not incongruencies at all. Perhaps these semantic changes do not affect the meaning of the prayer as much as a first glance might indicate. Let us look closer at the content of these formulae. The prayers describe different ascriptions: Saint Barbara or the eagle belong to the sky or to heaven, where they are "written," as the sand belongs to the valleys and the stars to the sky, and as the stolen object belongs to its owner. The concluding question in the prayer of the eagle, which is answered by the name of the owner, indicates the final and the most specific ownership. The person who recites the prayer, by denying her or his ownership of the stolen object, tries to persuade the animal to do the same and return it. Note that the prayer may be reduced to an essential opposition: sky/valley.

Sky : Saint Barbara (eagle) ::   SKY

Valley : Sands ::

Sky : Stars ::

Stolen object : Its owner   VALLEY

The eagle belongs to the habitat of the sky, like the saint and the stars; the stolen object belongs to the valley, like the sand, like the person reciting the prayer and the domestic animals. A metonymic association restores the order of the universe so that restitution may be achieved. The injury originates in the displacement of the eagle to a habitat where it doesn't belong. The prayer exhorts the eagle to return the object to the habitat where it belongs, the stolen animal to the valley, and to return to its own place, to the sky/heaven, the place of saints and eagles.

Storms also come from the sky, and the dangerous and accursed *truena* can destroy crops or burn stables and houses with its lightning. The prayer of the thunder brings blessed and celestial beings

THE PATH TO DEATH

and things: Saint Barbara, Jesus, the altar stone, the cross, and holy water. Traditional remedies against storms have included burning holy branches, sounding conch shells (which are also blessed), ringing the church bells, and even having recourse to the priest to conjure the storm.[14] The smoke, the noise, and the prayer, in a direction away from the storm, are ways to make contact with the sky and ward off its perils. The prayer of the thunder helps to remind celestial divinities to take charge of their house and the dangers that lurk there. The local substitution of an animal of the heights, the eagle, for a heavenly being, Saint Barbara, appears to be symbolically significant. Saint Barbara herself (truly barbarian!) stands in for thunder and lightning. The animal, the weather and the saint share the same place in the sky and certain ambivalence.

Interaction with the sky/heaven, in spite of its risks, is essential for survival in the same way that working the land is necessary, even at the cost of disturbing the beings that hide in it and contracting certain diseases from them. Fog, for instance, brings moisture that fertilizes the fields and allows cattle to drink. But it is also responsible for the death or injury of animals. It makes the wolf invisible so it can attack the animals with impunity, and it "blights" certain harvests. Like the prayer of the thunder, that of the fog [nublina] seeks to return to the sky what belongs there, with the help of the blessed beings that live there and their intermediaries.

Escampa, nublina, escampa,
que está el tchobo en la mia
　　campa,
comiendo la uvetcha blanca.
Ahí vien San Antonín,
con el suo borriquín
del rabo queimao.
-Muita agua truxo.
¡Donde está el agua?
-Muitas vacas la bebieron.
¡Donde están las vacas?
-Muita tcheite dieron.
¡Donde está el tcheite?
-Muitas pitas la bebieron.
¡Donde están las pitas?
-Muitos huevos pusieron.
¡Donde están los huevos?
-Muitos frailes los comieron.
¡Donde están los frailes?

Clear away, fog, clear away,
for the wolf is in my pasture

eating the white sheep.
Here comes Saint Anthony
with his little burro
with its burnt tail.
-He brought lots of water.
Where is the water?
-Many cows drank it.
Where are the cows?
-They gave a lot of milk.
Where is the milk?
-Many hens drank it.
Where are the hens?
-Many eggs thethey laid.
Where are the eggs?
-Many friars ate them.
Where are the friars?

-Muitas misas dixeron.	-Many masses they said.
¿Donde están las misas?	Where are the masses?
¡Todas subieron al cielo!	All went up to heaven!

The structure of this prayer shows the complete cycle of the interaction between sky/heaven and earth. The reason first given for wanting the fog to clear is the danger of the wolf attacking the animals. Then Saint Anthony, an intermediary between the inhabitants of heaven and earth, is introduced. He lives up above but is a protector of animals and appears with one of them in the prayer, a little burro. The fog, or Saint Anthony, begins its descent with water towards earth. Then two domestic animals appear, each with their respective products: cows and milk, hens and eggs. But the movement is circular and ends up where it began. The friars, other intermediaries, say their masses, and the masses go up to heaven. The cycle can be depicted as follows:

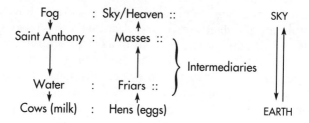

Water is a substance of the sky that comes down by way of the saints. Cows, hens, and their products are things of the earth that occasionally have been used as offerings to saints. Masses are offerings pure and simple.

Saint Anthony is worth special attention. His prayer, which is considered the most prized and effective of all the prayers, is used especially for finding things that are lost, particularly cattle and sheep, and divining the health of animals and humans. More concretely, the prayer serves to keep wild animals from attacking the domestic animals in the pastures or hillsides and keeps bad weather from destroying the crops or stables. The Vaqueiros have added to the beginning of the recitation of the prayer (which I do not include here as it is so well known and common to all of Spain)[15] the following verses, which take into account the specific favors the people of the *brañas* hope for from the saint:

San Antonio de Padua,	Saint Anthony of Padua,
en Padua naciste,	you were born in Padua,
en él te criaste	there you grew up,

dulcísimo cordón tendiste	a sweet cord you extended,
al Monte Calvario subiste.	you climbed Mount Calvary.
"¡Donde vas San Antonio?"	"Where are you going, Saint Anthony?"
"A buscar mi calvario	"To find my calvary
que lo he perdido."	that I have lost."
Tres pasos atrás,	Three steps back,
con el nombre de Jesús	with the name of Jesus
te encontrarás,	you will find
que lo has perdido.	what you have lost.
Tres pasos alante,	Three steps ahead,
donde tu ser llamado	where you are invoked
no caiga piedra ni rayos,	let there not fall hail or
ni de lobos es furado	lightning
	nor be pierced by wolves
ni de raposas sangrado.	nor bled by foxes.

This prayer, like the others, has a spatial progression, here both vertical and horizontal. Saint Anthony is born and grows up in Padua (actually in Portugal), the earth, but climbs Mount Calvary, a place near the sky/heaven inhabited by the divinity. The dichotomy up/down returns, associated this time with the transformation of an earthly person into a supernatural being, movement that repeats the ascent of the hart:

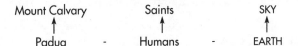

The movement backward naturally replicates the process of tracing one's steps when something is lost, the return to the immediate past. The movement forward indicates future action: protection against lightning, hail, wolves, and foxes. This dual movement represents the double nature of what the Vaqueiros hope to get from the prayer. Saint Anthony, the most popular saint, is a shepherd who, together with his little dog watches over sheep when humans are at rest.[16] Thus the prayer is a plea for divine protection. But the prayer also serves as a kind of oracle. The prayer people of the *braña*, determine whether owners of lost animals have a good chance of finding them, depending on whether the prayer has been said correctly or incorrectly. The saint cannot always save the lost animals, but at least he can say what has happened to them.

One must communicate with the saints in the correct way, but even so, they cannot always help. The saints and the wild beasts have their respective spheres of influence, and even their respective schedules.

Once I had the prayer said, and the wolf ate [the sheep] anyway. Sometimes the wolf is more powerful than the prayer. But people pray a lot; they say that the prayer of Saint Anthony is very powerful for many things. That night it happened that it ate the sheep, but that doesn't mean anything.

The wolf will eat them. It will eat animals that have been prayed for; it has certain hours for eating. At times you'll have a herd of goats or sheep in the hills and they've been prayed for, and even though the wolves are nearby, they don't touch them. But other times they have certain hours for killing and eating. If the prayer worked, saying it every day, or every eight days, then the wolf would die of hunger. That's why it has certain hours.

The dichotomy blessed/accursed classifies not only animals but plants as well. Some, as we have seen, are blessed because of a putative relation with the divine (for example, the holly), others because they are blessed on Palm Sunday (bay leaf) or because they received the dew on Saint John's Day [*sabugo*]. Some plants also owe some of their blessedness to their physical features (like trees that retain their leaves in winter—oak, holly, bay, eucalyptus) or to their medicinal properties (like rosemary, fennel, and rue).

The olive tree is blessed, too, and the laurel, whose leaf doesn't fall off either.

Broom, which grows in the wild, has a flower that they say is blessed. It is blessed because they say it is medicinal.

The plants considered blessed grow spontaneously in the wild, in the *monte*, which is a kind of transition zone in many respects. Most of the houses of the *braña* own sections of wild or untilled land [*monte*], which is plowed on occasion for conversion to pasture. Aside from attempts at domestication, the *monte* is a transitional zone between the *braña* and the outside world, a place where the Vaqueiros' animals find nourishment when the private pastures are exhausted, but also the scene of many accidents and tragedies.

Many of the occasions on which blessed objects are used correspond to a change of residence: candles when the cows go off to the high pastures; medals and incense when people or children leave the *braña*; and crosses when one "crosses" the thresholds of stables and houses. Many of the rituals seek to counteract the dangers that

THE PATH TO DEATH

come to the *braña* from the outside; from nearby (mainly wild beasts or pests who dwell in the *monte*) or from above (lightning or fog). The church and also, to some extent, all the places where Vaqueiros live are blessed. Beyond these zones, including a transitional zone that surrounds the *braña*, the accursed territory begins to appear. That is why the briars and brush that threaten to overrun cultivated land are considered accursed. Yet the *monte* holds blessings as well as curses: it is the location not only of the transition between the domestic and the wild but also between the divine and the human. The association of divinity, *monte*, and blessed plants can be seen in a prayer against erysipelas, a skin infection:

San Idelfonso por aquí pasou	Saint Idelfonso came by here
al Monte Calvario foi.	on his way to Mount Calvary.
Non foi buscar pan ni vino	He didn't go after bread or wine
porque aquí lo hay.	because here we have those things.
Foi por tres hierbas benditas	He went after three blessed herbs
para esta ferida curar.	to heal this wound.
Y tu, ferida,	And you, wound,
ni entumezas,	neither swell,
ni entestulezas,	nor get pussy,
más que las llagas	any more than the wounds
de mi Señor Jesucristo. Amén.	of my Lord Jesus Christ. Amen.

This prayer, like the others, seeks help from a supernatural being, Saint Idelfonso, to try to heal an ailment. The saint comes to the earth ("por aquí pasou") and goes toward a height, the cosmological Mount Calvary, where the blessed herbs that help humans are to be found. These herbs are divine products in the same way that bread and wine are human products; so, too, the wounds of humans correspond to the wounds of "Lord Jesus Christ." These oppositions could be rendered schematically as follows:

Here (earth)	::	There (sky)	::	sky ↑
Cultivated land	::	Mount Calvary	::	Saint Idelfonso
Bread and wine	::	Blessed herbs	::	↓
Wounds of humans	::	Jesus Christ		earth

Saint Idelfonso is an intermediary between the two universes posited in the prayer: here, earth, where there is bread and wine, where people have wounds; there, sky/heaven, the place on Mount Calvary, where the blessed herbs grow, where Lord Jesus Christ has wounds. The cosmological mountain has its equivalent in the *monte* around the *braña*. The lands the Vaqueiros cultivate produce bread and wine but not wild herbs; the uncultivated *monte* that surrounds the *braña* is the home of the wild beasts, the habitat of the undergrowth that threatens to devour the ploughed land, but also the habitat of the herbs that bring health to the Vaqueiros.

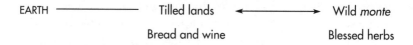

EARTH ——————— Tilled lands ◄————————► Wild *monte*

Bread and wine   Blessed herbs

The dichotomy blessed/accursed also has a temporal aspect. The week has two accursed or unlucky days [*dias aciagos*], Wednesday and Friday, and the month has an unlucky period, during the crescent moon, when one should not sow, cut timber, make repairs, or kill pigs, among other things. There is one day of the year in particular, June 24, the Day of Saint John the Baptist, that is especially blessed. Just as the priest blesses the laurel branches in church, so Saint John blesses the Vaqueiro universe during the night with water, the dew, which is holy.

> At the break of dawn you get up and take out the cows and pigs and everything because the dew is holy. And you used to have to drink water from a spring without having eaten first . . . and decorate doors and windows and stables with ash boughs. And we took out the bedclothes; in my house we took mattresses, sheets, blankets, and laid them outside to catch the dew.

To receive the water of Saint John, the house is literally turned inside out, and its effects are surrounded by moist green branches. The Vaqueiros' animals participate in the blessings, and Vaqueiros themselves come in contact with the dew. The dew is thought to prevent sickness in general and provide general well-being, but Vaqueiros single out two kinds of sicknesses against which it is particularly effective, those of the skin, especially scabies, and goiter.

> On Saint John's Day you get up early and you roll over naked in the grass to pick up the dew. There used to be something quite common called scabies or the itch. This was cured on Saint John's Day if you rolled over in the water of the field; it got rid of it. Hard to believe, eh? It happened to me once. I had it and got rid of it.

THE PATH TO DEATH

On Saint John's Day, if you have those lumps that come out, if you're getting a goiter, you have to go to nine springs, take a drink in each one. There have to be nine springs, or seven—not an even number, and after fasting. That way your neck won't swell out.

The therapeutic properties of the dew or water of Saint John also apply to herbs gathered on Saint John's day. The flower of the elder (*sabugo* or *beneito*) is blessed on that day. If gathered, these flowers will cure different ailments all year long.

On Saint John's Day it is customary to gather the flower of the *sabugo*. The white flower is very medicinal, and we gather it that day and leave it out to catch the dew of the night, and the dew will bless it. Then we take it in before the sun comes up and dries off the dew. The wetness the night of Saint John brings is said to be blessed. Here almost everyone gathers a handful of flowers and keeps them all year. It's very good for lots of things. For colds, cooked with milk; or for a pimple or a swelling, the flowers are warmed [in water], put on a cloth, and applied like a plaster. It is also very good for the eyes, for when you have erysipelas, too, it goes away when you warm some up and sprinkle it on.

In addition to providing medicine, Saint John and the vernal equinox with which he is associated bring hope of fertility. The water of this day, for instance, makes bread rise. "They say that the water of that day, before it is touched by the sun, is so good for mixing bread that you don't need yeast with it." Notions of fertility also are involved in the legends about the power of the springs on Saint John's Eve. Marvelous things are supposed to have happened near the springs, all of them related in some way to gold: the appearance of a golden horseshoe at the source of a little stream, the *pinto* bull who arises from a pond and changes everything that is put in his mouth into gold, or the famous "*encanta* of gold," whose story is recounted below. With this *encanta*, just as sickness was changed into health, poverty is changed into riches.

The *encanta* of gold is in some boulders near F called El Fontanón. There, on Saint John's Day, at dawn, an *encanta* of gold comes out to comb her hair. She has a golden comb and a brush. What's needed is a brave and valiant man; it can't be a woman. He has to carry a basket with some old rags, a part of a jacket, pants, underpants, all in the basket. And he gets there and says—he has to use the *tu* form—"Take from my poverty and give me from your wealth" [*"Toma de mi po-*

breza y dame de tu riqueza"]. Then she grasps the basket
and changes into a snake and begins to wind up around him
until the snake's head reaches the top of the man's head; and
when it gets to the top, it begins to go back down, to unwind,
and changes back into an *encanta,* which is like a siren.
Then the *encanta* says to the fellow there: "Turn around."
She puts the basket in his hand and says, "Don't look in the
basket until you get home, or else it will change into a serpent that will swallow you." And when he gets home, he
looks into the basket and finds it full of gold. But it has to be
a man, powerful and brave, who will be able to stand her
changing into a serpent and wrapping herself around him,
who will not fall down. Because if he falls, he curses it, and
she can never come out again, and he'll never be able to
marry, and if he does marry, he won't have children or ever
enjoy his life. He will live like an idiot.

On Saint John's Day, rags, the lot of the Vaqueiro in his everyday
misfortune and misery, are changed into gold, the always unattain-
able happiness. No one ever actually gets the gold, although there
is at least a possibility of getting it during one day, once a year.

And my father told my mother to prepare the basket for
him and maybe he'd come back loaded with gold. He would
keep saying it, but he never did it. There was another man, X,
who wanted to go; he wanted get rich, too. But the fact is no
one ever did it. Yet the *encanta* is there, and even though it
snows for a year straight, the spring of the *encanta* never
freezes.

Although there has never been a Vaqueiro brave enough to try to
make the bargain, any Vaqueiro may go at dawn on Saint John's Day
to drink from the spring of the *encanta* in search of health if not of
wealth.

Let us examine more closely the relation between man and
water, Saint John and the *encanta.* Aside from other meanings,[17]
the legend is a description of the interaction and communication
between man and a supernatural being, the *encanta*/snake. A man
initiates this contact by going to the spring and establishing the
terms of a transaction in the appropriate ritual language. But the
relation is not posed in economic terms. The female *encanta* is
combing her hair provocatively in the water of the spring when the
man arrives (and note that it must be a man); the man offers her
pieces of male clothing (jacket, pants, and underpants); and finally,
as a snake, the *encanta* coils around the man's body. As a reward for
this bravery, the *encanta* offers the man a part of herself, the gold

THE PATH TO DEATH

from which she is made. But there is an associated threat of a severe punishment—death (being swallowed by the serpent) or sterility (he will not be able to marry, nor not have children, nor enjoy his life). And the *encanta* will not be able to come out again. This tale contains a series of dichotomies, some explicit, others implicit:

Man/Woman
Rags/Gold
Poverty/Riches
Sterility/Fertility
Asexuality/Sexuality
Earth/Water
Ground/Underground
Sickness/Health
Unhappiness/Happiness

The *encanta* appears to personify the power of water that comes up from the depths of the earth. Note that this is the place attributed to the snake, and also the place where gold is supposed to be. The fact that the *encanta* may be able to punish the man with sterility implies that she is also able to bestow fertility, which is the essential feature of water.[18] Man must be brave enough to confront the power of water. If water is misused it will destroy; if used well it will ensure fertility. The ambivalence surrounding the *encanta* (gold and the serpent) replicates that which exists in the sexual relations of humans beings. The woman is a source of pleasure and a source of life, but she also can cause sickness and death. These dichotomies reflect Vaqueiro attitudes toward the sexes and fecundity as well as their dependence on cows, female animals.

The dawn of Saint John's Day places man in communication with the different levels of his universe, represented by supernatural beings and the water that blesses or cures. One is Saint John, an inhabitant of the sky, and the dew he sends down to the earth, whence comes the water from the springs. The man who goes to the spring on Saint John's Day to drink the water from the earth and receive the dew from the sky is an intermediate level. Just as the legend poses the possibility of contacting the underground supernatural, so there is a possibility of contacting the heavenly Saint John by way of smoke, by jumping over the bonfire, which is a source of blessings. The dew comes from the sky, and the smoke of the bonfires of Saint John returns to the sky. Both dew and smoke cure illnesses. It is no coincidence that *fumazas* (braziers of coal from the fire and branches that have been blessed) are one of the most frequently employed therapies for human and animal ailments at any time of the year. They are a prime form of communication with the power of the sky and a symbolic transaction with the powers that cause the ailment. Whereas earlier prayers showed us partial aspects of the interaction of earth, underground, and sky, the legend of the *encanta* contains this complete cycle:

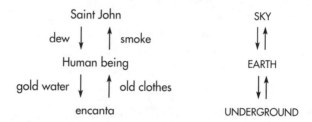

The ambivalence of the *encanta* suggests that good and evil are not always wholly opposed, antagonistic, and separate; the line between them is weak and broken. This can be seen in the objects considered to be blessed—some because they bring good luck and most because they are considered medicinal (an important aspect of what is blessed). It is very significant that some of these objects are parts of accursed animals: the tooth and the stomach of the wolf, the hide and the fat of the bear, and the head and tail of the snake.[19]

The tooth of the wolf is blessed—the mark of the tooth is good when the burros get the colic [*tarazón*]. They say that by passing one of those teeth over the gums, the colic goes away. For the cow, too. When the cow has a sick udder, they run a wolf's tooth over it, on the back part, nine days. In the house there is a wolf's tooth about so big.

Bear fat is a very powerful medicine. The old folks said that cooking it a little and adding some water is good for rheumatism and for the strange ailments that come out under fingernails and toenails. And the wolf's tooth is also medicinal; and the stomach of the wolf also has something very medicinal, for medicines.

The snake is an accursed animal, but its flesh is good. Once there was a man sick in bed, and it was a hopeless case. Then someone up and says, "Go get a snake." He cut off the head and tail, where the venom is, cooked it in an omelet, and served it to him. And they say it cured him. The skin shed by a snake brings good luck and cures headaches. The

THE PATH TO DEATH

skin is put in a handkerchief, which is put on the forehead or wherever it hurts, and the pain goes away.

The wolf, the bear, and the snake, which are regarded so negatively when alive, become useful when they are dead. Humans appropriate nature using certain parts of these animals as medicine, converting some of their substance into culture.

The accursed, what is evil, is also found inside the *braña*, just as the blessed may be found outside. The dog, for example, a faithful companion in herding and a domestic animal that frequently fights off the wolf, is nevertheless an accursed animal. One of the version of the *cosiyo* or *espina* prayer includes both dogs and men among the evil beasts, and orders it as with the others, to its rightful place: *"Se sos de can, al monte a tsadrar"*["If from a dog, go to the *monte* to bark"].[20] The dog likewise is regarded with ambivalence because of its capacity to bite and give rabies. Although it is classified as accursed, the dog has a blessed tongue.

> The dog, no, but the tongue of the dog is blessed. Blessed because they say it is medicinal, like any other thing that is blessed in church. One time a dog bit me in the thigh, attacked me. And I remember that my grandfather got them to bring the dog to my house to lick the wound; for it is very good if the dog licks it. That's why they say a dog's tongue is blessed. I got well, thank God.

The dichotomy blessed/accursed that Vaqueiros associate with the concepts of health and illness reveals the importance of religion in their classification of good and evil, well-being and misfortune. Although the Vaqueiros usually refer to a specific historical moment to explain the origin of the dichotomy, the time when supernatural beings roamed the earth, their classification system is nevertheless in flux, and the possibility of new blessings or curses remains. These local traditions are atemporal and ubiquitous. That is why local mythology deems certain elements of the environment blessed or accursed because of small favors or unpremeditated offenses humans give to supernatural beings. The fact that a plant that accidentally served as a hiding place for a divine being should be blessed, or that an animal that ate hay from the manger should be cursed, would seem to suppose an excessive degree of supernatural intervention. It betrays a need to include the natural universe within the moral order. It is because of this inclusion that animals, plants, and other aspects of the Vaqueiro environment seem to exhibit a consciousness and will acquired by contact with the supernatural.

Sickness and the Vaqueiro Cosmology

COSMOS	SKY		EARTH	UNDERGROUND
SPACE	Mountain		Valley	Holes
BEINGS	God	Saints	Persons	*Encanta*
ANIMALS	Birds		Domestic/Wild Animals	Pest
PLANTS	Blessed herbs		Bread and wine	Briars and brush
TIME	Holy days		Work days	Unlucky days

FIGURE 4 UNIVERSE CLASSIFICATION

In mythic times divinities granted their blessings by their mere presence; today sacred images of the region do the same. Contact with the sacred image renders objects holy or blessed. Religious intermediaries can also render things holy or blessed with their prayers, and so can laypersons when they make the sign of divinity, the cross. These gestural blessings have the power to preserve the health and well-being of people and their domestic animals.

The words of ritual prayer appear to be the key weapons in the struggle against evil. Ritual prayer is a combination of religious prayer, therapeutic formula or recipe, and dialogue between the forces that provoke illness and the forces that cure it. The healing forces are often mentioned explicitly: the Virgin, God, or a particular saint. Other times these figures are implicit, as in the sign of the cross, the reciting of an Our Father before or after the cure takes place, or the general religious context in which the therapy is performed. The forces that cause illness may be a group of accursed animals, the animals of sickness, pests, reptiles, and parasites that transmit evil or disease by their contact, tracks, or presence. Blessings and curses are transmitted in the same way. Blessed and accursed are terms that allow the Vaqueiros to order and classify the cosmos, nature, and society. The structure of Vaqueiro prayers and legends is based on a tripartite division of the universe that applies to space and time, beings, animals and plants (see figure 4). In this classification, the most elaborate and refined category is that of animals. It should not be surprising that in a herding culture the physical, social, and metaphysical distinctions should be expressed in a lexicon of beasts. In this symbolic zoology, humans observe animals and classify them by their benefits or drawbacks, by their habits and habitat, and by physical features. But this classification based on animals is also applied to human nature. The domestic/wild dichotomy is carried over to the social and supernatural spheres.[21]

THE PATH TO DEATH

Bendito and *maldito,* translated in this work as blessed and accursed, in fact have more complex meanings and connotations.

Bendito	Maldito
blessed	accursed
good	evil
domestic	wild
brings luck	brings misfortune
medicinal	poisonous
fertility	sterility

These oppositions would seem to reflect a dichotomized view of reality. But the schema is not so clear-cut, for there is a broad range of exceptions. The mule and the dog, domestic animals, are nevertheless accursed. The eagle, a bird, is accursed as well. The dew of Saint John's Day is blessed, but not the mist, which also comes from the sky. Saint Barbara, the eagle, and thunder are interchangeable and get confused one with another. Herbs, which are blessed, are located in the wild. Water from the underground will cure on Saint John's Day. Fertility is associated with the *encanta* serpent that dwells below ground. And certain parts of accursed animals—dogs, bears, wolves, and snakes—are blessed and will cure the Vaqueiros. What is the meaning of these ambiguities?

The fact that a good part of the Vaqueiro universe falls into the categories of blessed and accursed is not just the result of a purely intellectual, cognitive need for order. The placement of elements responds as well to the need for an affective and moral order. While good and evil comprise two distinct spheres, they are in permanent contact, connected by an ill-defined, permeable boundary. Communication between the two spheres is facilitated by ritual as well by the beings, animals, and objects that, because of their ambivalent positioning, serve as mediators. The relation of spheres could be represented as in figure 5. In this model we will not find the moral fanaticism that derives from the radical separation of abstract notions of pure good and pure evil. Life and the world, human and supernatural beings, do not belong to either of the two spheres totally or absolutely. In other words, the Vaqueiros understand that there is a relation between good and evil that finds expression in the ambiguity of human relations and human beings. Theirs is a sophisticated vision of the world seen as a complex reality, not as a simple Manichean opposition.[22]

Behind the "words that heal" we also find a cultural model of sickness, which is understood as disorder, something out of place.

Sickness and the Vaqueiro Cosmology

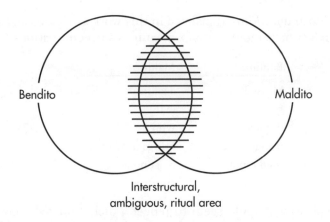

Interstructural,
ambiguous, ritual area

FIGURE 5 RELATION OF SPHERES

By implication there exists an order, a symbolic classification that I have tried to describe. For the Vaqueiros these disorders originate in differents parts of the cosmos, in the displacement of animals from their proper habitat, in the interference of wilderness in the domestic area. Disease and misfortune are seen as cosmic disruptions, and therefore health and fortune are achieved by restoring the order of the universe to which the sick person belongs. This metonymic restitution is accomplished by symbolic means. The evocative and expressive power of words, in the form of prayers, works this miracle poetically.

CAUSES OF ILLNESS: THE BODY IS A SYSTEM

Certain ailments are considered the results of anomalies and imbalances in the body. *Relajadura* [relaxedness or relapsedness] occurs when some part of the body has fallen out of place—belly, intestines, or sexual organs—and also is called a *herni* or *herniadura:*

> *Relajura,* yes, that is the hernia. When you're inside out, when your guts come out, you can also be herniated in the belly or in the sexual organs. This happens to us just like cows. We have two skins, and the inside skin bursts and maybe the guts come out, or a lump, or whatever, to the outside. The outside skin does not break, and the guts don't fall down to the ground, but you have to operate on it, and when you have *la estrangulada* there's hardly ever a cure for it.

> My mother had a fallen womb. She had it for many years. Some punishment, eh? Then she had trouble with her legs

THE PATH TO DEATH

after falling from a horse when she was young. Her kidney was hanging loose; she couldn't move and couldn't go out. She was like that for a half a year. She wasn't that old, but she got to the point where she wasn't eating anything, and seeing herself so bad off. . . . I said to her, "But how can you stand this, you're in very bad shape." And she said, "No, as soon as I lie down it goes back into place." But towards the end it didn't go back.

Quite similar to *relajadura* is another ailment common in the *braña*, in which one or more organs in the body shift out of place. This happens especially to the stomach and is called "fallen stomach" [*estómago caído*] or *sesgadura*.

I have *sesgadura*. That's when the stomach comes detached here, falls down, and then hurts a lot. They operated on me, but since then it's just the same. And I've lost my appetite, my kidneys hurt from it, and as my stomach isn't in place I vomit a lot. What happened is I maimed myself [*me manqué*]. When I work I maim myself all over again. If I didn't work so much I'd get a lot better.

As the informant states, this kind of imbalance often results from the hard work of the *braña*. There are similar instances in which one's chest or back "comes open" or "comes apart" from carrying very heavy loads—of earth, grass, or hay—up the steep slopes of the *braña*. In such cases the body "opens up" internally. The external signs of this problem include the inability to stand up straight or to move the body correctly. An opening in the chest is considered more dangerous than one in the back.

You can open the chest if you make too much of an effort. The person with a chest that has come open has the chest ruined for life if it's not fixed in time. Like C from B, when he picked up that stone, a very big stone, he hurt his chest—he felt a pain, *ras!* That doesn't heal well.

This ailment is thought to involve the slippage of one of the two horizontal parts of the body. Hence the cure for the "open chest" attempts to restore the equilibrium of the body by manipulating the affected part.

First you measure from the mouth of the stomach on one side to the center of the back, and then you measure the other side. When someone has an open chest one of the sides is shorter, the measure is not the same; the two sides are not equal. One side is shorter than the other if the person is

Sickness and the Vaqueiro Cosmology   57

open. And then you have to rub it with oil and butter this way on the front until they are the same. It has to be something smooth in order to rub it so it draws out the affected side until it gets even. And then it is trussed up well and they don't work for a few days, not at all.

More frequent and less serious is the opening of the back, also termed *espinitcharse* or *tirarse la espinitcha*. Here the bones of the back are thought to come detached from the *espinilla* or backbone. This also occurs as a result of an excessive effort.

Well, opening the back comes from lifting a weight too heavy for you and carrying it on your back, and the bones of the back come loose a little; but it can be fixed. I've had my bones separate from my back two or three times, and grandfather here fixed it for me.

The first part of the operation for fixing the *espinilla* is the diagnosis. The patient sits on the ground with ankles together and hands joined on the top of the head with the body relaxed. The *arreglador* or fixer lifts the patient from the ground by the wrists and sees whether the body is twisted, or has one limb longer than another, an unequivocal sign of the illness. If this is the case, the patient once more assumes the initial position, links fingers and makes a bow with the arms, which the fixer grasps, shaking the limp body of the patient repeatedly up and down. This sharp motion puts the bones back into place, and then the healer lifts the patient up, grasps the patient around the waist from behind, and presses the patient's body several times to confirm the correct positioning of the bones, which are then held in place by a truss. According to this informant, who later performed the operation on his own daughter, the incidence of this ailment has decreased.

I sat down on the ground with my two feet together, my ankles together, and my body like it was dead. And he took me by the wrists and shook me a little so that with the dead weight of the body it would go back into place, become even. And then he put his arms around me and pressed me hard against him, a series of embraces that made my back crack, *tras! tras!* . . . And then he tied me up with a truss tight against my chest . . . and a few days without working, and eating well, and then *ala!* back to work. Now nobody opens his back anymore, because they don't lift such heavy loads as before. And since nobody lifts the loads, how are they going to come open? When I was like X [ten years old] all day long I was carrying loads of grass, of ferns, of firewood, and as I carried more than I was able to lift, that's why it happened to me.

The dislocations of bones and muscles in other parts of the body, especially in the limbs, are considered in the same light. Such dislocations are common because of the farm work Vaqueiros perform. They are treated by a combination of gentle massages and more vigorous manipulation. Because this sickness involves something "out of place" that affects the equilibrium of the body, the treatments attempt to return the affected parts to their original places.

In addition to these disarrangements "on the outside" of the body, there are other sicknesses "inside" [*de dentro* or *cosas de adentro*] that are much more dangerous and less manipulable from the outside, problems requiring "apparatuses" for diagnosis and surgery for treatment. The Vaqueiros consider the weakest or most vulnerable parts of the human body (and that of animals, too) to be the thorax, which includes the lungs and the hearts, and the stomach.

The thoracic sector is where sicknesses attack you most, both in people and in animals. It's in the thorax that you get pneumonia, colds, flu . . . and in the intestines, the stomach.

The heart is the main base of the body. When the heart stops beating, then you're missing everything. A person can have an operation for a lung or a liver, but when your heart fails you, you're a goner. It's like when you kill a pig, eh? And if you put the knife in its heart, it dies instantly, without a . . . it bleeds a lot and dies. The same goes for a person. That is, the pig as a pig, an animal, and a person as a person, with the heart, good-bye!.

It is because the heart is so crucial that it divides the human body into two different parts, the left and right, a dichotomy that expresses negative and positive values respectively. For example, in the case of pneumonia, "They say that death comes to the left side before the right, that the right side holds out longer than the left. If the sickness comes on the left side, it gets to the heart right away." The heart also stands for the most interior part of the body, the source of noxious products, in contrast to the exterior of the body, which includes the best of the human being. The values bad/good associated with interior/exterior appear through a plant metaphor as follows:

The heart of the potato is the worst part; the part with the vitamins is near the skin, but the heart has the bad things. Notice that when you cut a potato in half, you can see what they call the heart of the potato, like some rays or veins, marked on the potato in the middle, and near the skin you see the potato clean. In the middle you see things like branches going in one direction; they say that is the heart of the potato. See, we are the same as a plant, the same as an animal. Inside is the worst, and on the outside the good part is covered. I mean to say that what you and I and everybody expel are the bad products, what has no value for good, because when you take everything in, the stomach mixes it up, and when it goes into the intestines, the good part goes into the blood, and you expel the bad part.

The human body has the same configuration as the potato, where the nerves replicate the potato's "branches" and "veins." The sickness of nerves attacks both vital parts of humans, the heart and the stomach. People say that "nerves affect the heart," or "he suffers from lax nerves in the stomach." If the heart is the center of the human being, the stomach maintains life and health. A correct diet ensures an internal equilibrium while hunger produces a multitude of ills. Internal illness will be visible externally in such symptoms as a change in physical appearance and loss of weight. At times such an illness can lead to death.

They say when a person is very thin, that person is heading for a *tisis* [literally, phthisis, consumption]. It is like tuberculosis. They start drying up and die with all their wits alive, as we are talking to each other now. There was a girl here who was fully alert and heard the bells of the cows and said, "Mama, I know the names of all the cows in the village," and I think she had tuberculosis. That came from hunger. It was after the war, and her bones got weak. It came from being weak, and from being hungry yesterday, today, and tomorrow, and there was nothing you could do for it. When you get hungry you lose your appetite. That girl was raised hungry; she didn't eat because there was no food. First she had a *reuma* in her bones, and when they realized it, it was too late, and every day she was worse. Some get tuberculosis in the blood, and she got it in the bone, until she got weak and couldn't walk. You can also get an anemia, because from anemias bad things come as well—everything you see to eat looks bad to you. You don't want anything.

While lack of food can lead to sickness, so can overeating, especially of foods considered "strong." This is the cause of "cerebral congestion," as explained here:

THE PATH TO DEATH

Cerebral congestion—that's when the congestion attacks you in the brain; sometimes there is no cure for it. A woman from X here filled up on chestnuts and couldn't digest them and died. And the mother of Z from Y, too. . . . *Hombre*, if you eat a heavy meal and you can't take it, it's the same. A lot of chestnuts is bad; they are very strong, hard to digest when you eat a lot. A person who's a little sick can't eat them. Once I almost died from them—I just about died; I knew I was dying. And *la fabada* [roughly, pork and beans] is also heavy meal. Look at V's father. When he was in the army he almost died, too; he was very hungry and ate the helpings of five, six, or seven people, and then got a congestion, and luckily he got diarrhea, otherwise. . . . In cows it's the same.

At the slightest symptom of illness one needs a mild diet, rest from work, and reclusion in the house. Bad weather, especially the cold, causes many illnesses.

He got sick when his sister was ill, and he went for the doctor to X; he already had a fever, he was a little sick, too. And on his way back on the path, the doctor told him he ought to be in bed rather than out fetching doctors. And the man, his idea was that as long as one is able to, one should be up and about. And when he came back, instead of going to bed, he went to work. And it was a bitter, killing cold. And then he got very sick.

In addition to the risks inherent in the life of the *braña*—the work, the food, and the cold—some illnesses appear to be caused by the female condition. The most common illnesses result from disorders in childbirth, or lack of care during menstruation, times that are considered very sensitive.

She had been sick in the guts for many years, and then she died. It was a pain she got in the belly the day I was born. I was born in X, in a hayloft, and the kitchen was underneath, and they grabbed me and left her up there without help. When they went up she had fainted. They left her alone, she got cold, and from that day on she had a pain in her belly, until she died.

Some died from filling up on chestnuts. When a woman is bad off [has her period], it's bad to eat chestnuts. My aunt, they called her from H house to take sheep dung out to the pasture. And what with taking out the dung, and then the beans they gave her for lunch—she probably didn't tell them anything—in any case, they gave her beans, and she being a girl of about twenty, strong and pretty, she came back home and got sick, after hauling sheep dung and eating beans and being bad off, and died.

Marriage can also cause sickness. Sexual relations are dangerous in certain cases, as with this girl who "didn't take to marriage" ["*no le pinta casarse*"].

One of my daughters died. She was married; she married here but died in Madrid. She died of a "chest" problem. She didn't take to marriage, she married very young, and I don't know what happened to her but she got sick. Oh my God! She was in hospitals for thirteen years, and they did her no good. She was very young, not even eighteen years old, but she insisted on getting married. I don't know what she had, the doctors didn't say. She had a baby when she was already sick; then the baby got sick and died, and then they went back to Madrid, and then she got very sick. Here she got much better, but she got worse as soon as she went to Madrid. Her father-in-law said that is wasn't good for her to be with her husband. Because while she was here, *vaya!* she was pretty well. She had had a congestion in a lung, and I'm not sure she was really over it.

Men can also get sick from females, especially if they have sexual relations with women who have their periods, because menstrual blood is contagious. Certain kinds of tuberculosis are thought to have this origin.

There are two kinds of tuberculosis. One comes to men through women. Now there are many medical advances, but that couldn't be cured, because it was even inherited through families, they say even through seven generations. There are various kinds but one is worse than the others.

Women can give you tuberculosis, but not those here— those from other places. I saw that in B, in T's house, in a brother who came home from Madrid sick. We were there sewing, and he ate a lot—they even killed sheep for him to eat, and he ate big pieces of goat, but every day he was worse and worse, from that thing that was gnawing at him. And he would go out in the sun, which he liked a lot. And that is how he died, each day worse until he was stiff. He came from Madrid sick, for they had infected his blood.

The categories female/male are used to designate a greater or lesser degree of sickness. Sicknesses termed female are more widespread in the body and more serious; while male sicknesses are slower and more limited. This dichotomy is applied to traditional illnesses like *icema* [eczema] as well as to more recently diagnosed diseases like cancer.

Cancer is something that can be female or can be male. It's like *icema*, which can be female or male. *Icema* is a skin infection, and there is male *icema* and female *icema*. The female they say spreads more, and the male spreads less. If it is female, you are more contaminated; if it is male, you just have an infection in a little patch, in one place. The female kind is worse.

The category of female includes, on the one hand, the aspect of fertility—the female *icema* "spreads" (*puebla*, literally, "peoples"). On the other hand, this category implies a certain intrinsic contamination or dirtiness derived from women's situation during menstruation. The emphasis placed on women "from other places" does not keep men from having a certain fear of those "inside." Nevertheless, it is thought that many illnesses originate on the outside, contracted by Vaqueiros who leave the *braña* for military service, especially during wars or in the years immediately thereafter.

They used to call that the chills [*calenturas*]. During the war in Melilla there was a lot of that. X also had the chills. They are fevers. It was said they could be cured with the honey from a new hive. And they cured one fellow that way, who came home from doing the *mili* with those chills. In Africa, that is where they caught those fevers, yes, because of the water and the climate. Almost all the soldiers got it there, or had it when they got back here. That X came back very sick, aching all over. He had a high fever, and then they gave him honey from a new hive, and he got well.

Theories about sickness and health that people from the outside world attempt to transplant to the *braña* are also regarded as dangerous. The owners of the house discussed below had lived in a tropical country in Central America.

She had a pretty baby, four or five months old. . . . They were farm managers [*caseiros*] here in X, and the owners of the house, since they were from the outside world. . . . There were a lot of drafts and ventilation in the house, and they had the baby naked in bed, with nothing more than a string on its chest. One day I said to her, "But this baby is going to catch cold." And she said, "I don't know, they want him that

Sickness and the Vaqueiro Cosmology   63

way. . . ." He got sick and died soon after. They said that in the outside world babies went naked. They were very strange. They said that you didn't have to cover them up, that they grew up better, healthier. He had to get cold that way, catch pneumonia or something. You have to cover up those little babies. I think that day it was cloudy and there were a lot of drafts, with so many doors and windows as that house had. And the baby was cold, just had some strings covering its belly. He died.

While "new advances" from the outside cure some sicknesses, progress also results in new illnesses caused by chemicals.

Now they bring in chemical flour. Who knows where it comes from? And all these chemicals are an excuse for the cattle to get sick. Because it's not the real thing; it's artificial. And also they put guano and nitrates and garbage like that on the fields—there are more chemicals and the cattle get sick. Before it was the rare cow that got sick, until it had a fall, or had an *asiento* of water, something that didn't sit well on the stomach. And now with these advances . . .

The Vaqueiros regard prepared foods bought outside the *braña* with similar suspicion. Vaqueiros send their city relatives homemade foods for Christmas—beans, potatoes, butter, and particularly meat products. The city relatives send toys and clothes rather than food. It is not only that the most healthful and natural foods are to be found in the *braña*; the basic medicinal products are to be found there as well. In addition to herbs,

They say that we have medicine here. Look, there are some hats here in the pastures. No, not hats, some white things, like eggs. My uncle said this year: "Look, they make penicillin from this, we have it here."

The *braña* is also a place of fertility. Some Vaqueiros who have been out in the world come home to combat sterility.

One of my uncles spent many years in Buenos Aires, married, and came back to Spain, here, and when he came back he had three children right away. I don't know if the doctors ordered him to come back to Spain, but he came back for that. I have it from my mother that he came back in order to have children. And N of C, how many years was it she didn't have children? And she came back to the village and had one. Since they were born here and spent many years here, it must be the change in water, climate—anyway, they went back there pregnant.

Vaqueiros will go to the city for drastic remedies like opera-tions, or for diagnoses in the case of complex diseases, or to consult specialists, but the *braña* is the place for convalescence. Vaqueiros' relatives, too, will come to the *braña* to recuperate from their own ailments.

The equilibrium that obtains in the cosmological system sky/ earth/underground is reproduced in the configuration of the human body. As we have seen, disease results from something being "out of place," whether living creatures or objects. In the case of the body, imbalances stem from the disarrangement of the body parts: certain organs, bones, or members shift from where they belong. Specific remedies seek to reinforce the unity and equilibrium of the body system. The affected parts are manipulated externally in an attempt to return them to their original position. In this sense, then, health consists of harmonious control of the body as a sys-temic unit. This unit is divided into halves that should be kept in strict equilibrium with the spine forming the vertical frontier be-tween the two halves. In illness, the body ruptures internally, caus-ing displacement to the right or to the left, on the front of the body or on the backside.

Disturbances "inside" the body are considered more difficult to diagnose and treat than those "outside." Today the Vaqueiros con-sider "inside" diseases the province of the official specialist who can observe them with his equipment. The Vaqueiros give certain body parts special attention. Aside from the lungs,[23] the key organs are the heart and the stomach. Together they divide the human body horizontally into two halves. The heart is considered the weakest point of the body, but it is also the body's vital center. Left and right seem to have negative and positive values respectively. Also, the exterior of the body is deemed positive while the interior is deemed negative because of the noxious products that issue from within. These products are expelled selectively thanks to the stom-ach, the motor of life. The functioning of this organ is held vital for the maintenance the health, as one can see from continual refer-ences to elderly persons who have a "good stomach" in spite of their age. The stomach, located in the lower half of the body, thus represents the physical and biological aspects of the body. It admits all kinds of food, with no moral connotation. The upper half, by contrast, corresponds to the emotional part of a human being. "Having a good heart" means being generous and affectionate; "a bad heart" connotes evil and social and moral danger. The heart is the moral center of the person, the source of obscure feelings and disorderly passions. The expulsion of noxious products from the body is a metaphor for the expulsion of the evil within, the biological exorcism of each person's devils. This expulsion is accomplished through the stomach. Heart and stomach are two symbols of the human being and its basic antinomies.

Hence the Vaqueiros attribute great importance to food for maintaining internal equilibrium. Hunger is seen as the origin of many illnesses and disorders. Chronic in the past, it fills the childhood memories of adult Vaqueiros and is exorcized in their many ritual banquets. But although hunger kills, so, too, may overeating. The danger of excess, especially of "strong" foods like broad beans and chestnuts, demonstrates the fine equilibrium and the fragility of the body. Matters of diet point to ecological causes for illness. The body is worn down by everyday work and by the interaction with the habitat of the *braña*. Hard work, bad food in times of hunger, cold weather, and humidity are the Vaqueiros' facts of life. But diet also points to social behavior. Sickness thus becomes a symptom that enforces a break from overwork. The sick person demands special care, no matter what the disease—abundant and choice food, total rest from work, and reclusion in the house.

Other causes of sickness seem to arise from a Vaqueiro's interaction with other humans beings. Women get sick due to the risks and wear and tear inherent in being female—childbirths or menstruation. The Vaqueiros associate these situations, which one might consider "natural" rather than disorders, with other "natural" circumstances, including the cold, work or certain strong foods. Yet they also attribute sickness to "cultural" causes like the contagion of the blood by contact with women, or the frequency and risks of coitus (not taking to one's marriage). Both men and women can get sick through sexual contact. I treat the matter more extensively below, but it is interesting to note here that the category female [*hembra*], which normally connotes fertility, a positive connotation, becomes negative in the context of disease. Women are considered fertile, but fertility in the context of disease means an increase in the amplitude and rapidity in the spread of the sickness.

Sickness can also come from outside the *braña*. It can be a result of the changes in the conditions of life entailed in trips outside the *braña*, especially in times of war or military service. These situations often have resulted in the loss of young members of the group by death or desertion. More benign emigrations for work also provoke moral traumas, which are thought to entail physical traumas as well, like sterility. Vaqueiros believe that these traumas are caused by changes in water and climate. By implication they believe that an equilibrium between nature and culture exists at

THE PATH TO DEATH

home. Just as illness is "something out of place," so Vaqueiro emigrants are "people out of place," who suffer disorders and other negative consequences because of their displacement. In spite of the generally negative valuation of many aspects of work, life-style, and culture in the *brañas*, when Vaqueiros consider the outside world they reaffirm their own. Like the body, it is thought to be a systematic, "natural" one.

ILLNESS AND HUMAN ENVIRONMENT: ENVY

Envidia, translated here as envy, is one of the Vaqueiros' most elaborated cultural concepts. Here I will discuss the symbolism of envy in relation to sickness.[24] The Vaqueiro saying "An evil envy will break the biggest rock" indicates the concrete and menacing power of a supposed abstract sentiment. Envy makes things sicken and die by way of a glance.

> There are some women around here that are said to have the evil eye. Do you know what it is? It's like you are here and envy the baby. And she begins to get sick. Then we would say, "It's because she was seen by an evil eye."

In this precise definition, the essential ingredient of the evil eye is not the look but envy, the act of envying. The eye is only an instrument, the localization of an evil envy. But who has this eye? Who envies? Consider the following examples:

> Sometimes you'll take the child to mass, at N, T, or C— this [girl] or another; and afterwards, maybe on the way back, she gets sick. And they say that some evil eye saw her. There are children who are very cute. I wouldn't envy them from anybody, eh? But there are those who envy them. Maybe there's a man who doesn't have any children, or a woman who says, "Ay! Who will give me this child, how cute he is!" or something like that. That's what they say. And maybe, I don't know, they hurt them! And the child begins to get sick, and we say that an evil eye saw it.

> Yes, there's a lot of that. Say you have a cow that gave birth not long before, and you take it out on a fine sunny day and meet someone who might or might not be a neighbor, and she says: "Well, the cow gave birth, eh? This must be a good cow. Look at that udder! And those tits! It must be good. . . . What a cow! May blessed Saint Anthony take care of it for you. . . ." And the cow comes down with a *recayo* [a sickness of the udder]. They would say it was caused by an evil eye.

Sickness and the Vaqueiro Cosmology

When you envy, you envy something good: a good meadow, a good cow, a good boy. Say a poor woman was asking for alms and saw the cattle. They might say, "It was so-and-so who bewitched it, because the stable door was open and she was staring at them." Some poor people will envy a rich house. It might be a poor woman you give alms to; deep down inside her she envies you, coveting what you have.

The people who envy are the extreme opposites of those who are envied; a sterile man or woman, a neighbor with less luck, a poor beggar woman. The Vaqueiros are very reticent in singling out persons with the evil eye. Although accusations of specific individuals do exist, always made privately and very confidentially, the most common accusations are ambiguous ones that center on unknown persons outside the group, those who pertain to the "world." The "world" includes everything that is not *aldea*, *braña*, or the surrounding territory. That is why the Vaqueiros often attribute the evil eye to someone in the crowd on a fair day in the big *aldea*, or to unknown beggars (visitors the Vaqueiros treat with suspicion and fear). When it is not possible to ascribe the evil eye to a stranger, when the evil eye is located in the *braña*—a neighbor, for instance—evil eyes make the internal tensions of the system visible. Both the eye and its focus, then, demonstrate antisocial behavior. This can be seen in the following analogy:

When cows start fighting, it's as though there were envious. And for that reason, although they might all be sisters, they hit at each other because they have been evil eyed. It's like if we were a herd of siblings in a household and we were all fighting with each other, if we had been envied; the same thing happens with animals.

In general, those who have the evil eye in the *braña* are those the people refer to as "bad neighbors," that is, they are "troublesome," "selfish," "not satisfied with that they have and want what others have," "a friend of strife and vengeance," and, of course, "envious." Women are often referred to as "gossipy," "hypocritical," "thieves," and "envious." Everyone agrees that "envy is the worst thing there is." There are many sayings that encapsulate this opinion: "He who is happy because of his neighbor's misfortune has his own coming" ["*El que se alegra con el mal del vecín, el suo vien por el camín*"]. "An envious person never flourishes," and so on. Note that the defects attributed to the envious affect the harmony of the community, and the maxims condemn problems between neighbors. By ascribing the evil eyes to this outside world, group solidarity is intensified and divisions within the group overcome.

I said before that envy causes sickness or kills by means of a glance. This phrase is in no way poetic; it must be taken literally, as the Vaqueiros themselves do. Evil eyes cause very specific and well-defined illnesses in the children of the *braña*. The two most important are the *mal del filo* [thread sickness] and the *mal de las lombrices* [worms].

The women of the *braña*, especially the mothers and paternal grandmothers, are those most concerned with the sicknesses of children. These are the women most directly responsible for the health and instruction of the younger children.[25] There can be no greater praise for a Vaqueiro woman than to be told how good-looking and healthy her children or grandchildren are. When a child is not well (all too often, according to the woman), special care is taken and worry sets in. It then becomes necessary to see a specialist, either the doctor or an *entendido* of envy. One kind of illness and its specialist excludes the other. For example, when I asked women about rituals of envy, I obtained responses like this one:

It's good you learn about this because maybe, *Ay Dios!* there are so many people in the world that . . . and so many children who die . . . How many of the poor things will die because it wasn't known . . . ! Doctors don't understand about this, about the bewitched worms and the *mal del filo*; of course, doctors don't know about it, because the kids get sick, sick, and they order medicine, and look at one thing and another, and the child gets worse each day, each day worse.

The "thread sickness" got its name from the use of a thread or string in the therapeutic ritual. It is a very common illness among children. The symptoms are: "they begin to stop eating, and get thin, it seems that they shrink, and don't grow at all, that they waste away. Then you have to measure them." The *entendida* is the one who measures the child in order to decide whether the child really has the thread sickness or some other illness. First she will make the sign of the cross, then she crosses herself and tells the child to stand up with arms outstretched in the form of a cross. Then she takes a thread or string and measures exactly the distance between the tips of the child's third fingers (that is, the horizontal dimension of the child), and, with the same measure, the child "from the tip of the head" vertically to the center of the foot. In the words of a famous *entendida*, the diagnosis is made as follows:

We have to have the same this way [horizontally] as up and down. If the thread reaches the ground, then the child has not been looked at, and if the thread only reaches halfway down the leg, or to the knee, then that means the child has been looked at, that he has the thread disease. Because the thread is the same, but if the child is sick, then it's not the same, it doesn't turn out the same.

If the result is negative, the *entendida* can check and see if the child may have the disease of bewitched worms or another disease of the *braña*, or she may diagnose an illness "of doctors" and advise a visit to one of these colleagues. If the result is positive, that is, if the child turns out to have the thread disease, she applies the ritual therapy.[26] To "cut" the sickness, the *entendida* takes the measurement thread and passes it around the child from top to bottom circularly nine times. Each time, she takes the two ends of the thread and puts them around the head of the child saying,

Filo te meto,	Thread I put you on
Filo te saco,	Thread I take you off
En el nombre del Padre,	In the name of the Father
y del Hijo	and the Son
y del Espíritu Santo.	and the Holy Spirit.
Dos ojos te vieron	Two eyes saw you
y un corazón malo.	and an evil heart.

Then she cuts the thread into nine pieces and throws them over her shoulder into the fire, one by one, at the same time saying:

Así seque quien te echó	May whoever gave you
el mal del filo,	the thread disease go dry,
como se secó este filo;	just as this thread went dry;
así seque quien	may whoever gave you
el mal del filo te echó,	the thread disease go dry,
como este filo secó.	just as this thread went dry.
El mal del filo te corto,	Your thread disease I cut,
el mal del filo te paso.	your thread disease I remove.
En el nombre del Padre, y del Hijo	In the name of the Father, and the Son
y del Espíritu Santo.	and the Holy Spirit.
El qu'el mal del filo t'echó,	May he who gave you the thread disease
seque como el filo secó.	go dry as the thread went dry.

A piece of the thread remains tied around the neck or the wrist of the child for a few days until it, too, is burned in the same way. These days form the period of convalescence. It is significant that the Vaqueiros refer to the disease not by its cause, an evil envy, or by the instrument of this envy, the evil eye, but by the most note-

THE PATH TO DEATH

worthy feature of its therapeutic ritual, the thread. This would seem to indicate that they are more interested in the diagnosis, therapy, and cure of the disease than in its hypothetical cause.[27] Nevertheless, the words of the ritual contain information about the "cultural" cause of the illness: two eyes that look and an envious heart.

Signs, invocations, analogies, and words provide strength; they are the medicine for envy. The curative agents are the *entendida*, the thread, and the purifying fire. The victims of the thread disease tend to be growing children. Although one theoretically can get the disease after adolescence, this is quite rare. The symptoms are invariably thinness, weakness, and loss of appetite. The sickness is slow, cumulative, and will consume the child unless the ritual therapy is administered. The eye, then, seems to administer envy in small doses. But we must look at the beginning of the ritual: the thread disease is diagnosed if, and only if, the thread is not the same both ways. As the Vaqueiros say: "If the child is sick, then [the child] is not the same, so [the thread] is not the same [length both ways]." By this they mean that the child does not grow as it should, or that it grows unevenly, out of proportion. This is the key to the thread disease. The sickness is a growth disorder, the destruction of harmony in the human body, a disturbance of the process of the child's development. Fear of uneven growth explains the high value the Vaqueiros place on harmony and physical strength, and their negative attitudes toward those with physical defects.[28] This fear must have been much more acute in the past when infant mortality was much greater. After the visit of the *entendida*, the child generally improves or at least the mother or grandmother appears to believe so. Concern for the health of the child has been allayed by the application of the therapy. The child also seems to be calmer, and at times, since it is no longer watched so excessively, it eats more. In other words it may be that love can kill as well as envy. In any case, if the therapy does not have the desired result, one alternative is to change *entendidas* and try again. Over time, the child normally stabilizes.

The evil eye is also thought to cause worms. This ailment strikes children, too, but unlike the thread sickness, it is sudden. It can be fatal and is always considered very dangerous. This disease affects small children. The name in this case refers to the cause, not the cure. The theory is that an evil envy, by way of a glance, introduces small black worms into the body, "the bewitched [*maleficiadas*] worms." These should not be confused with the more common tapeworms, which are clearly distinguished by the Vaqueiros. Tapeworms are included in the category of "white worms."

These white worms are believed to be produced by an excess quantity of milk and are remedied by a simpler ritual. They are "cut" by snapping scissors in front of the child's belly above her or his clothes, at the same time reciting words and giving the child a medicine bought at the pharmacy. The worm disease is caused by a different, malignant worm.

> These worms are said to be worms of persons who envy your children and look at them. And the children get very sick. . . . If they have a little blackness under the eyes, it means they have been envied. [The worms] are some black things that form between the flesh and the skin, which is like a *mecromio* [sic]. It's as though, if the child were an animal, a sickness formed between the flesh and the hide; these things grow that way.

In this quote one clearly sees the specific cause of the disease and its translation in "scientific" terms. The worms are believed to be *"mecromios"—microbios* [microbes].

The therapeutic ritual has a certain sense and revelance. It can be seen in the clinical history of one of the victims of the disease, whose mother speaks here:

> I had a very beautiful boy, fat and very handsome, who was never sick. One day an old woman came from another village, asking for alms. I gave her some potatoes to eat, but she seemed to think it wasn't enough. She went up to the child and started saying, "What a handsome, beautiful child; how well he is! I have a grandson his age, but not so healthy as this one." She talked this way for some time, and then she left. The next day the boy got sick and the following day worse, and the next worse, until he was almost dying. It was that woman who was looking at him and did some witchcraft, because she thought the alms weren't enough or because she envied the child. And since the child was getting worse, P [the *entendida*] came and cut the thread sickness out of the child for me. And it was worms. I hadn't known that P knew about it [worm disease]; she didn't say anything to me. All she did was cut the thread disease, and it didn't do him any good. And the child got worse. And then the child's father went with him to the doctor. And the doctor didn't save him either; said he had a "chronic sickness," and there was no cure for it. The child was four months old. He completely changed in just a few days—his eyes sunk in, and he was left with only his skin. The doctor couldn't find anything wrong, and the child was by then starting to make

death noises [*boqueando para morir*]. Then, when he was really dying [*del todo muriendo*] my father said—maybe he heard it—"That woman knew . . . did you look and see if he had those bewitched worms?" Old P came and cut them. She looked to see if he had the worms, and he was full of them. She took out big ones from all over his back, from his kidneys, from his whole body.

This case illustrates the way official and local medicine are typically used in succession. Furthermore, the whole tale is marked by the anguish of death. In the face of sickness, it is not possible to remain with arms crossed; one has to do something. The same woman continues:

Old P cut them from the child. He was already dying, completely dying. *Hombre!* By then he wasn't crying, or licking, or anything. You could just hear him breathe a little and open his mouth as much as he could. But she took care of all of them. For a while the child was as if he were dead. But the next day he began to get better and better, and in fifteen days he was perfectly all right.

The cutting of the worms is done as follows: (1) The *entendida* crosses herself, takes a small quantity of soap from a bar that has never touched water (because it "has more strength"), a little ash [*sarrio*] from the stove that has been previously sifted [*pineirada*], and some clean water. She mixes the ingredients and makes a pap or batter. (2) She makes the sign of the cross on the child and applies the mixture on the lower part of the child's spinal column. (3) At the same time, she recites the following formula nine times:

Córtote las cocas,	I cut your false worms
córtote las todas	I cut them all
córtote las malas	I cut the bad ones
déjote las bonas.	I leave the good ones.
Córtote las del renaz,	I cut those of your back,
déjote las del arcabaz.	I leave those of your belly,
Córtote las cocas	I cut your false worms
y las largas y las cortas	Both the long ones and the short ones
Sólo te dejo las del cordal	I only leave the ones in your heart
para tu corazón alimentar.	so they will feed your heart.

(4) Then she thins the mixture on the child's back with water and carefully examines the child's skin. It is believed that "when a child has them, the heads of the worms appear; they appear on the

back like the points of needles, but without coming all the way out." (5) The *entendida* then rapidly cuts off the heads of the worms with a knife she has ready. "The worms die and the child gets better."

As with the thread sickness, the ingredients of the cure include gestures and words, but they also include water, soap, and ashes. All three ingredients denote cleanliness. Soap and water, especially clean water and fresh soap, wash anything. Ash, which has been purified by fire and sifted, has traditionally been used as a detergent in the *brañas*. For a long time ash was the only detergent, used for laundry and to clean the stove, the dishes, and so on. So the symbolism of the ritual is fairly clear: soap, water, and ashes, which signify cleanliness are used to fight disease, considered to be dirt and pollution. The cleaning agents of everyday housework—the clean, the simple, the orderly—are employed against the bewitched worms, which are dirty and anomalous.[29] The Vaqueiros think of health and sickness as a battle between cleanliness and dirt, order and anomaly, and, in the final analysis, life and death.

The therapeutic formula contains local notions about anatomy. The worms come in two kinds, bewitched and white, the first derived from envy (the worst feeling) and the second from milk (the best food). The bad worms are extraneous, accursed, fatal; the white worms are natural and benign. The bad ones lodge behind, in the back; the others in front, in the belly. Those of envy are *cocas*, false, and destroy life; the ones from milk are "good" and needed by the body. The belly, storehouse of eaten food, makes the heart, the human motor, work, as the spell implies. The Vaqueiros take great interest in the body and how it works, and have a good idea of anatomy and the treatment of animal sickness. Every year several pigs are slaughtered in each house, and occasionally a cow as well. Vaqueiros also have a certain notion of evolution, as may be seen in their saying, "We Christians have the same organs as the pigs."

The evil worms come from envious persons who pass them to children with looks. Lice are communicated the same way.

> There was a woman here who envied, who bewitched an aunt of my mother. You know what lice are. Well, the next day she said to her: "Did you get lice, Fulana?" "I never had lice, girl!" But her shirt was black with them, and her armpits were full of them. . . . [I ask him for the cause] It's from envy, *hombre!* of course. How else would she gave gotten lice at that time? Because lice come from dirtiness. She wasn't dirty; she was clean in everything. But what happened was that [the other woman] sent them with her eyes.

　　　　　　　　　　　　　THE PATH TO DEATH

Evil eyes can be thought of as agents for the "contagion" of evil. Contagion would come from those most dirty, the frequent carriers of germs, like the beggars of the region—old, poor persons living in unsanitary conditions. Contagion can occur in the crowd at a cattle market, the day of the fair, and may be produced not only by a glance but also by the custom of kissing and touching, common and familiar Vaqueiro gestures toward children.[30] The belief that evil eyes are infections might explain the phenomenon on one level, or might be one aspect of the phenomenon, but not the only one.[31] The cultural responses to death demonstrate basic ideas about good and evil, luck and misfortune, order and disorder, in human relations. With pain and suffering, human fragility and proximity to death constantly present, life is conceived of as a struggle. Only in this struggle there can be some hope.

Here sometimes we have them smoked [cows and children], because we are mistrustful. We don't know what to do, because nothing does anything for them when they have it [the evil eye], so in order to do something . . . in case it might have an effect.

The words don't do much. They help, but you have to actually do something to them [the sick]. Medicine is worth more than words.

This [ritual] is to undo the bewitching of the girl, because they might have envied her. She was so nervous, so excited, the poor thing, that we said, "Let's smoke her." And look, it seems she's calmer now. It's not bad for her; it might not do any good, but it doesn't hurt either.

Local persons with physical defects are often suspected of having the evil eye. This is especially true of persons with any kind of ocular defect: eyes that are skewed, sunken, small, of different sizes, unbalanced, unsteady, or simply "ugly" according to Vaqueiro standards. The eyes are thought to express internal envy externally.

They have a different eye. A little bent toward one side or another. They have some defect of vision. That's why they say a "bad" eye [malo, translated throughout as evil but also meaning bad and sick]. Normally they don't look at you as other people do who look at you face to face. They look with anger, with an eye like this [turns one eye, twists his head], with anger.

Physical defects or imperfections have moral values: imperfection is bad while perfection is good. That is why not only eyes but also any other obvious physical anomaly can be the sign of an evil glance, as in the following case:

> In France, M said, there was a Vaqueiro who had a child that was sick, sick, sick, and more sick, and she wouldn't eat anything, and she was sick. And someone told the woman that there was a woman in France who knew many things, who did divining. And they told her, of course, what was happening to the girl. And she [the diviner] said, "Well, it's a woman who is doing that to the child; don't let that woman see the child!" And they had to change apartments. It was a black woman who was envying her for the child, and there was no way for the child to get better. And as soon as they left, the girl was well, completely well. It was a black woman who was bewitching her.

This quote shows how the belief and the therapy continue beyond the Vaqueiro boundaries. In this case it was easy to find a scapegoat. These Vaqueiros, who probably had never seen blacks before emigrating, viewed the black woman as a strange and different being. Note that in the story it was a woman who "bewitched" the girl. Throughout the quotes in this section, one may have noticed that the Vaqueiros use the verb "to bewitch" [embrujar] as a synonym for "to envy" [envidiar] with evil eyes. They are quite explicit about the connection.

> With the evil eye and the thread sickness someone is bewitching; that is, someone is envying them.

> They say there is witchcraft; we call the thread sickness and other things witchcraft.

The evil eyes, then, bewitch their victims, and envy is an act of witchcraft. This idea is perfectly expressed in the practice of *afumar*, smoking or fumigating children and cows, a simple preventative and therapeutic ritual against the more minor effects of evil eyes. The practice is very common among the people of the *braña* and does not require the presence of a specialist. First a woman mixes hot coals from the stove with holy bay leaves (blessed on Palm Sunday in the church), or other holy and aromatic herbs, in a small metal plate of a brazier. When the mixture begins to produce smoke, the brazier is placed on the kitchen floor (when it is for children) or in the stable beneath the affected cow. The mother of the child makes the sign of the cross devoutly and has the child that may have been evil-eyed and other children jump over the pyre.[32] If the child is too young, the mother passes the child back and forth through the purifying smoke several times in her arms.

THE PATH TO DEATH

When smoking the child or cow, the following words are spoken: "If I bewitched you, I will unbewitch you; if another bewitched you, I unbewitch you" ["*Si otro te embrujó, desembrújote yo; si yo te embrujé, yo te desembrujaré*"]. It is always a woman, the mother or grandmother, who performs this ritual. As the formula indicates, it is considered possible that the woman may have bewitched her own children or cows. The Vaqueiros believe that women are the primary possessors of the evil eye. A woman speaks:

> *Hombre*, it could be anybody, but generally it's women who do it more. Haven't you noticed that they're more gossipy, always spreading rumors about each other? I have always held women to be more gossipy than men. And I think women envy more. Like if they keep looking at you for a while, without taking their eyes off you . . . then it's said that it was a bewitching.

> There are not male witches; witches are women. . . . A witch is a woman who has evil eyes and bewitches men, and who has the power to dominate what she looks at.

Human gender divisions also have moral connotations: Bad is to woman as good is to man. Children and cows are the main victims of envy, but not the only ones. Young, unmarried men and women, as well as more mature adults are also subject to the capricious glances of evil eyes.[33]

> There was a man in N, a couple in that house, and when their son was ready to get married, twenty potential fiancées were presented to them, because the house was close to the road and they made money every day. There was one girl who was particularly interested in [the son] and counted on his not dropping her [for another]. Because girls would rather go, if possible, to a rich house than to a poor one. But there was another girl who was family, and the parents and the boy favored her. And on the very day of the wedding the poor thing came down sick from envy. They were in a car, and they escaped death by a hair. Because they went off envied on their honeymoon. And she was already unwell because she was having her period. And the bride's father got sick [from sorrow]. Because the doctor said she was dying, they bought her a coffin and everything, because the bad blood got to her heart. Then her father offered a promise to the Virgin, in case there had been an evil shadow [*mala sombra*], so she would remove it. And they went to Oviedo, and because of this

Sickness and the Vaqueiro Cosmology

promise, such a big one, she got better, and now she is working in the house.

I have quoted this tale at length because it shows how the struggle between the sexes is not just symbolic but also real, that of a girl trying to get a boy and his "good" house. This opposition between the sexes pervades Vaqueiros consciousness and becomes explicit on many occasions, as in the traditional *lutches* or tests of strength between a man and a woman, where the aggression of both is markedly sexual.[34] In this particular case, the aggression comes from the woman who has lost; she makes the bride ill on the day of the wedding. Considering the economic importance of the wife for her work in the *casa* and the Vaqueiros' values about sickness, the revenge affects both bride and groom equally. The doctor, the profane specialist, always a man, can do nothing for the bride, for the sacred and curselike nature of the illness requires the help of sacred and holy powers to mediate between men and women. That is why a woman, the Virgin, is evoked against the ill will of another woman. She is of the same gender but has somewhat anomalous traits.[35]

Both the reference to the bride being "unwell" because she was having her period and the description of her ailment, "the bad blood got to her heart," point to a special situation. Menstruating women are believed to have fewer defenses against malign influences,[36] as symbolized in the disturbing powers of their menstrual blood, known as "bad blood." The situation is structurally similar with a woman who has just given birth. The following lines refer to a practice intended to destroy the influence of evil eyes on women giving birth.[37] The opposition of men and women is evident.

Do you know how a woman whose time to give birth has come, and who can't, is bewitched? Well, the woman has to be accompanied by a man, who has to be her husband. When she begins to have pains but does not give birth, some corduroy pants of the husband are brought; they have to be the husband's. It's all right if they were once someone else's, but at the time of birth they have to belong to the husband. These pants are passed over the woman, who is in bed, from her feet to the tip of her head, while she is stretched out, with her belly up, and the pants *esparraos*, with the two legs up. They are passed over her nine times, and you go to the door of the house and hit the pants nine times. Then they are passed another time between the woman and her husband another seven times [they have to be uneven numbers], and taken to the door of the house and hit seven times, and brought back,

THE PATH TO DEATH

and five times, and hit five times, then three times, then one time. Finally they are burned at the door of the house, and these words are spoken: "May God permit the female witch [bruja] who bewitched you to be burned like these trousers of the man." This is what the other woman says. And then the pesos, that is, the pains, begin, and she gives birth. You do this to unbewitch a woman who is going to give birth and who has been envied, or was seen by an evil eye.

So it seems that the witch is fully part of the female world, the place where evil, envy, and evil eyes are located. This accursed half of human nature can only be counteracted by the other half, the masculine world, which signifies the good. In the birthing ritual, the influence of evil eyes is checked by corduroy trousers, until recently the exclusive attire of men.[38] The part of the pants that touch the woman could not be more symbolic of sex, for the pants are *esparraos*, that is, opened out where they come in contact with the male genitalia. Nor will just any pair of pants do. Note how care is taken to specify that they must belong to the husband and that he must participate actively in the ritual. But what is punished, and eventually burned, are the pants themselves, the symbol of the man, of the good. What does this mean? The man is helped by a woman, perhaps the *entendida*, but even more frequently by his own mother (another intermediary between her own sex and her son), who both directs and controls the ritual. The malignant effects of envy, of a woman, are gathered up by the pants, by the man; then they are beaten and cast outside the house, where they no longer pose a danger to its inhabitants. The envy is destroyed by destroying, by denying, the struggle between sexes that was at its origin. This is clearly expressed in the simile "let the witch [bruja] be burned [the feminine] as the pants are burned [the masculine]." The woman's "sickness," that is, her difficulty in giving birth, and the symbol of the man, the pants, offer the key to the origin of the problem. The woman has been hurt sexually; she must be cured in the same way.

Both men and women get sick from sexual contact.[39] Vaqueiro men say:

He who wants to live to be old has to keep the oil in the skin. This is what the old men say. A piece of advice. One wasn't to give in to the vice too much, for whoever dedicated himself to women didn't live to be old. Women little by little take it out of you. The reserves run out. It's like a little hole in a tin can. The women suck, take out a man's roots. You have to save yourself. Of course, if you have a certain level of heat, you say to hell with old age.

Compared with men, women receive much less harm in sexual relations, but they are much more dangerous than men, especially during menstruation (when sexual relations are completely forbidden), but also at any other time, since some diseases, like tuberculosis, are thought to originate in sexual relations with women. This is why the witch, always a woman, attacks men sexually.[40] Aside from giving evil looks, the witch "bites" areas of the body that are not visible.

They say that a witch has power with her sight, and if she looks at you in a bad way, has something against you, you may arrive home and find a black and blue mark; these marks are the bites of a witch. And we begin to suspect a woman we already had doubts about.

Envy brings out the economic, social, and sexual differences that are connected with illness. The belief in the powers of envy works to level social differences as it penalizes economic inequality with the group. Furthermore, it provides a cultural explanation for the sickness and loss of cattle, an explanation that is a confession of one's own defects as well as those of others, an expression of individual and collective responsibilities. When one ascribes the evil eye to someone within the group, one emphasizes the defects that make it hard for people to live together, stigmatizing those who cause the most conflict. By ascribing the evil eye to persons outside the group, as is so often the case, the relations of those within the group are reinforced. This way its members resolve the contradiction between, on the one hand, the internal tensions and disputes due to scarce resources, and, on the other hand, the need for mutual aid and cooperation dictated by its ecological niche. From this angle, illness is the expression of conflicts and tensions in the group.

If fear of the evil eye is in fact fear of contagious disease, the only problem I see is one of translation. But Vaqueiro rituals indicate that something much more ambitious is involved: the ordering of a universe in chaos, the overcoming of the disorder that comes from sickness. Note that the victims of evil eyes are never the elderly but cows, children, youths, and adults in the prime of life. It is the sickness or death of those who have not yet lived, who have not yet completed the natural cycle, that surprises, needs explaining, hurts the most, and is most unjust. The old folks are expected

THE PATH TO DEATH

to die when their time has come, to fulfill the fate of all that is human.

There are two sides to the envy that especially preoccupies the women of the *braña* by way of their children. On the one hand, illness, like the thread disease, is an expression of a growth disorder and a lack of harmony in the human body. On the other hand, the worm disease is a product of dirt and contamination, a violation of boundaries. The evil ones (in this case, the bewitched worms) occupy not only the habitat of the group but also the human body. Evil is within us.

Sex does not escape from this kind of dichotomizing. The sexual dimension of envy ascribes to one part of the Vaqueiro population the power to give death as well as life. This differentiation of human nature (division by sex is the most basic kind of social division) is not absolute. Rather, it provides a balance: the Vaqueiros understand and accept the relation between good and evil, and its expression in human ambiguity. Illness and health, life and death, are the lot of human beings. This cognitive dissociation of human nature, of masculine and feminine, gives a certain order to the Vaqueiros' universe. They believe that witches *should* exist. But why are they always women?

Let us consider the woman's position with regard to men. When a child is born in the *braña*, the father will feel very satisfied if it is a male, especially the first male. A son will be "preferred" in due time and represent the descendants, the continuity of the house. When the child is a girl, the father must think about another dowry. The girl must work until she is married in a house that will never be hers. It will go to her brother, the *mayorazo*, who one day may bring a strange woman to the house to be its *ama*, or mistress. If the girl is not able to marry, she may remain in the house where she was born as long as she accepts her brother and sister-in-law as its owners, and works for them without pay like a servant. It is more likely that she will marry and, like her sister-in-law, will enter a new house as a stranger. There she will do the hardest jobs in the fields and work an exhausting schedule in the house. She will not even be able to dedicate herself to her children, as her mother-in-law will be in charge of raising them, but she will be blamed for their misbehavior and defects. As time passes and her husband's parents die, she will become the *ama*. She will finally obtain control in the kitchen and over her children, but, even then, if she needs to buy anything she must ask her husband for it. Her preferred son may marry a girl who helps her with the worst work, but it is also possible that her husband will die before she does, and then she will be in the same relation of dependence to her son, the new *amo*, as her son's wife is. When she is aged or dying, she will fear that she may not receive the care she deserves.

The woman is a kind of currency for the man, an object in his house.[41] But the woman is also a critical factor in maintaining the continuity and prosperity of the home, for she is the one who cares for and milks the cows, the animals on whom the economic survival of the house depends. She is also an indispensable element in the wise administration of the house. She is, further, a "good" daughter, neighbor, wife, work companion, sister—that is, she is also a person. In their effort to treat the woman both as an object and as a person, the Vaqueiros make use of the concept of envy. The woman's lack of economic power and control is compensated for by ritual power and control. The responsibility of men for material things is counterbalanced by that of women for mystical things.

SPECIALISTS OF CURING

In one of the parish death registers of the zone under study one finds the death notice for one of the specialists of the official medicine, Don José Fernández Blanco, "official surgeon [*cirujano*] of the district." Don José, a native and resident of the parish *aldea*, died at age seventy-nine in 1854, a victim of what was called *fiebre catarral*. Other *cirujanos* appear in the books, certifying the causes of death of well-to-do parishioners between 1869 and 1896.[42] Apart from this vestigial information, we are also informed of the death of Don José's wife, Rita Fernández, a professional "healer" [*curandera*]. She died at age eighty in 1892 and probably succeeded her husband in his profession. The couple formed by Don José and Rita, surgeon and healer, and their likely professional collaboration, would not have been considered anomalous. For their two specialties are not seen as opposed or antagonistic in the treatment of illness; rather, they might be said to form a continuum.

Most older Vaqueiros agree that one of the greatest changes they have experienced has been what they call "the change in medicine," which took place after the Civil War. People constantly allude to "advances" of the present over past ignorance, the number of doctors at present compared to in the past, and the greater knowledge that today's doctors have of diseases and cures that in the old days had not yet been "discovered." Vaqueiros have experienced this change and are well aware of a decline in mortality rates in their group. Most of them clearly remember the deaths of children, siblings, or other relatives in the prime of life. When they remember those deaths, they also remember what they were sup-

THE PATH TO DEATH

posed to have died of and attempt to translate the old diagnosis into a more modern one.

> It seems like there wasn't so much of that cancer thing in the old days. They died from whatever they had; there were no doctors. My mother-in-law, may she rest in peace, had it first in her gut. I think it must have been her appendix—that wasn't known in those days—there were no doctors, and the doctors didn't know anything. . . . It was her appendix, because the pain was on that side. She was stretched out there, I remember, and the doctor came. And I don't know what he gave her, but it didn't do her any good.

Certain diseases seem to exist only through the doctor. People emphasize the lack of diagnosis as a problem of the past. According to the Vaqueiros, "people died from a thing and you didn't know why," or "the old people died from the latest diseases," which produced among the group a certain uneasiness and insecurity. Even today it seems that giving a name to an illness is a cognitive necessity. Naming it locates and individualizes the illness, allows the possibility of taming it with a therapy or, in the worst of cases, of accepting death as inevitable. Perhaps for this reason local categories emerged to define, however vaguely, certain ills from which the Vaqueiros died, like *fiebre, calenturas,* and disease that is "natural," "sudden," or "internal." [43] By naming diseases, the doctor has made them part of the Vaqueiro experience. The doctor is capable of deciphering and explaining what illnesses mean, though he is not infallible in his diagnoses and, at times, is not accommodating in providing the knowledge that the people of the *braña* need.

> Before, diseases were not known. The doctor only explained pneumonia to you—they did know that one. But if you had a cancer, the doctor didn't know it. Well, tuberculosis existed then, too, but the doctors wouldn't tell you or explain it to you.

> Look, the doctors are bastards [*cabroncetes*], too. They wouldn't say anything, just "Well, you should do this and that." They never gave their opinion about anything.

It was not just that people were unaware of diseases. People felt fear and awe of the first X-ray machines, whose rays were associated with the *rayos* from the sky that burned houses and stables. And the techniques of the official specialists provoked a certain fascination among the Vaqueiros as well, especially when they used "apparatuses" like the thermometer.

This cow used to get sick, like a person, sick with a fever. What did we know then? When a doctor came to give you a thermometer people wondered what it was. "What's that?" they said. "I dunno. The doctor came, put something long under his arm, left it there a while, and looked at it. I dunno." "And does he cure people with that, eh?" [To the doctor] "Are you going to cure him with the wire, dear?" And the doctor, he wouldn't want to get into an argument, he'd say, "Sure, we'll heal him."

The lack of communication between doctor and patients is not necessarily the fault of the doctor. The Vaqueiros didn't like to ask questions because, as they would say, the specialists in medicine "were imposing," and besides, even if the specialists did speak, they could not always be understood.

In the old days a person died and they would never ask any questions; people were afraid. Now it's different—you've had dealings with *inteletuales* [the doctor and the veterinarian]. Before one wouldn't talk with an intellectual except for words you didn't know. You'd go with a horse to fetch him, and you came back holding onto the horse's tail, and you weren't on familiar terms with him, nor he with you.

Until recently (and it still holds true for some *brañas*), the doctor could reach most Vaqueiro settlements only on horseback or on foot. In spite of what was usually great urgency, the doctor's trip had to be well planned. He would come up to the *brañas* only on certain conditions, and not always even then. Many doctors stayed in the region only until they could get a practice in an easier location, but the people gratefully remember certain doctors who spent many years going up to the *brañas*. They refer to these doctors as "slaves," a very flattering designation in local usage.

They would come by horse. They would go for the doctor to P [*aldea*], for X, who is still alive. They would say, "A horse has to be taken down that is well-equipped, and so-and-so has a saddle we can borrow." And they went after the saddle, the best there was. And they brought the doctor up on the horse, and then they had to take him back down again. When they went with the horse I'm not sure they would actually mount it; they might come up on foot holding onto the horse's tail.

Hombre, of course they came up, when you went for them. No, those who were the most slaves mounted a horse and came up. Now, unless it's by car or in an accessible place, they don't want to come up, even though there are more doctors. In those days there were few doctors.

The doctor did not always arrive in time, given these conditions. Often his presence merely served to confirm a fatal outcome. Many Vaqueiro stories about illnesses revolve around the fatal delay. Occasionally the delay is said to be due to the absence of the doctor, but more often it is said to be because Vaqueiros waited too long before sending for him. In addition to the distance, poverty was a powerful reason for not calling the doctor at once. The hope that a patient would get well without having to spend scarce money meant that people died by neglect, *abandono*.

Since there was no money, and you had to go and fetch him so far away, until a person was very bad off, people would hope he got better, hope he got better. Many died from neglect. Many illnesses could have been cured if they had acted in time. And it seems to me that many people never sent for the doctor at all—the patient was old and . . . *ala!*

At times the Vaqueiros doubted the efficacy and skill of the official specialists, especially when they worked in the areas of competency of the local Vaqueiro experts. One doctor who helped in childbirths was dubbed a butcher [*matarife*] because of the use he made of one of his tools.

The daughter of T from B died in childbirth—she was the wife of my brother-in-law E, his first wife. When she was in labor a doctor from X came up and took out the baby with some hooks they used to use, not like now, and made a mess of her. She lasted a day or so, must have had a hemorrhage or something. She died because he split her open. F, who went to see her and take her some soup, said, "She was just as if she had been thrown out a window!" He's dead now. He killed a lot of women.

Yes, well, there was one here in X who was said to be a doctor for childbirths. He was a butcher! He would put hooks in their bellies, get a hold of the baby. But how did he know what he was getting with the hooks inside? He cut them up and almost all of them died. He would get a hold of the baby and pull, and *bueno!* He left a lot of [babies] marked for life, and others with their necks twisted so they had to be operated on. There's a woman still alive with her neck twisted; he pulled her out, too.

The visits of the doctor to the *braña*, or those of patients to his office, were followed by those of some young adult Vaqueiros to specialists in the city, especially to Madrid and Oviedo. They would go there, staying with relatives, and have operations. But one would think that medicine on the outside was little better than that in the *braña* from the way Vaqueiros tried to avoid it. At present, the Vaqueiro attitude toward official medicine is quite different. Vaqueiro's frequently go to see doctors in nearby towns, and the doctors come to most of the *brañas* by car to visit the bedridden or the critically ill. The worst cases are treated in hospitals. According to the people of the *braña*, there are more doctors in the region now, perhaps even too many:

> Here in L there are so many doctors. There is no town in
> Spain with so many doctors, eh? If I count the ones here,
> there are at least seven. Then there are the retired ones, three
> or four who are still working and practicing.

> I saw my husband die; he had so many things wrong with
> him. He had been sick for many years, died five years ago.
> Lord! He was so tired of doctors and drugs, dear heart . . . the
> number of times they came, several of them, eh? And he
> went to Oviedo, too, for his heart and all.

In contrast to the past when there was little medical care available, and that used only in extremis, Vaqueiros now make use of a full range of medical services. They not only go to the local internist but also see specialists, pediatricians, dentists, and others. People will say ironically that the most minor headache or an aching fingernail is reason enough to see one of these private doctors, which may be an overreaction to the deprivation of the past. Traditionally, the doctors of the zone have been private, for Vaqueiros have had access to the Social Security medical system only recently. At present, Vaqueiros will use the Social Security system for hospitalization, but otherwise the "insurance doctors" do not appear to be popular among the Vaqueiros. They complain about the lack of attention these doctors give and the production-line atmosphere of the office care.

> The other day I went to the insurance doctor. Just the
> other day B said to me, "You old folks have it all—the doctor
> and medicine all paid for and everything." Sure, I went to the
> insurance doctor; he doesn't look at anybody and didn't give
> me anything for my blood pressure after he saw it was 22; no,
> just told me I shouldn't eat salt. So what am I supposed to do
> about it? I'll keep on going to the doctor in L [a private one]
> because I'm happy with him. Because it costs me more to go
> here to N [*aldea*] than to go to L [town], even though an ap-

pointment there costs me two hundred pesetas. Because in order to get back home after the insurance doctor is through . . . he was seeing people until ten at night, but as though he wasn't looking at them, each one the same. He doesn't have anywhere to see them. He sees them there in the pharmacy. When we got there the doctor didn't pay any attention. We had hurried, running to get the form. They told us "Hurry to get a number." We went to get a number and there were twenty-four ahead of us. We got home very late, after waiting, waiting, me anxious to be home in bed, and we got here late at night. *Oy madre mía, madre mía!* This cannot be! What a time to come! He came late because he lives over in T [town]. Everyone left there disgusted. *Hombre. . .* and what about the ones from F [the most distant *braña*]? This isn't worth it. The insurance doctors don't have a room to examine people. I was sitting in a chair. "What do you want?" "I want to have my blood pressure taken." He took my blood pressure. "You have 22." "*Uy, Dios mío!* How can it be so high?" "You must be eating salt and everything." "I don't eat salt at all." "Well, be very careful with the salt." And that's all he said.

In spite of the abundance of medical care now, some doctors still "don't get it right." People still, occasionally, die young.

She had some kind of urinary problem. Look, they went to the doctor in N [*aldea*], and I don't know how many times he came to the house, but she kept getting worse—the same or worse. So one day M [her husband] went to N so they'd give him a form so he could take her to Oviedo [to the hospital]. That day the doctor wasn't there, maybe he was on vacation, and he left a substitute, a woman doctor. And she said she wasn't giving any forms out without seeing the patient first. So he said, "Fine, come on up if you want to go to the house and see her." And she said it wasn't that serious— "*Hombre*, it's not that bad that we have to send her away; let's leave her until tomorrow and see if she gets better with what I'm prescribing for her"—that there was plenty of time to send her to Oviedo. And I don't know what she gave her, but she got it wrong and that night she died. They weren't expecting it.

Most doctors who work in the region stay there only a short time[44] and for that reason, with a few exceptions, they are held to be poorly trained and inefficacious. People believe they gain their experience and expertise on rural patients before moving to the city or other places where life is easier.

Sickness and the Vaqueiro Cosmology   87

Here we get the worst ones. The worst ones go to the worst places. Occasionally there's one who has a good head on his shoulders and gets better here, but as soon as they can, they leave.

As for doctors, no one can say which are better and which are worse. But if a doctor applies for a job in public competition and doesn't get it, it means he's not well prepared, right? Well, the ones here didn't win any competitions.

Perhaps following this kind of thinking, when Vaqueiros have illnesses difficult to diagnose or treat, they begin a kind of pilgrimage to doctors, first the local ones, then those of the nearby towns, and finally those of the cities, Oviedo and Madrid. At the same time they go to see the unofficial specialists, like healers, and also make visits to churches and shrines for divine help.

It happened suddenly and the doctor from X [large *aldea*] came and said he wouldn't take responsibility "I won't take responsibility for it." And my son said, "Well, what do you say, Don X, shall we call another doctor?" "If you want to, yes." It was my head, my mind would go off, without any pain at all. I don't remember the name of the disease, it was a rare one, it had to do with the eyesight. I couldn't stand brightness. I had to put a kerchief over my eyes, only look down. And the doctor said, "You have to take him to L [town]." And I said, "I'm not sure I can go on horseback." And my son said, "If he can't go by horse, we'll take him in a car." I went to L, to an eye man, an oculist, and he didn't know what it was I had. And he told me there was a resident doctor in L and asked if I wanted to go to him. "Sure, of course I do." He looked at me right away, told me he didn't know what this could be, spoke well to me. And he said, "Listen, you could enter [the clinic] here in L, but we haven't got the equipment to examine you. So I recommend that you go to the general hospital [for the province]." He saw that I had something wrong in my head, you see. And of course, in the head there are many different diseases. So we went to admissions [at the hospital] and there they put me on a bed, and a young lady [he looks at me and laughs] began to undress me and put pajamas on me. Then a pile of people gathered there, men doctors and women doctors asking a lot of questions, checking me to see if I had lost my memory. I saw that's what they were doing, and as soon as I got a chance, although they hadn't finished asking me questions, I said, "You people"—I said, lying there—"are studying me, but so far my memory has been fine." They all shut up, looked at each other, and made a sign to a nurse, who took my stretcher up to the fifth floor. And they examined me, oh how they examined me! with X rays, radioscope; they even put a wire on me and electrical current, in order to find out what I had. The doctor from L was no fool. He was experienced. They didn't have the stuff in L, but they did in Oviedo. In the general hospital they have all kinds of equipment.

Perhaps the greatest change in what the Vaqueiros call medicine has been their recent acceptance of surgical operations in the cities. A stay in the hospital is an adventure for Vaqueiros, and, on their return, they give a detailed account of what happened there. The above speaker continues:

They put me in a room, in a bed that was empty. There were six of us, and the next day I say to myself, "Well now, where are my clothes?"—referring to what I had been wearing, undershirt, underpants, everything. One man said, "See what the number of the bed is, and then look under that number in the bureau—that's where you'll find your clothes and your money, if you brought any. They don't steal things here." I went to look, and there it all was. And a young lady took me to the bathroom [smiles]. But they began to give me two injections every day, and I took some pills they gave me, and by the fifth day I could go to the bathroom by myself. And I said, "*Joder*, that medicine is making a difference." Each patient is all set up there, each one with his bell by his hand. But a month is a long time to be shut up. Doctor X, who took care of me, said, "Hey F [last name] don't you want to get out of the hospital?" "If it was up to me, I would have left fifteen days ago, but I'm here under your orders. How am I going to insist that you let me go? No, you know when I can go. Because I've seen some fellows pressuring the doctors to let them go, and the doctors don't like it, they don't say anything out of politeness, but they don't like it." And he said, "You're right, well, let's see if I can let you out in three days." "Good, I'd be grateful to you, I'm happy about it, doctor." And so I came home. It was a day we were going to plant potatoes.

This extensive account brings out, among other things, the deferential or submissive attitude of the sick of the *brañas* toward the official specialist, whom they try to win over with gifts and demonstrations of obedience and submission. They show the same attitudes toward the saints, for both saints and doctors can save their lives. The doctors have acquired this power through study, the use of equipment, and their knowledge of medicines. The other official health specialists, veterinarians, are thought of and treated similarly.

As we have seen, because of the isolation of the *brañas*, prolonged contact with these "intellectuals" is a relatively recent development. That is why the local *entendidos* or experts as well as the saints have been called on to perform similar tasks in the *brañas*. Let us see what they do. The *entendidos* are persons who *entienden* [understand] some special skill. There are *entendidos* in carpentry, electricity, haircutting, and pulling teeth. Sometimes such a person is referred to as a *curioso*, but this term generally refers to a lesser degree of professionalism, a certain interest in a specialty but less dedication or preparation. The health *entendidos* lack a degree, although some may have studied on their own or are known to "own books." Their school is that of experience paired with a natural vocation, interest, and certain gifts that may be thought of as natural or supernatural. The distinction between the categories "study" and "talent" is explicit in the following comments:

> They're no good, those [healers] didn't study. It could be that some have a good head, but they don't convince me. And they may be able to give out home remedies that keep you going, but they sure can't cure you.

> Here in N there was a man who was an *entendido*; his son is still alive. That man was a talent, without having studied or anything. Now this E [a different *entendido*], he studied; he has books.

Many of these local health specialists help with births. Female *entendidas* help with human births while male *entendidos* help with those of animals. Other healers [*practicantes*] know about the same kinds of illness that doctors and veterinarians treat. These specialists are local replicas of the official specialists; they use the same medicines and tools, and try to emulate them. Indeed, *practicantes* often counsel their countrymen to go to the doctor or veterinarian, anticipating the correct diagnosis and the steps that must be taken for a cure. Hear one of them:

> There was a woman who knew a little nursing. In this village for instance, when a woman was going to give birth, there was one who knew a little more about it than the others, that's all. There wasn't anything else in the way of medicine. As for animals, look, I was the one for the entire village who knew a little bit more; now it's my son. All of us in this

house give shots. Only P [wife of his grandson] didn't know how, and now she gives them. One time I said to her and my granddaughter "Now you both are going to learn, today one of you, tomorrow the other," and they both did learn. Now it is my son who married in the house who goes whenever a calf is going to be born in the village; he puts his hand inside and feels whether the calves are coming out twisted or the wrong way, and he sets them right. And he also goes out to the nearby villages—they come for him, too. Now, since there is a road, people grab a car and go for the veterinarian quick if necessary, but in the old days. . . . Here, look, in almost all the houses now, they all are acquainted with medicines; for in this house not a day goes by without giving drugs, shots, or treatments, whether for rheumatism or whatever. In the old days people were completely backward; there was witchcraft.

Midwives have been very common in the *braña*, though now they have less work since the trend is to give birth in hospitals. They have always been women, and learn their trade through their own experience as mothers, and by helping other midwives.

I have helped a lot of women and that's a fact. I learned after marriage, because there was a woman in X, named Y, and she came to me twice, and we were good friends with her. And the first time it took me a long time to give birth, and that woman knew a lot, and I, from what she did to me, I . . . Now they go to hospitals, but . . . I always was the one at R house (look at all the children she had), F house, H house (all seven of them), the whole village. I came to this village for O, for L, and once to G house when her afterbirth didn't come out and M [another midwife] didn't dare to pull it out. I pulled it out, yes, that was the first time here. We had been near her house, and when she got in a bad way they sent word and the afterbirth had to be taken out. Mine was taken out by R, may she be in heaven.

Vaqueiro mothers usually gave birth standing up, with two women supporting the mother and a third receiving the child. Nevertheless, in imitation of births in the hospital or with doctors, in more recent times an occasional birth was attempted with the mother lying down in bed, an impractical position according to the midwives. While the midwife is no longer in such great demand, this is by no means true for animal births, where the *entendido* continues to be indispensable. The human birth rate has gone down, but there has been a great increase in animal births. The veterinarian lives far away, it is not always possible to call him in time, and his fees cut into the profit from the eventual sale of the calf. Under these conditions, the local *entendidos* may substitute for the professional in cases without complications. They will indicate the need to call the professional when the birth presents serious problems. In addition to directing the birth, these *entendidos* will give the animals shots, prescribe medicine, and slaughter pigs and cows when needed. They do not charge their neighbors for this work.

Over the years, some of the local experts acquire experience and fame not only in their own *brañas* but also in others, where they are called in cases of complicated births. On such occasions they might be thanked for their work and their visit with a small present, but, regardless, they are always ready to give a hand. The knowledge that these specialists acquire through experience and observation is a response to the basic need for help and mutual solidarity in a dispersed habitat with few professional services. For this reason, in the most isolated areas—the high transhumant pastures—the *entendidos* and their cures are even more essential.

A veterinarian asked why I bother myself so much with births, giving shots, and slaughtering cows. And I told him, "The day my house catches fire, do you think I'm going to try and get the workers at L [a distant town] to put out the fire?" You have to help folks out of necessity; there has to be someone in each village.

In addition to the *entendidos* and *curiosos*, there are other persons in the *braña* who act as professionals. Such persons are known to have books and tools from abroad, and they are informed about medicines. People pay for their services, although less than they pay for the veterinarians. Hear about one their performances.

Yes, there is a man who is not a veterinarian but knows a lot more than a veterinarian knows. For getting calves out of cows, that is the man who knows most. The veterinarian doesn't have to come up to this whole neck of the woods.

It was an enormous calf, dear. The cow was saved, after a lot of struggle. . . . It was a young heifer, her first birth, and it was an abnormal calf, dear. And we tried to pull it out, six or eight men, and no way! They couldn't get it out. So many people were pulling. So they stopped pulling and said, "*Ay Dios!* This way we'll pull the cow over, and the calf won't come out." So they talked about sending for an *entendido*. X and my son went off to a distant place—it took them five

THE PATH TO DEATH

hours to go and return—for a man who knew much more than a veterinarian does. So the man came and *Ay Dios!* the cow's body was split right open, like the door of an oven. Poor thing! *Ay Dios!* Seeing that cow bellow and bellow, and not be able to . . . but then that man got it out. He had an apparatus that I think he brought from Germany, an apparatus that you turn and it pulls, and then it holds, and then you keep pulling little by little. And the cow was exhausted afterwards, that's for sure. I don't know how long it was before it got up in the stable. And he is a very smart man; he gave it shots so it wouldn't get infected, and powders to heal it, because otherwise the cow would have gotten gangrene all over. The result is that the man got the calf out while the veterinarian would have cut it out, in pieces, with a saw.

These somewhat more professional *entendidos* share with veterinarians an air of authority and even authoritarianism toward country folk. Some of those I knew used excessively arcane language (at times ridiculously so) with many supposedly refined and scientific terms. They also show their open contempt for traditional local practices, practices to which even they, at times, have recourse.

E [an *entendido*] gives himself more importance than he deserves. He's stuck up and doesn't talk much. I didn't understand him at all, and he was showing off what he knew. He's got some books, and as a result of going around looking at cows . . . he's picked up things. You learn through practice.

They're running out of local skilled veterinarians. That fellow was going to replace me, but he has left. Of course, not all of us were any good. When I went to Madrid, there was one guy who wanted to take my place [as *entendido*] and they finally had to call the vet for help, and the vet gave them hell [for calling him when it was too late] and ended up pulling out the calf dead, then charged them and said good-bye. That vet has a bad temper, because when women begin to say things like, "Uy, you have to do this or that," he says, "I'm the one who gives the orders, got that? Just me."

Let me present in some detail one of the local *entendidos*, whom I will call Lulín. I got to know him shortly after I came to the zone, after I gave him a ride one evening when he was on his way back to his *braña* after helping at the birth of a calf in a nearby village. When I told him about my interest in local medical and veterinary practices, Lulín adopted me as a kind of apprentice, in-

Sickness and the Vaqueiro Cosmology   93

viting me to be present at several births of calves where his help had been solicited. Very often he would come to my house in the evening, order me to turn on the "apparatus" (my tape recorder), and instruct me on some ethnographic subject that he had been thinking of during the day. He was an excellent informant who quickly understood what interested me and what did not, although at times he would complain ironically that "people from the city are very ignorant, and the people who study are only interested in what they study, and do not think about anything else." At age sixty-two he had a prodigious memory, an exceptional mind, and unlimited curiosity. His only defect (for the purposes of my study) was his powerful imagination, which meant I had to verify carefully what he told me. In his youth, Lulín spent five years out of the *braña*. At age seventeen he went to Madrid, where he worked as a butcher. Then he did his military service in Africa. At age twenty-two, he married his Vaqueira girlfriend and returned to the *braña* to his wife's house, which was a relatively poor one. No sooner had he arrived than he began the first of the many innovations in Vaqueiro life he was to make, both in the area of "medicine" and of life-style.

The first person to use a thermometer here was me, when I came back from Madrid. If you asked, "Does he have a fever?" people might answer, "Is he not supposed to?" As soon as I began to explain it, they began to buy thermometers, but there are still many persons today who do not understand what it is. And they wouldn't go for the veterinarian. Instead they would do things to the cow. If they saw that the cow was sick, we [sic] would begin to douse it, *venga!* They would bathe it with water, oil, and soap, lather it up as if it were a piece of clothing.

There have been a lot of improvements, thanks to me, if you can believe it. You start by making a feeding trough for the cows, or bedrooms in the house; you start because there isn't a certain piece of furniture, and you make it and install it. You start because here in this village there was no cast-iron stove, and in 1940 I installed one. At that time there was only one machine for spreading sulfate, that of X in [another *braña*], because he had spent some time in Madrid and was a man of refinement. In this village there was none, and I went out with twenty-five *duros* and bought one. When I came back with it in a bag, *uy!* My wife made a lot of noise about it, saying I was crazy. Then in 1942 a group of boys took their first communion, both mine and others, and no one talked about anything except my son, because he went dressed for first communion. They almost came and got me out of bed. He was dressed up in a blue sailor suit, and wore gloves and a crucifix. He went as one was supposed to go. He was the first in the village to stand out dressed for a communion. Still it took years for things to change, and now more recently it has begun.

The death of his first child and the illness of his second were probably crucial reasons for his interest in medicine.

My first daughter died of pneumonia when she was four months old. We hadn't taken it seriously because we thought it was something else. In those days there weren't medicines or anything. When I took her to the doctor, he said, "*Caramba*, I'm afraid you've gotten here too late. She's got a bad case of pneumonia." And he was right. She only lasted three days after we took her to the doctor. In those days you didn't take her to the hospital; everyone went back home. They gave you some powders to take orally, with a spoonful of milk. A lot of people would just waste away. Thirteen days later the son who lives in the house now was born. And he got sick and I had to keep him a year and a half without any food from the house; everything was from the pharmacy: cream of wheat, Astrobactol, Estrolactina. Milk had to be made for him, and you couldn't give him anything else. He would get intestinal infections that would give him a very high fever that we couldn't get down no matter what.

Another factor in Lulín's vocational choice was the Civil War. Lulín participated in the war, traveling over much of Spain. Before he left he saved the life of a friend, a local doctor who was in political trouble, by hiding him in his house; during the war he picked up pointers from army doctors.

I hid here the doctor who used to come here on calls, hid him in a hayloft, between blankets, because they were after him. All he would eat was the boiled milk we prepared him at night. He almost died from it. We took him two bottles of boiled milk, one in the morning and another at night; he had a bad stomach condition.

In the war each batallion had a sergeant major or a second lieutenant who was a doctor. And I, since I was a messenger, would walk with them when I had nothing to do, or I'd be in the clinic talking awhile, and I would ask them things. And my captain, when we were in the shelters, would give me classes, because he said, "*Coño*, it's too bad you haven't had an education." He would explain things to me; he'd say, "*Venir, subir, bajar*—all are written with b's." [V and B are pronounced the same in Castilian, hence commonly confused in spelling.]

He first attempted to heal his own cattle out of necessity. He began to have more confidence when he saw that his diagnoses were confirmed by the veterinarian.

My interest in healing began out of necessity. Necessity at times forces you to get involved in things you shouldn't, but you do it because the cow has to be saved. You start with your own, then they begin to call on you in the neighborhood. One of the first cows that I took care of was one of X's. I put my hand inside and said, "No, it's not giving birth." "Ay, *hombre!*" he said. "No, I'm telling you, it's not!" I looked again, and the opening of the womb was no bigger than a finger, not yet dilated. The veterinarian came and said, "No, it's not giving birth; it can give birth when it wants to." He gave it some shots, and the cow gave birth normally two or three days later.

Lulín's interest in medicine leads him to cultivate good relations with the "intellectuals" of the area. Here he speaks of one of them.

Don X, until he was very old, was a doctor in the villages. [To me:] Take note of his name and go to see him. He came here as a doctor in 1929, came to Y. He attended my wife when she gave birth in '32. I am the most backwards Vaqueiro around here, but I have always been on good terms with this gentleman, and we still are. He was the family doctor, and whenever I was in doubt about something I would consult him. Because one time a veterinarian said to me, "Do you believe everything that's written?" And I said, "Yes sir, in the case of medicine I do, but not in the case of history." "Well listen, in medicine there is just as much nonsense as in history. Mark my words, if we don't use our wits a little as well, we'll all be bad off—we and you."

Although an advocate in the *brañas* for science and progress, Lulín rejected traditional practices selectively; some he would retain and use, attempting to rationalize them. His genuine interest in experimentation is clear from this account of his dialogue with another "intellectual," the parish priest.

These are things that come down from antiquity, like when we cross ourselves and say, "God before us [*Dios delante*]." I do it, we all do it every day. One day I was talking to the priest we have now. I said, "I don't know, nowadays we're so bland, *desaboridos*, to use a Vaqueiro word, that we don't believe in anything. I grew up among sheep as you must have, since you're from around here over near X." And he said, "Right." I said, "And the sheep when they come in from the hillsides, sometimes there is one with a nose swollen up this long [makes half a meter with his hands], a snout! They would say she had been bitten by a snake. Because the sheep has a very fine snout and inserts it in the undergrowth in search of green grass, and gets bitten. And people would take a nettle and repeatedly prick it to make it bleed, would say some prayers, and rub it with a cloth and honey, and, *coño*, the sheep would get well, that would actually happen. Now I don't want to argue for the sake of arguing. Because we would have to get a snake and grab a sheep and get the snake to bite the sheep and wait until it got infected, and then prick it. We'd have to do this in order to be convinced, and since we're not going to do it, we can't really know." And he said, "No, you are very mistaken." "I may be very mistaken, but you won't be able to convince me." "Look, what happens is that they get pricked by the furze, and the furze is very infectious. And, of course, you lance it and make it bleed a little, and put some medicine on it, and it gets better. But if it had been bitten by a snake, there wouldn't be anything you could do for it." People had that theory, that way of healing it, and that belief.

In spite of his skepticism and arrogance toward local practices, Lulín occasionally showed a certain kind of humility, as can be seen in these philosophical comments.

Yes, they say you have to understand this world. As your way of life gets more modern, you say, "How could we have lived that way?" But things are no different now. They change a little—the same dogs with different collars—but it's all the same. They say everyone is a lot smarter now; I think people are a lot dumber, because people vainly think they know everything, and they don't know anything. We don't know anything at all.

These local *entendidos* share an attempt to imitate the methods and knowledge of the official specialists. One may distinguish them from another category of *entendidos,* whose methods and knowledge have less to do with formal training, and who often compete directly with the official specialists. Among these *entendidos* I would include the *curanderos* [healers] and the *arregladores* or *compostores de huesos* [bonesetters]. These less professional practitioners also may be referred to as *curiosos.* As with the official specialists, bone setters also have their defenders and detractors. For example, two persons gave quite different evaluations of the bonesetter.

> I went to her, Doña Q, because this arm got dislocated when I went to put the bridle on the old mule and my shoulder popped. So we went and as soon as she saw me she said, "Your son has to help me." And I said, *"Ay de mi,* poor thing, kill me!" And after doing this to me [pushing up] three times, the shoulder went back in its socket. That woman had such hands. . . .

> There was a woman [Q] who set bones in X, too. She's probably still alive, but she must be very old. We went to her with L [daughter] because her arm got out of joint. It happened twice, and once it was fixed by G [a *curioso* of the village]. That woman was old, and she charged for what she did. And once there was a girl whose knee was bad, and she grabbed her knee and said, "Yes, you can see it, you can see it," and she was holding the knee that was all right! That's why I lost faith in her. I thought, "Bah, this woman doesn't know anything."

The advantage of these specialists is that they divine [*adivinar*] or diagnose [*acertar*] like the doctor but their treatments are simpler and shorter. They also speak the language of their clients.

> Doctors don't know anything about that. When I went to [a bonesetter] because of my leg, she said, "I'm going to make you some real coffee." "Is it that bad?" I had broken leg. And she said, "If you go to a doctor you'd be in a cast for three months." And she told me to stay in bed for forty days. And it came out fine, and furthermore she didn't wrap the bandage too tight, so it wouldn't cut off the circulation of the blood; the doctors make it very tight.

The bonesetters work with their hands, the official specialists with equipment. The specialist is seen as having formal training and gadgets; the bonesetter is thought to have a special gift. Doctors belong to a professional class whose services require payment while the bonesetter is more like an artist. He or she works altruistically, charging only *la voluntad,* a voluntary contribution. Another difference is that the doctor uses chemical products while the bonesetter uses only natural ones, generally herbs. In this respect, the bonesetter resembles the *curandero,* and, in fact, many persons have both skills or arts.

My horse threw me against a rock. And from here upwards [my arm] was all black. And I said, "I'm going to lose my arm." But the healer/bonesetter said, "No, it's just that some cartilage [*una ternilla*] broke and you spilled some blood." And he set it and wrapped it and I got better. I never thought I'd be able to use the arm again. Every day that man has his stairway full. He only sees people from nine until two, because after that he has another job. And he only charged what you wanted to give. I gave him 150 pesetas and told him, "If it's too little, tell me." And he said, "You gave me enough. Some people don't even pay enough for the bandages." And my girl, she cut her leg to the bone, and she went to him also. And he told her to put poultices of rue on it, boiled rue, right there. And he told me to put on poultices of camomile, there in Oviedo, of course. I had to buy them and they put it on me. He's very famous. I was going to go to N [to a healer in the area], but my son-in law said, "No, he's got a different kind of medicine. Let me and the child go with you to Oviedo, for that man sets things very well.

The medicine the healer uses is what was used in the *braña* before the doctors turned up. Healers employ what are termed "household remedies" or "old things," which are available to any Vaqueiro aware of their properties. The ingredients can be found in any household, or in the country around the *braña,* without having to go to a pharmacy.

Rana disease was something very bad in the past, because the critters would die. Now the veterinarian comes and gives shots. And when snakes would bite there were also household remedies. R [an *entendida*] knew a lot of those old things. Now you go to doctors. Before you didn't go to a doctor, but now my granddaughter who's a year old, I don't know how many times she's gone to the doctor, for shots and one thing or another. Before you'd get by, there wasn't any doctor. When people had colds they would give them a frumenty of lard and milk. I had a book, the *Herboristería Franco-Belga,* what a good book! It had all the herbs.

When confronted with a problem, the healers try to come up with some response, even if they have to improvise. Some of these improvisations win the approval of doctors. In following instance, a poultice soaked in kerosene was used. Kerosene was the main source of light in house prior to electricity. Observe how the healer behaves with the doctor.

> She knew a little, but three of her children had died young. She would say, "What am I to do? More than I did for my children, because I couldn't do anything for them." She knew a lot about it, from being in Buenos Aires eight years. Doctors don't know anything about that kind of thing. As soon as people got sick she'd have them put on a cloth soaked in kerosene. And one day a doctor called X came and said, "This girl already had a plaster, right?" "No, I put something hot there." She didn't want to say what it was. And he said, "Well, that was a good idea" (smiling). Look, my older son had a pain, and one day it was in his shoulder, the next in a leg, and every night he'd get the pain, a sharp pain that made him cry and wouldn't let him sleep. And one night the boy began to cry because he had the pain up above his ass. And I moistened a cloth in kerosene and put it there, and his pain went away for good. I put the cloth on him following her instructions; she was right there watching.

In spite of the antiquity of their art, *curanderos* are now a kind of alternative doctor, one of the many specialists that Vaqueiros may consult in turn. As with their colleagues with diplomas, the most famous healers are those who live in the cities—Oviedo, Santander, Madrid, and especially a famous one from Alcalá de Henares—where, thanks to improved transportation, Vaqueiros can visit them with relative ease.

> People who heal are called *curanderos.* The one in Madrid has a very good hand; a lot of people have gone from here. Over in Santander there is another famous one. I think my brother was going to go, but then changed his mind. For his "nerves." The one in Oviedo is a *curandero.*

While experience has shown that doctors are more effective at curing certain diseases, the *curandero* knows more about other illnesses, for example, a "fallen stomach."

> He had a low stomach. He went to three doctors in Oviedo and they told him he had gas on the stomach, and then he went to L [town] and this woman told him he had low stomach, and then she reset it and cured him and had

THE PATH TO DEATH

him gain weight and rest. She was a woman called X; she died two years ago. She told him to come back, but then we heard she had died. We felt bad, since she had cured him.

The *curandero* is less effective at curing other illnesses, but the treatment these popular specialists provide, while it may not be effective, does no harm because the methods and ingredients used are benign. That is why Vaqueiros will pay a visit to the *entendido* before undertaking the more drastic solutions of official medicine, particularly surgery. Note that the official specialist was no more successful than the *entendido* in the following cases.

I haven't been out of the house for over twenty years. It's because of an arthrosis of the hip in the year '53. I went to N [*aldea*] to see the doctor and the practitioner; they gave me shots, did a lot of things to me. I went to a healer called F, in X, went to him. He ordered me to be given shock baths, throwing water on me from above, but *qué coño*, it didn't do anything for me. This all began when beans were being harvested, in October, and in April I began to take butter—there was a lot of it—and it did me good, but nothing else did.

Yes, they went to healers—beyond Madrid, in Alcalá de Henares, twice. And that man gave him some herbs, and he said he got better a little, but afterwards I don't know, I guess there was nothing that could be done, the sickness was so advanced, and then it was all over. They had gone to Oviedo, to many doctors, and to visit the [female] saints.

Let me profile one of the best-known healers of the region, the famous Cura of C, a parish priest. Unfortunately, I never knew him personally, because he died shortly after I began my research. The Cura of C was much loved and admired by Vaqueiros.

He was a blacksmith, veterinarian, doctor, and bonesetter—he could fix people's feet. And he gave classes in his church as well as saying mass.

Now he's an old man, he can't see patients any more, but he was really good! There wasn't anybody like him. He was more than a doctor—he was a . . . nurse! He was very *entendido*, a doctor for people, a veterinarian for animals, a carpenter, and a priest. He was very smart, a man who had studied a lot. You can see how learned he was because he always consulted books. He came from around here, from a village called A, and we were all delighted with him; he was better than a doctor.

Because the Cura of C was from the area, he had no trouble communicating with the people.

He was like a country person. Once when he got off a mule he was riding, the mule stepped on him and he said, "Get away, mule, I shit on Christ!" He was just like an old *Vaqueirón*. He said this in front of us; it probably slipped out against his will, out of custom. He came after partridges here, hunting and fishing, and people would invite him into their houses to have a glass of wine, and he would come in and drink and talk just like we're talking now.

This *entendido* was known for his disdain for social convention. It seems he had the same weaknesses as the rest of the rural folk.

Yes, I saw him many times. One time I went with X's son-in-law—the one who got married before he did his stint in the army—while he was under army discipline. And one priest here didn't want to marry him, saying, "You [*Tu*] are at present under orders from your superior, you are not under my control, and I won't marry you without permission from your superior." And then they told him that the Cura of C would marry him, and we went there, and he said, "Sure, *hombre*, sure, go ahead, get married."

His nickname was Pepe *las nenas* [Pepe the girls]. They say he liked the girls. Yes, it's true they called him that. The servant . . . well, the woman he had in his house had two children, I believe—at least one anyway.

The medical specialties of the Cura of C covered a wide range of skills. Here are some of them:

He was very much of a healer. He put back up the stomach of C's wife after it had fallen, put it back up with a gadget he used to raise mine, too. He cured with herbs. For rheumatism he had people gather *carqueisas* [broom] and apply steam to where they had it. F of X, how many times he's told me—he suffered a lot from rheumatism—that he was told to do that. A lot of people go to see him.

There was a couple without children from M [*braña*] and the woman was in very bad health, and they went to see the Cura of C, and he told her, "You must do what you are told. When you have your period, you don't take care of yourself at all. You go out for grass, and you go and do washing. Your blood is very thick, and for two or three days you have to take care of yourself and drink soups, and not go out for grass or to wash, and keep a diet, because you're getting anaemic." And right away, in four days of dieting, she got better, but then she abandoned it. And her husband took her to Madrid where she went to see three doctors, and they told her the same thing the priest had. That shows how *entendido* he was. And everyone decided that the priest was better than a doctor.

The Cura of C was also very *entendido* about cattle, something for which the Vaqueiros were particularly and sincerely grateful.

People loved him because he was very *entendido* about things. One time they went to him from X—some cows had just been grazing in a field and they all got sick. And he told them—he was there for a mass—to go to [the pharmacy at] N for some kind of bicarbonate and some camomile, and they all got better. He sure did know a lot. About people, too.

There's nobody left like him. He knew about cattle like a veterinarian. He could take a calf out of a cow, too, and turn it around if it wasn't coming out right. The people of the villages went often to consult him.

Although the Vaqueiros greatly respected him, and have good memories of him, it seems the Cura of C had his detractors, apparently in his own parish and among the most educated parishioners scandalized by his unusual behavior. At the end of his life he suffered some kind of ecclesiastical suspension and was replaced.

He cured with herbs from the fields, and with some books he had—I don't know if he sold the books or not. He lost some [of his faculties] because of a head injury, and now he can't say mass. Now there's a new boy saying mass, and they like him, but this one doesn't do any healing at all.

In contrast to the *curanderos*, who are not usually Vaqueiros and who tend to get along better in cities, another category of *entendidos*, the prayer people [*rezadores*] and the diviners [*adivinones*], are native to and do their work in the *brañas*. The prayer people not only pray in order to heal but also may divine, protect cattle, and direct prayers at wakes. These distinctions are made below:

My grandmother knew a lot about praying. No, not about healing, for that there was a woman in B [a nearby *braña*] who prayed in order to heal. The one who prays real well now is the girl of M house, at wakes; they come here to pray for everybody [at wakes].

My father prayed for the cattle every day because that way he would know they were safe from the wild animals, and he prayed for them before he went to bed. He would also pray a little to find things that were lost, but he wasn't as successful at that as he was with the cattle.

T was a diviner. In the old days there was one here in L— she was a diviner, she prayed, and knew that way if an animal had been stolen. Yes, they went to her, too, the diviner of L. She died many years ago, I remember that my grandfather, one time that they stole a cow from him, went to her and asked about it, and she said there was nothing to be done about it.

Knowledge of the prayers or words that can heal is transmitted through the house, from fathers to sons or mothers-in-law to daughters-in-law. But this transmission has its risks, for an indiscriminate spreading of the knowledge will cause the prayer person to "lose the hand," that is, to lose the power to heal and to divine.

I don't know about that old woman of M [*braña*], T. I'm afraid she's not going to tell anyone the prayer either. She's very religious. It's because they lose the hand, because if they tell it to someone else they lose the power to guess right.

This man from here only prayed; he must have had the hand. I don't know about this, dear. It must be that some people do it better than others. There are people who can do it, and we say that they have the hand. Not all of us can do it. The person who can, it comes out of him alone.

The transmission of special knowledge takes place within the family just prior to death. There were times when a sudden death would make it impossible. Also, the person chosen to receive the knowledge might be inappropriate because she or he did not have the hand, interest, or skill.

Old L, who's dead, knew them, too—she was the mother of the woman who's in the house now. But the daughter didn't learn it, couldn't do it, didn't take the trouble to learn it, probably learned other silly things instead. I know some of those words, my child, because I was taught them by S, may she rest in peace. [Recites a prayer] S taught me that, because I was dying to learn some of that.

Those are words we ought to know, people can die [without them] because the doctors can't treat it. I don't know the prayer of *dicipela*; I wanted to. M of S knows it, I don't know if you know her; she does know it—her mother cured it, cured it well—but she probably won't tell it because she'll lose her hand; one loses it, and then it wouldn't work if she recited it.

The prayer woman recites a prayer to treat diseases, including envy. Let us see who combats the effects of the evil eyes. When an animal, a cow for example, or a calf, gets sick because of an evil eye, its owners are the first to apply the remedy—simple rituals that everyone knows. But when the sickness is persistent or the animal gets worse, one must visit the specialist. The veterinarian does not know anything about envy, so he either is not called, or if he is called, he does not cure the animal (by definition, if he does cure the animal, it was not a case of envy). The specialists for envy found in the *braña* are also referred to as *entendidos*. *Entendidos* of envy usually have a clientele limited to the *braña* in which they live, but there are a few who, because of their fame or specialization, have a sphere of activity as wide as a parish. People go to them or ask them to come when they are needed. All of them belong either to very poor or very wealthy houses.[45] The knowledge and skill involved is transmitted with the house and derives its continuity from the house. The only difference is that the richer *entendidos* regard the possession of this kind of knowledge as a kind of pastime, since they do not charge anything for their services, aside from an occasional small gift. But for the poorer *entendidos*, the skill has an economic value and can even be a primary source of income, which is received in kind, as a percentage of a harvest, eggs, or cured meat. In odd cases, poor *entendidos* have even sold the secrets against envy (normally jealously guarded within families on the pretext of not wanting to lose one's hand at it). An *entendida* [female *entendido*] speaks:

> My mother knew many things; she taught me. But the thing about that [she refers here to a ritual against envy], it was another woman who taught me that. She's dead now. She was from here, from F, she was asking for alms. I gave her something, and she told me. And furthermore, she cured my sons and the cows; because I didn't know about that.

Nevertheless, both for poor and rich *entendidos*, there exists another kind of indirect compensation.

> Over in C there were other *entendidas*, a mother and daughter, both single. The mother was called S, and she knew how to pray very well, and cure. She probably had . . . how can I say it? She probably had faith when she prayed, but if

Sickness and the Vaqueiro Cosmology 105

she was angry at you or me, and say we went to ask her to pray, then she would say, "Well, it can't be done, it's not good; I pray, but it does no good," because she had something against us. One time here the boys of S house were playing with the sheep at her house and killed a sheep in the mountains by hitting it. And later she found out it had been them. And she went to their house to see the parents, and the parents argued with her and told her it wasn't their sons who did it. And time went by, and for some reason they sent to ask her if she would pray for something; and she told them no, that it couldn't be done, that she prayed, but it didn't do any good, because she didn't have the faith that she needed to have, in their case, because she was mad at them. And that it didn't do any good to pray.

In other words, *entendidos'* knowledge provides them with a way to defend themselves against others. The richest and the poorest thus receive the respect and deference of those who are, respectively, either worse or better off than themselves.

The specialists of envy are usually persons who have a limitless curiosity for knowing and understanding the meaning of things. They pay careful attention to details. Since they cure through "words," they know various prayers and at the same time serve as prayer people. They are noted for their fervent religiosity, quite uncommon in the *brañas*. It is said that these persons are "very saintly," that they "use saintliness a lot." Occasionally their birth is said to have been accompanied by certain supernatural signs.

My mother-in-law, speaking of one of her daughters, the one that died, said that when she was eight months pregnant with her, she heard her weep in the womb. She said this, that we have to weep in the womb of our mother to be able to understand these things [concerning envy]. And you have to be born on Maundy Thursday to have this powerful hand and be good at it.

I do not know any *entendidas* of envy who conform to these conditions. The ones I know are almost all elderly women who spend a good deal of time praying and chatting, not much time working. My impression is that they are quite well informed (even though some of them are shut up in their houses) about the news of the area because of the many visits they receive, and because their help is sought when people or animals are in difficult situations. I think that what these women have in common is a good knowledge of human nature, which they see more objectively because of their age and condition. They seem to be above the pettiness, the little ambitions and interests of the more active portion of the population. In other words, the community finds a use for a person who is intelligent and unusual, no good for physical labor but valuable for her knowledge. One *entendida* says, "You have to know many things, a little of everything." In spite of the legend of saintliness that she herself subscribes to and others ascribe to her, most persons regard her, and others like her, "not [as] a healer, but she knows something. Over the years she has come to understand things, and she has the experience of old age."

The *entendidas* of envy have one thing in common: they are all women.[46] Among other specialists like bonesetters or prayer persons, there are a considerable number of men. But envy, which comes from women, is cured by women. Sometimes there is a genuine division of ritual labor within the family, as follows:

> My father prayed and my mother healed. But there are women who pray as well. My parents got used to that, each doing one thing—him praying and her healing. But he didn't just pray; he worked in the fields as well, like the other men,[47] and she did too. In Oviedo I've heard there's a man who heals very well, a healer [*curandero*], but around here for healing it's women, always women.

The women who cure envy have an ambiguous position in the community; their charismatic power is both needed and feared. The *entendidas* are more like witches than normal people and thus are regarded with a certain mistrust.

> There were some women who, because they knew other things, were called witches. But the women who cured this [envy], no. Well, yes, they would say that this was witchcraft [*brujería*]. Those who did the cures were never known to have harmed anyone. But maybe they did it and nobody knew.

> The woman who is a witch will bewitch you as well as cure you. She's just as quick to nail you as to save you. If you go to her to complain, "Ay! I'm really bad off! It's like they bit me, such bad luck . . . ," she'll say, "Hush, I'll cure you." And since it was she who nailed you, she's the one who lifts the sentence.

I will discuss a specific healer once again: a prayer woman/diviner named Eusebia la T. She has since died, but I came to know her well as she was quite well known in the region. When I met her she was an elderly widow who lived alone. She had always been particularly religious. According to her neighbors, she learned her prayers in her parents' house, and she herself said she had always wanted to be a nun, something very unusual in the *brañas.*

When cattle were missing, or whatever, people would go there for her to pray. She had to know how to do it before she married, because in X house [where she was born] they knew a lot of prayers. There was a woman there who knew how, and the other women learned from her. She liked to go to church a lot . . . saintliness [*la santidad*]. She would say, "Chachina, chachina, it's time to go to mass."

I have some relation with God and with the Virgin . . . that's why I wanted to be a nun. Then my family sent me to marry this man, who was a relative, and we were very happy the time we were together, but my true state is to be a nun. From the time I was ten years old I have wanted most to read and pray. Yes, I help everyone, for we are like brothers; I like to be good for everyone.

Eusebia, who was rather unattractive physically, married a widower. They had no children and lived together quite well.

No, he was little like me and ugly, but very good; he was good and led a good life. We would pray in the evening. He was a widower and lived in this house, which had been his wife's, and I came to live here with him. When you are angry and tired, you get home and start talking with your husband. If you get along well, you eat together, chat, play footsie, and if you feel like it, kiss each other, as if in paradise [*como en la gloria*]. And in the winter it's very nice to sleep next to each other. And if you want to have children you do, and if not, then you have one or two.

While her husband was alive, she lived like the other women of the *braña,* aside from her specialty as a prayer woman. But when she was widowed she began to lose interest in work and human affairs, and to intensify her relations with the divine. She sold her cattle, devoted herself solely to prayer, and was in frequent communication with a convent of nuns in the region.

Eusebia was married to one of my uncles. She was very devout, but she didn't work at all. Her husband was the one who worked. As soon as he died she sold all the cows and never again planted a potato or anything. When you would go to see her she'd say, "Sit down, chachina, you must be tired, you'll get yourself sick. I got sick; I can't work much." That's what she would always say. She was not bad to anybody.

As long as she could, Eusebia liked to go to mass a lot.
And she would take bouquets of roses. You know what that
is? They're not [wild] flowers, they are roses from rosebushes.
I've seen her put them [on the altar]. And they say that later
she spent a lot of time with the nuns of X, that she gave them
all she had; she didn't go anywhere else; they said she'd
rather go hungry in order to save up to give money and things
to the nuns. No, she wasn't a hard worker they said, everything shut down when her husband died. He was a hard
worker, had four or five cows, the finest in these parts, but
she began to dispose of everything so that in just a few years
all she had left was one sheep. She must have gone hungry; I
don't know what she ate. If she had kept one cow, even
though she couldn't gather much fodder, it could have grazed,
and maybe she could have rented out a field or sold the hay
from a meadow or two so they would give some back for the
cow. . . . The fields would have been worth something in
rent. . . . But even two hens would have been better than one
sheep. She kept the sheep so she could give wool to the nuns.
As long as she could walk, she would go to X to take things to
the nuns. And the money they gave her for the fields, instead
of spending it on food and clothing, she bought things and
gave them to the nuns. While her husband was alive she
wouldn't have done that. She would have worked some.

Thus Eusebia went hungry and depended on the charity of her
neighbors, which she accepted with a certain dignity. She helped
them out when she could, especially in caring for children. A
neighbor woman speaks:

Maybe we had to go off in the hills to gather furze, and if
grandmother wasn't here, my husband would say, "Leave the
child with Eusebia." The child was three years old, and she
would distract him so he wouldn't see me go off, and the
child loved being with her. She had a sheep, and the child was
with the sheep all the time. He called her Ubesia, but in the
last days before she died, he began to call her Eusebia—isn't
that something? One day we were cutting up potatoes to
plant, and she said, "If you gave me some—some of those
that aren't any good to plant, I'd take them." I said, "So
you've run out of yours, Eusebia?" She said, "Just about." She
really had run out. So when the potatoes were all in the basket, my boy took a bag with maybe three or four potatoes for
"Ubesia," and gave them to her. When she had boiled them,
without lard or anything, just a touch of salt, she gave some

to him and they ate them as if they were the best thing in the world. She would have bread and sugar—she'd moisten him a piece of bread with water and spread sugar on it, and I won't tell you how eagerly he ate it.

Aside from the charity of her neighbors, Eusebia also received food for her services as a prayer woman and diviner.

She would pray some and they would give her something. We would give her something, too, like at the pig-kill or carnival. We would take her a bag of food, because she went hungry. Maybe the neighbors gave her something; in her later years she couldn't work much.

She didn't work—she was real lazy. One time someone, I can't remember who, took her a lot of meat [from pig-killing]. My daughter-in-law passed by on the way to X. Because she had sent word that the big loss of cattle we had suffered—that we should be careful, that maybe the dead of the house needed something. She said that masses and I don't know what else be given.

I don't charge anybody for healing. I do it as charity. But since I'm poor and cannot work, they give me some of their produce—beans or potatoes or whatever.

Given that her knowledge of prayers provided part of her sustenance, she was not eager to share it. Another prayer woman speaks:

No, she liked to pray, she prayed a lot. I don't know who taught her, but she knew them, knew a lot of prayers. I asked her one time if she'd teach me a certain prayer, and she said, "I'm afraid of losing my hand, girl." And I said, "Then who told it to you?" Because you have to say it. I tell it so they'll know, so when I die. . . . She had the hand, eh? Many times she was right.

The prayer of Saint Anthony and her good "hand" for divining were the principal tools of her trade. Here she explains how and when she used the prayer:

I know the prayer of Saint Anthony. And you can apply this prayer to all of the saints you want. And if the prayer comes out of me right, I have faith that the item will turn up. And if the prayer comes out of me wrong, the item is lost. If the prayer comes out right, I have hope that if an animal is sick, it will soon get better; and if it comes out wrong, if I stumble when I say it, then it's possible that the animal will

THE PATH TO DEATH

not stay well, or will get sick, or have some accident. Yes, you have to recite it with complete faith, a lot of times for that. Good hand . . . you have faith, much faith in whatever you do, and make the sign of the cross. Each healing you undertake, when you start, you make the sign of the cross.

People recounted several instances of her prayers and divinations having to do with healing. Here is one of them:

When I was sick in a breast, X went to see Eusebia one day at nightfall. And he told me they went there, and when they were in the courtyard he said, "Hey Eusebia." "No, don't say Eusebia, be quiet." She went off to one side by herself, said the prayer for me, and told them, "She's quite sick, but it's not something bad." And the next day she prayed again for me, "She's already better—nothing serious."

In addition to human illness, Eusebia also dealt with crises of cattle, and provided information about persons or things that were missing or absent.

Yes, I pray for everything—for animals and for people. For instance, if someone is in Venezuela and doesn't write for awhile, his mother comes and says, "Pray for this son and see if he's dead or what's going on." And I pray, and I might say, "Well, the prayer came out all right." You see, this prayer is very good for many things. [She recites it.] That's all, then you cross yourself, pray some Our Fathers and Hail Marys, and *ala!* It starts taking care of itself—whatever is lost or is sick. If you don't make a mistake while praying, the lost thing turns up and the sick will get well. If a cow is going to give birth, and forgive the comparison, a woman is going to give birth, this prayer also works so that the mother has a good birth and the child lives. For a woman you also have to pray to the Virgin of the Birth, that she give a good birth.

Eusebia sometimes made mistakes in her divinations about the births of cows, which her admirers do not deny. Her advice seemed to be based on the idea that nature had its course, and she did not take into account human interference in that course—artificial insemination or hybridization—that produced larger calves and more difficult births.

You know when she would make mistakes, at times? Because now cows carry large calves, and you have to reach inside and pull them out. She would say the time for birth had not yet come, but if we left the calf inside any longer it would die. She would say, "No, leave it there, probably the time hasn't come yet." But when the men see how things are going, they don't wait.

Eusebia herself recounted to me two cases of divination, including one in which she erred. They are interesting because both refer to searches for a product of modern technology, a wristwatch, demonstrating her efforts to catch up with the times:

Well, two years ago a boy from X [*braña*] lost a wristwatch when he was cutting grass in a field. A woman from his family came here, and they asked me please to pray about the watch. I said, "Well, it's not lost; it will turn up if God permits. He thinks he lost it near the house, but he lost it in the field." And after two or three months it turned up in the field. And a man from N [*braña*] came asking please would I pray for a watch he lost in the *monte* one day he went for furze. It was a gift when he got married, and he didn't want to lose it by all that was holy. And I said to him, "It's not lost, dear; nobody's found it yet. You have to look in the fuel you brought home, where you threw it in the stable; keep looking because nobody has found it yet, look and see if you find it." It didn't turn up. I think he lost it in the *monte*, but horses had gone there, and they probably stepped on it, and it didn't turn up.

Eusebia always received me very cordially and graciously, offering me at least at least a cup of hot coffee in spite of her poverty. After a couple of visits, she had no objection to reciting the prayers she knew and transmitting much of her knowledge about healing and divination. Perhaps she understood that because I was "lettered," I would not be competing with her. During one of those visits, she surprised me with this divination about me.

I have said the prayer to find out what you are going to be. Have fun with all the men, but when you get your degree you will meet a student from a good family. Yes, you are going to be very lucky. Go ahead, have not just one, but fifty boyfriends. Speak with all of them, but when you meet one from a good family and who has studied, take advantage of the opportunity; it's better than slaving in the fields [*estar picando en el campo*].

I met Eusebia as soon as I came to the *brañas*. After three months I took a break and went back to Madrid, where I found a couple of old religious books in a flea market and sent them to her. When I was in the *braña*, I, like everyone else, had thanked her for

THE PATH TO DEATH

her help with small gifts of food—a couple dozen eggs, for instance. But I was told that she greatly preferred the books. On my return, I found that Eusebia had died, and people said her death, which she herself had predicted, was accompanied by supernatural signs.

Among health specialists, the doctor is the newest addition to local experience. Official medicine has revolutionized the traditional theories of disease by giving names to certain illnesses, and by that very naming giving them a place in the Vaqueiro world. People define doctors as having formal training and a diploma. Like the rest of the intellectuals of the area—the priest, the teacher, or the veterinarian—they are seen as having acquired their knowledge through an elaborate initiation that depends on the possesion and reading of books, together with the knowledge of other techniques, including the use of equipment or gadgets. Books are seen as tools for knowing and understanding how things work in general; doctors specialize in the understanding of the process of disease in particular. Nevertheless, any other intellectual, because of the custom and ease in reading books, is also seen as capable of acquiring medical competence. For instance, when I began my research in the *brañas*, people often consulted me about certain ailments because they knew I had advanced schooling. I finally was able to convince people that I was not competent to make medical diagnoses.

In order to be a good professional a doctor must have more than a title or diploma. He must have a "good head" and the possibility of developing it, that is, practice and experience. Given the hierarchical valuation of the city over the country,[48] rural doctors have less prestige than urban ones. The city has better means of communication, better schools, and better services than zones of dispersed settlement, and the *brañas* are an extreme case of dispersion. That is why Vaqueiros in search of health services believe the cities are the places where they can find the best professionals with the best equipment. Of course, the fact that the hospitals—with their elaborate bureaucracy and their abundant supply of *aparatos*—are in the cities reinforces the local point of view.

Not all doctors, however well equipped they may be, are equally adept at "guessing" an illness. The diagnosis on many occasions requires that the sickness be "divined." Vaqueiros very rarely attribute a bad outcome to human error or ignorance on the part of the doctors. When they do, those cases often concern illnesses that the people themselves cured traditionally.

The relationship between doctors and their Vaqueiro patients often involves serious failures in communication. The doctor, sometimes in spite of a continued residence in the area, is a stranger to the community, uses words difficult to understand, and has an idea of sickness and health that Vaqueiros cannot fathom. In the face of local medicine, these official specialists show a mixture of disdain and irony, dismissing traditional rituals and practices with the facile label of superstition, and offending the dignity of their local lay colleagues. Nevertheless, Vaqueiros treat doctors with respect and deference.

The *entendidos* of health are local substitutes or interfaces for the doctor, since they basically follow the official model of medicine. The *entendidos* lack official titles, but they try to "understand" the processes of life and health by means of the same tools—injections, powders, and medicines from the pharmacy. On occasion they use complicated equipment and even books. The fact that *entendidos* exist is a result of the scarcity of doctors in the past and the lack of official medicine in the *braña*. But *entendidos* are also an example of the mutual aid that has developed in the isolated habitat of the Vaqueiros. Women in labor cannot always wait for the doctor to arrive; certain ailments require immediate treatment. These *entendidos* are more available to the people and are examples of group solidarity. Note that they perform their work gratis or semi gratis, according to their degree of professionalism. Even when they compete with doctors, their specialization is the result of a vocation, an interest, experience and practice, combined with intellectual and natural skills that the people are continually checking and evaluating.

In a sense, an *entendido*'s knowledge comes from the group, and it is certainly directed towards it. The *entendido* is an intermediary between the group and the outside world, one who makes official knowledge accessible by interpreting it and adapting it to local cultural needs, using a meaningful vocabulary, and selecting those aspects of medical practice that will help Vaqueiros. Note that these persons are innovators among their neighbors in various fields, not just in medicine, in an attempt to improve the quality of Vaqueiro life.

But these *entendidos* often adhere to outside ways of thinking they do not understand (many use medicines as if they were prayers for healing), and they profess rejection of local practices and ritual that deep down they still believe in. What is more, they imitate not only the doctor's methods and his acceptance of progress, but also his gestures and behavior. The grotesque conduct of some *entendidos*, normally the most professional ones, who use a recherché vocabulary and an authoritarian attitude, caricatures the official specialist. It reveals the two features that the local people consider essential in a doctor, authority and unintelligibility.

In the continuum of popular medicine, the bonesetters and healers are representatives of an old, traditional knowledge. Both are qualitatively different from official specialists. In contrast to the studies of doctors, they offer the power and wisdom of sensitive "hands." Rather than using drugs made from chemicals, they offer herbs and natural concoctions available to all who know about them. Quite significantly, today both ways of curing coexist and on many occasions are tried successively or alternately. Often popular medicine corrects the tendency toward excessive compartmentalization and specialization of official medicine. The popular knowledge of healing is integrated into the local ecological system.

It is no accident that the *entendidos* of envy come from the *braña*, since this is the place where the envy is produced. The *entendidos* of envy are found like the hexed and the hexers at the top and bottom of the social structure. Their too high or too low position distances them from their neighbors. They have a perspective on the society in which they dwell because they do not actively participate in the rhythm of work, in the ambitions and daily struggles, in the pettiness of the social interaction. Their religiosity and experience, age, curiosity, and specialized information allows them to understand human nature and thereby become guarantors of the social order. Illness represents disorder within the group, disorder in feelings and passions out of control. The *entendidos* of envy mediate these conflicts and tensions within Vaqueiro society.

Finally, the prayer people and the diviners broaden the narrow definitions of sickness, placing human health in a wider cultural context. According to these specialists, sickness involves a cosmic transgression, and so the therapies mainly involve prayers. Prayer brings the earth into communication with the underground and the sky, people into communication with the divinities, in an attempt to restore the order of the universe. That is why the abilities of both kinds of specialists have a supernatural origin, expressed through the power of "having the hand" or "relation" with God. To have the hand is an innate feature similar to the skill of the bonesetter, but here technique, practice, or expertise counts less than a relation with the divine, that is, religiosity or devoutness. It is not coincidental that prayer people and diviners help to uphold the moral order. In the final analysis, health and sickness come from God; prayer persons and diviners are intermediaries who succeed in bringing the saints and the Vaqueiros into contact.

The preceding pages demonstrate the syncretic character of the healing specialists, how they combine "traditional" and "modern" symbols and elements in their work. The doctor must "divine" the illness; the prayer woman prays not only for the return of health but for the lost wristwatch. These two specialists are not opposites or antagonists but rather stand at the two ends of a whole range of healers. This range is even more extensive, as we will see below, including saints, spiritists, and other beings. But even among the human healers described here, there is a great variety in terms of specialization and professionalization as well as a considerable amount of overlap. The extent to which these healers combine and blur approaches and etiologies should lead us to question the applicability of standard classifications of "traditional" and "modern" medicine (Smith 1973).

The healing specialists' role as intermediaries points to the transactions between the group and its environment, the group and the outside world, between persons within the group, and between persons and the divine. Underlying these transactions is a cultural model of illness. Illness from contact with the environment, with the outside world, within the group, or with the supernatural is cured by means of the same channels that produced it.

1. View of a *braña*

2. Household surrounded by its fields and meadows

3. Three generations in front of the wooden storehouse

4. Working at seedtime

5. Woman and cows in the field

6. *La feria* (cattle fair)

7. *El trato* (cattle deal arranged by a middleman)

8. Transhumant woman

9. Mowing

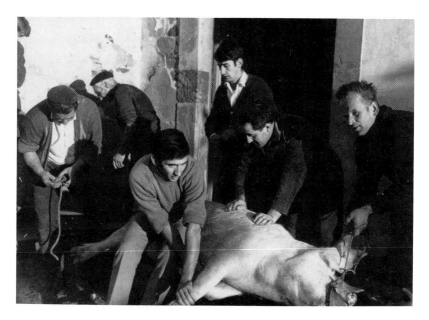

10. Killing the pigs

11. Girls playing "birth of a calf"

12. The farewell: leaving the *braña* at the burial of a
suicide

13. The farewell: approaching the church at the *aldea*

14. Burial at the cemetery

15. Visiting the dead on All Saints' Day

16. Flowers for the dead: All Saints' Day

17. Food for the people: *Romería* at Acebo

18. Offering to the saints: the *lacón* of Saint Anthony, or the *Ánimas*

19. How much is the *lacón* worth?

20. *El Acebo*: lights for the *Ánimas*

21. An *embolubrao* (shrouded live man) at the Acebo

22. Procession at the Acebo

23. Christ at the *aldea*

24 and 25. Offerings
at the Acebo

PART TWO

DEATH

Introduction:
Kinds of Death

Vaqueiros distinguish between three different kinds of death: "good death," "bad death," and "tragic death." By examining what they mean by these distinctions, I will outline the conceptual aspects of the phenomenon of death, treating its organizational aspects later. These distinctions, naturally, involve concepts and values specific to the culture of the *brañas.*

The positive and negative aspects of "good" and "bad" deaths do not refer only to the moment of death itself but also to the circumstances that precede it. A "good death," among other things, is rapid while a "bad death" may mean weeks, months, or even years of slow agony. For that reason, a good death is also known as a "sudden death" [*repentina*] while a bad death might be classed as a "death of chronic illness" or a "slow death" [*accidentada*]. In all the definitions of good death, there are two additional constants: the absence of pain and the absence of an awareness of dying. A good death that fulfills these three conditions is known as a "happy death" [*muerte feliz*], or even a "nice death" or "pretty death" [*muerte bonita, muerte guapa*]. This is the way all Vaqueiros, irrespective of age, want to die. The happy death comes peacefully during sleep when the dying person is not aware of it.

> A happy death is what would happen if I went to bed now and was stiff the next morning. It's not being aware . . . and not knowing about anything. It's not thinking about anything, just going to bed and not waking up, without suffering at all. It's what I would want. (Man, age 38)

In contrast, a bad death involves sickness with pain and an awareness of the imminence of a death without cure. A long, drawn-out agony precedes this kind of death.

> Bad death is that of some people who suffer, God save us, a lot of pain. Some more and some less, everybody dislikes pain and suffering. The more you have to be in bed, the more you suffer and dwell on death and think about those who remain. (Woman, age 62)

A bad death, then, comes from any long illness, especially cancer. A good death will have had no symptoms, and that is why a heart attack is one of the more preferred types of death. This kind of death allows one to work and lead a normal life until the last moment—another aspect of a good death. A bad death is not only painful for the person who is dying but also for the household, those who must care for the sick person and see the suffering. The foreknowledge of one's own death, or the observation of a painful death in others, produces "apprehension":

> If the Divine Lord prohibited dying when you know you're dying, I think it would be better, eh? When you realize it you get an apprehension, you see that you're dying and you die. You're dying with a disease for years and years, suffering there, seeing that you don't get any better and that you have to die. You are a burden for the family and those who are around you, and you lie there thinking, "Well, now I have to die." A bad death was that of X from F, who would spend all day going "Ay, ay, ay!" She must have had cancer, and she couldn't stand it; it was painful to hear her. (Man, age 65)

A good death ideally takes place when a person has completed the life cycle, in old age. It should occur in a "natural" way, without illness or violence, so that a person is unaware of it and feels no pain. Death of old age, also called "natural death," is a subcategory of the good death. It differs from the happy death in that the latter may occur at any age while the former takes place at around eighty years. Those who die "old" do not have a specific illness; they simply "terminate," which means they eat less and less and their blood ends or runs out [se agota]. People who die that way have a tranquil and soft conclusion; it is said that they "died like birds." Sometimes they lead normal lives, even doing work appropriate to their age up to the last moment. It is thought that this ending closes the cycle of a full life.

> The man from C house died completely healthy, but he ran out of blood. And the grandmother here was the same; all

she had was rheumatism, and she began to decline, eating little and kind of faded away, until she didn't have any strength left. She was eating less, and getting thinner, and declining with less strength, because the blood comes to an end, until they end up like a bird. (Woman, age 66)

This kind of death represents for humans the continuation of the general cycle of nature. Plants and animals share with humans some elements of this final process. Compare, for example, the following observations on the cycle of plant and animal life with the preceding statements about the natural death of humans:

December is known as the dead month because it's the last one of the year; it's the month that the blood declines. The grasses decline and the sap goes all the way down. It's something, I think, that's the same in humans; humans grow until they are thirty years old, and then they slowly get smaller. The grasses and plants grow in the spring until the end of autumn, then they are flattened by the wind or bad weather; they dry out. It's like dying; they lose their sap, their blood, and they have less strength. (Man, age 79)

A good cow gets sold when it is fifteen, sixteen, or seventeen years old. It may last until it's twenty-two or twenty-three, depending on its mouth—if its teeth aren't so worn down that it can't graze and eat. That's the main reason cows give out. Their teeth wear down and fall out; they waste away, getting thinner; they can't ruminate and they die. But no one waits until they die. When the cow gets old you to dispose of it, because the same happens to them as with people—rheumatism, etc., until they pass away. Me, they won't throw me out until God or the devil calls, but the cow, since it's useful you sell it, but not for much, since by then it's hard to fatten. (Man, age 65)

The death that forms the sharpest contrast with natural death is known as the "tragic death" [*muerte desgraciada*]. In natural death, one dies from intrinsic and entirely predictable causes; the tragic death is caused by external agents or accidents. First and foremost, tragic deaths occur in mortal accidents in the course of the traditional activities of the *braña*, but they also include more modern deaths in automobile accidents. Those who die in these ways are said to die tragically [*de/por desgracia*] or by accident. Another kind of death is known as "violent death," a form of tragic death that includes all deaths caused by humans, both murder and suicide.

Someone dies tragically who goes to hitch up the cart to the cows and gets caught and trampled. Or if a tree falls on him, or a landslide, like the one that fell on those here. Tragic death is when you fall from a roof, or a stone falls on you, or you fall off a cliff, or you're run over by a cart, or a car hits you and flattens you, since you end up pretty tragic. There are a lot of accidents. . . . No, hanging yourself is not an accident. That's more like a crime; that's violent death.

Tragic death shares some of the features both of the good death and of the bad death. It is usually quick like the happy death and consequently it is often without pain or an awareness of dying. But it is not always instantaneous; the moribund may have the long agony of the bad death. Although many Vaqueiros prefer a tragic death to a painful illness, they do not prefer it for those around them, for a tragic death is always a disagreeable surprise for those who remain. It can happen to persons of any age; in fact, the active population is especially susceptible to it. Furthermore, this kind of death involves the courts or a police investigation, an autopsy, and other legal problems. So Vaqueiros are ambivalent about this kind of death.

An accident is not a good death, woman. Well, it's a rapid death—but what if you barely stay alive? You could smash your hands or a leg, and God knows how long you'd be dragging around. *Hombre*, if you don't feel anything, then there's nothing quicker than an accident, because you die instantly. Nobody wants it, because it's a surprise for those who remain. Because it's a rapid death, but not for the family. (Woman, age 19)

The contrast between death of old age and tragic death is made clear in the following quotation. Death of old age is expected and inevitable, the conclusion of a natural process. Tragic death interrupts this process unexpectedly and prematurely. The subject came up when a cow was injured and had to be slaughtered.

The animal is destined to die. But this animal, like a person, shouldn't have died yet. It should have lasted a few years more, or however many it would have lasted; it's a pity. The cow, like a person, dies one way or another; you have to take it to the fair to be sold. But it makes you sadder when it's lost tragically, like that day. And with people it's the same. You have an apprehension when you lose a family member tragically. But it's very different when they've fallen ill or come to an advanced age and then die, because that way you knew they had to die. But when you lose a person by accident, tragically, who was young, or middle-aged, *Ay Dios!* It's a different pain, a different feeling, a different sadness than when you get to the right age, you're old, and you die. (Man, age 67)

This same "apprehension" is felt when one merely talks about death. Any middle-aged Vaqueiro reacts to the subject with worry, distress, *aburrimiento,* or bitterness, when noting the inevitability of death. It also leads them to think about the futility of life, the selfishness of everyday life, the contrast between pleasure and entertainment, and the obligatory ending that must occur sooner or later. Often Vaqueiros prefer not to think or talk about this matter.

Death worries everybody. Just thinking about it. Because one never dies without having thought about it. But just to think that no matter how long a life is, it won't be more than a hundred years. So that all that work, all that slaving and all that loving . . . and then to think "I have to die." You almost get depressed [*te aburre*] thinking about it, eh? You almost get demoralized, and it's like you don't feel like working anymore. But we shouldn't be so bad or so selfish for the little time we have to live. Of course, sometimes it's not fun, but there are always moments of pleasure, good times at fiestas and fairs, of going from one thing to another . . . and then, nothing! Everybody dies. (Man, age 40)

If they told me I was going to die tomorrow, I wouldn't be afraid; I'd be sad. The sadness of going away forever and not coming back. Death. Here we are four days on loan. That's what the whole world is if you stop to think about it. But one can't talk about this, eh? I don't want to talk about it. (Woman, age 47)

When people get old, they often lose their fear of death. Thus certain elderly persons lose all awareness of their coming death; they are said "not to feel it." Others resign themselves to it or even accept the idea. And finally there are those in severe pain who "ask for death." The quotes that follow provide examples of these three ways of facing one's death.

There is a saying that when we get to be old we are like children, and it's true. In terms of the way of thinking and awareness. Old P, I think, is someone who doesn't even know he's going to die. He's already half sleepwalking, doesn't know when he's hot or when he's cold. He has no feeling in his body. He's shivering from the cold and doesn't realize it. That fellow doesn't feel death.

No, I've been counting on it. Can't you see that I'm tired of life . . . it's not like you who are very young, and you haven't yet enjoyed anything in the world. Life is that way. I've seen everyone in this village die. And I'm still here. I don't know for how long—not long. And if I don't want to die, well, I have to die. Death comes and you have to *pelear*, eh? You have to die. As my mother would say—she was in fine shape, died when she was seventy-five. She went out of this house to go down the hill and she got tired. And we had to go get her and put her in bed, and then the woman she . . . I don't remember what I said to her, and she said to me, "If I have to die, then I'll have to die." (Man, age 84)

You see some people with a lot of pain, and worn out, and they say, "The sooner I die the better." They are afraid because they have those pains. Someone who is very bad off asks for death, of course. A lot of them do! And they say, "Suffocate me, finish me off, I'll forgive you if you stop my suffering."

In the worst cases of bad death, both the person who is dying and those who are witnessing the suffering desire a quick ending. Life ceases to have meaning in some circumstances. Here one of these cases is compared with a case of tragic death.

When somebody old dies, you feel confused. On the one hand it makes you sad, but on the other you are wanting death [for an older person]. Because when one is that way, nothing helps, and one can't enjoy the world at all. If you're going to be in bed all day and in pain, then what are you doing in the world? But a young person is different. Poor E [who died after an accident], what he went through! So young and healthy. Look, he was the same age as I am now. Think about if I died now. And he just went into a coma, and there was nothing that could be done. (Woman, age 18)

It should be clear by now that death is not only a universal biological fact but also a complex cultural event. The Vaqueiros use language to express their perception of similarities and differences among the different ways of dying. By giving these different ways names, they give a certain order to an inherently chaotic human phenomenon. They are able to classify death, even if in arbitrary and subjective ways. The local taxonomy of death could be represented as follows:

DEATH

GOOD DEATH		BAD DEATH	TRAGIC DEATH	
Happy or sudden	Of old age or natural	Slow or chronic illness	Accidental or by misfortune	Violent

Following the local procedure of expressing general distinctions by citing specific cases, I will conclude this introduction with three descriptions. Each shows the ethnographic context for the different ways of dying. I hope they bring color and spontaneity to the more formal exposition above.

A. Good death (happy)

Three years ago on Maundy Thursday, over in N [aldea] a woman died suddenly. She was from X house in M [braña], and she had gone down with her grandchildren to mass, by burro. That was something! If she had fallen off the burro on the way they would have said that the burro killed her. Anyway, down in N we were all in X's place [a bar/store]. I was standing up, getting things from the counter, and the woman was sitting on a bench. And she began to get purple, and stick out her arms and lean against a chair, and go over backwards, and the people went to grab her. And ala! She up and died in J's arms, just like that, without saying a word, she died. They called the priest, who must have been in his house, and she was still breathing and moving. And the priest said, "We have to get a mattress." J went upstairs and got a foam mattress, and they laid her down on it. By then she wasn't moving at all. And he said. "This woman's not right here among all these people. Why don't we take her upstairs?" And everyone carried her upstairs, and they sent word to her house that she had died. She wasn't aware of anything. And that day they took her up to the house. Yes, dear, she didn't suffer at all. That is a happy death.

B. Bad death

"Bring me my clothes to lay me out in them, now! I don't have a reason to be here anymore," she would say. Her illness lasted four months. Sometimes she would say, "No, instead of suffering like this, it would be better if the devils took me." When she would say silly things, P would say to her, "Hush, you don't know what you are saying, don't say that." And she'd say, "I'm crazy, crazy, I know it, I'm crazy. You're not going to remember me; you complain a lot. If you had to stand what I stood, you wouldn't last so long!" She said, "If you'd only give me something to choke me, or if you'd choke me yourself . . ." And she offered a mass of one thousand pesetas to the Santo de los Dolores so that God would take her as soon as possible. You could see that she wasn't getting better; she realized that. She said, "*Ay Dios*, dear, if I die today I won't have to suffer tomorrow." She thought she had cancer and that we didn't want to tell her. She knew she was going to die, because she said, "Ah, ah, ah, don't go, don't go." "What do you have grandmother?" "Can, can, can." At the end she spoke badly, until we realized that she was saying what we didn't want to say—"cancer." When she was going to die, she had three or four blood blisters on her feet and on her body. And when they broke we looked at her, and she said, very faintly, "What is it?" That's all she said. And I said, "Nothing! Just a little blood." And she said, "Nothing . . . go and lay me out," very quietly. She could hear well. She got the blisters from being in bed so long. I don't know if it was that night or the next day that she died. It smelled of blood and pus. What she suffered! She had a very bad death.

C. Tragic death (by misfortune)
With my father it was by misfortune. We were together cutting a tree down by the river. And as I told you, for the felling of a tree, we had attached a rope high up, to pull for the direction of the fall. And when I saw the tree was falling I called to him, and he ran full speed in the direction of the fall. A branch caught him on the head and felled him on the spot. He died there. All you could see was that he gritted his teeth, his mouth and nothing else! It slayed him instantly. He was dead, but he could not be brought home because of the law. Some neighbors counseled me to take him home, others not, because someone could report it, denounce it, and they would take everything we had. The judge from T came here and men from B [a nearby *braña*] volunteered as guards as well, two of them, day and night, almost twenty-four hours until the judge came. It was winter, but they made a fire, since there was wood. He wasn't even sixty years old; fifty-six, I think. The doctors of N, when they performed the autopsy, said, "What a shame! What a chest this man has!" I saw him die right in front of me. Thank goodness there was a man from B nearby. I called him, and I cut

the branch and he lifted him up. We looked to see if there was any hope, but no. I was pretty afraid when he died. When the tree fell that got him, he must have suffered a lot, but if you think about it, it was something sudden, maybe a second. Because those who die with a lot of pain, maybe over a number of days, they suffer a lot.

In the following chapters I will discuss at greater length natural death and violent death, the two poles of the categories the Vaqueiros have established.

2
Natural Death

THE DYING AND THE HOUSE

The elderly have traditionally considered the Vaqueiro system of inheritance as old-age insurance. The *manda* or *mejora* assures them of daily sustenance, someone to replace them in their work, assistance in illness, and company at death. One of the main obligations of the inheritor or married son at home has been to take care of all the elderly "of the house," not just direct family members but also servants and affines. In a sense, the elderly are an obligation inherited along with the material and spiritual possessions that form the household. The aspect of inheritance as old-age insurance does not always mesh with the need to maintain the unity of the patrimony. All Vaqueiro adults wish to die in their house and hope that the house continues. The following quote illustrates the fierce desire to die in one's place.

> Some people would rather die there, poor and abandoned, blindly insisting, "I don't want to go anywhere to die." But if this person knew anything at all, Dear God, how could you be better cared for than in a hospital? But we have this thing that we don't want to leave our houses. A nephew of X came and told them, "Listen, if you don't want to go to the rest home in L, I can get you into a rest home in Madrid." No siree, "No, no, no, no." There were two bachelor brothers, and one said, "No, I don't want to leave my house." It's very hard to leave. People should die where they laid their foundations, where they've spent their sweat.

128

The desire that the house continue, not only during one's life but after one is dead as well, is expressed as follows:

The inheritance is used so that they take care of you and the house does not come to an end. The essential thing is that they take care of you while you're alive; then once you're dead, God only knows what will become of the house. I would want to have the house continue, but if they don't want to take care of it. . . . It's the business of those who come after. . . . But everyone's way of thinking is that the house should continue forever, even if it is in others' hands, that someone should take over and run it. That it shouldn't be broken up, with one neighbor having one piece of land, and another, another; that doesn't satisfy you. What satisfies you is that your house always stays united under a couple who have children, and always continues that way. Even if it's not your own family, it's the same idea. It's powerful, this thing, this faith you always had, the love you have for the house. Even if your children go away and are well employed. What are you going to do here? You have to leave, too; you have no choice. But then you think, "*Ay Dios!* How much I worked in this house, and the season is coming on for gathering the corn. . . ." And that this house should come to an end. *Hombre!* that's a lot for someone to bear, eh?

The situation of the elderly person varies according to whether he or she has descendants, is the owner of the house or not, and also according to the kind of property inhabited. I begin with the most common situation, that of the old *amo* with descendants. His choice for the preferred son takes into account the two desires I have already cited, the care of the aged and continuity of the house. Although in theory the eldest male son (or *mayorazo*) is the preferred heir, he is not always the one chosen. In addition to their capacity for work and administering the house, the candidates are evaluated on how well they get along with their elders. The old *amos* choose among their sons and daughters the one they prefer in conduct and character, who they expect to continue in the house and best care for them in their last days. The choice of an heir is formalized when the *amo* makes his will before a notary public, in which he "improves" [*mejora*] or prefers one of his children, who, very frequently, is already married, has children, and has been working in the house for years. Sometimes the *amo* postpones this legal transaction, either because he is unsure of his choice or simply out of neglect. At times, also, death unexpectedly intervenes. In these cases, an effort is made to have the old man make a will on his deathbed in order to give legal preference to one of his children; if he does not, the house will be divided equally among the children, which involves the liquidation of this single family enterprise. That is why the notary is a familiar deathbed figure, together with the doctor and the priest. The ideology of the unity of the house has so much weight that in a few of these instances in which the *amo* dies intestate, his relatives collectively accept the moral rights (as opposed to legal rights) of an heir and avail themselves of various subterfuges so that the house will continue under one leader, in spite of the financial losses this would mean for many of them.

> In this house up here, when the old man died, he didn't dictate what was written down. He had a stroke and died. The daughters were here from Madrid, and the whole family, and everyone agreed that the oldest brother should be preferred. But he [the dead father] didn't dictate anything, and the document was written as if he had dictated it. And then we all went as witnesses to testify before the judge. Some have time to dictate it, but not this one. He was dead.

The *amo* who leaves his house divided equally among all his children is criticized very severely. The duty of the *amo* is to maintain the house as it was left to him, without selling any parcel of land or any other property. If at all possible, he should enlarge his house. That is why he must leave all papers in order before he dies, or others will call him lazy, stubborn, a disaster, and selfish. At the hour of death, "the idea of the person dying is to leave to house to someone who will look out for it, someone who will continue to operate the house of so-and-so."

The survival of the house becomes a problem not only when there are too many survivors but also when there are none. For couples without children, single owners, or widowers without descendants, there is a conventional solution: the *heredeiro* [literally, heir]. These persons without direct descendants "bring a *heredeiro* into the house" so that someone will care for them in their old age, work in the house, and inherit it. This person is generally a relative, typically a nephew or niece, who, although he or she belongs to another house, has no possibility of inheriting.

> In the past, and it's still true today, when there were no children, a couple always obtained one, as happened in R house. They had a son, and on Saint Anthony's Day he was killed when he fell from a horse. This couple then brought a niece to the house, as *heredeira*, and she's still alive today.

Others without children do the same, maybe with a neighbor.

Sometimes the inheritor begins by working in the house as hired hand, drawing a wage. If the *amo* likes him, that is, if he works well and behaves well over time, he becomes the *heredeiro*. This means that he loses his wage but inherits the house when the *amo* dies.

One of our sisters went as a *heredeira* to A. She was married to a man from F who wasn't an eldest son. And there was a house with an unmarried brother and sister, who had no family. They both were over sixty years old, and they took him on as a hired hand, paying him so much, and they liked him and they made him *heredeiro*. As soon as they made them *heredeiros* they stop paying them. And they had him recognized as their son, and when they die, everything will be for him. They've been married there at least seven or eight years. They get along well, take care of the old folks, and the old folks aren't bad either. The days they go out, the old people give them money, just as if they were their children.

The obligations of the *heredeiro* are the same as those of the preferred child: work in the house, care for the elderly, and obedience. The contract is beneficial to both parties, and both try to fulfill it, though not always successfully. On occasions there are frictions and arguments stemming from the inevitable incidents of joint households. While such friction is bad enough with one's own kin, it tends to be worse with *heredeiros*.

They didn't get along; they fought; they could not live together . . . and the man [the *amo*] was left alone. Because it's hard, living in the same house is hard, because the owner, for any little thing, he won't like it and say it's badly done, and then the divisions arise, and getting along badly, and fighting . . . and the *heredeiros* have to leave.

When *heredeiros* leave, the accounts must be settled, that is, the *amo* has to pay the ex-*heredeiro* for the work done for the house. Then he begins to look for another heir. Sometimes many are tried. At times a *heredeiro* may be chosen over direct family members, for example, when the *amo* has not wanted to or has not been able to cede control to one of his children, whether because of personality differences or because they have migrated. In one of these situations, a widower took a *heredeiro* into his house when his children, who had emigrated to Latin America, suggested it. They did not expect to return to the house since they had prospered abroad, but they shared their father's desire that the house should continue. In this kind of situation, whether or not the children are in agreement, the *amo* uses unorthodox legal procedures to leave the house to the *heredeiro* so that it will remain intact.

When all attempts to bring a *heredeiro* into a house fail, the old person who is alone has one more recourse, although it is usually viewed as a last resort, a step to be taken only when he is sick or incapacitated. He may go to the house of one of his neighbors and offer them everything in exchange for care for the rest of his life. This is a very favorable offer, and it is almost always swiftly accepted. The old person doesn't usually last long, and one's house can often double in land and buildings. This is the way that some of the small houses of the area have ended, because, being small, their owners have been unable to find a *heredeiro*. The neighbors obtain the house, money, land, and so on as a donation while the *amo* is still alive. He lives his last days in comfort and dies surrounded by people.

> You give it, give what you have. Before you die you give away what you have. Many times you can't find someone to bring in—you might find people for a good house, that could support a couple, but for a house like that one, that can't support two cows, who are you going to find? Nobody. When he was left alone, he came to this house to say that if they would take care of him he would leave them everything. "Yes, come on over, we'll do everything that needs to be done for you." And then everything was left to them—the fields and the pastures and everything.

The same thing happens when the old person is not the owner of the house although he lives in it. These "old persons of the house" typically include uncles, single brothers of the *amo*, who have lived and worked in the house to which they brought their part of the inheritance; old hired hands, considered part of the family and therefore no longer paid a wage; and old emigrants who have returned to die in the house. Until they die, all of these people participate in the work of the house as much as they can, and they leave their savings and belongings to the people of the house, in particular to those who gave them the best care in their last days. Often the quality of this care corresponds to the quantity of savings, although there is a recognized moral obligation to care for these old persons "who did so much for the house" regardless.

The forms of property transmission I have mentioned try to maintain the difficult balance between the security of the elderly and the continuity of the house. Inheritance by will ensures both

DEATH

aspects by making possible the substitution of different children or *heredeiros* if those chosen don't fulfill their obligations to the house and the elderly. The last cases I referred to emphasize the care of the elderly in their last days. Some purchase this with money, since they have nothing else; others are forced to give away their house. This exchange, in which the integrity of the house is sacrificed for the integrity of the body, is the extreme opposite of another situation, in which the old *amo* releases most of his rights to the house in order to ensure its continuity at risk of his own security. This is the case of property transfer by *escritura*, or deed as opposed to a will. This transfer is made while the *amo* is still alive and is irrevocable. Vaqueiros use a blunt popular dictum for those who negotiate this type of transfer: "He who gives away what he has before he dies deserves to be hit with a club" [*"El que manda lo que tien antes que morra merece que le den con una porra"*].

Property transfers by deed tend to occur either under pressure from heirs who threaten to leave the house, or voluntarily when the son "marries in the house," his parents are pleased by the match, and the bride brings a substantial dowry that increases the house. But, as the saying implies, deed transfers can have unexpected results for the parents, as they themselves recognize:

> There is a law that when you make a contract of property in joint society for gain, a third of the house is taken. This law should not exist. Because the parents sell a third of the house to the son for no money, and it's not right that a son married in the house should be there for only six months or a year and then say that he's leaving and wants his part, and they legally have to give it to him whenever he says so. That way the house is broken up! This deeding is a bad thing, very bad, because the old folks should come first; it's only fair. If the children have the money, they can treat their parents badly. And then where are we? Because we're all good, but things change and . . . I have seen men with sacks on their shoulders, asking for alms because a son married in the house, they were weak, and then they were left without a house or anything, in the street!

In these lines one reads every old person's fear of abandonment in the last years of life. The house provides them with capital in order to obtain the care and attention they require. In this clash of interests between generations, the lack of confidence is mutual, but the person who stands to lose the most is the old one, because of age and situation. That is why a deeded inheritance is often considered to have been obtained by trickery, ignorance, or weakness.

Natural Death

It's rare that it happens. It's likely to be done by ignorance, by not knowing what they're signing. Because if a son is bad to his parents, there's no way to change it.

More than someone tricking the parents, they let themselves be tricked. They are very weak, with little ambition, and they give in. Because look, when I married, my parents deeded my inheritance to me without my asking anything. And my father even wanted to leave me part of the house in case we ever separated. My father was very weak, poor guy, he didn't know how to stand up for himself. And the notary said to him, "*Hombre*, you can sell it to him." This was two or three days before my marriage. I could have treated them badly but it wouldn't be fair. And after that they bought fields and wanted to put them in my name . . . and I said, "Today you have a good son, but you are being very soft. When you are in need, you have to be a little tough."

A kind of middle way between the deeding of inheritance and inheritance after death is relinquishing of the administration of the house [*ceder el mando*]. An old man may do this voluntarily in favor of a son or a *heredeiro*, but he will reserve for himself at least part of his savings and the legal title of the house until his death. In this way the succession of generations takes place within the house: the heir not only takes on the obligations, the work of the house, but also the rights, the administration of money and decision-making, without having to wait for the death of the *amo*. As this is a verbal, nonlegal contract between the two parties, if the old *amo* is not satisfied with the way the heir administers or the treatment he receives, he can take back the direction and even change the will. Accustomed to power, the old *amos* sometimes resist handing over control and try to postpone it as long as possible, although they admit it is a much better solution than deeding for inheritance.

Handing over control is an advance. Because I hand over control but I don't make a bill of sale or give away my rights, which is an important difference. Because already with my son I had various arguments on this point. [Handing over control] doesn't take anything from me. I get relieved of a burden. Many do not relinquish control, because not all houses produce the same. The house that is good, well, of course, the person with control . . . has a lot of money to make or lose. But do you know what it is to administer a house that barely makes a red cent? You have to know how to administer. The treatment [of the father by the son] is going to be the same. . . . So if this son one day denies that his father preferred him, I can say, "Look, if you're not going to care for me, then you're not going to have the good life and order me around." He has to understand it. I continue to be the owner just the same; I continue as the *amo.*

As implied above, the way property is transmitted depends on the size and quality of the house. Inheritance by will generally occurs when the house is strong economically and various siblings have an interest in it. They keep their hopes up until the end, because if the preferred child has a run-in with the father, does not care for him well enough, or does not do enough work in his father's eyes, the father can change his will and prefer another child. Indeed, many times these siblings succeed in manipulating the situation to the detriment of the preferred one. Hence the preferred child cannot demand the inheritance by deed without running the serious risk of being supplanted.

But when the house is weak, small and of poor quality, there is little competition among the sons, who quickly abandon the house. Then the heir is freer to demand the transfer of property, under threat of leaving the house and the old *amos* alone. The heir's main argument generally stresses the continuity of the house: "If you want the house to come to an end . . . because, what are the two of you going to do here alone?" The transfer of the administration of the house is also sought using the same arguments, in the same circumstances.

Yet the values of the house seem to hold less weight for the younger Vaqueiros. Some of the poorer houses have disappeared in recent years because the children have preferred to seek their fortunes in the cities or in other countries. Military service provides all male youths with a chance to leave and not return. An old *amo* might say, "He who stays at home hasn't been to Oviedo," an Asturian version of "How are you gonna keep 'em down on the farm after they've seen Paree?" Even in the wealthiest houses, which have a number of candidates, the old folks complain that the only interest the potential heirs have in the house is strictly economic.

The old days are over when you made your will for a son or daughter and passed away in peace because you knew that they were going to take care of your house for the rest of their days. Because up to ten years ago the father who made his will could die and did die with the tranquillity that came from knowing that the house would continue to be run by a son or daughter. If it was a daughter who was preferred, the daughter was married in the house, and if not, a son. But now, in order to get what the father has, they'll say, "Yes, yes, I'll take care of [the house]," but *ala!* four days after you die, they say, "All right, I'm the *amo* and I can do what I want with it."

However, the problems of inheritance are less severe now than in the past due to old-age pensions [*el retiro*]. With this government aid, the old *amo* tends to transfer control earlier and more often, since one of the reasons he retained it was for economic security. This, in turn, has prevented many conflicts with the young heirs, previously frustrated because of their total lack of participation in the decisions of the house. This change is part of a more general shift in attitudes, way of life, and customs that the older Vaqueiros have seen coming for a long time.

The grandparents get pensions and hand over the control of the house to the young folks so they can make the decisions. I myself have given control to my son-in-law, because if the youth do the work they should have control, right? If we're no good anymore for working, we're not going to run things. When I had to do the buying and the selling, then, yes, I went to the cattle fairs and had to know the prices; when you sell things you have to find out. I don't go anymore. But the youth now isn't the same as before. When I want to change something—actually, I just leave it to them now, but say I see something that's not right, that's not feasible, and I say something; they say, "But now everything has changed." And everything *has* changed. I am getting a pension for my own little expenses, and my wife, too; that is to the good. And since everything has changed . . . it's true, because in my lifetime, it's like a change from white to black. The way of working here, everything. And the old days will not come back.

In addition to causing this small revolution in domestic organization, the old-age pensions have ensured the well-being and tranquillity of every old person in his or her house. The single uncles, for example, or the *amo*'s widow, can now contribute to their household small donations of money in exchange for care, in addition to ensuring themselves a certain independence and extra food. The subsidy provides "hope" to those who are nearing the end of their lives and to those who will be in the same position in the future.

It is a different hope to live in the countryside now than it used to be. Now we have the probability [of a pension]. You make an effort, you start paying [the monthly contributions], and what a difference! Life in the country, and in the *braña*, when you get to be sixty-five, each day has to get better for the individual. No longer do you have to think, "The house was a poor one and I couldn't put anything aside. What's going to happen to me? Am I going to die a pauper? What if I need an operation or am bedridden here?" Uh-uh. Now you can know that when you're old you'll have enough money until you die. Yes, something can still happen to us, a calamity, but when you know that in fifteen days you'll get a payment, then you perk up a bit. This is a great thing. My son and daughter-in-law, the day I'm no longer here, if they keep the house going, when they get to be sixty-five and are alone in the house, they won't live high off the hog, no, but they'll get along all right on it. Because if they pay me three thousand pesetas after fifteen years of payments, he who has thirty years they'll give seven or eight thousand at least. That's why since '58 when they started the old-age subsidy, life in the *braña*, in the country, is very different.

One might even say there has been a positive reevaluation of self-esteem. The subsidy seems to have reduced the old feeling of inferiority on the part of the person of the countryside toward the worker in the city.

Being a farmer, being old and going down to L [town], and seeing a worker from L with his good suit and his cane, strolling, enjoying the fresh air, you'd say, "This fellow, who was always a worker, look how he lives at age sixty-five; and the rest of us, with all we've worked, twenty times as much as he, and we haven't got a penny." But now, this fellow, I don't say I'm like him, but I don't envy him at all. He gets seven, and I get three, but since I always grew my own potatoes, and I have a cow to milk . . . it all works out. This thing of the subsidy is very important, no matter what they say.

Many Vaqueiros complain about the cost of the monthly Social Security payments, and almost all of them are afraid that they will not able to benefit from them in their old age, either because they won't live long enough to receive them or because of a hypothetical war that would destroy all kinds of security. The following statement is typical: "I hope we get there [sixty-five years old, to receive payments], that there isn't a war and they don't take it away. It's a wonderful help."

The transfer of administration marks the beginning of the transition towards death. Over a period of about ten years, say, from age sixty-five to age seventy-five, depending on the person's health, the old Vaqueiro gradually relinquishes the decisions of the house. And although he does not stop working entirely, he reduces his work load considerably, doing things that require less strength and more patience, like watching cows at pasture, work traditionally relegated to the elderly or to children. His experience in administering the house is also valued. The Vaqueiros appreciate the saying "The old ox doesn't plow, but he knows the furrow," which affirms the wisdom and expertise of the elderly. Being able, in spite of one's years, to contribute to the work of the house is very highly valued by the elderly and those around them. Indeed, this one of the features of the happy death.

In addition to a diminution of work, the diet of the older Vaqueiros begins to change. Although there are old Vaqueiros proud of their "good stomachs," examples of "hard and strong old men," or "people like there used to be," at a certain age most stop sharing the strong foods of the active population and replace them with foods considered more bland. The elderly have to be "looked after" to prolong their lives. This care should be given

> not only at the time of death, because at the time of
> death, there isn't much you can do. It's the same as a horse
> you starve and whip on until finally it falls down. And then
> you give it oats, the oats you should have given it long before.
> As soon as a person gets to be old, you have to look after him.
> You shouldn't push him to work, and he needs some foods
> like an infant. The young person has health, can eat every-
> thing, but the old person cannot.

A third factor that gradually serves to distinguish the elderly from active adults is more subjective, but it is something that inevitably appears with age: the loss of "grace" [*gracia*]. It is said that an old person loses *gracia* when life begins to escape from him and death is nearby; one loses one's pleasure in living and begins to die a little.

> When you get to have as many years as I do [80], you
> think about when it's going to happen. I don't have much
> left, eh? When you get to this age, you're not as alive as you
> ought to be; you're half stunned, without *gracia*, because you
> are thinking about death, and when it will come.

The practical result of the loss of *gracia*—of the pleasure, fun, or interest in living—is that the old Vaqueiros begin to turn inward and gradually isolate themselves from the world around them, begin to lose ties with other people. First they cut back on their trips to the towns or the larger *aldeas* where many of the Vaqueiros go for the cattle fairs and markets, and for the pleasures of socializing. For a while the old folks continue to circulate in the *braña* and its environs, chatting with neighbors and friends, but ultimately they seclude themselves in the house.

I don't have any interest in going out. I don't have *gracia* for anything anymore. It's been years since I went to N [large *aldea*] or L [town]. I lost the *gracia* of going out. It's like I don't dare to go out, maybe because of my age. Because three or four years ago I would go to N or L to the markets, just like a dog going out of the house, perky and with *gracia!* When I was in the bus it seemed like a liberation. Put me in a bus and it was the limit for me; I'd come home all happy. And now I don't want to go out of the house, I've reached that age. Because I already know, I've always seen old men in the village who, when they got to a certain age, wouldn't go out of the house. "Going to N?" "No." There are people who get very old with a lot of *gracia* . . . but me . . . I had the *gracia*, but for the last two or three years I haven't gone to the markets, with friends and all it was too much, too dull. I go out very little; I don't feel like it. A lot of the *gracia* is gone.

When the old Vaqueiro stops making his trips away, the younger people are starting theirs. It is very common for there to be a dispute in a house about who gets to go to the fair. Usually everyone wants to go, but someone has to stay home and take care of the animals. First preference goes to the adults who run the house: to the men who normally buy and sell cattle, and therefore have to be up on the latest prices; and to the women who shop for the household at the fair. For the youths of the house, the fair is only a place of entertainment, a way to find a mate, especially at the dances held at most of the fairs. They are the logical ones to stay at home since their activity at the fair is not directly productive for the house. But as the loss of *gracia* helps the old Vaqueiros to cede their roles in social interaction to the younger ones, they stay home to feed the animals. The old person begins to feel out of place at a fair among the young.

Before I went to the fairs when I had to buy or sell. You see your friends and you talk a little. I don't go now, not anymore. Sometimes I go to L to have a game of cards or two among friends, but *Ay Dios!* you start losing *la gracia* and you're out of place [*no pinta uno*] among the young.

In old age, new alliances are formed. Differences in diet and work often result in a separation of the aged from the active adults and the alliance of the aged with children. The hours of their meals do not always coincide with those working in the fields. And even if all age groups eat together, the difference in foods and their different preparations already marks a separation. Such a separation is especially significant among the Vaqueiros, for whom rituals of commensality have great symbolic importance. The type and rhythm of work also separates both children and the aged from the active adults, and many chores are assigned indiscriminately either to children or the elderly. Furthermore, both the very aged and the very young often have to stay in the house, either because of bad weather or bodily weakness and lack of equilibrium. The transhumant trips, for instance, are made by the strongest, while those who are losing their strength and those who are beginning to gain it stay in the house or make the shortest trips by cart. For all these reasons, it is the old Vaqueiros, particularly the grandmothers, who very often are in charge of the education and care of the infants in the house until their schooling begins. At the same time, they also do other easy jobs in the house, like feeding domestic animals or caring for sick cattle, while the adults work in the fields and meadows, and travel substantial distances with the cattle. As the aged get older and lose *gracia,* this pattern of the elderly caring for the children reverses. Then the adolescents care for the old folks, maintaining the bond of solidarity between the two groups, which the elderly often reward with small amounts of money when the youths go off to the fairs. Many times it is this bond with the children that keeps some *gracia* in the elders' lives.

Today I'm interested in the grandchildren. First the one in Madrid; now the one we're raising here. You always have to have some reason to keep going, and you say, "*Coño,* if it weren't for this girl I'd . . ." for this baby, let's see if we'll see her a little older.

According to local thinking, the loss of grace is not only a psychological phenomenon but a physiological one. *Gracia* is lost with the blood. As one gets older, the blood gets heavy, dries, and ends together with life itself.

When the years come that weigh on you so much, something happens to the blood; there isn't any blood, the *gracia* gets demoralized, that *gracia* is lost.

Eighty years is very bad, very heavy. The blood and everything is finishing up. The blood does not have *gracia.* Blood is life and soul; when the blood ends, everything ends. There is a time in life when the blood is wasting away, and one loses one's forces; this is because the blood is not quick, one is failing, one gets dry.

The disinterest in social interaction and the diminution of strength coincide with the lack of pleasure in other earthly things, like food, or even survival itself. The old man whose words I quote below has not lost interest altogether. He still takes care of himself and enjoys receiving his pension. It is said that "he's afraid to die because he's receiving his pay," in spite of his loss of *gracia*. He expresses this contradiction.

> I don't [fear death]. Why should I be afraid? It doesn't make any difference. It's all the same. Since I'm old, I can't do anything, there's no *gracia* anymore, it's all lost. The second book [a school reader], when I went to school—now they don't have them—said that the time comes when the pleasure in all things is lost. And it was right. You even lose pleasure in eating. Don't eat and you don't have your health, and you don't have anything. Yes, as long as you can get around . . . and anyway, this money they give us, it's a great thing.

When he suggests "I can't do anything, there's no *gracia* anymore," one concludes that the loss of *gracia* corresponds to the activity of the individual. As long as one works, albeit slowly, takes care of oneself, and can walk around in the *braña*, there is *gracia*, there is still life. This is not case with the aged person who cannot move. At this point there is little or no *gracia* left. A paralyzed person indicated this indirectly when I asked him if he was afraid of death. "Not me, dear. What do I do here? It's been a long time since I went into the courtyard." In other words, it could be said that as long as the older Vaqueiros feel useful and are not a burden on the others, life is still acceptable. When all of their strength fails and they have no recourse, they take to bed. They have entered the last phase of dying.

THOSE AROUND THE DYING

As soon as an older Vaqueiro takes to bed, there is an inevitable reorganization of the division of labor in the house. One or some of its members will have to take care of the sick person's basic needs—cleanliness, food, and company. At some time in their lives, almost all Vaqueiros have taken care of a sick person, whether parents, parents-in-law, *amos*, or the aged emigrants who come back to die where they were born. The *braña* traditionally has been the place for convalescence and dying.

My brother-in-law was in Madrid, but he began to feel bad, and worse and worse. I don't know how long he was sick in Madrid, but when it began to look real bad he came here; his other brother brought him here and left him. And he was here for a while until he died. And he died here because there was no one to care for him in Madrid then.

The scrupulous care of the sick is considered an important moral obligation that all the people of the house must fulfill, but the obligation rests with the preferred child in particular. As long as he is healthy, the old *amo* may blackmail the heir with the threat of a change in the will, but on his deathbed he is at the mercy of his family. Sometimes this moral obligation and the fear of criticism from others keeps the heir from taking revenge for the many years he has been dependent on the *amo* and subject to his will.

When the time comes that you're flat out in bed, it doesn't depend on obligations of the [preferred] son, it depends on their morality. Because you can't get out of bed and say, "*Hombre,* if they're going to treat me this way, I'd rather go to the rest home." It depends on morality. *Hombre,* but at this time you will have another son or daughter who will be able to move their conscience and say, "Listen, this isn't the way to care for him, not at all."

By and large, fulfilling the obligation to the aged requires a great sacrifice on the part of the people of the house. One sacrifice is the labor spent in sick care, which they would have spent doing other work. This work, in turn, must be assumed by the rest of the household. Especially in the cases of bad death, the fine equilibrium that exists between the work of the house and the members that compose it is so affected that eventually everyone, sick and well, begins to hope for the end.

The washing and feeding of the sick is considered women's business. If the sick person is the *amo,* it is the obligation of his daughter-in-law and granddaughters; if it is someone else, then some member of the house in particular will take on the job, a niece for example, who will often inherit the dead person's belongings. Keeping an aged person clean is considered essential, but it is very difficult, since there are no washing machines for the sheets and an old person who is bedridden is often incontinent.

When there is a sick person, you have to change the sheets every day. Yes, otherwise there are smells, you know.

DEATH

And for him, when he did everything in the bed, yes. I would just finish changing it and . . . no, that was awful. S [niece] was the person who did most of it, and he left everything he had saved to her. She had her fill of washing and changing him and doing things. He loved her most [of the house].

The way this work is organized also depends on the composition of the family, the number and sex its members, and how much work there is to be done. Some houses have several women; others have only one. The care of a sick person is more or less onerous depending on these factors. Note the difference between these two cases:

Well, one thing is true, I was worse off than they were [the parents-in-law]. They didn't let one rest even a little, or dress up or anything. In three or four months I didn't lie down, or undress, or anything. He died before she did, but she was very bad off, too. You had to put her shoes on, take them off, help her change her clothes. I had to do everything; the children were little and my husband in Madrid. Yes, I've worked some in my life. You had to go and cut hay, and feed the animals and leave food all ready, and when you came back start all over again.

We had to change her very often. Wash her and put the clothes in the kitchen to dry. As if she were a little baby. I think we were four months caring for her. From washing so much, your fingers get chilblains. Of the three of us, we said that A was the chambermaid, and we, my mother and I, the nurse and the washerwoman. She said, "It seems like God punished me," with all the diapers she had washed for the baby, Little Carlota. And she said, "Before it was Little Carlota and now it is Big Carlota [*Carlotón*], and now you have to wipe the bottom of Big Carlota."

When the elderly Vaqueiros take to bed, their diet becomes even more restricted. The food given them is either very special—that served at fiestas or in life crises—or very soft and bland, often both. Everyday foods like stew, white beans, and pork are prohibited, because they are considered excessively strong for the invalid. The foods recommended are easily digested and will provide the invalid with strength, for example, quinine wine, milk, coffee, hot chocolate, veal steaks, eggs, green vegetables, fruit, sweets, and above all, chicken soup, the panacea for all illnesses. The slaughter of barnyard hens is necessary. This attention to diet is due in part to the fact that lack of appetite is considered symptomatic of the more general malaise of loss of *gracia,* with its associated sadness and *aburrimiento.* It is because of this sadness or jadedness that much of the food that the aged invalid eats is special. The theory is that since they eat so little they should eat what they want. Whims [*antojos*] are an important part of an old person's diet as death approaches; catering to them is almost a moral obligation, regardless of the (at times considerable) expense.

When someone is going to die, the doctor says, "Look, there's no hope. What you have to try to do is keep him clean in bed and see that you satisfy his whim [*antojo*] if he wants anything." Because they say at the hour of death there are many whims. I myself was never a wine drinker and never tried it. It may be that at hour of death I'll say, "Bring me a little wine." Or you may ask for some grapes, or oranges, things you get an urge for. All these things, when possible, should be made available to the sick person.

In addition to physical care and food, one should provide the aged invalid with company in sickness and death. As long as the work of the house allows it, the sick person is accompanied day and night by a family member. Since someone has to sleep in the same room, it is usually a person of the same sex, but not always. The Vaqueiros often cite a saying that is to the point.

"Said the meat to the bone, at the hour of death God give us our own" [*"Dijo la carne al hueso, a la hora de la muerte Dios nos dé algo nueso"*]. They say that when we are prostrate in bed and sense death. It means that there should be someone from the family to attend us.

For this reason, as we saw above, many Vaqueiros resist the idea of dying in a hospital, impersonal if clean. Accompanying the sick does not just mean observing them; it involves the exchange of human warmth, which in most cases is lavished with great generosity. An effort is made to distract invalids from thoughts of death and to accept their caprices and quirks patiently.

Her sickness lasted four months on the button, that in bed. And before it happened, fifteen days without sleeping, because she got the idea she had a wooden shoe on one foot. She had a thrombosis. There were moments in which she had all of her wits, and other times when she would get dopey and imagine things about her granddaughters. She was in the driest room in one of the beds, and three of us—my mother, my sister, and I—were in the other bed. She would dream with her eyes open; she was awake. We wouldn't contradict

DEATH

her. She said that her granddaughter was falling down, and if we said otherwise she would say, "But don't you see her? How can you say that when I am seeing her?" What do you think that could have been? Something that she was dreaming about the baby when she was wide awake. She was like that until she died, sometimes all right, other times not. She had her sleeping reversed; she slept in the daytime and at night she was awake. When we went to go to bed, she would give us a sermon! That so-and-so was coming. "Shsss," she would say, "be quiet, the police are coming; don't say a word." She was funny at times, eh? Because she would start laughing and laughing. And when she would fart, "Pum!" I would say, "Pepa, shut the door," and she would say, "They say the prisoners aren't happy in jail; you have to let them out once in a while." Sometimes we would jiggle her bed, for the fun of it, because she'd get bored there all day. And she would say, "Wretch, don't shake my bed," and she would giggle, "Go ahead, jiggle it, jiggle my bed." And I would say to her, "You don't want to dance or jump anymore." And she would say, "Yes, I've done all my dancing and all my jumping." And she knew she was going to die.

Death in solitude is considered a miserable end, a beggar's death.

C from E was a woman who lived alone. She worked around here spinning and people would give her milk. She lived where those of C are, in a little house they took down. She would go away for as much as a week at a time to help out somewhere or ask for alms, without coming back. One time days went by and she didn't appear, and she had cats and hens, so people went to the door to see if the key was there or if it was locked from the inside. And they got worried when they saw it was locked from the inside, because I think she had been sick. So some of the neighbors called others, and they broke down the door. The law came. She had been dead for days. It wasn't known when she died. I believe she just lay down in bed and died like a bird. Nobody knew about it.

When old persons take to bed, they are not totally isolated from the outside world nor are the people of the house left to care for them alone. As in all life crises, Vaqueiro solidarity makes the course of an illness easier to bear, both for the sick and for the household. Neighbors and relatives from the *braña*, family members who live in other towns and *brañas*, and even those who have

Natural Death

emigrated to Spanish cities or other countries assist in different ways. Emigrants usually provide financial help, since they cannot always come to help out at the house. In addition to sickness, other misfortunes in the family, like the death of a cow or the funeral of a family member, often occasion monetary contributions or loans from those who have moved away. Indeed, they send help at other moments of special expense as well, like weddings or the building of a new room. But these absent relatives are especially generous in the hour of death, which is considered the key time of human solidarity. "An old person dying gets help from the emigrants. In this world there has never been a man without another man."

Neighbors and relatives in the same *braña* are the first to hear the news and help out. Although in theory the obligation to help a house in need falls on the closest relatives in terms of kinship, in practice it is those who live closest, whether or not they are related, who arrive first, especially when sickness occurs unexpectedly. They will be the ones who spread the word, call the doctor, and do some of the essential chores in the house. It is not unusual to see several persons working on their own initiative in a field that belongs to the house of the sick person in order to feed the cattle, or a group of neighbor women in the stable milking the cows. At such times, there are always people ready to help.

> When someone is sick, there are always people there from other houses, taking turns, making sure the family is not alone. If hay has to be cut, some will go and do it, and another will take their place, if there are a few people in the house. That's the good thing here, at times like that everyone sticks together. When it happens, one neighbor or another, there is always someone. This is true in all the villages.
> There is always a person or two, and sometimes six or seven.

While they may not be the first on the spot, the greatest burden falls on the immediate family, whether they live in the same *braña* or in an adjacent one. The news must be taken to them as soon as possible. If the illness is very serious, they will be expected to come at once. If possible and necessary, some may come and stay with the sick person until she or he dies or gets better. This happens especially when the old folks live alone. Their children deal with sick care collectively.

> Those two daughters were talking quietly to each other, next to my bed. They weren't even sitting down, uh-uh, that day I was in bad shape. They asked me if I wanted something to drink, and I told them no with my head and I didn't drink anything. My daughter from B, the one from V, and O, each

was here for a few days. I think the one from V was here the most, twenty-five days she said she was here. They all came for a few days, but since she lives farther away, she stayed for awhile.

A procession of visitors comes to the sick room. Everyone in the *braña*, or at least a delegation from every house, will come in addition to immediate neighbors, relatives, and friends. This is known as the visit [*visita*], an important obligation to the elderly Vaqueiro and the household. Thus begins a period of intense social relations for the old person who lies in bed. The visit is always made with some gift of special food, and indeed the word *visita* is used both for the visitor and for the gift. One is said to "give" or "take" the *visita* when indicating bringing the gift in person. Because of the large number of visits received, a large stock of delicacies is amassed. Now these foods are essentially supplemental to the food the invalid is served in the house, but in the old days, they probably constituted the main part of the invalid's food. The visit is more than a social gesture; it seems to involve a moral obligation toward the sick Vaqueiro.

When one is sick, or going to give birth, they bring the *visita*. Those who came to see him would say, "Do you know who I am?" And sometimes he got the name right, other times not. They came from B, C, A, B [*brañas*]. From T house the two girls came and brought him a can of peaches, Nescafé, grape juice and cookies. It is customary always to bring something.

The visit has a fairly set pattern. Once the visitor has been identified by the sick person, the conversation includes discussion of the course of the illness, desires for a quick recovery, and news of the area. The sick person normally gives an exhaustive account of his or her symptoms.

One says, "How are you? How are you feeling?" and he says, "All right" or "Bad." "Go on, you're better already; soon you'll be well." And when one leaves, one says, "Now get better," as I said to F, whom I went to see. He was in bed, and I took him a couple of cans of peaches; I didn't know what to take him. Well, he wanted them, poor guy; as soon as I got there and gave them to him, he told S to open one for him. And he told me in detail how bad off he was, and then I said to him, "Well, get better, *hombre*," and he said, "*Ay!* don't say that, because I'm never going to get better." And I said,

"Yes, *hombre*, yes, of course you'll get better, if God wills it."
He said no, that he wouldn't. And he was right.

With this kind of attention, it is even said that some invalids enjoy themselves. The visits certainly help them to maintain their interest in life. The visits also serve to monitor the treatment the invalid is getting from the household. The little society is always aware of the old person's well-being, since neighbors have the right to enter the house to visit at any time. If the invalid is not clean or well fed, they will complain about the lack of care. A lot of criticism could ruin the good name of a family. So the visits serve to keep the family from avoiding their responsibility to old Vaqueiros. This aspect of social control is implicit in the following quotes:

> For example, X said that we weren't treating grandmother well. She came one day to visit and that day my aunts from Madrid were here, as if I were going to have the sheets dirty when they were in the house, no way! Thank goodness that they were here to witness it; otherwise people would have believed it.

> Yes, the problem is that a sick person needs a lot of cleaning. Because if . . . well, if you know on a given day someone is coming to visit, then naturally you want to have her looking especially neat, even if she isn't that way every day.

In summary, aspects of the visit are worth noting. First, this occasion serves to renew the ties of blood, neighborhood, and friendship. In the face of the possible disappearance of one of its members, the family, the group, respond selflessly. People try to repair the fissures that a sickness imposes on a house, in spite of the inevitable selfishness and petty problems of everyday life. Illness, sooner or later, comes to everyone. The visit will be scrupulously returned when the visitors of today need it tomorrow.

Second, the visit contributes to the feeding of the invalid, even assures it in the poorest houses, as it supposes a collectivization of a small part of the community property. It is a final reward for the person with whom one has shared one's life and work, who has maintained and created a family, in this way contributing to the strengthening of the community.

Third, for these reasons, the group takes responsibility for the lot of the older invalid, comes to the bedside and provides company and food, which is the highest form of thanks in the *braña*. The group helps the household in the farmwork and in sick care, but it also serves as a zealous advocate of the rights of the weak, checking on sick care. The contact between the visitors and the old Vaqueiros show the visitors' attempt to retain the invalid, to keep him or her alive and participating in the little society, yet the visit also can be a farewell when all hope is lost.

When the illness becomes critical, a feverish activity begins in the *braña*. In the division of labor that occurs as death approaches, a couple of people have to go out to contact the specialists that may be needed in these critical moments: the doctor, the notary, or the priest. Those assigned to inform these professionals are usually neighbors of the sick person, often young people who can get to the villages or towns quickly. Until a few years ago, this trip was made on horseback or on foot, depending on the distance. Today those asked to go have a car or a motorbike. At the same time they telephone the city and send word, by different means, to the relatives of the sick person who live in the area.

Sometimes there is a certain competition over whom to notify first: the doctor who heals the body, the priest who heals the soul, or the notary who settles legal and earthly problems.

People waited until they were very ill, many of them. One would be in critical condition, and *ala!* Send out for the doctors, the priest, and the notary, whoever came first. The first who had to come was really the doctor, but if the notary or the priest got there first. . . .

Doctors, notaries, and priests are official representatives of the outside world in their respective fields. Of these three "men of studies," the priest is the one with the greatest impact on community life because he lives permanently in the area, and his opinions weigh heavily on local decisions. His visits to the *braña* are no more frequent than those of the doctor, but he has more contact with and a greater knowledge of the Vaqueiros through their intermittent attendance at church and their use of the sacramental services the church provides. At the hour of death, a notary will not be needed if a will has already been made, and a doctor may be unnecessary if there is no hope of improvement, but it is virtually obligatory to call a priest. The request for the last sacraments is due to the pressure of the priest on the family members of the invalid.

Well, you had to inform the priest. It has always been the custom. Because if the priest didn't confess the sick person, later he wouldn't want to bury him. I'm not sure, but I think that he wouldn't want to bury him without having made the extreme unction. He would bury him, but not willingly. Always, even at midnight or at three in the morning, the priests would come when they were called.

The priest's visit is always a kind of intrusion in the life of the *braña*. He is used to contacts and social relations with the Vaqueiros in the church and the *aldea*, but death brings him into the most intimate spheres of the Vaqueiro homes. Several of the stories the *aldeanos* tell making fun of the Vaqueiros have to do with the administration of the last sacraments and attempt to show the Vaqueiros' ignorance of religious ritual. The sources of this kind of anecdote are the *aldeanos* who at times accompany the priest, particularly the sexton. The stories told today refer to the past and make fun of Vaqueiro speech.

In the old days, once when they called the priest to confess people, afterwards they told a story about one man from X house, I believe. Well, this one didn't die, although normally they call for the priest when they're on their last legs. The sexton told a story; he was a very funny fellow. ["A Vaqueiro said:] 'I was shored up against the door of the yard and what should appear over B Hill but a man on a horse with a white sheet on and an altar boy in front with a little dingaling, going dingaling dingaling. And they pulled up in the yard, put me on a bench, took off my shoes and confessed me. Then I says to him, "O *señor* priest! That thing you want to give me now, put it here on my hat, I'll have it later, because I don't want the cats to get it." The body of Christ on his hat! "No, *hombre*, no, you have to eat it now, it's Christ's body." "Well then, give it here!" And he put it in my mouth and I chawed on it.' "

These kinds of stories, although distorted, reflect the intromission of the *aldea* into the private space of the Vaqueiros. Faced with this interference, the Vaqueiros close ranks. The priest traditionally brought out a good number of the inhabitants of the *braña* to meet and accompany him to the house of the sick person. His presence, nevertheless, provoked in all a certain mixture of respect, preoccupation, and fear, according to the Vaqueiros themselves. A woman says:

When the priest who came to confess a sick person appeared at the tip of the *braña*, for he'd always appear there, they would say, "Hey, the priest is coming to confess here, and you have to meet him; change your clothes"—if you were a little dirty—"you have to go and pray and accompany him." And we would all go trembling, of course; we weren't prepared to see the priest at all. Fearful, we would take a candle and *ala!* to the house.

DEATH

The administration of the last rites, extreme unction, and, if the patient is conscious, confession and communion, is called *sacramentar* [to sacrament] by the Vaqueiros. Everyone in the *braña*, or at least a good delegation from each house participates in this ceremony. The ritual has several phases.

If there was time, the priest was called in order to sacrament, if someone was suddenly dying. Still now, if someone is gravely ill, they say, "We have to go for the priest." The custom was for someone to go from every house, and two persons were better than one. The people of the village came with a candle to meet the priest, to assist him, and this was called going to *sacramentar*. The priest would come with a cross, dressed in white, with the sexton, who rang a little bell. Then we would all kneel when they passed us, and we would cross ourselves. And we would enter with the priest to where the sick person was, everyone with a lighted candle. And when the sick person confessed, the people would stand back, outside, until he confessed, and then they would go back in; and when the priest gave communion, everyone kneeled. If the person didn't talk anymore, extreme unction was put on their feet. He who was no longer speaking was not confessed; because, of course, some were breathing their last when the priest was called. And when you went in, you would be wondering how the sick person was, but until the priest came out [from the confession], you couldn't go in. The priest would come out, and we'd all go in to see if he or she was talking or not. And then the priest would leave, and everyone would go home. Everyone brought his own candle. It was the candle that was used to make crosses on the haunches of the cows, when they left for the high pastures; it was holy.

Although this commentary refers to the past, the ceremony is observed today, albeit with less ritual content. The priest is now dressed in lay clothes, comes to the *braña* by car or motorcycle, and confesses the sick before they are in critical condition. This visit, more social than ritual in appearance, can still cause a certain alarm in the elderly ill because of the connotations of such visits in the past.

When the agony begins, it is said that "the bride of death is courting" the dying person. The comportment of the old Vaqueiros in their last moments depends on the illness and especially the person's degree of awareness of their approaching end. This is the *deje* or destiny of the individual.

Some die completely drained of energy; others die completely alert, giving you a running commentary; others will tell you, "I say good-bye to you forever." In short, each of us has a particular way or style [*deje*] at the hour of death. As soon as the bride of death begins to court us, we have our own way of saying farewell—looking off in one direction or at the people. Each of us has a destiny—how we conduct ourselves at the hour of death.

Although a happy death is characterized by the absence of awareness, most old persons die knowing they are dying, for Vaqueiros take virtually no tranquilizers, except in cases of painful illness. The acceptance of one's end appears to be traditional among the Vaqueiros, as the following anecdote told by an *aldeano* implies.

Also in B [*braña*] in X house there was a fellow who got very sick and they called the priest to confess him—this was maybe a hundred years ago. After the priest confessed him and left to go back, the sick man went out in the yard and called him, "Ah, *señor cura!* these robbers from T [city and administrative center], will they make out a death certificate?" It's true, eh? He died soon after, and they went down to tell the priest. They came here to say that he had died so the priest would spread the word and ring the bells and everything. But he was still able to go out and ask if they would make out the death certificate. Among the country people, those of T are thought to be robbers.

When all hope is lost, many of the moribund, if not surprised by sudden death, make their last wishes. One of the most frequent is the choice of clothing that one will wear when laid out. The most self-conscious women pay attention to the smallest details of their final outfits.

We said to my grandmother, "Look what a nice dress you have." And she said, "That will be my shroud." I said to her, "Go on, now you're thinking about a shroud already, you'll still go dancing in it." What else are you going to say? Yes, you're right? You have to make believe. But she said, "The day I die, dress me in my knitted sweater, my knitted skirt, and my knitted jacket," because she was always cold, and always liked knitted things best. She had the clothes all ready, for she had made them for her granddaughter's wedding. And

if you had to go and buy it, at what hour of the day? She had
the clothes all ready in her bureau. She had them buy her
some panties and some stockings. She told grandfather one
day to bring her some pantyhose for when she died. Before
she got sick she wore stockings with elastics, but for her
death she wanted some pantyhose because the others would
hurt her.

Many use these last moments to make or change a will, settle
other legal problems, repay old debts, tell family members about
unfulfilled promises to saints, and finally to distribute their savings and thank people for their care.

I think the woman knew she was going to die, or something like that, because she, poor thing, even helped us with
[to pay for] the road. She didn't give much, but she gave something. She hunted up some money here and there, and during
those days she got together all she could and gave it to us.
Yes, she said she didn't want to owe anybody anything when
she died.

Quite often Vaqueiros tell those around them that their death
is imminent and anticipate the events that will happen after
they're gone by asking for their laying-out clothes, or refering to the
disposition of their body. This is the context of one of those deaths.

My grandmother died of . . . she just came to an end; she
was ninety plus years old, the mother of my father. She died
very well, poor thing. We were roasting chestnuts, checking
on her all the time because she had already had a bad spell in
the afternoon. The doctor had been here, and had given her
an injection, or pills, and said she was dying. Once when I
went to see her she said, "What are you doing?" I told her,
"We're roasting chestnuts, grandmother, do you want some?"
"Yes, bring me some." And I took some with a cup of milk
and brought them to her. And she looked at them a little, and
said, softly, "I don't want them, I don't want them . . ." And I
said to her, "Take one," and I gave her one, and she took it
like this, and put it up to her mouth, and dropped it in the
bed. And she said when she had the chestnut in her hand,
"Leave it, leave it." You could see she was saying this with
her head. Then she up and said to me, since there was an old
chest next to her bed, she said, "That way," as if to put her in
the chest. She had told me this many times, so I knew she
meant that I had to put her there. She died with all of her
wits. At that moment a fear got into me. And she pushed

Natural Death   153 back the sheets and blankets on her bed; I thought it must mean that it was the time of her death, or it was coming soon. She was all hot, suffocating. And then she lay back in a certain way, and I went running out. "Grandmother is very badly off. I think she's going to die." We were all around the fire, and everyone got up and went in to where she was. She didn't last much longer, about half an hour, and she died little by little, little by little, and did not move at all except to push back the sheets, and so, looking at us, she passed away.

Death is considered an extreme occasion that demands everyone's immediate help and solidarity. While in the case of illness there is a certain hierarchy of preference for who should be told and who should pay visits, at death there is no choice or doubt. "In a case like that [death] or an accident, or when a cow gives birth or has an accident, even your worst enemy comes to help. In these cases you call the first person you meet."

A natural death generally occurs with the house full of people. When the end is imminent, the members of the house stay up watching day and night. When necessary, other relatives in the *braña* and neighbors take turns so those of the household may rest. Even if the death takes place unexpectedly or very late at night, it is very rare for the household to deal with it alone. The nearest neighbors often are notified first; they pass the word on to the rest of the community. In a few minutes groups of people gather around the dying person, people who have "dressed on the way." Collective decisions are made about the laying-out clothes, whom to notify, and the paperwork. As soon as it is certain that death will take place various persons are delegated to perform these tasks. Amidst this coming and going around the dying person appear the feelings that death provokes in everyone—fear and sorrow primarily, surprise if the death is sudden, and *descobertura*, a feeling of empty space that the person leaves when dead, especially if the person is not very old. People cry, share their tears.

There sent me there, to the room, to see how she was. . . .
I went to her, and how shall I say it, she was passing away. . . .
I called my mother and my aunt, and grandfather was crying.
They told him to go to bed, because what else would he feel
like doing? Everyone came running, and grandfather crying,
he cried a lot, and they told him he should go to bed, because
he'd just feel worse about it. She died like a bird. That night
the whole family was there, those of X house, and those of Y,
those of Madrid, everyone. She died at night, and that's why

only the family was there at the time, everyone else was in bed.

The symptoms of death, according to local opinion, are manifested above all in the respiratory tract. Moribund persons suffer sensations of stifling, faintness, and "pressure"; their last breaths are "mouthfuls," the choking of the agony. The absence of breath, pulse, and motion define death, and certain changes in physical appearance, like pallidness and deformation of the face, also occur.

Death is something that . . . I have seen many people die. You get a choking in the throat, you begin to get weak, like something that rises in you, and you gag at the mouth, and then they're dead. They saw that he was dying and they sent word. He was already without a pulse. I looked at him . . . he breathed once in a while, but then, nothing. He stopped breathing soon . . . something rises in them as if they are drowning.

The fundamental cause of death is the loss of blood. There is not much consensus about where this substance that produces life goes. For some it becomes solid, for others it goes to the head, or degenerates and disappears inside the body. The decay of the body is manifest in the diminishing force of the blood. The equilibrium of the individual, the energy, terminates with this red liquid.

He was already suffocating, the hour of death, for the blood throws one off, I think. Something has to happen for one to end with nothing, white; they say you run out of blood. The blood keeps going away, or the thing that chokes you, you feel pressing on you, or it must be something. They get white, and this is because they are left without blood. It ended, it was consumed, I don't know where it goes. The last blood goes up to your head, because it doesn't go out below.

The blood ends when a person dies; it becomes stationary. Blood doesn't go out of your body unless, for instance, you have a wound. The blood becomes paralyzed, and then it must become the same as flesh.

3

Violent Death: Suicide

STATISTICS: THE PROBLEM FROM OUTSIDE

In 1965, Rodolfo Soto Vázquez published an article entitled "El suicidio entre los Vaqueiros de Alzada Asturianos" in an Asturian
scholarly journal (Soto Vázquez 1965). The author was at that time
a magistrate in the *concejo* of Luarca. He had noticed the high rate
of suicide among the Vaqueiros in the course of his work. I will
refer to Soto Vázquez's article extensively, since as far as I know it
is the only work on the subject, it is not well known outside of
Asturias, and it is a good introduction to my ethnographic material.

Aside from his use of terminology derived from the manuals of
legal medicine (he classes suicides as leptosomatic, *picnicos*, ath-
letic, etc.) or criminal psychology (psychic and somatic failure,
schizophrenia, psychosis, neurosis) that is either outdated or difficult to diagnose retrospectively, Soto Vázquez is generally cautious
in his conclusions and rigorous in his method of analysis. In the
first part of his article, he presents three findings as a justification
for his research: (1) the number of suicides among the Vaqueiros is
proportionally much higher then that of their neighbors; (2) the
percentage of Vaqueiro women who commit suicide is much higher
than the local or national statistics for their sex; (3) The number of
suicides for absolutely unknown reasons is also higher among the
Vaqueiros (Ibid., 168).

Soto Vázquez's work is divided into five parts. After providing
some brief information on the method and sources used, and on the
Vaqueiro way of life, history, and habitat, he then focuses on sui-

cide. He based his work on the judicial archives of the three districts where most of the Vaqueiros live—Luarca, Tineo, and Belmonte—during a period of about twenty-five years from 1940 to mid-1964. Over this period in this zone there were 273 cases (93 in Luarca, 80 in Tineo, and 100 in Belmonte). Soto Vázquez personally examined 165 of the dossiers and obtained information from the others. Fourteen of the cases were attempted suicides that failed. Of the total number, 111 were Vaqueiro (including six of the failed attempts). Soto Vázquez identified Vaqueiros by the combination of typical Vaqueiro family names and residence in the *brañas*. He excluded cases in which the cause of death was in doubt, or in which it was unclear whether or not the suicide was a Vaqueiro.

Out of the population of the three townships, a total of 110,000, Soto Vázquez counted 7,000 Vaqueiros (4,000 in Luarca, 1,500 in Tineo, and 1,500 in Belmonte). He then roughly doubled this figure because of the difficulty in obtaining the exact number of Vaqueiros registered outside of the *brañas* and living in other settlements of the zone. In my opinion this doubling is excessive.[1] It supposes a total of fifteen thousand Vaqueiros, which would be one-seventh of the total population. Even so, the Vaqueiros provided two-fifths of the total number of suicides.

In this period [25 years], then, 7 per thousand of the group under study [Vaqueiros] living in these districts have committed suicide. This figure represents not only a coefficient greater than that for the rest of the inhabitants of the districts (approximately 1.5 per thousand), but also is equivalent to an annual rate of 28 per 100,000, much higher than the Spanish national average (barely 7 per 100,000), and amply exceeding the national coefficient of any European or Western Hemisphere nation (Soto Vázquez 1965, 85).

These coefficients for the Vaqueiros would be doubled if the original figure of 7,000 Vaqueiros were maintained, but even when Soto Vázquez overestimates the Vaqueiro population, he shows the importance of suicide among the Vaqueiros.

Vaqueiros put an end to their lives mainly by hanging, and to a lesser extent by drowning themselves and jumping from heights. Table 1 represents the causes of death for Vaqueiros in the three districts.

According to the author, the cases of the use of knives and poison are exceptional in the sense that in four of the six cases the suicides were physically incapable of using other procedures. Information was not available on the remaining two cases. Thus it appears that except in cases of physical disability, the alternatives open to the suicidal Vaqueiro are hanging, drowning, and falling from a height. The figures for non-Vaqueiros in the zone show a wider variety of procedures and a greater number of unknown means.

According to Soto Vázquez, what the two tables show is that the Vaqueiros seek to assure themselves of a death that is rapid and certain. This is the case, he points out, with hanging, jumping from a substantial height, and drowning by jumping into water when one cannot swim or with attached weights. In contrast, he notes, the use of poison or self-inflicted knife wounds is slow and uncertain; a gunshot may attract relatives or neighbors who may frustrate the attempt. In any case, these alternative methods involve a higher possibility of intense or long-term suffering. But the author does point out that on occasion Vaqueiros, too, have recourse to different

TABLE 1. MODE OF SUICIDE OF VAQUEIROS

MODE	MEN	WOMEN	TOTAL
Hanging	54	33	87
Drowning	3	4	7
Knife, razor	3	1	4
Fall from height	0	3	3
Poisoning	0	2	2
Unknown	3	3	6
	63	46	109

Source: Soto Vásquez 1965, 178.

TABLE 2. MODE OF SUICIDE OF NON-VAQUEIROS

MODE	MEN	WOMEN	TOTAL
Hanging	52	23	75
Drowning	9	8	17
Fall from height	4	7	11
Gunshot	6	1	7
Knife, razor	5	2	7
Poisoning	2	1	3
Electrocution	2	0	2
Unknown	?	?	(40)
			162

Source: Soto Vásquez 1965, 181 (adapted).

DEATH

procedures. He cites three cases in which two methods were used: knife wounds and hanging, for example, although all three cases involved some kind of mental illness, a factor not present in the five non-Vaqueiro cases of this type. As for the specific procedures, there do not tend to be differences between the Vaqueiros and their neighbors. Generally the suicides hang themselves by climbing into the branch of a tree, tying the rope to the branch, putting the noose around their necks, and jumping. The noose may be a rope used in farming to tie up bundles of grass or hay, or a leather belt. Vaqueiros also committed suicide by hanging in haylofts, stables, buildings under construction, the home, and even in the barns of the upper pasture by making a hole in the upper floor.

In regard to the persistence of suicide, Soto Vázquez cites four cases of Vaqueiros (men aged 71 and 62, women aged 69 and 28) who had tried to commit suicide once previously before succeeding. Except for the oldest man, who attempted it six or seven years previously, the others consummated their efforts from a week to a month after the first known attempt. The four non-Vaqueiros who had tried to commit suicide did so not once but many times. Furthermore, Soto Vázquez found only two Vaqueiros who verbally and repeatedly warned of their suicides—a man who was a habitual drunk and a woman, mentally ill. The three non-Vaqueiro women who gave warning were apparently normal. Soto Vázquez finds no pseudoattempts at suicide.

The Vaqueiros not only commit suicide in a quick, sure, and effective manner; they (and only they) also do it in a manner that is at times exhibitionistic. Soto Vázquez found that seven out of 171 cases were of this type. One was a fifty-four-year-old man who hanged himself from the balcony of the parish church after having assisted the priest in the mass. Two men, aged sixty and seventy-four, hanged themselves in a public road at mid-day. A twenty-seven-year-old woman, five months pregnant, who believed that she had been abandoned by her fiancé, hanged herself in his hayloft with his photograph in her pocket. An elderly woman who lived alone hanged herself wearing her best clothes, having placed on either side of herself stools with lighted lamps, as at a wake. At 7 P.M., a forty-three-year-old man buys a rope, a bottle of brandy, a piece of stationery, and an envelope in the nearest village. The owner of the store asks him jokingly, "When are going to hang yourself?" He answers, "Within four hours," and hangs himself at nightfall. Finally a sixty-one-year-old man tried to commit suicide with a razor blade, and then went to the village cemetery where he finished the attempt.

There do not seem to be differences between Vaqueiros and

non-Vaqueiros as to the month of the year, the day of the week, or the hour of day of suicide. Although Vaqueiros leave suicide notes less frequently than non-Vaqueiros, the notes tend to be similar for both groups, consisting of detailed lists of debts owed to them and to others. Sometimes the notes give reasons for the suicide. But even more revealing are the direct testimonies of those who fail in their attempts, or who survive long enough to give their reasons. Of the fourteen cases of this type examined by Soto Vázquez, six were Vaqueiros. Of the Vaqueiros, three were men who tried to hang themselves or to cut their veins; three were women, two of whom fell from a height and one who attempted death by poison. Two of the men mentioned family problems and physical incapacity for work due to sickness as reasons. Two of the women gave as their reasons, respectively, as mental illness and fear of legal prosecution. The remaining two cases presented an interesting reason. Soto Vázquez writes that there were

> unexplainable references to *aburrimiento* [boredom, loss of interest] in the other two cases, both of persons aged 62, in which there was not even an attempt to present a coherent explanation, limiting themselves to declare they had committed the suicide *"because they took the notion to do it"* ["porque les había dado por hacerlo"]. (Ibid., 177; my emphasis)

To correlate the cause of the suicide with age, Soto Vázquez drew up a table of the 158 cases for which he had complete information, excluding two subjects under sixteen years of age (see Table 3). When there were two or more reasons given, he placed the person in the category of the reason that seemed the strongest. First Soto Vázquez remarks on the high percentage of "unknown" motives among the Vaqueiros. This factor, which does not exceed one case in ten in the national Spanish statistics, is normal for the non-Vaqueiros (4 out of 48 for men and 1 out of 28 for women) but much higher for the Vaqueiros (9 out of 48 men and 8 out of 34 women), where it represents about 20 percent of the total suicides.

Soto Vázquez recognizes the figures for mental illness as normal for both groups. According to the dossiers, which are usually not very specific, he found among the Vaqueiro male suicides three schizophrenics, two manic-depressives, two mentally retarded, three severely neurotic, and an epileptic; among the women were two manic-depressives, two severely neurotic, and one mentally retarded. After a similar count among the non-Vaqueiros, Soto Vázquez concludes that psychosis among the Vaqueiros and neurosis among the non-Vaqueiros distinguish the two groups. His sample,

TABLE 3. CLASSIFICATION OF SUICIDES BY MOTIVE AND AGE

MALE VAQUEIROS

MOTIVE FOR SUICIDE	AGES OF INDIVIDUALS	TOTAL
Mental illness	18, 24, 25, 26, 28, 35, 44, 48, 48, 55, 62, DK	12
Serious physical illness	46, 59?, 60, 61, 62, 65, 65?, 70, 70?, 71, 74?, 75, 80	13
Serious economic conflicts	25?, 44?, 48?, 65, 84?	5
Serious family or marital problems	43, 61F	2
Misadventures in love or jealousy	20?, 30	2
Poverty	41, 51	2
Fear of legal prosecution	85	1
Severe melancholy	42	1
Great nervous stress	27	1
Unknown	24, 40, 42, 42, 45, 54, 62, 65, 77	9
		48

FEMALE VAQUEIROS

MOTIVE FOR SUICIDE	AGES OF INDIVIDUALS	TOTAL
Mental illness	22?, 28, 29, 30, 50, 54, 58, 69, DK	9
Serious family or marital problems	17?, 20, 23, 29, 40, 60	6
Serious physical illness	50, 54?, 58	3
Misadventures in love or jealousy	25, 27, 28	3
Serious economic conflicts	62, 63	2
Severe melancholy	45?, 62?	2
Fear of legal prosecution	41F	1
Unknown	17, 22, 22, 23, 24, 24, 59, 62	8
		34

Table 3 (*continued*)

MALE NON-VAQUEIROS

MOTIVE FOR SUICIDE	AGES OF INDIVIDUALS	TOTAL
Mental illness	30, 30, 31, 35, 35, 36, 40, 42, 43, 44, 49, 50, 51, 61?, 63, DK, DK	18
Physical illness	14, 25, 28, 42?, 44, 77, 78, 80	8
Family problems	17, 21, 21?, 27, 31, 62, 66	7
Love or jealousy	34, 39, 39	3
Economic conflicts	58, 61, 64	2
Fear of legal prosecution	56, 57	2
Severe melancholy	16, DK	2
Poverty	49	1
Unknown	24, 28, 41, 75	4
		48

FEMALE NON-VAQUEIROS

MOTIVE FOR SUICIDE	AGES OF INDIVIDUALS	TOTAL
Mental illness	18, 31, 36, 38, 44, 46, 48, 50, 52, 52, 60, 63, 65, 87, 88	15
Physical illness	53, 62, 63, 77?, 78	5
Family or marital problems	39, 52, 59	3
Love or jealousy	22, 28	2
Poverty	35, DK	2
Economic conflicts	40	1
Unknown	19	1
		28

Source: Soto Vásquez 1965, 76 and 78 (adapted).
Note: When the age of a person is not certain, the letters DK are used. The age followed by F means a failed suicide; a question mark indicates that the reasons for including the individual in the category were weak.

however, is not large enough to confirm this conclusion, even if these vague labels held some sort of meaning under the circumstances.[2] He goes on to point out the higher percentage of physical disability among older Vaqueiro men as a motive for suicide. "Among male Vaqueiros over age 60 any physical ailment, even though it may not be serious, last long, or be particularly painful, may serve as a reason to initiate the idea of suicide" (Soto Vázquez 1965, 79).

Soto Vázquez then presents a table of Vaqueiro suicides by year, including unsuccessful attempts (Ibid., 81–82). From this table he draws the conclusion that suicides among the Vaqueiros are a cyclical phenomenon, occurring in greater number in three-year intervals until 1954, the most suicides occurring in the years 1941 (7), 1944 (7), 1948 (8), 1950 (10), 1954 (12), and declining thereafter. The fewest suicides occurred in 1942 (2), 1946 (1), 1953 (1), and 1959 (1).

Finally Soto Vázquez compares Vaqueiros' and non-Vaqueiros' age at suicide for the 160 suicides for which he could obtain the information (see Table 4).[3] Here he points out the large number of young Vaqueiro women (aged 21 to 30) who commit suicide. Out of fifteen, six did so because of love or marital problems, four because of mental illness, and five for unknown reasons.

Furthermore, citing the statistics for total suicides, not just those for which the age of the person was known, it appears that the suicide rate for Vaqueiro women in general is especially high. "The proportion of (Vaqueiro) women who commit suicide is that of four out of every five men (49 cases compared to 62), while that of the other residents of the area (non-Vaqueiros) is barely six out of every ten (59 cases compared to 103). The rate (for Vaqueiro women) is above the national rate, and even above that of England and Wales, which, according to the United Nations Demographic Yearbook of 1955, had the highest [female suicide rate]" (Soto Vázquez 1965, 85).

Soto Vázquez summarizes his conclusions and attempts to offer an explanation of the suicides, referring to two contrasting hypotheses he proposed at the beginning of his research: the "characterological biotype" and the environment in which the group exists. He is convinced there is no somatic or psychological degeneration factor that would explain the abnormal frequency of suicide or the apparent lack of motivation for it. Thus he reaches the conclusion that his hypotheses are not alternatives but rather complementary.

The root of the matter, as we see it, lies in the sociological influences of isolation and the real (although now decreasing)

TABLE 4. SUICIDES OF VAQUEIROS AND NON-VAQUEIROS BY AGE AND SEX

VAQUEIROS

AGE	MEN	WOMEN	TOTAL
16–20	2	3	5
21–30	9	15	24
31–40	2	1	3
41–50	12	3	15
51–60	6	7	13
61–70	10	6	16
71–80	6	0	6
81–	2		
	49	35	84

NON-VAQUEIROS

AGE	MEN	WOMEN	TOTAL
16–20	3	2	5
21–30	8	3	11
31–40	9	6	15
41–50	10	4	14
51–60	6	6	12
61–70	6	4	10
71–80	5	2	7
81–	0	2	2
	47	29	76

Source: Soto Vásquez 1965, 83.

inferiority complex, which like all complexes of this type, at times takes the form of a false superiority and spectacular exhibitionism; these influences are combined with certain constitutional throwbacks or reversions [atavismos], which are not pathological but merely traditional (Ibid. 87).

As for the suicides categorized with "unknown" motives, he affirms, "Public rumor always offers an explanation for a suicide, even though it may be erroneous. We therefore reject the idea that those Vaqueiro suicides classed as being of 'unknown cause' occur for reasons that are mysterious, solemn, and at the same time unfathomable."

Finally, he invites further study.

DEATH

The field of suicide is inexhaustable in regard to classifications. Probably the desire to penetrate behind the mask of the suicide is the only reason that a matter so intrinsically arid is examined from all imaginable perspectives. For the criminologist it has interest only as an exclusion . . . in this sense, whatever more is known about suicides, methods, motivations, or customs will make it that much easier to reach a positive or negative conclusion in given cases; but once a conclusion is reached, the interest of the criminologist fades, and with great pleasure he gives way to the sociologist or the statistician. This is not surprising, because in spite of all the research, there is as yet an inadequate understanding of suicidal persons (Ibid. 75).

In the pages that follow, accepting the amiable invitation of Soto Vázquez, I will attempt to offer an anthropologist's point of view on the cultural dimension of suicide.

CULTURAL IDEOLOGY: THE PROBLEM FROM INSIDE

I will present an ensemble of ideas, opinions, and local values about suicide as well as descriptions of a number of cases of suicide recounted by my Vaqueiro informants. While Soto Vázquez approached the topic from the outside, I will try to offer a view from the inside, from the point of view of the actors. It is obvious that, strictly speaking, the main protagonists are the suicides themselves, who logically remain inaccessible and inscrutable. Nevertheless, if culture is, as we understand it to be, a collection of shared and transmitted understandings, these understandings, as they refer to death in general and suicide in particular, belong to the entire group of which the suicides form a part. Perhaps by analyzing the conditions in which this phenomenon occurs, or at least the reasons why it is deemed acceptable in the popular perception, we can understand in some way why some persons choose this kind of death. It is also the way to avoid as much as possible the imposition of categories, ethnocentric values, and moral considerations that frequently impede an understanding of the matter.

The relevance of this perspective or *emic* view of the matter became evident to me on the occasion of a suicide that I was able to study in considerable detail, since it occurred shortly before my stay in the field. I followed the entire process, including the visit of the magistrate and "the law" [*la justicia*], the wake, and the burial from the house of the deceased, where I remained for more than twenty-four hours. During this time I listened to Vaqueiros' private and public comments, most particularly to their declarations to the magistrate. The discrepancies between the ideas and considerations of the local people and their official testimony seemed very significant indeed. I was struck not so much by the fact that the Vaqueiros lied to these representatives of the law (they did not, at least not consciously), but rather by the fact that they used different language, values, and categories to communicate among themselves than with the persons from the outside. The comments neighbors made in the following days, and even after a couple of years had passed, ratified my initial sensation that this was a cultural problem. Among other things, people mentioned, compared, and gave many details of other suicides in the area, which, given its small population, seemed quite significant.

Given the kind of material I use, it is evident that the cases I present below do not have a statistical value, since they are based on the memory of the people and memory is selective. Spectacular suicides appear frequently in local descriptions while less striking cases are forgotten or mentioned only briefly and rarely. Among the latter cases are those of women or bachelors, which I will discuss later, and those that occurred longest ago or farthest away. These cases have come up spontaneously in conversations in the *braña*, often as illustrations of local theories on the matter, and the list does not pretend to be exhaustive. All of the persons interviewed easily came up with a half-dozen instances of suicide, which they expanded to a dozen with a little insistence on my part. By this means I found out about thirty-nine suicides, thirty men and nine women, out of which three were failed attempts. Five of these took place outside the area (four in Madrid and one in Buenos Aires); two took place in a nearby town where the suicides lived; and the rest in the sixteen *brañas* of the area under study, the nearby vicinity, or in the mountain pastures. In eleven of the *brañas* cited there was more than one case; one *braña* had five cases.[4]

In regard to the methods the Vaqueiros used to end their lives, I found slightly different alternatives than those cited by Soto Vázquez (hanging, drowning, falling from a height), but his conclusions as to the desire of the Vaqueiro suicide to have a quick and certain end are amply corroborated by the people of the *braña*. They told me about twenty-seven deaths caused by hanging, two by drowning, and two by poisoning. The cases of drowning (one in a river, one in the ocean) are likely to be fatal because there are no good swimmers in the *braña* ("Here nobody knows how to swim; if we fall in the river hole we drown there"). The two cases of poisoning, although atypical, were cited very often for this very reason. But it is hanging that has become a synonym for suicide. Indeed the immediate cause—the rope or cord, and frequently its affectionate disminuitive, *el cordelín*—is used to refer to this kind of death ("take to the cord," "catch the *cordelín*," equivalent to the English "stringing oneself up"). The few remaining cases, except for two in which I did not learn the method, were by gunshot (three cases), knife or razor (one successful, one failed), and falling (two cases). All of these cases, except one of the shootings, were committed by Vaqueiros in towns or cities. In other words, within the region, Vaqueiros normally commit suicide by hanging themselves; away from home, they use other methods. At least by reputation, the most typical form of Vaqueiro suicide in cities involves jumping out of a window (both cases cited were from the sixth floor); this is quite difficult in the *braña* for obvious reasons.

While I reached similar conclusions about the methods of Vaqueiro suicide, my findings about motivation differ markedly from those of Soto Vázquez. Methods are objective, confirmable facts, but motives are subjective estimations. This subjectivity is more cultural than individual, for the personal opinions of Vaqueiros about a given case tend to be quite similar, although there are exceptions. There appear to be certain biases, both theoretical and methodological, in the dossiers of the magistrates, given the nature of the magistrate's role and image.[5] He tends to choose, among the various motives, the one or ones he cognitively understands to be appropriate as reasons for suicide and to reject others, for example, *aburrimiento*. Like anyone else, the magistrate has preconceived ideas on the matter. In the testimony, which is generally brief, he unconsciously provides cues for the witnesses, who invariably will follow them. Furthermore, as a magistrate, he tends to reify the categories of the legal manuals and tries, often forcibly, to fit the suicides and their motives into them. The emphasis on quantifying this kind of death leads to facile simplifications, for in certain cases there is a combination of motives, any one of which alone would not have led to suicide. Finally, the frequency of certain motives in the dossiers suggests that the magistrates make negative moral judgments on the act of suicide. This explains, in part, the frequent designation of "mental illness" as a cause.

The people of the *braña* have their own conditioning. For them the magistrate represents *la justicia*, with which the best form of relation is no relation at all. The Vaqueiros' ignorance of the law (aside from the laws they need to know in order resolve disputes derived from the administration of the house, such as those over land, pastures, or inheritance) leaves them relatively defenseless when dealing with the magistrate. Vaqueiros fear coming up against "the law" because they think that sooner or later they will have to pay substantial sums ("the law will bring the house down"), there will be extensive legal complications, and, most important, they will be punished for something. A magistrate's visit to a Vaqueiro house always brings out fear, suspicion, and anxiety. The Vaqueiros' behavior is a combination of caution and desire to ingratiate themselves with the outsiders by acting very respectful and polite. The formal testimony takes place in this context.

For all of these reasons, Vaqueiros will say that they do not know why their relatives or neighbors committed suicide (this would explain some of the supposed "unknown" motives), or will use labels or categories that do not compromise them. "Insanity" might be one of these. By the same token, they systematically suppress motives like family disputes, which might morally (or legally) implicate Vaqueiro survivors. Furthermore, they will magnify or reduce motives at will, converting what was a "serious marital dispute" into a "minor argument," or, inversely, a quiet or taciturn personality into "suffering from nerves" (their equivalent of "mental illness"). In casual conversations and among friends (especially outside the family circle of the suicide) there is no need for these defenses, and the comments are quite different. This can be seen clearly in the quotations below.

The people of the *braña* are aware of the high frequency of suicide in their group and try to explain the reasons. The easiest suicides to explain are those that occur as a result of exceptional circumstances, such as the Spanish Civil War, or after committing crimes punishable by the state. One of the few Vaqueiros who took a side in the war, the losing side, ended his life when the war ended so as to avoid reprisals because of his public stance.[6] Another committed suicide, as they tell it now, because of his supposed membership in a secret society, considered in Spain to be leftist, which obligated him to commit a homicide. A third man tried to kill one of his neighbors and then committed suicide to avoid his trial and probable imprisonment. These three cases, then, have in common the suicide's fear of legal prosecution. (I number the cases to facilitate subsequent references.)

CASE 1. Here during the war they came and beat a man up, and he had to present himself at X [district, post of the local civil guard], and rather than present himself, after they had beaten him up, he killed himself, and he left a letter saying why he did it. He was very "red," because once he got drunk and said to the priest (who was called Don José), "Screw you, Pepe, aren't you swell!" ["*Para joderte, Pepe, cómo te cuidas*"].

CASE 2. It seems that fellow was one of the Masons—those that are paid and told, "You have to go and kill Franco or another general." And you have to go and find a way to kill him. And it seems he had to go somewhere and kill someone, and rather than do it he killed himself. He got . . . that guy got very rich in just a few years, and they didn't know where he got the money. Because those people are well paid.

The following quote, which refers to the same suicide, supplies a new reason for the alleged wealth. Given that in the *braña* nobody gets rich from the everyday work of cattle-raising, those who stand out among their neighbors are thought to have achieved their wealth by devious, external means. In spite of the doubts that appear in the last lines of this quote, suicide here becomes an example of the price to be paid for selfishness and immoderate ambition.

CASE 2. There was one here in X who had a lot of money and hanged himself. He got involved in some things that got him a lot of money, but when the time came for him to kill someone—you had to do it when your turn came—he hanged himself. That fellow had a lot of money but he wanted even more. That fellow, at harvest time, when potatoes were worth more, would go and sell them at L [town]. He would ride back on his mule, stop at the edge of the village, eat something (he didn't eat anything in L so he wouldn't spend money), and go back to his field to pull up more potatoes, all by hand. He'd get his mule, load it with another two hundred kilos of potatoes, and go to L again on foot, then home to bed.

The third case occurred after a murder had been attempted. I will refer to other aspects of this case below. Here I particularly wish to point out the local justification for this suicide.

CASE 3. In X one of my relatives hanged himself. There was a reason for it. He was on very bad terms with Z's father and gave him a terrible wound with a knife. And they referred his case to Oviedo, and they were going to bring him to trial. And he was old, and got scared that he might get a life sentence, that he'd have to go to jail for years. In the meantime, he came back to the village. He had said he was going to feed the cows, as always—he had his cows in a stable apart from the house—and he hanged himself in the stable. [He must have said,] "Well, I followed my fate, for I was in for it anyway."

Physical illness or infirmity is one of the few reasons that in itself explains a suicide, for these are the circumstances that would lead to a bad death. Cancer is the prototype of this kind of illness. The illness itself, or fear of it, puts the individual in a frame of mind that is favorable to suicide. In such cases, suicide becomes "logical," even among persons who are sensible and normal. The disease itself weakens one's resistance. But just having the illness is not considered a sufficient justification for suicide, not even cancer, if drugs can ward off the pain.

So if I saw I was impeded, bothered by some kind of illness, even if I didn't know what it was—you imagine the worst—I might assume it was this or that . . . and when people have cancer, the very mechanism of cancer pushes us on. And so with fear, depression, and dwelling on it, many people take that path.

Look María, before many people hanged themselves because those who had cancer had to suffer pain like fire; there wasn't any alternative. Now they give you morphine and you have no more pain. Before there wasn't morphine or anything. You would hear people screaming in their houses and moaning, and there wasn't any recourse. . . . Maybe it existed, but the doctors didn't know about it; now they give you injections or something to spare you from the screams.

The terminally ill also suffer because of the work and trouble they are causing their relatives. All involved think of suicide as a possible solution.

What she suffered . . . seems like it makes you want to take something that will finish you at once. No, a mother or a daughter won't do it for you. But when you feel that way. . . . She had some drops; if she took the whole bottle, good-bye! What happens is that one looks towards life and doesn't want to die that way . . . and they're not going to help you do it either! Not a son to a mother, or you to your son.

There was a woman in X house; she had asthma. She was Z's mother-in-law. Poor woman, she asked her family members to help her to the window so she could get some air, and they carried her in the sheet; and what she wanted to see was if she could get a hold of the window so she could jump out . . . but she couldn't. . . . That woman went through a lot.

The cases of suicide due to illness are those most easily understood by the people of the *braña*, especially when there is no hope of cure and/or the sick person is very old. But, in fact, the actual number of suicides for this reason is quite low. As one person told me, "Yes, there are those who do it so as not to suffer, but very few, it seems to me." The Vaqueiros often mention illness as a probable reason for suicide, especially when speaking with outsiders. But it was the reason for suicide in only four of the cases I studied, and two of those were unsuccessful. In the two successful attempts the motive seems to have been combined with a desire to avoid the expense of continued medical care.

CASE 4. But the other man from X, he was sick, and he told them not to buy the medicine, because it was expensive and they were poor. He was between forty-five and fifty years old—he was sick, and needed a lot of medicine, and there wasn't enough money.

CASE 5. Well, I had a brother who also, unfortunately, had cancer—my younger brother, the youngest of the family; he was in Argentina. It's too bad I have to say it, but that man knew what he had, and rather than see himself suffer, and his wife and a child suffer and be left with nothing . . . well, one day he threw himself from the sixth floor. That's enough about that. That is *aburrimiento*. That happened about four years ago.

In the other two cases, both failed suicides, the protagonists both said they thought they had cancer, apparently mistakenly. It is easy for a person to have such suspicions, since family members rarely inform a sick person if he or she has cancer out of fear as to how the person will react. In these particular cases, there may also be a possibility of mental instability on the part of the attempted suicides.

CASE 6. Here in X it was; now he's seventy-eight. It seems he had something wrong with his liver. And they told him the truth, but I heard he said one day, "Well, it's all the same if you tell me one thing or another. I know well what's wrong with me. I know better than you do." And he suspected he had a cancer; that's what he declared afterwards. And one day he ate, went to bed, and I'm not sure whether it was with a needle for vaccinating animals or with a knife point, he opened the vein of his arm a little, and it began to spurt out. And a servant girl saw the blood beneath the door and began to scream, and at that point he was already saying good-bye, eh? The doctor said, "Here we have a tiny bit of life left, bring all the family." And he began to draw blood and give it to him from all of his brothers. They saved him.

CASE 7. X from X, he's still alive, the old man. They got the rope off his neck when he was blue. He, too, had been acting a little strange, a little funny, for about three years, until one day a neighbor saw him and told the others. "Hey, he went up that way with a rope." They went after him, and when they got to him he was already blue. They cut the rope and laid him on the ground. The civil guard came to take his testimony. He said he wasn't well.

That guy was wrong in the head. They took him to Oviedo, he got a little better, but then he'd get sick again, and they'd take him back to Oviedo. And one day when he couldn't climb the tree, he got up on a burro to be able to tie the knot. And someone came in time to see him and get him down. He must still have the rope mark on his neck.

Soto Vázquez claims that "physical illness" is the motive that leads to the greatest number of suicides among male Vaqueiros (13 out of 48) while this motive is much rarer among the women (3 out of 34). By contrast, he holds that "marital or family disputes" are a greater cause of female suicide (second only to "mental illness") but a minor cause for the men (6 out of 34 for women, 2 out of 48 for men). At first glance the above figures do seem to point to a significant difference in reasons for suicide between the sexes. If, using Soto Vázquez's figures, we compare the average age for male Vaqueiros who end their lives because of illness and female Vaqueiros who do it for domestic reasons, we find that the former are more than twice as old as the latter (sixty-six and thirty years, respectively). This difference in average age is similar to that between the sexes of suicides for "unknown" motives (fifty and twenty-eight years, respectively). Soto Vázquez claims that these figures show a surge of suicides among Vaqueiro women between ages twenty-one and thirty years of age and that physical illness triggers suicide in Vaqueiro men.

My material indicates that physical illness is a reason frequently adduced in theory but is, in fact, an infrequent cause of suicide. However, what we might call "family and conjugal disputes" affect quite a large proportion of suicides. Of the thirty-four suicides for which some sort of motive was given to me (including those classed locally as unknown), twelve (more than one-third) explicitly involved this motive, and the motive appears implicitly in other cases. Given that the house is the basic family unit, the Vaqueiros believe that many suicides originate in the tensions and conflicts inherent in the workings of this institution. While the house resolves certain problems, it creates others, which, in extreme cases and for certain kinds of persons, are resolved by this sort of death. Suicide thus can be a critical indicator of the negative aspects of the house system, showing up its weak points and dark corners.

From this point of view, suicide becomes an act with a strong moral content. The vox populi, when it indicates the particular family circumstances that surround the suicide, emphasizes the failures of human communication, the selfishness and the pettiness of daily interactions. Yet instead of a direct accusation or an open denunciation, Vaqueiros prefer to use a vague rumor, the implicit suggestion that permits them to continue living side by side with the survivors, what they call "living with the living" [*vivir con los vivos*]. The suicide itself is sufficient punishment for those who survive because of the social stigma that it supposes; there is no need to add to it hypothetical expiation by means of "the law." A Vaqueiro presents this point of view below:

> There is no way to find that out, not by a magistrate or by anybody. There's a saying, "You have to live with the living, since it's no fun with the dead." You'd have to be evil-minded to say, "Well, yes sir, they treated him very badly, and they even beat him publicly." How are you going to go and say that, because all you're going to get out of it is that they'll put the others in jail for six months or a year. If it's proven officially that they were ungrateful children or even that they had hurt him, yes, they'd put them in jail; it would be a way to have people straighten up and prevent it from happening to others. And there have been many who have committed suicide and left a note so it wouldn't reflect on the family of the house, saying, "My time has come, so don't blame anybody. They don't deserve it." A letter in their pocket, or that they send to the magistrate.

The persons who are most defenseless within the organization of the house are those most likely to commit suicide because of family disputes.

> You know who the people are who hang themselves? Well, they're people who have become *aburrido* and who can't defend themselves anymore. People in the houses where there are others, people who are old, no, and even some who are not old, and who see things going wrong in the houses, see maybe everything going the wrong way. There were some like that. And others hang themselves and who

knows why—because they are *aburrios*. There are people who jump off, people who are old and can't defend themselves. Because when one is young and new, you don't do it. . . . Well, there may be a young person who does it, like a woman, because of problems in her life; that happens a good deal—major problems, things that are misfortunes. There are also persons who are *aburridos* and live in a house where everyone is against them, and so they try suicide. And others do it who are young, for whatever misfortune they have suffered. These things come easily. There are always misfortunes and bad living situations . . . these things happen to people.

Defenselessness inside the house is closely related to the rules of inheritance. In the previous chapter I concentrated mainly on the place of the *amo* in the case of natural death and its circumstances. As we saw, the expectation of a transition in administrative control accompanies the entire process. Here I will concentrate on those who are not *amos*, that is, the wife of the *amo*, or the uncles, or "other old folks of the house." I will refer to certain extreme cases involving *amos*.

Since the *amo* is typically male, the *amo*'s spouse is typically female. Except in the cases I will speak of below, it is the first-born son, or *mayorazo*, who inherits the house. It is necessary that this son "marry in the house," quite often with the active involvement, or at least the approval, of his parents ("they approved of the girl" [*eran gustantes de la chica*]). A woman enters her new home by marriage under these conditions. Although she enters with some kind of dowry, such women occupy positions of low privilege and status. It is said that mother-in-law and daughter-in-law do not mix [*cuecen mal*], and it is common for there to be competition and confrontations between them. Some women remember that in times of hunger the *amo*'s wife would distribute the food selectively, giving the smallest portion to the "newcomer" [*la nueva*], as these women are called. Food was doled out very sparingly to *la nueva*. Even those best treated remark insistently on how their fathers-in-law would say "eat what you want," as though it were a favor. The "newcomer" remembers her home with nostalgia for a long period. Even today young women will say, "When you come from outside and you want to live in peace, you have to keep quiet a lot, eh? Keep quiet and work." These women do work a lot. Many young men leave the house to work as laborers in the area (on pine plantations, for instance). Much of the work of the house and farm, then, must be done by the wives. The mother-in-law at most will care for the smaller domestic animals and do some of the house-work while the young wife takes care of the hardest work in the pastures and fields. This work limits the short and infrequent excursions of the young couple to the fairs and fiestas of the area, which they may attend only if the *amo* and his wife have no interest in going. On these occasions they must ask the *amos* for spending money, since they have none of their own. Any other necessity, including clothing, must be obtained in the same way. This dependence and the tensions it generates sometimes leads to the young couple abandoning the house, either by their own decision or by that of the older couple. This decision is made only in extreme circumstances and under certain conditions, because the young couple will have amassed very little capital, even after working many years in the house. If the house is "good," that is, has enough land, the preferred son will try as hard as he can not to clash with his parents, even allying himself with them against his wife, since one of his brothers could easily take his place. Under these circumstances, life can be very hard for the newcomer.

If a newcomer is widowed while the old *amos* are living, they will pass the control of the house directly to her son, their grandson, on the condition that she does not remarry.[7] If she has no children, then her husband's brother may be preferred, and he may marry her if he is single and his parents get along well with her. But if there have been conflicts, the widow will have to go back to the house of her parents and her own preferred brother. These cases of the death of the preferred son show the precariousness of the newcomer's position in matters of inheritance and residence in the *braña*.

The newcomer's difficult position lasts until the old *amo* dies or becomes physically disabled. Then the power in the house passes to her husband, something that tends to the coincide with the marriage of her son. Then the *nueva* becomes a mother-in-law, and it is no wonder that she takes revenge on her young daughter-in-law after so many years of "keeping quiet and working." When her husband dies she loses her power, since the power then passes to her son. If he does not maintain a fine equilibrium between his mother and his wife, then one of the two, frequently the mother, may suffer the consequences. Older women often worry that the newcomers "won't be good to them." In this situation, strained alliances in the house are aggravated by the age of these women. If life in the house becomes intolerable for them, they do not have the alternative that the young couple does of going elsewhere.

This state of affairs changes drastically when it is the daughter who is the preferred child. She then becomes the *ama* and acquires many of the social characteristics of the male. Some of these women sell and buy cattle, get their husbands to do work normally considered women's work, and take charge of the house, its money, and its distribution. I knew one *ama* who, when she argued with her husband, would say, "You, since you brought nothing, will take nothing away with you. Take your jacket and go back over X mountain" [to his home *braña*]. In these cases, not only is her husband at a disadvantage, but so is her son and especially her daughter-in-law. A clash with a mother-in-law could mean the loss of a husband's inheritance in favor of one of his siblings. It is difficult for an *ama* to accept the fact that her own daughters have to leave the house so that an "outsider" can enter by marriage.

Even less enviable is the situation of uncles and other "old people of the house," a category that includes very different kinds of people. Most of these people are siblings of the *amo*. For example, one might be a widow who had to go back to her natal house because she didn't get along with her in-laws. When their parents die, these women become servants without pay in the home of the preferred sibling and his (or her) spouse. There may also be other siblings who do not leave the house, hoping against hope that the inheritance may be changed in their favor, and others who, although once preferred, waited too long to marry and thereby lost their chance because of the marriage of another sibling. A preferred son's brother will have difficulty marrying and remaining in the area unless he marries a preferred daughter, or unless someone will take on the new couple as *heredeiros*, a relatively infrequent occurrence. Except in these situations, those not preferred must emigrate with their spouses on the small portion of the inheritance that belongs to them. If these siblings do not marry, they may remain in the house, but only if they renounce their inheritance in favor of the preferred sibling. The bitterness of some of these frustrated siblings is typified by the following comments:

> The *mayorazo* is the eldest, or the one who marries in the house; he's the one who stays as the *amo*. For the one who stays in the house, the parents get to choose, to approve whom he marries. If everybody wants the house, then it is for the first one who marries, or who marries someone who gets approved. If the father gives control to the last born, then the first born has to get out [*tocar espuelas*]; the others will get little in the division of goods. Sometimes there are fights and bad blood. That's why, since the *amos* are the parents, they decide. Like what happened to me and him. This boy is the *mayorazo*, as I was. Now I don't have anything, because now

DEATH

I am—in the house there are two brothers and a sister. And
they all solved their problems of love and got married, and
now I'm the oldest and . . . now, until they kick me out, here
I am in the house. My brothers married outside the house,
but my sister married in the house [was preferred]. I help
them out when there is a lot of work in the house and when
I'm not out earning a wage for myself. If you get married,
there isn't enough for all, and you have to leave. You can ask
for your due, and you leave. You can come back, unless you
leave in anger. If you leave on friendly terms, you might
say, "Well, I'll be back here when I can, to visit for a day or
two."

While they are young, these aunts and uncles of the house may
work outside it; if the situation is tense, they may decide to leave.
But as they get older, they have fewer alternatives. The old uncles I
often met in the houses did the most disagreeable tasks and had no
say in family decisions. Sometimes they even ate separately from
the rest of the family. Their position in the house was identical to
that of aged servants who exchange their salaries for terminal care,
given the impossibility of returning to their parents' house. They
become part of the household, the butt of the remarks and practical
jokes of the youngest members. The more benign *amos* and *amas*
tell the children that the aged servants merit their respect "because
of all that they worked for the house."

Given these structural tensions built into the inheritance system, some of the cases of suicide may be seen in a new light. The
Vaqueiros themselves are aware of the frequency of disputes between mothers-in-law and daughters-in-law, the weak position of
old people in the house, and the relation of these situations to the
decision to commit suicide. "It used to be the case that the two
couples in the house got along badly; that it was bad between
mothers-in-law and daughters-in-law, and so they resorted to this
procedure. Yes, the old man resorted to this procedure."

This kind of suicide, unlike those in the case of serious illness,
is considered avoidable by separation, up to a certain point. But for
the older suicides, separation would mean a situation comparable
to suicide itself, for without an inheritance they would have to live
off public charity, begging while they could and ending their lives
in a hospice. This situation leads to contradictory comments on
suicides who are either "cowards" or "brave," depending on one's
point of view.

That still remains to be studied. Some say it's people who
are cowardly; the way I look at it, if we consider it a little, we

might even say that it might be people who are brave. Say there's no point in my living, because nobody can set my life right—that I have certain family problems in the house, and it can't be fixed no matter how you took at it, and so you take this step. It might be a lot easier to say, "Let's go off begging, and the day we can't do that anymore we'll go to the door of a poorhouse so they'll take us in." For while you live, maybe you live disagreeably, but you live.

Well, the person who does this finds himself somewhat *arrepentío* and is a little cowardly or timid, who finds he has to do this. No, he's not brave, because life doesn't just leave you that alternative. Rather than do that you can take a bag and beg from door to door or at a poorhouse.

Here are some of these cases as they were told to me. These suicides were motivated by the conflicts between mother-in-law and daughter-in-law, mother and son, or even father-in-law and son-in-law. In no case did the suicide own the house. Observe the explicit remarks in this respect:

CASE 8. It was because she had to care for a calf, and he told her, "Don't make the big-assed calf suck milk because it might get sick." And it got sick. The son had the power in the house, and he came up and said, "If the calf dies on me, you can get out of this house." And a pig got sick, too. And she must have said, "It's all happening at once; I'd best take a rope and hang myself." And that she up and did.

And X's mother, they say he wasn't a good son to her. She had a son in the house and a daughter-in-law, and they say they got along badly. The son had control over the house, for her husband had died.

CASE 9. Here, too, a woman took poison. They say her daughter-in-law had criticized her to other people. She had a son married in the house, and they weren't good to her. She cried a lot at first, and then she decided to do it. . . . No, she didn't have control; the *amo* had been her husband.

CASE 10. In this village a woman hanged herself when I was a boy—the grandmother of X here. His grandmother hanged herself in a tree on my land. She got along very badly with her daughter-in-law, very badly. She herself was not *ama*, her husband was. But that didn't have anything to do with it; she had recourse to this procedure. We knew they got along badly, because, of course, if you don't know how to control your disposition, it can lead you to a bad hour. She had a bad hour.

CASE 11. Many people hanged themselves. X, Z's grandfather, hanged himself, too. His son-in-law would hit him. He got along badly with his son-in-law and hanged himself. It was his wife or his son-in-law, and he hanged himself. It was his wife who had the *manda*.

In the following two cases the conflict involved the spouse or family, but here, too, the suicides did not have the *manda*.

CASE 12. Here in X a man hanged himself, too. They say he got along badly with a son who was married to Z. He got along very badly with his son, and his wife didn't care for him. He married into the house and didn't bring anything. He was a chronic drunk and would be in the bar and keep drinking spirits.

CASE 13. Yes, here in the village a man committed suicide. More than forty years ago he threw himself into a pool in the river. He was going out with his lover, and then his family did not want her.

I courted him a little myself [laughs]. He already once tried to jump into the river and they stopped him—there were people nearby, and they saw him on a cliff, and they stopped him that day. And another day he did it. I'm not sure if it was in the same place. The water took him downstream; I don't know where he ended up. Here no one knows how to swim; if we fall into the river, that's where we drown. He had problems with his family. No, he wasn't the *amo*; the house belonged to his wife.

The suicides of unmarried aunts, uncles, or other "old people of the house" do not inspire much commentary, just as their "natural" deaths cause little mourning and few people attend their funerals. It might be said that people ignore the disappearance of these "dead branches" of the family tree because of their slight social significance. The weak position these people have in the house culminates in their almost anonymous deaths. I suspect that a couple of suicides I know were of his kind, but I do not include them here because I do not have enough information about them.

I do have considerable information about one recent case, summarized below. A was a nonpreferred son who, at age twenty-five or thirty, joined the house of a widow with a number of young children as a servant. Over time he came to be considered a member of the family since he helped to raise the children and cohabited with the *ama*. After about forty years, the widow went to the city where one of her children lived so she could have an operation. After the operation, she did not return to the *braña* and appeared to have no intention of doing so. A took charge of all of the work of the house, with the help of a young servant who was mentally retarded. All this time he anxiously awaited the return of the *ama* and her children. He was used to obeying, and he did not like the responsibility of buying and selling cattle, killing pigs, and so on, especially because, it is said, he was illiterate. When one of the widow's relatives in the *braña* referred to him as an idiot, he is said to have replied, "Yes, you say I am an idiot, and you still give me all the work to do." During this time he complained that he was "nobody" in the house. Finally it was rumored that the house would be closed up, and he would end his days in a rest home. The night before his suicide A said things like "Tonight I will go to bed, but tomorrow . . . ," or "Let's go to bed; there won't be another day. . . ." In making his preparations, he locked the room where he kept his small savings, fed the animals, and even left ready the corn flour they would need the next day. Then he sent the young servant to work with some neighbors so he wouldn't discover the body. He hanged himself in the stable near the house, using a rope with several knots.

When the magistrate and the civil guard came to investigate the suicide, the widow's relatives received them and busied themselves, with other neighbors, getting the body down and testifying. People declared that the deceased had no problems, was normal, had a disease of the urinary tract, and that they "don't know why he hung himself." Once the authorities had left, the funeral, like any other, took its normal course.

But immediately afterwards, rumors began to circulate. In private people claimed that the man's alleged illness could not be considered a reason for his suicide, since he had gone to a specialist who merely said that his urine "was dirty" and that it wasn't serious. The *ama*'s family insisted that there were ample provisions in the house for his use: "But the house was full of food. How could he have done that? He did what he wanted to; he was the *amo* of all this; nobody told him what he had to eat." To support their claims, they showed those present the pantry: "Look, he had everything— soup, coffee—he was the boss—four hams, one open." A neighbor spoke up, "He said, 'I didn't even touch it. The *ama* might need it when she comes back.' He didn't want to cut into it." Obviously these affirmations and their emphasis were an attempt on the part of the widow's relatives to head off possible accusations about lack of care for the deceased. The comments of the neighbors brought out all of these aspects. Some were milder while others were quite severe:

CASE 14. A? Oh yes, he was Z's man, Z's lover. Poor man! What a life . . . he came to that widow, worked like a nigger all of his fucking life, and then, at the end . . . she takes off to the city with a disease and doesn't come back, and him there alone, seeing himself *aburrido*, and so he does it.

And this boy entered the house when he was young, and Z was a widow, and then they say he began to sleep with her, and then they say she got some kind of paralysis and went to the city, where one of her sons was married, and she said she wasn't going back, that he should kill the pigs. He had to kill the pigs himself. And seeing himself alone there and *arrepentío*, and being a little sick, too, well . . . "All right, I'll end my life." And so he did. He was *aburrío* when he considered his situation. He put the noose around his neck.

And the man from X house, nobody knew why he did it. He had enough to eat, and worked as much as he wanted to, because he was alone there when it happened. Maybe it was being there alone . . . loneliness isn't good for anyone. He would have thought that the *ama* wasn't coming back, that he'd have to be the *amo*.

The tensions of Vaqueiro houses do not only touch these persons with no inheritance. Some *amos*, too, have ended their lives because of situations of exceptional conflict. The following suicide is one of these cases. The *amo*, who was in conflict with his wife and daughters, took care before he died to pass the *manda* to a young son.

CASE 15. Others take strychnine—you poison yourself and you die right away. They say a man from X did it, with that poison for killing wild animals, wolves, the strongest there is. All you have to do is taste it with your tongue. Who knows why he did it? He got along badly with his wife and daughters, they say, for they all went one way and he went another; they wouldn't get together with him. Maybe he was sick, too. He planned it in advance, because he went down to Z [town] and made out the *manda* to a young son, and everything was all arranged.

If the family is one cause of suicide in the house, loneliness is another. When an old, widowed *amo* committed suicide after all of his children had emigrated to the city, and he had made an unsuccessful attempt to live with them, local opinion attributed his suicide to loneliness. Observe the emphasis on family disagreements, even outside of the region, as alleged contributing factors in the act.

CASE 16. X committed suicide quite recently, hanged himself in a cherry tree next to his house. He had food in the house, but they say he was *aburrido* for some reason. . . . They said he went in another house the night before, at a spinning circle, as usual, and he left as he always did, and the next morning he was found hanging. He didn't say anything to anyone. Z was the first person who saw him—came to bring the milk with his dog and saw him hanging there. Yes, he left a letter on the bed and his shoes clean beneath the bed, and his bed made. In the letter he said that one person owed him a thousand *duros*, another a thousand pesetas, and that the twenty thousand pesetas in the house were for his daughter, and that there were thirty thousand pesetas in the bank. They usually hang themselves in old clothes, but they leave their good clothes ready so they can be changed in the laying out. It was at night; they do it that way so no one will see them. They know that if they are seen they won't be left to hang themselves in public.

X's in-law did it, but there have always been and will always be cases of this. He found himself all alone. What we don't know is how he got along with his family, how they treated him, how much affection they had for him. This thing comes from not living well together. The man lived alone here. When you live alone, when you get old, the nights seem very long, you start to dwell on things.

He was in Madrid once and couldn't live with any of his sons or his daughter, so he came back here. He must have been alone here a year—came in September and stayed. He had been married, and his wife died, maybe two years ago. . . . He has a married sister in the same village; she must have done some things for him, if only wash his clothes, I don't know. They didn't have much money, somewhat poor, the sister, too. They have poor houses, seem to be badly off. His children, some married and others not, went off to Madrid. The house was poor, and it seems nobody wanted to stay.

I think someone said he was a man who saw his children in Madrid—one a good-for-nothing, others in bars and street-life, and saw they had turned out bad, all coming in at four in the morning, so he came back here. And then he made up his mind, and left a letter saying he was owed money—the thousand pesetas—and twenty thousand he had in the house.

In these comments, people consider the possibility that the suicide occurred for economic reasons. People remember that in the past there were many beggars, and there were "many people and much hunger" in the houses. This led some people to end their lives. Today people are considered to live in relative prosperity. The poorest houses of the region have been depopulated by the emigration of their members or because their *amos* have not been able to marry or find *heredeiros*. The houses that remain are supposedly those that permit—with more or less ease and considerable work— the raising of a family by local standards. But the remaining houses are still vulnerable to occasional crises caused by natural disasters (a bad harvest, the death of one or more animals, the burning of a stable caused by lightning, etc.), social obligations (a number of successive weddings or funerals), or other unusual circumstances (litigation over inheritance or the purchase of land). Such crises produce debts that are paid off slowly with much effort. The work of the house requires good "administration" and a lot of patience. It is not surprising that the most ambitious or impatient Vaqueiros seek other means, more rapid but less secure, to repay their debts, for example, by becoming cattle dealers. The next two cases of suicide involve persons of this type; the third case is also related to commerce.

CASE 17. And in this village another hanged himself, too, beneath Y house. It's a terrible village with four families. This was a little man who became a cattle dealer, buying calves, and he didn't know how, and spent all he had, and ended owing a lot to many people. And when he was too ashamed that he was finishing off the house, he went into the stable and hanged himself.

He got into a mess with deals and was in a bad way. And the other dealers wanted to finish him off. And they even took him one night to a brothel and got hold of his money. They got him into a house like that, and I think they robbed him; in any case, the man came home on his last legs, and went up to a stable and there he hanged himself. Many hang themselves. What happens to a lot of them is that they get in debt for ten thousand *duros*, and it seems to them that they'll never pay it off in their entire lives, and then they find themselves *aburridos*.

CASE 18. Another killed himself because of debts. He was a cattle dealer, and he killed himself for that reason. He was a boy from my age set, an excellent dealer.

A man from X was ruined and hung himself. Furthermore, he was in bad health; he married, and when he married he was unwell. He married late, and he got worse and worse. He wasn't a particularly good man, because in the war a lot of them tried to pass cattle through the lines, and he swindled them all.

CASE 19. In Madrid I saw a bar owner married to a young filly start to go downhill fast. He was from a house in X [*braña*]. And he had always been an old bachelor, and at the last moment he married a young girl. And he was badly off; he couldn't pay his debts; he was losing money. And one day he got a revolver and went to the Puente de los Franceses, got under the bridge and shot himself. And the widow, a filly, was pregnant.

Suicide for economic reasons is almost exclusively a masculine phenomenon, since it is usually the man who is in charge of the household economy. The suicides and their local descriptions serve to warn *amos* not to run risks that jeopardize the integrity of the house. They also stigmatize an untoward interest in becoming rich at the expense of others (given that the dealers have few scruples in this respect and cheat the Vaqueiros when they can get away with it). Two of the above cases also serve as a warning against marriage in old age or between persons of disparate ages. Vaqueiros attribute certain problems to such unequal marriages, including jealousy and infidelity, sometimes given as reasons for suicide. In my opinion, suicides for these reasons are not common. The following cases were referred to me by my informants with a certain perplexity.[8]

CASE 20. Another woman hanged herself in X. She was seeing a man and got pregnant, and she knew he wasn't going to marry her, and hanged herself in his stable with his letters.

CASE 21. This happened a long time ago. My father told me about it. A certain boy had two children by a girl of X, a baby boy and a baby girl. Then his mother said to him, "Well look, since you've had two children with her, if you're not going to marry her—because that was common in those days, eh?—bring her to the house at once." Because she was from a very poor family, too. And he went and brought her to the house. And he, of course, was from a house just as poor—in those days there was a lot of hunger. And he told his mother he was going to Madrid to make some money and send it, in order to raise those children. And what should happen but that when he got to Madrid he got involved with a girlfriend there. He was really in love with her, eh? from what he did next. He wanted to get married to her at once. People then were like people now: they gossiped about everything to the girl in Madrid, that he had a woman with two children in his mother's house. And she didn't take to the fact that he already had a woman. And one day when he went to meet his girlfriend, she said, "Do me the favor of getting out of here, scoundrel, shameless one, pig, what do you have at home in Asturias? Go and take care of those children and the woman you already have!" And she turned away. And he said, "Listen, let's not end this way. Please give me back my things, and I'll give you yours." They would have exchanged photographs; it was customary to give as presents a pair of stockings, a handkerchief. "All right." So the next Sunday, instead of taking her things out of his pocket, he takes out a revolver, shoots her in the head, and shoots himself; both were killed.

Mental illness, in its various degrees of severity and forms, is another cause of suicides. In local etiology, it is generally said that mentally ill persons "suffer from nerves." Some illnesses of nerves are said to be permanent; people who have these permanent conditions are said to be "incomplete" (we would say they "have something missing"), crazy or crazed [alocadas], and wrong in the head. People say, "If someone is suffering some from nerves, he'll hang himself for no reason at all." The association between the sickness of nerves, which is not uncommon, and suicide is not automatic, but it is predictable. Sick persons of this kind, whether they are permanently or temporarily ill, are more likely to suffer "a spell of craziness," "a mania," "a bad hour," or a seizure [remate] that can lead to self-destruction.

Those who hang themselves, they are people who are *arrepentida*, or who are not right in the head, or who find themselves *arrepentida* and say, "Oy, I shit on the mother, bah, better out of the way than live." Something must happen to their heads, because you've got to be pretty bad off to do something like that. It must be some spell that hits their heads, or very turbulent blood; I don't know what it is. . . . It's like I am in a certain way, or a sickness makes me bad off, and I say, "It would be better to get rid of myself, drown once and for all." It may be one of those seizures that people get.

The nerves help such people to put an end to their lives in the face of difficulties that ordinarily would not provoke suicide—a curable disease, or one without pain, or even a minor family problem or argument. In other words "nerves" help to explain doubtful cases of suicide. In the following quotes Vaqueiros weigh the possible influence of "nerves."

CASE 22. In X another girl hanged herself. I think she suffered from nerves. She was married, but I don't think they got along badly because her husband ended up marrying her sister later on.

CASE 7. They found the man from X in time. They say he got sick, suffered from nerves, and the people who suffer from nerves have moments when they're very badly off, when their wits get addled. He had a case of testile [senile?] dementia.

He must not have been well in the nerves. That's something that for any little reason makes people go off [commit suicide].

Clear and diagnosed craziness is distinguished from "nerves" in these two cases, the second of which concerns an attempted suicide.

CASE 23. It was a few years ago. I had to be with the body at night in the wake, with another fellow. The man was wrong in the head. He would go to Oviedo [to the hospital] and when he came back he would say, "Well, they didn't even get rid of my evil thoughts." He would be sick, they would give him shocks, and when he came back from the shocks he would be pretty good but. . . . The evil ideas were to hang himself, because he had already hung himself once, but either the cord broke or he thought better of it, and they were able to save him. . . . This is something in the head, *hombre*, it comes from the head. They kept a close eye on him, but one day he got a chance; he said he was going to some meadows they had, and he hanged himself.

This fellow from my village, it was in the head. Already a brother of his had gone crazy; it was in Africa, in the war. He got sent to Africa in '21 and came back worn out. . . . They also get this from weakness, and some is inherited, too.

CASE 24. My husband was going by on the path above, weeping, weeping. "What's wrong?" I asked him. And he said . . . the child had come from the school—that we should send the child, four or five years old, to school. And that's where the craziness came from. He began to say that the school-teacher was a fascist and I don't know what else. He went crazy and nobody knew why. When I got to the house, I asked the children where he was and he was already at X, in the house of his parents, in a stable there, with a cord to hang himself. He went plumb crazy and had to go to an insane asylum. He went crazy, and then got it into his head that they were going to kill him, and before that he would . . . it was when they were coming through here, when the reds and the fascists were doing so many killings and all that, that was when he got sick.

The suicides of the mentally retarded, those who are "not right" or dullards, do not require explanation because these are persons whose behavior is always considered unpredictable.

CASE 25. One from X, he was a dimwit and one fiesta day he went and hanged himself. He was a dimwit and that's what he did.

In X a boy apparently wasn't quite right and hanged himself. His brothers went to the fair and didn't let him go and he hanged himself. He wanted to go to the fair.

CASE 26. And in X another boy also hanged himself. His father and his brother went up in the hills for gorse, and he went off and hanged himself from a pine tree. They say he wasn't right in the head either.

Another common explanation for suicide is "inheritance." This factor applies when a suicide comes from a family in which other people have committed suicide. People believe the tendency to commit suicide can be like a biological trait.

I think there are families that inherit it, we inherit it . . . there are some germs [genes?] in the family; just like there is a germ of tuberculosis, so is this thing of ending your life.

But those people seem like they have some kind of inheritance, like when tuberculosis explodes in a family. Two more have hanged themselves, a brother and a sister. They had an inheritance.

Some cases of suicides are explained by citing other cases with reasonably close degrees of kinship. The kinship need not be genetic but may be affinal, or mere membership in a house. Compare the following two cases:

CASE 7. The fellow from X, he already had the inheritance. His father and his brother hanged themselves. That house was very bad; they say they stole things and so on, but then they were well off, and he didn't hang himself because of poverty.

In one family the grandfather and the father hanged themselves. The grandson, no, not yet. I knew both of them; the first hanged himself in the hayloft and died there. And his son tried to hang himself but didn't succeed. And the grandson, who is there now, is deaf.

CASE 16. This fellow who hanged himself [A] was married to a sister of this other fellow [B] . . . who also hanged himself [case 14]; they were brothers-in-law. They were from the same village, the one who hanged himself [A], another of X house—no, that one hasn't hanged himself yet—and two sisters, one of whom was married to B.

From biological inheritance one passes imperceptibly to cultural inheritance. Ending one's life, like a skill in singing or dancing, is a trait that is transmitted with the house, a kind of destiny or family fate.

That is a family in which it seems to me they are not complete, that they've got something missing. Those are inheritances, I don't know, a strain [ramo] that makes them that way, so that for any little thing you get pessimistic and start to think about it and . . . a bad wave in the head and you're off. A strain that makes them that way, like others like to sing and dance. All of us have a strain that affects us in some way—that makes you want to study rather than be a cook, for instance, or another want to be a nun. You took to studying; you have the strain for studying. Each person, we have something different from others; I think those people who hang themselves have that character.

That is why the people of the *braña* worry about family members of a suicide who show symptoms of wanting to die in the same way.

Because this fellow from X, another brother died the same way, and also their father. And now one's afraid that the other brother in Z will also take a mind to hang himself. He, too, got a little crazy, got the idea that he was sick and wasn't getting better, and they say he really didn't have anything wrong with him, just an obsession that took hold of him. That's why any day he's alone in the house, he might up and do it. He easily might do it. He's not working now, and he doesn't want to go out anywhere or anything. Before he liked to go out everywhere; he played cards, and he was always joking with everyone. And now, for the last seven or eight years, he gets up to eat and that's all. He doesn't go out of the house and doesn't want to see anybody or anything. It is a sickness of nerves that he doesn't want to see anyone. If he's in the window he leaves it so they won't see him. He wants to see, but he doesn't want to be seen. Well, you still don't know if he'll do it, until the end comes.

The threat of imitation affects the entire Vaqueiro group. The suicide of one of its members makes people "pessimistic." This social inheritance can affect everyone, including "normal" people.

People say: "What a shame, *hombre*, what a bad hour God gave him." When someone hangs himself it makes you pessimistic. You start to think, "But what really happened?" Given that you knew him, that he was a normal person and not unstable. And someone says to you, "I'm going to end by hanging myself, eh?"—they might say it to you a long time before, years before. And you take it as a joke and then. . .

I think it's very wrong, those people who hang themselves, because after they can no longer go on and for that reason hang themselves, maybe because they have a series of problems. Well, I think that more than for any other reason those who come later know that so-and-so hanged himself and follow suit. So-and-so hanged himself and the others do the same, yes, yes. The people, when they see that someone hangs himself, say, "A lot have done it already." Do you think that on that day only X hanged himself? Unh-uh. So did another fellow in Y. He wasn't related, but a lot have hanged themselves.

Vaqueiros may also interpret suicide as a form of divine punishment, one of the ways God chastises injustice. This affects not only the persons who commit the sins but also their descendants.

I believe, that is why when I leave on a trip I cross myself and say, "God in front of me [*Dios delante*]." That fellow from Argentina, when he saw me make a cross on the horns of the cows, he laughed and said to me, face to face—and he is intelligent—"But why do you use this word 'God?'" "Look, fellow, that's how we were brought up, doing it that way. It's something that doesn't do you any good, right? but it doesn't do you any harm, doesn't cost you a red cent or any trouble." Because if it were a case of stopping, picking up a heavy weight, and putting it on your back in order to say "God in front of me," then it would be different. But religion says that God asks of us the Ten Commandments of the law of God, but nothing else. In Argentina this doesn't exist. And that's why I say to you, and I have observed it, that whether it is God or some other powerful hand, or a path that exists for each person, a destiny, we could say any of these things. But if you have seen someone who did a thousand misdeeds [atentaos], me caso con Dios! If things go well for him, then you don't have to be afraid of anything. Things might go all right for him, without problem. But then there is a disaster, and you say, "But what fault did his son have, or his grandson?" Caramba, the guilt lies with the one who committed the crime. Why should someone else suffer? It's like a father whom God gives a crippled son. What fault did the son commit that he should suffer? If the father committed a crime, punish the father in accord with the crime. Why the son? Well, that's the way it is. Here in X there has been a disaster.

This extensive and heartfelt declaration suggests that the "fear" of God and the observance of his rules may prevent the sufferings that lead to suicide. In the last analysis, everything comes from God, including the kind of death one will have, but people provoke God's wrath or benevolence with their behavior. Thus suicide is a kind of moral punishment. Consider, for instance, the "disaster" to which the man quoted above was referring.

CASE 27. Here in X there was a louse who married three times and finally hanged himself. You'll see why. This scoundrel was a real son of a bitch; every time he had a wife, he took a lover. He took a widow for a lover when he was married to his second wife. And the lover got pregnant. The lover lived in her own house, along with her father, who was a widower himself, and who was quite sharp. So that everything was well arranged, eh? And when she got pregnant, then how was it to be fixed? Well, he gets the idea that she blame her father—that it was the father who made her pregnant. "Say it was your father." She and he were a pair of scoundrels. I don't know why that man, with the brains he had, didn't tell the police: "Take this girl to jail and make her talk, so we know where this comes from." And so her father, when he was humiliated in this way, took a rope and here in these stables he hanged himself one afternoon. And the man and the people said her father had been crazy. Some craziness! The guy got disgusted and fed up and hung himself. Well, then the wife of this bastard died, and he married his lover. After marrying her, he took another lover younger than her, and wanted to bring her to live in the house. And his son and his wife said no, and he began to insist and make trouble in the house. God, what a mess it was, arguments all day long. He began to drink a little. And one day he went down to Z and invited everyone for drinks, "Drink, because I won't be inviting you again." "*Coño*, why?" "I'll pay no more." They had a sewing woman in the house, and he told her, "Take this, this is the last I'll ever give you while I live. I'll pay you no more." He went down one day to the funeral parlor. He was a friend of the director, and he told him, "X, they'll be buying a coffin from you soon." "For whom?" "Hush up, you'll soon know. Make it a good coffin, the best you have, eh? Charge what you want." And they had a little hut off the house, and he told them he was going to sleep there. He dressed himself in his laying-out clothes, put on a decent suit, tied the knot, and hung himself [case 28]. Because he had committed crimes, he made his father-in-law hang himself, with a slander. That was a powerful hand [*una mano poderosa*], I swear. . . .

In this way, then, the law of God is the law of humans. One must live peacefully, avoiding hatred and confrontations as much as possible. This moral aspect of suicide serves as a corrective to the exploitation and bad treatment that might drive others to end their lives.

Finally, there are a few suicides for which the people of the *braña* can find no explanation—some because they took place long ago or far away, others because of the discretion of the suicides themselves. ("Sometimes they find themselves *aburríos* for something they don't tell anyone about, and decide to do it.") This latter type is exemplified in the following case, in which people examine different hypotheses.

CASE 29. Yes, here the man from X house hanged himself. We don't know why. These are designs, who knows? It wasn't because of sickness—he was a little hoarse, but nothing to worry about. It must have been a strain of craziness, or something like that. They can have something that only they know about, something in their lives that no neighbor or family member knows, and then comes the time when they think about hanging themselves. So, yes, I saw him hanging here. Nobody knew anything; we hadn't noticed anything about it in him. He wasn't nervous at all, and he had money; none of us knew anything, just that he had a run-in with some neighbors here down behind the house, but it wasn't the kind of thing that would make him do a thing like that.

These lines subtlely and implicitly put part of the blame on the community in addition to the mysterious nature of human life. In the face of death, life prevails: one has fulfilled one's obligations to the dead, but the difficult task of living with the living remains. Some of my informants understood exactly why I was interested in the subject of suicide but had considerable difficulty answering my specific questions.

But look, suicide has always existed and will keep on happening. You're hitting your head against a wall. What you want to find out is how the brain works, why they do it, how does the person who hangs [himself] know, what the brain of these people is like. Even when it happens in the village, and we know it; because we have to live with those who remain; we already did what we could for the one who left.

Conclusion:
Kinds of Death and the House

The different values accorded to death apply both to the Vaqueiros who die and to their survivors. A good death is one that is hardly felt at all, rapid and without pain; a bad death supposes a long illness or a slow and painful agony together with a consciousness of the approaching end. For those who attend the dying person, the good death is discreet; they say "it's almost not death," and it happens while the Vaqueiro is still participating in the collective work of the house. A bad death becomes a heavy burden for those who remain, adding to their other work and forcing them to share in the suffering and impotence.

While it might seem at first that the Vaqueiros refuse to accept death, these descriptive categories in fact involve a rejection of sickness and pain, and raise the problem of the selectivity of death. Vaqueiros consider the age of the person who dies very significant. They complain of the injustice involved when persons die who have not yet completed their life cycle, who have not worked and taken pleasure as they should have, those who still enjoy the *gracia* of living. When such persons die, even in the most benign cases of happy death or mortal accident, members of the group experience "surprise," "worry," and *descobertura*—a sense of loss and absence, which is not only affective but also economic for the people of the house of the deceased. By the same token, one hears muted criticism of those who, when they are very old and have amply fulfilled their life's cycle, "do not feel death" or "do not know that they have to die." When these persons die, survivors feel serenity and also a certain relief. Vaqueiro attitudes toward death thus depend on the context in which the death occurs.

My analysis of natural death and violent death brings out the contrast between these two different ways of dying. Death of old age means the continuation of the cycle of nature on a human level. Old Vaqueiros "dry up" like the grass of the meadows in winter, "finish up" like the animals of the Vaqueiro stable, "die like birds." Birds exemplify a sweet and quiet end, one that is barely noticeable and in accord with in the laws of the universe. Some Vaqueiros achieve this ideal: death finds them gathering wood, on a quiet walk, or shopping in the *aldea*. Without a period of sickness and suffering (these people are said to die "healthy"), death results from a physical exhaustion or emptying in which the dying person never loses his or her social personality. Those who are with them accept the fact of death with tranquillity.

The house is the context for death in the *braña*. This family enterprise provides the frame for death as it does for life, the last recourse even of those who had to abandon it so that it might survive. With each change of generation, the house, along with its old *amo*, suffers a crisis that the various legal dispositions governing the transmission of the property attempt to overcome.

The transmission of the house presents a dilemma for the Vaqueiro who is going to die. On the one hand, the house, through its continuity, offers the only possibility for immortality. The old *amo* who in his day received the house from "those who went before" and "who sweated" there, who raised a family there, wants the house "to go on" with "those who come afterwards." The duty to increase the house, or at least transmit it without loss to the next generation in an orderly succession, involves a lesson of humility— the recognition of one's own transience in relation to the permanence of the institution. Human beings die but the house survives. The old *amos* thus are linked in the collective but anonymous chain that built the house. The fact that the house survives even when there are no bonds of kinship, when transmission from father to son is not possible, demonstrates the importance of the house. Perhaps even more significant, when the old *amo* must choose one of his children as the heir, he thereby virtually disinherits the others, doing a kind of violence to his own blood, especially when he must take into account, among other things, the aptitude of the preferred child to continue the house in spite of his own personal preferences. When the two roles of the elderly Vaqueiro, *amo* and parent, come into conflict, the dilemma is usually resolved in favor of the *amo*. Being a "good parent," that is, favoring all of one's children equally, is inconsistent with being a "good *amo*" and choosing the child best suited for the house. If an *amo* vacillates in making this choice or he refuses to make it altogether, he will be criticized severely by the Vaqueiro community.

The house holds other more practical and subjective interests for the elderly Vaqueiro. Traditionally the system of inheritance provided a way for the *amo* to ensure himself a peaceful old age, providing for care in sickness and company in death. From this point of view, the house is a property that one offers to those who might be interested, children or *heredeiros*. At times, when relations are strained and especially when the property is small, the old *amos* have to offer the heirs something more than the tenuous promise of preferring them in a will. The solution in such cases may be the deeding of the property or, more recently, the ceding of control, now made possible by the old-age subsidy. This subsidy demonstrates the endemic insecurity, both economic and affective, of the elderly, together with the efforts and legal ingenuity of the culture in protecting them. Until the old-age subsidy was instituted, the legal title to the house was the principal weapon of the elderly, together with control over the profits the house produced, in order to ensure dignity in old age.

The dying Vaqueiro must negotiate between two contradictory desires: the perpetuation of the house and personal care. The various cultural solutions aim at maintaining a difficult equilibrium between the moral obligation to continue a house and the peremptory necessity for personal security. But all solutions are inevitably partial: by placing the emphasis on one aspect or another, certain conflicts are resolved but others are created. One of the most frequent conflicts of this sort is the deterioration of relations between the older and younger couple within the house. The latter often resent their lack of independence and participation in family decisions, because they are doing most of the work of the house.

Today ceding control of the *mando* is perhaps the most viable attempt at solving the dilemma. In this respect the old-age subsidy also helps the young. Ceding control allows for an effective and gradual succession of one generation by another, compared with the definitive and drastic changeover of death or the deeding of the title. In such a situation, there is a possibility of combining the experience of years with the strength and vitality of the young. This method does not always work. At times there are clashes and conflicts between the two generations because of their differing ways of administering the house, and especially because of their differing ways of thinking about it. The old *amo* has a "faith" and an "affection" for his home that the young *amo* does not always share. The greater possibilities of emigration and work available outside the *braña* now make the traditional hope of becoming an *amo* less attractive. In local terminology, becoming an *amo* is now sometimes seen as becoming the "slave" of one's house.

Ceding control is also the first stage in the transition to death. The diminishing of responsibility and work coincide with a change in diet and the gradual loss of *gracia*. Learning to die is a process like learning to live. The child who is born in the *braña* stays in the house at least until he goes to school, a time that marks his formal entry in the outside world. He gradually begins to become interested in extrafamilial relations and creates his own kind of bonds to others. In old age a reverse process occurs in which there is an increasing disinterest in social life, eating and working, fiestas and entertainment, relations with neighbors, and interchanges with friends. At a certain point, children and the elderly coincide in their reclusion in the house. As Vaqueiros say, "You are a child twice." The elderly and children perform similar services in the house and develop a bond of friendship and solidarity.

Gracia signifies a pleasure in living, both everyday and social: traveling, seeing friends, going to the market, and playing cards. This social expansiveness is represented by metaphors of body expansion and lightness. Conversely, the loss of *gracia* means shrinkage and heaviness. Losing *gracia* is not just a matter of age, since there are some old people who have quite a lot of *gracia*. The main cause of the diminution of *gracia* is the increasing heaviness of blood. Blood is a metonymic sign for life; the absence of movement in blood or human beings is the characteristic trait of death.

Vaqueiros are able to maintain their *gracia* as long as they "defend themselves," that is, as long as they can can contribute is some way to the work of the house, maintain an appetite, get around the *braña,* or care for children. The old-age subsidy today helps the elderly to maintain *gracia* because it allows them to be economically independent, preventing them from becoming a burden on the house. Other Vaqueiros hold in high esteem the elderly who, in spite of their age, "defend" themselves with dignity; they praise those willing to do the small tasks they are able to perform. The loss of *gracia* signifies the entry into a phase of defenselessness that culminates in death.

Once the old Vaqueiro has taken to bed, he or she has reached the maximum separation in the process of reclusion. Nevertheless, it is at this point that a final and intense sociability forms around the sick person. Members of the household provide the three basic aspects of care: food, hygiene, and company. The rest of the community also participates in the process of sickness, helping in the work of the house in various ways, watching over the sleep of the sick person, and especially visiting. The same thing occurs when a Vaqueiro mother gives birth; the presents that she receives from relatives, friends, and neighbors are virtually the same.[9] Like the mother who has just given birth, the sick person has urges for certain foods, which are generously supplied by the members of the house and by visitors. Like the young mother's, the sick person's diet is composed of unusual foods, fiesta fare rather than the everyday food of the *braña*. The similarity of ritual in both transitions suggests that death and birth have many points in common. The group that welcomes the newborn and celebrates the woman who has brought a new life into existence also thanks the person who leaves the group, wishing her or him well on the final journey. The people of the *braña* who gather around the sick person help to maintain his or her interest in life and contribute to his or her nourishment. At the same time, the *braña* neighbors monitor the condition of the sick person, making sure that the family fulfills its obligations.

Representatives of the outside world—the doctor, the priest, and the notary public also appear at the house at the time of death. The visits of these specialists tend to occur when the house is full of people. This is particularly true of the priest, whose arrival brings out the *braña* residents to participate in the religious ritual. Grave illness or death is the only formal occasion on which the intimacy of Vaqueiro home is opened to the outside. Normally the Vaqueiros go to the doctor and the notary in town, and see the priest at mass in the *aldea*. The respective jurisdictions of these professionals—over the body, legal status, and the soul—define the Vaqueiros and provide official recognition of their deaths.

If death from old age may be seen as the culmination of a natural process, suicide involves a sharp and drastic interruption of this process. Suicide is in some sense the most "cultural" way of death because it occurs according to the will of the Vaqueiro. Culture not only provides a set of norms for dying but also the possibility of violating these norms in certain circumstances. The examination of the motives that lead to suicide shows the existence of conflict in the Vaqueiro society as well as a system of values about life and death—when and why it is worth living, and when and why it is worth ending one's life. I will summarize these circumstances below.

Many suicides are considered "normal" by the group, and many persons who commit suicide are not considered sick in any way. What is more, suicide, although it may be considered a mistake, is not regarded as a sin or a crime. In the proper circumstances, anyone may do it.

Suicide is something that gets into the head from think-ing wrong. I'm not sure, dearie, what I would do, I'm not sure. It is a mistake, of course, it has to be a mistake.

It seems to me to be something done backwards. That you should die when God wants it, and not before. Of course, when they're in pain, I don't know, since it never happened to me.

Among the circumstances leading to suicide may be a desire to avoid the punishment of the law. Vaqueiros generally agree that death in the *braña* is preferable to life in jail. They consider suicide a reasonable expiation or corrective for a crime or wrong decision. In the case of the attempted homicide, additional factors included an implicit fear of a serious economic loss for the house, the ad-vanced age of the man, and the probability of his receiving a life sentence. In the face of the law and the courts, the Vaqueiro, as we have seen, feels impotent and defenseless.

A similar feeling of defenselessness results from prolonged sickness. When there is no hope that the person will get better and a bad death is expected, suicide is considered a "logical" solution. The Vaqueiros regard suicide as humanly reasonable in cases of chronic or painful illness because they live in a society where the use of painkillers traditionally has not been an option. Those around the suicide may even look on this act as ethical and moral, because the illness of a member of the house, especially when the treatment is long and costly, can lead to the loss of the household savings and the amassing of substantial debts. The possibility of suffering, combined with the possibility of making others suffer, thus can be more unbearable than the idea of death.

Suicide usually has its meaning or its motives in the house. Those suicides that result from family or marital disputes show up the conflicts and inequalities in the system of inheritance and its corresponding distribution of roles in the house. In such cases, much of the responsibility for the suicide is attributed to the sur-viving members of the household, but in a way so subtle and diffuse that, while it serves as a warning to the guilty, it does not threaten their daily relations with the community. Given that all of the houses are organized in the same way, these diffuse accusations serve as negative models, behavior to avoid, and allow for a collec-tive recognition of guilt in which all Vaqueiros participate.

Within the house, certain persons appear more susceptible to suicide. The transmission of the property brings the *amo* security in old age and guarantees that he will be treated acceptably, for he can choose the child he prefers as heir and, by threatening to change the will, blackmail him or her into behaving well. But the other inhabitants of the house are "defenseless" when involved in the household tensions. Among the "disinherited" persons are the women, who very rarely are *amas*. Those women most likely to commit suicide are twenty-one to thirty years old, the age at which the "newcomer" women are adjusting to their new houses and to the difficult roles of daughter-in-law, wife, and mother.

The young woman faces a sharp change from the preceding period, *la mocedad* (approximately ages fourteen to twenty), which most women remember as one of the happiest times of their lives. *La mocedad* is a time of courtship, characterized by frequent attendance at dances, fairs, and diversions. It is a critical period in that the choice a woman makes will determine her entire future. It is necessary to weigh the candidates carefully. A good match would be a *mayorazo* with a good house that is easy to work in and has few relatives, but if the girl waits too long to find her mate, she runs the risk of remaining single or wasting her time. Hence in her late twenties, when she is in danger of becoming an old maid [*moza vieja*], a Vaqueiro woman will become less choosy. Marriage means the end of diversions and the beginning of a period of hard work, many obligations, and few rights. Many mature women lamented to me their choice of mates; they vividly remember their sorrow at leaving their own home and their conflicts with their mothers-in-law and sisters-in-law in the new house. Even after many years of residence in the new house, when they speak of "my" house, they refer to the house in which they were born, in contrast to "this" house, the one in which they now live.

The high suicide rate for women in their twenties must be understood in this context. But it is significant that few people spontaneously mentioned local cases of suicide of this sort, although they often admitted that this age is full of unpleasantness and "life problems." I think this avoidance of the subject has two sides. The first is that these are the suicides the people find most intolerable: they involve the disappearance of young persons "in their prime of life," for reasons for which all Vaqueiro feel a little guilty. By the same token, the suicides of older persons—mothers-in-law rather than daughters-in-law, for example—which are viewed as less morally unjust, are spoken of more frequently. In several cases, the suicides of young women were ascribed to "nerves," even though it was recognized that there were conflicts in the house. It seems that many women of this age have "the nerves," something I noticed myself. Once this condition is diagnosed, the behavior of the other members of the house toward the "newcomer" tends to improve.

A second reason why people were reluctant to mention female suicides is the lack of salience of women in the culture. According to Soto Vázquez, female Vaqueiros commit suicide almost as frequently as males (49 cases compared to 62). But in the cases of suicides mentioned to me, only nine women were mentioned compared with thirty men. It seems that the suicides of women are less frequently noticed and remembered than the suicides of *amos* because of the woman's weak juridical status in the house. As regards status, women, especially those who have not had children, resemble the bachelor uncle or any of the other "old people of the house." The distinction between women and *amos* becomes clear as well in the amount of publicity and number of attendees at their respective funerals and postmortem rituals. Note that in case 14 cited above, which involved an *ama*, the man of the house complained before committing suicide that "nobody paid him any attention," and that "he was nobody in the house." In the legal sense, all women who are not *amas* are "nobody" in the house, at least until they have children; even then, their rights depend on their sons.

Although conflicts in the houses principally affect women, some men find the role of *amo* unbearable. Because they are responsible for the prosperity and perpetuation of the house, a serious economic blunder that "does the house in [*acaba con la casa*]," or an error in foresight that leaves the house without a successor, can lead to much remorse and personal anguish. Both situations imply that the *amo* has made a mistake: either he does not know how to run the house or he has not exercised enough authority within the household. Being an *amo* demands an assertive personality. Given the difficulties of the Vaqueiro environment and the conflictive social organization of the household and the *braña*, the *amo* must sometimes be tough and aggressive. He must know how to defend himself in the family and in the *braña*, where some houses take advantage of the weakness of others in order to expand (at times in the crudest ways—by moving boundary markers or appropriating disputed fields). The role of the *amo*, with its implicit responsibility for the direction and decisions that affect the house, is the opposite of that of the bachelor uncle, who must work and obey. Some people are not at ease in their respective positions; for them, suicide is one way out.

Attributing a suicide to mental illness allows people to avoid the issue of responsibility. Mentally retarded persons who commit suicide are also thought not to have any responsibility for their actions. It is thought that because both the mentally ill and the mentally retarded do not follow the normal rules of reasoning, any in-

DEATH

cident may lead them to kill themselves. The Vaqueiros do distinguish a less serious and more transitory kind of mental problem: "suffering from nerves." As I have indicated, this may be an expression of conflict between the individual and the household. It is taken as a warning of the need for a change in behavior by the rest of the household lest the sick person have a "spell of craziness," an "attack," or a "bad hour." In these cases it is thought that certain physiological causes—violent blood and the bursting of the nerves in the head—can initiate the process of self-destruction if others do not avoid flare-ups and arguments as much as possible.

These spells or strains [ramos] that lead to suicide are believed to be "inherited," since they are transmitted in the house like other qualities or defects—the art of cooking, devoutness, studiousness, or thievery—although they affect some individuals more than others. The factor of "inheritance" implies a shift from the scrutiny of individual motives and social situations to that of the history of the house and its members. Vaqueiros intuitively relate personal disorders to the diachronic process of the family system as it unfolds within the confines of the house. Family precedents, repeated suicides in the same house or even in the same braña, pose with a certain starkness the eternal truth that we are all products of the past and models for the future, or, in local terms, that "there are things that go beyond persons."

Indeed, "inheritance" seems to have certain deterministic aspects that turns it into "destiny," which in the braña is thought to be directed by God. Suicide is thus a moral expiation, a settling of accounts with the heavenly court, either for one's own debts or for those of prior members of the house. Possession of the house thereby supposes not only certain material objects but also these old faults, which can be redeemed only by obeying the Ten Commandments. I will treat religion at length in a later chapter, but I note here that the loss of life in itself is considered sufficient punishment for the person who commits suicide and further expiation in the "other world" is not expected. After death, suicides are distinguished from those who have died naturally only by certain acts carried out by the civil and religious authorities; the Vaqueiros consider these acts efforts to discourage others from doing the same thing. Here is how the Vaqueiros describe these differences:

> And you know that they can't put those who commit suicide in the church either. That's right; the persons who commit suicide, hang themselves, or shoot themselves or things like that, they aren't put in the church. You know that they take dead bodies to the church. Well, I went to X to the

burial, and they didn't put it in the church. He hanged himself in a cherry tree there by the house. They say that such persons find themselves *arrepentidos.*

With them it's different. Sometimes they have to go to the cemetery and so autopsy, and open their heads. I've never seen that and I hope to God I never do, because it's bad to see it, but they have to lift up the lid on the brains.

In addition to the specific motives given as causes for suicide, local explanations often point to a process called *aburrimiento,* a concept I generally have left untranslated. The situations that this term refers to include all of those that may lead Vaqueiros to end their lives: the people of the *braña se aburren* because of sickness, because they cannot defend themselves, when they see "the bad things in the houses," or see "everything going wrong"; because there are people "who pick on them" in the house when they are old, because of the "problems of life" when they are young, and because of loneliness, lack of money, debts, and even "the nerves." All of these negative aspects of Vaqueiro life produce, individually or in combination, a state of mind that begins with the loss of *gracia,* disinterest in life, and culminates with an abhorrence of life.

That's it—they see that they are *aburríos* of life. No, they're not wrong in the head, no, I think they see that they are *aburríos, aburríos.*

They see that they are *aburríos* of life. They see they are *aburridos* and so they say, "So, I'll do this to end it." *Ay Dios!* They have to be in a bad way, a bad way in order to do it.

Life is *gracia*—interest in things, activity, and struggle; *aburrimiento* means being tired, irked, and loathing life. It is associated with the state of *arrepentimiento,* an express renunciation of living. The Vaqueiro *arrepentido* finds death is the only solution.

No, the one who does it is considerably *arrepentío. Arrepentío* is when one is worn out, *aburrío,* when one is not able to go out to another town, or do anything else, when one thinks about it, when one is oppressed by the idea of it, when it seems that it is the best solution, when one finds oneself forced to do it.

When that happens, it'll be because they are *arrepentíos;* they don't have another solution, and they find themselves alone, and they *se aburren* and they come to that. *Hombre,* I feel they don't have any other choice because in order for them to hang themselves they have to be really *arrepentíos.*

Aburrimiento is evidence of the stress, conflicts, and inequalities of the inheritance system. But in some way the violence is inevitable. The family system here and everywhere is always arbitrary; it solves some problems and it creates others. If the loss of *gracia* follows a gradual and natural process of disinterest and disillusion with life, *aburrimiento* implies that this process is hastened. Although physically alive, the *arrepentidos*, once they have lost *gracia*, can be considered as socially and cognitively dead. So suicides properly hurry on their own death. Living, in certain circumstances, makes no sense. Death is a flight from pain and human suffering.

Well, they are people who are cowards, who *se arrepienten*, who give up. Seeing myself in this situation. . . . Because you have to have *valor* for that . . . you have to be *arrepentío*.

I don't know what they think. They think, "Perhaps if I end my life, I'll end my suffering, I won't suffer anymore." Leaving is a way of getting out of the way.

In the next chapters I will examine where the Vaqueiros go when they "leave."

4

The Burial

PROCEDURES OF DEATH

Once it has been ascertained according to local standards that a Vaqueiro is dead, the body is immediately dressed for burial. This process must take place quickly: those around the corpse overcome their sorrow and prepare the body for its last journey before it stiffens.

Those in charge of dressing the body are likely to be the bravest or the least affected of the relatives. They are generally of the same sex as the deceased and are usually directed by an older, experienced person. In all of the *brañas* there has always been somebody "handy" at manipulation of corpses who has become an authentic specialist in the art of laying out the dead. They are likely to be older men and women with a certain serenity, who do this task efficiently and selflessly when asked.

There has always been a grave-digger and a man who dressed the dead. Old M, they always called him for the dressing. There were always one or two women, too, like old C; they would be for the dead women. There was always someone who knew how to do it.

No, it doesn't scare me at all. And the grandparents here, my parents-in-law, I dressed them, and I felt like I was dressing them when they were alive. I wasn't afraid at all. And my own parents, I also helped to dress them, and around here, when they call me. I've seen a lot of people die, that's for sure. It's not that I want to do it, but I'm not afraid to, either.

Amortajar, like English verb *to lay out,* refers not only to dressing the corpse but also to preparing it—shaving it if it is a man, washing and combing it, making it as presentable and dignified as possible. The person who lays out the corpse must also close its mouth and eyes. Special problems are posed when the body is swollen or deformed. The body is handled with a certain respect and tenderness.

My mother and my aunt dressed her. My aunt put a handkerchief on her that could be adjusted, because otherwise she would have had her mouth open. And they lowered her eyes because they were wide open. They had a terrible time putting on the dress, because it was a little small for her. Mother wanted to put a skirt on her because the dress wouldn't go on, and we were going to injure her. And C said—she's like a burro—"Since she's dead, she won't feel a thing." And I said, "Yes, you wouldn't feel it, but that doesn't mean you have to hurt her." And she said, "Whatever it is, she doesn't feel it now." And so, by pulling carefully, they got it on.

The dead are dressed in their very best clothes. The old folks often go out with the outfit that they first wore for the marriage of a grandchild or an exceptional trip to the city. Even the poorest people have an abundant stock of clothes in good condition that their relatives in the city have sent them at Christmas. They select the best of this almost new clothing for their laying out. If they do not have clothes deemed good enough for the occasion, new clothing is bought in advance. The dead must wear their best, for it is the last time they will be dressed up. Those who die young are dressed with special elegance by their parents, almost as if they were dressed for marriage. The following quote concerns a young man who died in an accident:

May X rest in peace. They bought a new suit for him, didn't they? His father bought it. His mother had brought him clothes from here [to the hospital], and his father told her, "Burn those clothes or throw them in the river; buy him a suit." When it was said that he was very bad off, when he was already in a coma and could not recover, she said [to another son], "A, take him his clothes." And A said to her, "No, these clothes I won't take. I'll go and buy others." And he told his father, who told him, "Yes, buy him new clothes from head to toe, for it's the last time he'll be dressed up." And they bought him new clothes from head to toe. Shoes, pants, coat, shirt, and everything he needed, undershirt and all. His father bought it.

The family's desire that the deceased be well groomed is an expression of affection, one of many in the funeral process. One must present oneself correctly dressed in the other world, as when one goes to the city, emigrates, or gets married. The trip to eternity is the last time that the members of the deceased's household can thank and bid farewell to one of its own.

They say that we go to another world, that we have to sleep in the bed that was with us in our lives, in the bed that will be with us for good, for one does not change where you are going once you are dead. That if you change your bed or your place, you do it when you are alive, but that once you're dead it's forever, the bed is forever, forever more. You see how they ask to have the most expensive funeral so that the priests sing and all, and that they be bought the best coffin and be dressed in new clothes. About those who don't marry [before they die] they say, "Poor guy, that good suit he's wearing is for his wedding and his funeral." It's the one he'll wear forever.

An elegant laying out is also a matter of social pride. Vaqueiros are surprised that other peoples wrap their dead in a shroud. Yet the oldest people remember that the shroud in fact used to be the traditional garment for the last voyage of the old-time Vaqueiros. When one old Vaqueiro asked to be shrouded after death, his family did not fulfill his wish out of fear of community criticism.

About when they were wrapped in sheets, and if they did it—we weren't old enough to see it, although I heard about it. S, A's grandfather, always said that he wanted to be wrapped in a sheet when he died, that he wanted to go out like in the old days. . . . But no, no, they didn't wrap him up, because the family didn't want to; but he did ask for it. And what difference would it make if they wrapped him in a sheet or if he went with a suit and tie, since it's all the same. . . . But now you have to dress him as well as possible. . . . Because in the old days . . . they didn't have many clothes, and furthermore it was easier . . . to dress them, so they wrapped them in sheets . . . but his family, so that everyone wouldn't talk about it, dressed him up as is the custom, because people could have said, "*Coño*, look at him, how they're throwing him out that way."

Once a cadaver is dressed, it is placed so it can be visited by relatives, friends, and neighbors. First the corpse is stretched out on a board, bench, or other smooth, flat surface until the coffin arrives. This generally takes place in the bedroom of the deceased, if there is one, or one of the more intimate areas of the living or sleeping quarters. Sometimes the deceased is covered with a sheet. While the body is in the house, it is always surrounded by light from candles or an oil lamp. Vaqueiros insist that light is needed to illuminate both death and life, literalizing a religious metaphor.

We put a candle to burn all night, or an old lamp. They say, "God give us light in death or in life." A dead person is in a house for two days. In the old days there was no electric lighting, but it seemed like a kind of protection to have a candle there at the bedside, yes, day and night. As soon as one burned down, you would light another and so on, or an oil lamp.

The custom of illuminating the dead, while a religious practice, was not so different from lighting the house in the *brañas*, where there was no electricity until recently. Wax is used in different rituals—the blessing of animals, the payment of promises, wax votive offerings and so on. It also has a central place in death. Vaqueiros traditionally received a good number of large candles from their relatives in Madrid to light up the dead on Holy Thursday.

Before they set aside a candle to light up the corpses. Now they set aside oil when there are no candles. Always light so as not to leave the dead in the dark the entire night. Now there is electricity, but before there were no electric lights . . . but there was wax; in our house there were always many thick candles from Madrid. These was a custom of always sending them the day of Holy Thursday. They came in crates, crates of thick candles; those who went to Madrid sent back wax like this, lots of it; there was enough for all of the houses.

A body is completely prepared once it is in the coffin. Coffins used to be made in the *braña* or ordered from local carpenters, but according to the oldest inhabitants, for many years now coffins have been bought in the funeral parlors of neighboring towns. Nevertheless, when small children died, a common occurrence in the past, those handy at carpentry in the *braña* immediately set to work.

I remember my father making coffins for children. F also knows how to make them. And they laid them inside with flowers, each dressed as well as possible. They went out to get the coffins for adults, but they made the coffins for children here, the small ones, because it wasn't worth buying them, they were so small. I don't even know if they stocked them in the town. I never went to buy one. They make them with thin boards, as tight as possible, and line them with cloth, blue for boys and pink for girls. In the old days so many used to die . . . they were nice little coffins.

Once the body has been laid out, feverish activity begins in the *braña*. If neighbors are unaware of the death, they are informed at the same time that preliminary funeral arrangements are made. The first step is "to be with the priest." A direct relative of the deceased will go to the parish church with another relative or neighbor while other neighbors stay with the family and the deceased. It is essential to visit the priest first, for he decides the exact day and time of the funeral, information that then will be communicated to the neighboring *brañas*. Notification is usually verbal, delivered by someone either on mule or horseback, or on foot.

Boys would go to spread the word, maybe those who went for the coffin. A boy would go on foot or horseback to the *brañas* of F and C and tell the first person he met. You say, "Please pass the word along that so-and-so has died, and the funeral is on such-and-such a day." Those who could would notify two or three places, for there could be relatives in several places. That's how it is done.

Today funeral notices are posted in shops and meeting places by those who used to spread the word in person. Of course, death is also communicated to much of the parish by the tolling of the bells of the parish church, and to the immediate *braña* by the laments of the family of the deceased.

Now you just go to Luarca and put up the notices on all the doors and that's it. But in the old days there were no printed notices, and someone had to go around and tell people that their uncle or grandfather had died. And one or two had to go be with the priest so that the bells would be tolled, "ton, ton, ton. . ." If a person was afraid to go alone, someone went with him. They told the first inhabitants they came across. In the village itself there was no need to tell anybody, because you could already hear family members sobbing and crying out in the house. You could even hear from C [neighboring *braña*] the people crying and lamenting.

The whole village would come; they'd leave their cows and everything to come to the house.

Depending on the time at which the death occurred, the body remains in the house about forty-eight hours before burial. During this time the neighbors perform the essential outside chores of the house in mourning, such as milking the cows, feeding the animals, or cutting the hay, especially if there are not enough family members or they are particularly affected by the death. During the daytime people come and go continuously, but it is at night that the house of the dead person becomes packed and the wake begins. To the wake [*velorio*] come first of all the inhabitants of the *braña* and of the neighboring *brañas*. These people often come sooner than the deceased's relatives, who sometimes have to travel long distances to get there. The number of people who come to a given house depends on their relation to the deceased, the degree of friendship or physical proximity, and the status and age of the deceased. The minimal delegation to a wake is at least "one from each house." In my experience, many people come from each house, and sometimes everyone in the *braña* comes. One attends the wake to express interest in and deference to the family of the deceased. The wake is an attempt to be with and console the living, and to stay up with the dead. If necessary, the villagers will set up a relay system to accomplish these tasks, in local parlance, "doing the mourning with the family" or "helping them mourn."

At the wake were the relatives and someone from each house. [On the evening of the wake] people would stay at home awhile, talk a little, and then say, "Right, let's go, we aren't doing anything here. The one who died is all ready by now, and this woman or this man is very upset, and we should not leave him or her alone." One or two or three people would stay with the people of the house until dawn. But not where the body was, rather in the kitchen, and they would talk there and wait for sunrise. And then they would say, "All right, it's all over, dear, don't cry, things have to be done right, and all will pass." Of course, those in sorrow weep, as is normal. They are the ones who stay to do the mourning with the family, to help them mourn.

Velorio also means spending the night with the body. The custom was stricter until a few years ago, but it has been relaxed to a certain extent today. Relatives and neighbors generally organize relays so that the body is not left alone. While the sick Vaqueiro is alive, everyone will visit him or her, but once the Vaqueiro is dead, only family members have the obligation to attend to and be with the dead body. Others outside the family receive a polite invitation to look at the body, which some accept and others do not. People's attitudes toward cadavers vary according to the condition of the body, but in general there is a certain fear or awe of dead bodies, both on the part of relatives and nonrelatives. In relatives, this fear is mixed with sorrow for the departed.

> Before, yes, before one stayed helping to . . . to watch them. I was scared; all I wanted to do was to leave. I couldn't stand to see people dead like that. I got a kind of fear inside me, something . . . that would wake me up in the night. I remember one day my sister said, the wife of S [weeping]: "Look, look at Daddy, for we won't see him again." I couldn't. One time a baby girl died in my house and I stayed up with her. Maybe I was ten years old. And my father had to deal with all the work, the animals, and the children. And that baby, I went to look at her, and I lifted the sheet a little to see how she looked [weeps], and I felt so sad . . . a terrible sadness came into me.

Death was much closer in the past, literally as well as metaphorically. The old houses in the *braña* had only one room, which served as both kitchen and bedroom, or had at most a kitchen and a *sala*, the family bedroom, where the dead was laid out. So if anyone wanted to lie down for awhile they were perforce close to the body. What this informant describes still occurs today:

> At the wake my aunt remained—how brave she was— she was a little woman, and she slept there with a dead body; in another bed, but still it's really something, in the same house. He was her uncle, and she slept in the *sala*, in the same house. I get very frightened when I see a body out of a coffin like that.

The bravest Vaqueiros will approach the deceased to see whether he or she is correctly dressed and laid out. Most are torn between curiosity to see the condition of the body and its attire, and fear of seeing its decay. This fear varies with age: the oldest people acquire a certain experience with death that gives them a sense of serenity the youngest lack. Fear of seeing the body is mingled with sorrow. At the sight of the body, depending on the degree of friendship or kinship, those at the wake express their grief with abundant tears and cries that spread to others, especially when one of the immediate family members arrives. Everyone shares the sorrow in the case of the death of the young; it is more limited and restrained for the very old who die after a prolonged sickness.

DEATH

Then there are cases that people weep according to the type of dead person. If the deceased was young, his absence was greatly felt [*queda mucha decobertura*] . . . of course, everyone is sadder; and if it is an old person who had already been sick for many years, then people are used to the idea, and don't get so sad about it.

One of the most important aspects of the wake is collective praying. The word *velorio* becomes synonymous with praying in certain contexts. No matter how short a visit people make to the wake, very few leave without participating in collective prayer, which might range from a rosary to a few Our Fathers, according to the tastes and preferences of the persons in charge of directing the prayers. Those who direct the prayers are generally specialists.

One went to pray the rosary, at the wake, to pray. There was always someone, man or woman, from the village who knew how to pray better than the others and would say, "*Bueno*, silence." One would go to where the dead was laid out, on some boards or in a coffin, and there one prayed. But then, after one was there praying some Our Fathers or something, then the person who had nothing [no kinship] with the dead, who was just a neighbor, would go home and the relatives would remain.

Now M's girl is the one who prays very well; they call her to the wake when someone dies and everyone comes to pray. When my sister died it was a beautiful night; it was a full moon, and the house and the yard were full of people. And M's girl prayed for the soul of the dead. She prayed a lot; she knows how to do it well.

As people express sorrow for death, they reaffirm life. After the initial grief, the prayers for the dead, and the solemn and sorrowful stances, the wake little by little becomes a social gathering. The thirty or so persons who attend end up chatting in the kitchen about any number of subjects, which might range from cattle, to local gossip, to memories of the dead person and other deaths, and even jokes and anecdotes. This kind of conversation is interrupted periodically by relatives of the dead arriving from distant parts and showing their sorrow. At such moments, the others readjust their demeanor and carry themselves more soberly, but such interruptions are short. The Vaqueiros themselves are well aware of this shift from death to life.

[At a wake] you can talk about whatever you want, about cows, or calves, or people, or anything. About the deceased as well, about his last words, his suffering or . . . well, you wouldn't talk about weddings, though, in fact, you even talk about them, too.

Food and drink are one special aspect of this reaffirmation of life at the time of death. In the past, feasting was as integral a part of the wake as prayers for the dead. The great banquets organized in the *braña* when somebody died have disappeared, but they are still remembered. These wake banquets [called *funciones*] were prepared as soon as the death occurred. The Vaqueiro would go to the stable and slaughter a ram or a sheep, or a number of them if necessary, and the women would make bread. The village women who specialized in cooking would help out.

I remember that in the old days when a person died they used to have a big meal in the house. They would go to the stable—in those days all of the houses had sheep—and they would kill a flock of rams. They would get rye flour and knead it and make bread, and get together a big . . . when there was a body in the house. I remember one of those in X's house. I don't know whether it was his father or his grandfather, but I remember one of those affairs, yes, a big meal that they gave like that. Then they said some Our Fathers or whatever. People came from neighboring *brañas*, but the meal was mainly for the people of the village and some of the closest relatives. They gave the feast while the body was in the house. There was one woman here who always did the cooking. And it was always A who did the praying.

Although, as we shall see, there are other meals in the course of the funeral, that of the wake was the first and the most intimate. Those present, neighbors and closest relatives, were those who have maintained the most frequent and closest contact with the deceased.

No, I think [the *función* of] R's father was the last one given here. I remember I was in F [*braña*] and they gave a dinner, with meat and everything, for people of the village and some from B [very close *braña*] as well. Yes, for a meal at night like that they invite those of the village. People from F and B are just as though they were from the same place; if someone dies in one of them, the others go to the wake.

Eating still plays a part in the wake but in a form much diminished compared to that more splendid past. Now guests are offered soup, coffee, chocolate, bread, wine, and above all liqueurs, brandy and anisette. At one wake I attended, in spite of the fact that the guests had already had supper, about thirty persons were given a soup cooked with ham, and sliced ham with bread and wine. The family of the dead man served the food with these words, "He is all set; we have to eat." Relatives from outside the *braña*—it was a sudden death—brought some bottles of anisette and brandy with them, which were finished off. The present tendency is to suppress all special food at the wake, which has been simplified and abbreviated. But the discomfort of staying up all night in the cold is part of the reason for these offerings.

Here, before the burial, people come at night to the wake. All night. One from each house. But when T died, and it got real cold right before dawn, S, a son of the dead woman, said, "Everybody can go home; it's too cold here." And in that case the dead woman would have been left alone. But normally the custom is to stay until morning. They serve some brandy or coffee or something. For the nights are long and you have to warm your body. Towards dawn it gets so cold that you give up. The people are in the kitchen, and the dead one is alone with a candle.

When dawn comes, activity begins again in the house. Those at the wake go to their homes, those who have slept a little awaken, and everyone gets ready for the new day, the day of the funeral.

Vaqueiro burials occasion the gathering of great numbers of persons from a wide geographical area, usually from a number of parishes. The inhabitants of the *aldeas*, who frequently criticize the Vaqueiros' lack of church attendance, admit that exceptional numbers attend Vaqueiro funerals.

Vaqueiros went for years without going to mass. They came [to the *aldea*] only to buy things and for funerals. When someone died in B [*braña*], every last one of them came. It is something special.

Every funeral does not command the same attendance. Generally, the death of a newborn child, especially in the past when infant mortality was high, does not draw more than the closest relatives in the area. The death of an *amo* will draw many more people than that of a unmarried uncle. The funeral of a youth, because it is unusual and striking, also gathers a large cortege.

Let us look at some norms regulating funeral attendance. *Braña* neighbors and close relatives make up the largest contingent at a funeral. If the latter are from a different *braña*, all able-bodied adult members of the house will come. If necessary, their neighbors will do their chores for them as they do in the immediate household of the deceased. Neighbors theoretically attend in small numbers, a minimal representation, but in practice their attendance is much more extensive. It frequently happens that the *brañas* are virtually depopulated for a funeral. Thus day-to-day relations and contacts determine, to a large extent, attendance at the final farewell. The solidarity shown when death takes place brooks no exceptions. Those quarrels that impede the entrance to the deceased's house, and even, at times, to a wake, disappear in the more impersonal context of a funeral.

The entire village and all the relatives go to the funeral. If [the deceased] is from the village, everyone who can has to go. . . . If I am upset with someone when he is alive, I don't visit him, but if he dies, then I do, even if I continue at odds with his family. When someone dies, you go to the funeral and give your condolences, that's for sure.

The neighboring *brañas* maintain a more diffuse level of interaction and contact. More diffuse still is the interaction of the *brañas* of the parish as a whole, then that of the market centers of the parish. The deceased's contacts in these spheres are obligated to pay their respects [*cumplir*] at a funeral. There are those from these wider spheres who, because of their professions have regular relations with Vaqueiros, for example, mailmen or utility collectors. This includes the people from the *aldea* with whom a Vaqueiro has normal business, such as bartenders and shopkeepers. The fidelity of such relations over generations has established ties such as being the godfather at a Vaqueiro wedding.

Aldeanos! . . . Hombre! of course, if we have friendships with them. I have seen them come to the door of a dead person's house to accompany the coffin when there is some friendship, as with the owner of a bar where [Vaqueiros] spend and drink. Because of the funeral notices, all this has changed a lot. Now they distribute the notice so you will go to [funerals at] N or P [*aldeas*]. Of course, if you have a deeper friendship it's different—you go by the house and you pay your respects as well.

Going by the house of the deceased before the funeral and accompanying the body in the funeral procession implies a special level of friendship. Those who do not have particularly strong ties wait for the funeral cortege in the parish church. There is even an intermediary position: waiting for the body halfway along the route and accompanying it part of the way.

Many people who attend the funeral never knew the deceased at all but are friends with some member of the household. The death notices include in large letters after the name of the deceased the traditional name of his or her house. At a funeral, then, one is not saying farewell to an acquaintance (it might be someone too old or too young to have known the person well) as much as fulfilling one's obligations to a household. The number of people from each house who attend the funeral is another indication of the level of friendship, geographical proximity, or kinship. Normally, one person from each house is the minimum delegation [la representación], but there is a standard of reciprocity: one must send as many persons to a house as they have sent to yours. Many people come from the native braña of the deceased, even if he left the braña at marriage and lived most of his life somewhere else. They also go to a funeral of the father or an immediate family member of a woman who married into the braña. In both cases, a minimal delegation is sent from each house.

Those who are neighbors, relatives from afar, and friends—three or four hundred come. The villagers come, one or two from each house, even if they are not on speaking terms. If it is a girl from this village who married outside, only one goes from each house, not two . . . only if they are related will they send two, or whoever has to go. Now if this girl marries into another village and her father dies here, then one person will come to the funeral here from each of the houses in the other village. And when those from here go out, someone has to stay behind to look after the animals.

In the case of physical incapacity, funeral attendance may be delegated to sons, nephews, or legatees who represent the house of the incapacitated person. This is made explicit when one delivers condolences. With these norms of attendance, Vaqueiro funerals are very large. Although the number of people varies according to the social standing of the deceased, in normal circumstances, there are rarely fewer than 150 persons. I have counted as many as four hundred persons at some funerals. Considering that many houses send only single representatives, very few are not represented.

The funeral is a manifestation and ratification of the widest and most diffuse bonds of friendship, neighborhood, and kinship, in contrast to the wake, which marks the most reduced and intimate of these kinds of relations. Persons attending funerals, with the exception of relatives from the cities, usually Madrid, Oviedo, and Gijón, come from a wide radius of several kilometers within the area studied. It is said that more people than ever come to funerals now, doubtless due to the spread of automobiles in the *brañas*. In the old days people came on horse, mule, or on foot; for this reason they came from shorter distances. It also meant that they were more likely to be men, because they had more practice in horseback riding and were more accustomed to walking long distances. Many people still come by horse or mule, but cars have diversified and increased the attendance at funerals. Whether people come in their own cars or in taxis, the cars are usually jammed, and doubtless have increased the average number attending from each household. Of course, a large funeral is a matter of pride and consolation for the family of the deceased. Long afterwards they recount the number of cars and people who came as a proof of the importance of the house and interest in the deceased. They take special note of the number of members attending from each house in case of future funerals. But in the old days there was a particular reason why the crowds of today would not have been so welcome.

In the old days fewer people came. . . . For then they served food, and that's why there were fewer people. They served bread and wine. Certain people were informed that if they wanted to they could come to the burial and have bread and wine; if people were not invited, they didn't go down. They've gotten rid of that now. At the masses of this village they give out bread, wine, and coffee, but nowhere else.

People remember funerals as gastronomic occasions on the same level as weddings. On the morning of the burial, following the banquet given during the wake, in addition to neighbors and close relatives, everyone who was going to accompany the funeral processions to the church would reassemble at the house. And all would eat lunch at the house of the deceased.

Funerals were very different than they are now. Over in E [*braña*], a funeral was like a wedding. They served lunch on the funeral day. They cooked up several kettles of food for those who came from far away, and coffee with milk, wine, and a liqueur for those who come in the morning—anisette or brandy. In the old days they would kill a sheep and serve it to all the people who came in the morning.

The menu varied according to fashion or the wealth of the house. In later years, the meal was reduced to bread and wine, although more food was probably given to those who came from far away. Young adults recall having had bread and wine in the house before the body was taken out. The custom has been discontinued in some places; in others it continues. A further stage in the reduction of food offerings was the serving of bread alone, called the *carito,* in some places. An almost religious care is taken to distribute the *carito* in equal portions. In addition to those who gather at the house to accompany the body, the *carito* is given to all of the houses in the *braña* of the deceased, taking account of the number of persons of each house, including those sick or absent.

When my father and my mother died, the baker-women were called, and they made some enormous breads. El C, who was an old man, was the one who cut up the bread at funerals; there was nobody like him for doing it. If there were six people, he would go like this and that, and right off cut six very equal portions. He would say, "Let's see, in V's house there are six, these six *caritos"*—they called it the *carito.* If it was all they could afford, they just gave out bread. If they had a couple of bottles of wine, one red and the other white, and couple of glasses, and they gave a glass to the people who came for the *carito.* They would send a kid at night to the houses to spread the word. . . . And someone might say, "In my house there are only four because the other one is in Los C or Las T [transhumant *brañas*]." And the man at the head of the table cutting the bread would say, "Well, he gets a *carito,* too." They took it home and ate it gratefully, because in those days there was want in the houses.

The *carito* was also called *limosna* [alms] or *caridad* [charity]. It was a kind of alms given in the name of the deceased to all neighbors and relatives, and because it was given from a dead person, it could not be refused. Those who received it evoked the dead.

No, the *carito* could not be turned down. They said that you had to take that piece of bread; that even if you didn't eat it, you had to take it home. Because it was handed out as if it was from the dead person, and people wanted you to take it. They would put it in a shoulder sack, saying, "*Vaya por el alma del difunto, por las obligaciones que fueron de la casa."* That is, for the soul of the dead and for all obligations of those from that house who had died. People went to collect this alms on the morning of the day of burial.

The ritual that surrounds the giving of the *carito,* the specialist who cuts the bread at the head of the table, its distribution to the entire *braña,* the obligation to accept it and recite a prayer in memory of the dead—all suggest that the custom is quasi-religious. In fact, today Vaqueiros say that this meal or *carito,* can be replaced by a mass. Furthermore, sometimes the priest who climbed up to the *braña* to go with the body was invited to bless these foods, although not all of them agreed to do it. The similarity of the bread and wine with the communion ritual is evident. In the second quote, a priest speaks:

> When somebody died a meal was given for the whole village and those who came from the outside; it was like alms for the soul of the person who died; now they give a mass.

> At the funerals here they ate bread, wine, and ham. And I blessed it. It was for the house; some of the dead willed it. An Our Father was prayed for the dead and for the obligations of the house.

In addition to its spiritual side as an offering from and to the dead, the meal serves more earthly purposes for the living. In the past, accompanying and carrying the body from the *braña* to the parish church was not just a gesture of courtesy; it was hard work that demanded compensation. Until recently, the coffins were carried on the shoulders of those attending the funeral, and such efforts, over long distances and often in bad weather, are remembered as nightmares. Now automobiles can reach the *brañas*, on dirt roads, and they carry the bodies. This is one of the reasons why those who attend the funeral no longer have as much need for food.

> They used to give food to people on the day of the funeral, but not anymore. . . . They fed the people who went down to M [location of parish church] on the funeral day because the coffin was heavy; it had to be carried on the shoulders, and sometimes it was snowing. When X's wife's first husband died (now she lives with his brother), it was snowing and sleeting, dearie, and they carried him to N, the priest going as fast as he could, and everyone else, too. When they got to L, they could go on by road, and it was raining, snowing, and sleeting, and their hands were freezing from carrying that man on their shoulders as far as N. But now a hearse comes to pick them up here, by the dirt road they've made, and it's all changed. Before, they would spell each other on the way to the burial, sharing the burden equally. They gave out food, and A says it's good that the custom stopped. People were very poor, and they had to feed those who went with a dead body to N when they really needed the food for themselves. The night before a funeral they started getting everything ready and cooking the meat for the morning.

Let us examine the Vaqueiro's last journey. The funeral is a ceremony controlled from the outside from the moment a priest arrives at the dead person's house to begin the trip with the body. Today the priest comes with some altar boys, but until recently he often came with some townspeople and especially the sexton. The sexton served as a mediator between the priest and the laity, and between *braña* and *aldea* where he carried news and gossip about the Vaqueiros.

They would say to the sexton, "At B, in such-and-such a house, I believe that they were very sad about so-and-so." And he would say, "Oh, they cry better than down here; I climbed up by way of A to B [*braña*], and you could hear them all the way, mother of my soul!" And the people would laugh.

As soon as the priest arrived at the house, after the usual greetings, he would sing the first responses in front of the dead body. The meal is not the only offering at a funeral, for the Vaqueiros pay for each response in coins as it is sung. This alms is thought to go to the deceased by way of the priest.

. . . before taking the body out of the house, when some Our Fathers were recited and the *arresponso* was given. The money all went to the priest. The altar boy or the kids went around for money because the priest told them to, and people would give maybe a *duro*, maybe a peseta each. People from the household would give more. One does this in order to do things right; maybe it has no effect at all, but one thinks that one can set things right by this, that when one gives more the deceased will be better off.

The time when the cadaver crosses the threshold to leave the house is particularly painful for family members, who express their sorrow with copious tears and expressive gestures. The family members most affected, especially the women, are advised to stay at home rather than go to the funeral. The departure of the cadaver from the house is typically accompanied by the singing of the priest and the chorus of lamentations of the family members.

Nosotras llorar y el cura cantar—we cry and the priest sings, is what I used to say when I was young [says a woman, laughing]. The priest came for the funeral to the house. And he went out singing and we went out crying.

There are strict guidelines regulating who carries the deceased out of the house. For a newborn child it is the godmother, or the woman who would have been the godmother, who carries the coffin on her head. For children and unmarried youths, it is comrades of the same age and sex. In all these cases, the coffin is white. When the deceased is an adult or is married at present, the closest male family members must carry the body out of the house, if they are strong enough. For the child who is dead pertains to his or her age and sex group of peers, and for adults, the bonds of family and matrimony are determinant. While immediate family members carry the dead adult out of the house and into the church or cemetery, between these points neighbors and more distant relatives take over (or used to, since the body now goes in a hearse). Women attend the funerals, but it is not considered appropriate for them to carry the coffin. Some Vaqueiros do not remember precisely whether in the old days, when coffins were carried on the shoulders, members of the household would take it out of the house and into the church. But they are sure that during the trip the body was *not* carried by close relatives. It appears that the weight of the sorrow exempted those who had lost a loved one from carrying the physical weight of the body.

Yes, on your shoulders, that was the worst of it. In the old days family members didn't carry the coffin; now they do. At least I remember that my father went to a funeral at my mother's house in F, and it was my grandmother who had died, a woman as big around as this table; and bodies had to be carried very far, to B, and I believe that in this case the people had to spell each other after short stretches. They said, "This can't be done unless more people come; she can't be carried," because she weighed so much and it was so far. And my father went to carry her, and someone said, "Don't you carry it; I'll do it for you." I don't remember who it was. No, family members did not pick up the coffin. That would not have been considered right . . . it would have been thought to cause them grief. They might say, "These people have already enough to deal with; not them."

While today carrying the dead is considered a privilege and a sign of deference, it was formerly a burden and an obligation. It was not a pleasant walk from the remote and badly connected *brañas* along small, winding paths. Those who did not carry the coffin accompanied the slow procession on foot or on horseback.

All of the *brañas* have a special path always used for the last journey of the dead, known as the *camino sacramental.* At certain points, people from nearby villages who had not gone all the way up to the *braña* joined the cortege. Today these paths are used only in those very few places that are still not accessible by car, or by anyone who has to go down to the *aldea* on foot. Nevertheless, there are some people who remember the old customs with nostalgia.

Yes, there was a *camino sacramental*. Now it's overgrown, and they go by the road. Now it's taken down by [the hearse called] *"La Pena."* When it was by the path it was on men's shoulders. There is a lady here almost one hundred years old; she had a fall and has trouble walking, but she's got a strong and healthy stomach. She says that when she dies she doesn't want any car to come for her. Because when another woman died, her body went off alone in the hearse and that the right way to go is on the *camino sacramental*. She doesn't want to go on any road; she wants to go on the old path, so that the people will go with her. Otherwise, she'll go off in the car and the people by the shortcut.

Those who accompany the dead also complain, since there are never enough cars, and many still have to go on foot or by horseback. Those who go on foot have to hurry in order to keep up with the hearse, and the cortege ends up rather disordered and bedraggled.

In spite of the difficulty of the terrain, the practice of carrying of the body on men's shoulders involved great solemnity and had a certain ritual character. At certain points, known by tradition and generally corresponding to crossing paths, the carriers stopped and were replaced by others. At these times, the priest would recite some responses. At each stop where responses were said, people would give alms according to their degree of friendship with the deceased, just as they did when responses were recited in the house. Popular opinion has it that the priest would lengthen or abbreviate his prayers according to the amount of alms given.

We would stop at the crossroads and the coffin was put down and some Our Fathers were prayed. There were eight or ten stops and responses were prayed—responses are said by the priest and would consist of Our Fathers and Hail Marys. Now they don't do this. Before when the priest came for a body in the village, the coffin was put down at certain places and the priest began to pray and pass the hat, and he went with a little hammer, hitting what the people threw in with it, and depending on how much money he had, he prayed so many Our Fathers, Hail Marys and Gloria Patris—that is, responses. And as soon as they stopped contributing there, he would say, "All right, let's go," and they picked up the coffin again and were on their way. And again the coffin was put down, and the people began to throw in *duros* again . . . no, not *duros*, pesetas and *reales*, for in those days . . . (laughs). Eh, María, one person spent one thousand *duros!*

Both in the old days and at present, the customs quickly become uniform, as new advances are adopted by everyone even in the smallest detail. One Vaqueiro, more original than his neighbors, wanted a very different funeral, a happy one.

How many times my grandfather said, "Have me taken away in a cart with bagpipes; the cart singing and the bagpipes playing." He ordered that on the day of his burial that we not mourn for him or weep, that his family should not sorrow because he had died . . . he liked the pipes very much.

What happened is that in his house they were going to do it, as he wanted . . . but his children came from Madrid and said, "No way, *hombre*, this is shameful, how can we do this? Here we will have a funeral according to local custom; we're not going to do something ridiculous [*hacer el indio*] because this man was off his rocker." They said he was soft in the head, and they didn't do it because of the children. But they wanted to do it, for what difference is there between a piper playing and a priest singing? It's the same. He's dead now. They should have done as he had instructed, but people get afraid.

In the *aldea* the last mourners join the funeral cortege, and all proceed to the parish church. Some *aldeanos* wait for the body at the door of the church, and family members carry the coffin inside. There the funeral is performed. In the past there were three classes of funerals, corresponding to the economic position of the deceased, with the type of coffin, the paraphernalia of the burial, and the performance of the mass (number of priests, vestments, etc.) varying accordingly. Today there is a uniform service, although there are still noticeable differences depending on the number of people present, the number of wreathes, and so on. Identical funerals are performed with the body absent for all persons born in the zone who have died elsewhere, whether in different regions, Spanish cities, or abroad. Each house is obliged to say good-bye to its dead in this way, even though the deceased left the house long ago.

After the religious ceremony, the procession continues to the cemetery. As final benedictions are said, the body is put into the grave. Graves were dug in the earth until recently in most places (and in a few places still are), but today people are usually buried in niches. When the coffin is lowered into the grave, those present

DEATH

throw a handful of dirt upon it. This widespread custom has the following local meaning.

> People had the custom of taking a handful of earth and throwing it on the coffin. They said it was a good sign to do this, that it would make it easier to go to heaven, or something like that. . . . Anyway, I saw others do it and I did it, too; don't ask me why. They said that the earth of the graveyard is holy, and that's why they picked it up. They said, "The day you die I will throw the first fistful of dirt on you." Someone who liked you would say that.

After the burial, the immediate family members of the deceased thank those who attended and say good-bye. The women kiss other women and shake hands with the men in front of the grave. Men who know each other will embrace. All present mumble *"Te acompaño en el sentimiento,"* or something similar, and the family members reply with thanks. Then the family members return to their homes. The funeral would seem to be over, but it is not. Once again there is a dinner.

Let us consider the traditional customs. The oldest people remember two varieties of postburial dinners in the *aldea*. Some meals were prepared in the *braña* and eaten somewhere, maybe in a meadow, near the church; others were ordered and consumed in a commercial establishment of the *aldea*. All who attended the burial were invited.

> The day a person died, in this house or another, in S [transhumant pasture] what they would do is grind some wheat and make it into bread, and then they brought down to the cemetery one or more entire fatbacks, cooked, and they gave out bread and wine and fatback to the people. This was on the day of the burial, the day you gave earth to the body. There in S, it was both Vaqueiros and the *aldeanos* who did this.

> The only meal that I remember was that of the house of C for the grandmother of X. It was given in P [parish *aldea*] at noon, in a tavern, and it was a real banquet. But by the time X's grandfather died, they didn't do that anymore.

Just as the death meals in the *braña* have been reduced, so the burial meals in the *aldea* have been simplified to an offering of bread and wine. This offering was given until quite recently and apparently was quite well received.

> The custom barely exists anymore. But in the old days as soon as earth was given to the body, one went to the bar, and

there they would have maybe twenty or forty loaves of bread, forty or fifty liters of wine, and hundreds of people. People would start talking as if they were at the market; they would chat away, dipping bread, soft as cake, in the wine.

They still give out something in many places. Here, previously, on the day of the burial, they gave to everybody who came to the funeral, whether *aldeano* or Vaqueiro, bread and wine. The *aldeanos* gave out bread and wine as well. As soon as the dead was buried, we had bread and wine, as much as we wanted; sometimes they put sugar in the wine and the people would dip the bread in it. They stopped doing this about ten years ago, no more; when X died, from La L, about seven years ago, M house still did that. It may be that there are still some villages where it is done now.

The grave-digger and the sexton were invited to partake of this postburial bread and wine. At times the sexton directed the prayers that were recited in the name of the dead during the meal.

The day of the burial, the one who dug the grave would be invited to have bread and wine also. He was from N [*aldea*]; he would be notified the day before, and he would go with a pick and shovel.

The last sexton we had was always invited to bread and wine, and he did the prayers. He had to remember all of the dead of the house in question in order to recite an Our Father for each, otherwise the people would be offended or would remind him. The last prayer was for the calves, the animals, and all those present. And he, too, stuffed himself and ate a lot, and got flushed in the face.

Today the relatives of the deceased give those who attend the burial only coffee and liqueurs. They advise one of the bars in the *aldea* that they are inviting those attending the funeral to a first round of drinks. Given the massive attendance at funerals, such events are occasions for socializing, and friends and relatives get together in animated conversation.

Back in the *braña*, the night of the burial, neighbors and relatives gather again for the *novena*. The main purpose of the *novena* is to recite prayers for the dead and to console the survivors. It lasts nine nights, counting the night or nights of the wake. Like the wake, the *novena* on the burial night is an intimate gathering, directed by the resident prayer specialist of the *braña*.

You have to pray nine days in the house. Nine days always reciting the rosary. And people come from each house, two or three per house. We all pray; that is, S prays for everyone; S prays very well. If it wasn't S, it would be somebody else, but S really prays well! And I think they provide some bread, wine, and coffee.

As with the rest of the funeral meals, today drinks often are substituted for solid foods.

THE HOUSE OF THE DEAD

Most of the local cemeteries are adjacent to the parish church; a few are on the outskirts of the settlement. Except for one, discussed below, all are in the main *aldeas*. Among the Vaqueiros, the *camposanto* [literally, holy field] is considered the last dwelling [*morada*]. This is not just a figurative usage, for many Vaqueiros refer to the tomb as "the house" [*la casa*] "the new house," or "the little house." They use ironic metaphors and puns to avoid referring to the cemetery by its name, for instance, *pataqueiro*, the place where old potatoes are stored, or the "if-you-know-what-I-mean" [*si-me-entiendes*].

We buried her in La F. She was always saying, "How nice the house down there will be when I go down there. I have to go down and see if I can look at it." They buried her with one of our brothers who died young.

In spite of the jokes and euphemisms, or perhaps because of them, few Vaqueiros dare to approach one of these places of the dead at night. In the last few years, however, the last resting place has become a frequent topic of conversation, especially among the most elderly. Until recently, the Vaqueiro was buried in the earth, giving meaning to phrases like "give earth to the body," "bury it," the "holy field," and so on, and providing work for the other specialist of death, the grave-digger, generally a poor inhabitant of the *aldea*. He did his work as follows:

Maybe you gave him ten *duros* and he took care of everything, but now nobody wants to dig it, the grave. Before the priest would say, "The funeral at such an hour and tell the grave-digger." And you had to notify him and pay him ten *duros* for the grave. This man first cut the turf, then marked the grave; then he began to dig and throw the dirt to one side. Then you went there and they put the coffin down; they put a rope under it, and four men would lower it down slowly. In the last years, if anyone went to the earth, the family members themselves had to dig the grave. There is no grave-digger anymore. No, the family members didn't actually do it. They would get X, the one who is very poor, or L; but now they don't dig graves. Before there was always a grave-digger.

Now burials are very rare, because edifices of brick and cement have invaded the *camposanto*. Most of the Vaqueiros bury their dead in niches. Each house has its own little hive, the pantheon, with three or four niches, also known as mouths, each for a dead body. The pantheon sometimes contains another opening to store bones, known as the *huesera* [ossuary]. The name of the house and the *braña* are clearly inscribed on the upper part of these edifices. These small and individualized "houses" (whence the term) receive the Vaqueiros, providing them in death with the same identity that they had when they were alive, that of their house. The switch from grave to niche has been quite swift, occurring almost simultaneously in all of the parishes. Death, too, has its fashions. One of the reasons Vaqueiros give for preferring this kind of death hive is precisely that "everyone has them." One of the advantages of the niche is that it protects one's privacy in death. Burial in the ground can mean being walked on by the living in visits to the cemetery, which is considered unworthy of the memory of the deceased and an injury to the feelings of the survivors. The niche also helps protect the privacy of the dead in that the bones of the long dead are uncovered when it is necessary to dig new graves.

Yes, my deceased husband bought [the niche] for himself and for me, for when it happens. And he took out bones of his father, who was in the cemetery near the entrance, saying that he didn't want everyone walking on him, and so he bought the niche and took out the remains and put them in the niche. And his sister who died here five years ago, she is in the niche with him as well, each one in their coffin. They're in there, each one in their little house. Because we go walking on top of them, on all of them who are there; and that's a lot. . . . No, one is better off in the niche than in the ground. There, at least, they don't step on you. . . . Well, it's all the same whether they step on you or not, but, just the same, everyone says, "so they won't step on me." That is why they do it, so they won't step on them in the ground. After you're dead, what difference does it make if they step on you or do anything else to you? But it's true that everyone prefers to be in one of the niches; almost all have one.

There are niches for all the inhabitants of the parish, all of them. I think that there were two houses who didn't have them, and they were ordered made for them. I prefer the niche. Because when you turn over the soil, the bones come up, and all those things. Those buried in the earth, in one row, today it's the turn of this row, the next day another, and when its the turn of this row again, the bones go out. If they had an ossuary to put them in, there would be piles of them. Some people prefer to be buried in the earth than to be put in . . . but here all of us have niches.

The richest inhabitants began to construct niches around 1965. The price for one of these edifices of three or four niches varied from parish to parish, from sixteen to thirty thousand pesetas in 1975. This amount includes certain duties for the church but does not include a cross or inscribed stone. Only the very poorest have no niche, because no matter how little one has, all want to be equal to their neighbors in this respect. Some older persons receive this quantity from their emigrant children as a gift, and although at times they have trouble deciding whether to spend it for a niche or for a television set, generally they decide in favor of the niche. Those who do not have the money on hand in case of urgent need borrow it to be repaid as soon as possible. Burial in the ground today is considered a *bajeza,* a lowering of oneself. It is a way to demean oneself and can be a cause for criticism.

Now the niche is in a fashion; before it was the earth. I don't know why . . . because it is *bajeza.* I have the money for it, because my son sent it from Germany, twenty-three-thousand pesetas. E has the money. We have to wait until there is room.

They buried her at N. No, don't think it was in a niche. Previously few people had them: first they were uglier; now they are more modern. X had one for many years; he was the only one around here who had one, and it was a nice house. Now he's made another and changed over; they'll want to sell or fix up the first one. Now everyone has one here. They say it is shameful to demean oneself by being in the earth.

In some parishes, more cynical people point out with a certain irony and a lowered voice that "this was something the priest cooked up to get money, because he charged almost thirty thousand pesetas for each."

Some zones of the cemetery are considered better than others. The holy field has its own stratification. The first distinction made, the classic and traditional one, is that between sacred and profane space. All of the dead are buried in sacred ground, blessed and "holy," except for those who are not yet Christians, children who died before baptism, and (at least in the past) those the Church ceased to consider as Christians, the suicides. The profane space, according to the Vaqueiros, is in the corners of the cemetery.

Oh, yes, as with my little baby girl who died without baptism—they did not put them in the middle; they buried them in the corners. Why should that be? Because it was not a religious enough soul, because it was not baptized. I don't remember who, one day, said to me, "Look, your little girl is buried here, as if she were not baptized. They bury them like that, near the wall, not near the center." They buried these babies where water came off the roof, near the entrance to the cemetery, because they said they were not Christians and they could not be given Christian soil.

One of those who hung himself they did not bury as a Christian; they buried him as an animal, not in Christian soil, but to the side of the cemetery, which they say is not blessed, at the entrance to the right. They don't do that anymore, but before they buried those who strung themselves up in that corner. They said they did this, this insult, so that people would not hang themselves.

Another important distinction in the cultural geography of the cemetery was the space reserved for paupers and beggars, as the parish records show. But there was also a space reserved exclusively for "vaqueros" or "brañeros," who even after death occupied a certain section of the cemetery separate from the aldeanos. I will now treat this ultimate margination of the Vaqueiros in funeral and burial.

The most striking aspect of Vaqueiro funeral customs is without doubt the commensality with which the burial is surrounded. The various meals are disappearing due to reasons both internal and external. Let us start with the former. Vaqueiros today primarily criticize the meals before burial, when the body is still in the house. They are not as critical of the other meals. Popular opinion now shows that there has been a shift in values so that the association of death with eating is now considered in bad taste. If the bread and wine is still tolerated, a formal banquet with meat today is considered scandalous. People now believe that the deceased's survivors should not have to busy themselves in the production of a feast at such a time. And those attending wakes and funerals themselves considered the consumption of food and beverages improper with the body present in the house.

Here, too, they serve mutton; they would kill a sheep or two, or whatever needed. I think that they were still serving meals when I married in, but since then people began to say that why should people have to provide food under those circumstances, and so they gradually did away with it . . . to serve meals in the house was very wrong, to have to get food ready . . . and people were, well, it would have had to have been another kind of people.

First of all, in the house of the dead, it is a little repugnant to go to eat on that day, both to offer it and to consume it. That is what people of villages around here would do, those who were dying of hunger, the drunkards, in order to fill up on wine and bread; it would be the only time they ate anything. Still today a round of drinks, anisette and brandy, is offered when you enter. I take my position from my father-in-law. He used to say that it was something low [una bajeza] to go and take bread and wine.

Because of the invitations to eat, the funeral, in theory an occasion for sorrow, at times loses its serious and circumspect character and becomes confused with its opposite, the wedding, the prototypical occasion for joy. People frequently compare the two, especially because of the similarity between the banquets. Vaqueiro excesses in drinking and eating led to behavior dangerously festive for funerals, provoking gossip and criticism, and ultimately hastening the demise of the funeral feast. The second informant, below, an outsider married to a Vaqueiro woman, shows his surprise at the funeral customs of the area.

The relatives of the deceased soon go back home. And the others stay in X [parish aldea] partying and boozing . . . as on a wedding day. . . . He who is not in sorrow stays down there and drinks and eats and has a good time.

What I found very strange here is that after the burial they invited everyone present for bread and wine. It seemed to me that there was an almost total lack of respect for the deceased. Because while the family was weeping and in pain, the rest of those present would drink until they lost control and do crazy things, falling all over each other, so that it seemed more like a fiesta than a funeral. That's why I thought it was wrong that they gave out bread and wine.

In addition to the wine, the food in the past served to satisfy the chronic hunger that permeates the childhood remembrances of adult Vaqueiros and aldeanos. A meal with meat, or even a piece of white bread, was an unusual event, typical only of fiesta days. The poorest people received the *carito* not only at funerals but also on local "feast" days. Thus the local association among funeral, meal, and fiesta is not surprising. Hear an *aldeano:*

> There has always been a lot of poverty here, even thought it is an *aldea.* At a funeral I remember they [Vaqueiros] brought wine down and bought bread here in the *aldea.* Now all this is over and done with, and there are some very rich people in the *brañas*—in B there are millionaires. And they were having a banquet when we left school, I shit on the sea, when did we see white bread? We only had bread made from corn or rye. . . . And they went to a tavern and one [Vaqueiro] said to his grandson, "We won't have a fiesta for another year." They like to drink a lot, don't they? This was on the very day of a funeral, just after the ceremony. They gave to the poor, wherever they were from, and called it the *carito,* the dividing of the bread. It wasn't so long ago that the poor, the women, came to beg for the *carito* at every house on St. John's Day and the feast of Jesus, and would be given a small piece of bread.

Today these funeral feasts no longer have the same meaning for the Vaqueiros, who no longer go hungry; if they need a meal they can always buy one at any of the taverns of the *aldea.* The old collective meals at funerals must have meant a substantial outlay for many of the poorer houses, and this expense must have contributed to the demise of the custom. About forty-five years ago, the total expenses of a death, including coffin, death certificate, alms, and the different funeral meals were equivalent to the cost of a cow.

> In the old days the funeral cost less. I did everything, with the help of P from B, when my mother-in-law died, may she rest in peace, because my husband was in Madrid. It cost fifty *duros* for everything, including the coffin, which was made in the village by some carpenters. The funeral was the first-class kind, and I had a candelabra for the wake—now they use electric lights. It was forty-five or forty-six years ago. Fifty *duros* is what a cow was worth, a cow I sold to C because I didn't have the money. I gave the money to P, who had paid for everything. He helped me out all the way. Now, of course, you don't have the meals, but that was expensive, too, if a lot of people came, what with the bread, wine, and coffee. In the morning I gave them all hot chocolate, and then bread and wine when they went to bury her, and again at night to those of the village.

Criticism from the outside was even worse than that of the Vaqueiros themselves. Tales of Vaqueiro funeral meals have become a minor literary genre for Asturianists. Today these stories form a major theme of the mocking and gossiping by the *aldeanos*, proof of their Vaqueiro neighbors' irrational customs. Yet, in the past, funeral meals were common to both Vaqueiros and *aldeanos*. Over time, criticism from the outside took its toll. "The funeral meals stopped because the *aldeanos* of X were laughing at them." But the outside critics who had the most effect were the priests. The older parish priests considered the funeral feasts scandalous, particularly because of the combination of eating and death. While they may not have articulated explicitly the possible competition between Vaqueiro rituals and the orthodox Catholic ones, the Vaqueiros themselves did.

In this parish, as in others, it was the priests who stopped it. They began saying "This is bad, this is bad . . ." Someone should have said, "Listen, this is bad, but what is given to you is also bad, and you just want everything for yourself, eh?" They, too, charge for funerals. Well, he who goes to accompany a dead person carries him on his back and doesn't charge a *céntimo*, so it is very logical that he should have a glass of wine and have a piece of bread. "You, because [you] come here and scratch your balls [*tocándose los perreñes*] and sing, want everything for yourself." He screwed us!

Many of the tensions between Vaqueiros and *aldeanos* came to the surface on the occasion of funerals. There were (and still are) very few occasions when so many Vaqueiros come down to the *aldea* at once. Such a massive outpouring may have helped to put an end to some of the overt discrimination that existed in some of the parish churches during the nineteenth century. Some of the mythical protest battles occurred at funerals.

Vaqueiros, at funerals, were not allowed to go to the front of the church. They had to stand in the back at funerals. They told me it wasn't allowed to have a first-class funeral or to carry anything of silver. Once, maybe in 1850, there was a funeral in my house, and the great-grandfather of this child was from Vizcaya—when they built the road he fell in love with my grandmother—and there were two funerals, one from C [*braña*] and the other from the *aldea*. And they got into an argument, and these two went out, two big young men from here, and they made a lot of trouble, and from that day on they could not go all the way into the church.

The people of the *aldea* also have their traditional stories that make fun of the Vaqueiros and their funerals. These occasions are carefully observed by the more witty *aldeanos* and amply described. An *aldeana*'s words, despite their humor, illustrate why Vaqueiros are at times hesitant to confront the external world:

There was a priest who was friendly with the people here. And a woman died in the X *braña*. And a man, who had spent stretches of time in Madrid as a vendor of giblets and entrails, came down to be with the priest and he said, "Don M, a woman died there in the village and they have sent me to talk to you because I am the one who knows how to speak the best in the village, shit on God. Will it be all right, in order to leave something with the survivors, if we only have two priests at the funeral?" "There have to be three." (Most probably the dead woman was well off.) "All right then, we'll have to swallow another priest, shit on God."

Because of the history of discrimination against them, Vaqueiros today are very suspicious of the way *aldeanos* react. Although the discrimination is no longer so overt or formalized, complaints continue on both sides. The parish church was not the only place where segregation occurred. The cemetery also traditionally had specific areas marked off for the Vaqueiros. Today plots for pantheons are awarded by lottery, but the Vaqueiros claim that the *aldeanos* cheat and get the places they want—the sunniest, most central, most protected, and so on. This may be true, because in some parishes the niches of the *braña* are all together, although the *aldeanos* generally had purchased them first and would have been able to have their choice. In any case, in spite of the desire of the young priests to eliminate the differences, in the popular mind they still continue.

In the *brañas* the people are more humble than in the *aldea*. There they are more proud. For instance, the priest proclaimed in the church that the crosses in the cemetery should be all the same. I don't have a pantheon because I am a poor woman, but they put up crosses different from ours. He said it should be the same for poor and rich, *aldea* and *braña*.

These tensions between Vaqueiros and *aldeanos* crated a curious situation in the *brañas*. At the turn of the century, the head of one of the richest Vaqueiro houses, heading the struggle against the margination of the Vaqueiros, attempted to create an exclusively Vaqueiro parish. He endowed his *braña* with all of the characteris-

DEATH

tics of an *aldea* by building a chapel, a cemetery, and a tavern. He planned to build roads that would unite the other villages with "his" parish center. Hear how a Vaqueiro from that locality tells of this dream of independence:

> Eighty or more years ago, this graveyard was set up privately by this house; it belonged to this house. It was an old man here, they called him C, who wanted to set up a parish here for these *brañas* because he had a place to sell wine and do business. Since on the burial day everyone is ordering bread and wine . . . he was fifty years ahead of his time. He also wanted to build a road from here to B and T. In the *brañas* there are no chapels or cemeteries. And we wouldn't have our own either if it weren't for this man who wanted to set up a parish here. So he got a head start, as if to say, "All right, now we have a cemetery and a chapel, let's have a parish." Of course, it would have been difficult to send a priest here, as it would have been a very poor parish, it seems to me.

This enterprising Vaqueiro ran up against the Church. Ecclesiastic authorities, by way of the parish priest, denied permission for burials in the cemetery. After a diocesan trial, permission was eventually granted:

> So then that man began to have trouble with the parish priest. And in those days priests were so touchy [*adelicados*] that this one went to inform the diocese, and they told him— they had already buried twelve or thirteen from the village by then—"Neither for him nor for anybody." So they suspended the cemetery; that would be about sixty years ago. Later another priest, Don X, who died suddenly, was told by the bishop, "Look, I saw the decision of the court about that man in the trial with the diocese, which went against the people of the village; but if they want to, they can bury there again." This was about ten years ago. The bishop of Oviedo told the priest he had in B that we could fix it up and bury people and say mass if we wanted to.

The time for a decision by the people had come. The lines that follow are an incisive and perspicacious analysis of rural sociology:

> For the moment we didn't know what to do. Some of us already had our niche in La F, others were undecided. The priest died, and it was the one we have now who got us going. The cemetery and the chapel are private; they belong completely to the man who built them. And the priest said, "*Hombre*, we have to make this cemetery a public one." For

awhile some of us said, "Let's go," and others, "Let's not."
You don't know how things are in a village. One fellow twist-
ing his beret, another with his hands in his pockets, another
holding back, another scratching his ear. . . . Some said that it
was demeaning to be buried there [una bajeza]. They said it
at the first meeting about it: "I don't want to see the cemetery, pass by there and see that someone is buried there, that
is demeaning," one of the rich ones would say. So that one
day the priest said in a sermon, "I believe you are somewhat
divided on the matter of the cemetery, and this should not
be." And everybody was whispering and holding off. So I told
the priest that I wanted to bury there. My friend, it was like
when one sheep from a flock takes the first jump. X piped up,
"Well, I want to do it, too, but first we have to write to the
owner to see which part of the cemetery he wants for himself." And the priest said, "That is a good idea. How could we
tell this gentleman that he should have the place he is assigned? Since he is the owner, we will give him his choice."

What happened next within the Vaqueiro group seemed to replicate what happens between Vaqueiros and *aldeanos*: preferred
places in the cemetery. Consider the angry response and violent
attack in a similar situation many years before, although now it is
a case of rather exaggerated social, rather than racial, discrimination.

Let us go back 150 years. You know well the customs in
the old days, the differences there were in the church and in
the cemetery. You must be tired of studying it. Since the *aldeanos* held us in such low repute, as the dregs of society, we
could not speak with anyone besides each other, and that
badly. And now in L [braña] it was all modern, and that had
ended. Now we were like them, like everybody. Our bodies
went in the hearse to be buried just like theirs. But we went
back, in a way, to 150 years before, to distinguishing the beggars from the rich. Because, *ay Dios!* they begin to hand
down laws. The rich people of the *braña* say, "Wait," says X,
"we want to be all together in the niches of the cemetery." X,
P, G, with the owner of this house, all wanted to be together,
you see? The niche of a poor person wasn't allowed, because
we are beggars and they won't allow a beggar next to them. I
told him, "I don't care about this, but if we do what is right
and lawful, these niches will be numbered and assigned by
lot. If you end up next to me, that's where you go; and if you

end up next to a general, you go there. But this kind of sepa- ration of the rich from the poor . . ." They didn't want me to have my compartment here, then one of a rich man, then one of another poor person, the rich between the two of us. They want the rich all together and the beggars all together. Isn't that something? Worth writing about, eh? It's like going back 150 years to what went on between *aldeanos* and Vaqueiros, and what went on in the city of L. Just as the city people looked down on the people of the *aldea*, so those from the *aldea* looked down on us. Now they come here and say, "Hey, what pretty niches! Whose are they?" "Well, from here to there are the beggars, and from here over, the rich." So that here a distinction has been made; no mixing at all. And the same in all of Spain.

Such firm words indicate that external segregation reproduces in- ternal segregation. They also indicate that the desire for equality continues in some Vaqueiros even after death.

THE RITUALS OF LEAVING

The funeral and burial of a Vaqueiro are profoundly social acts. The entire process, from the moment the individual dies until the body is put in the ground, and even afterward, is a collective matter in which the entire community participates without exception. Within minutes after the individual draws his or her last breath, neighbors and relatives spontaneously develop a division of labor efficiently and selflessly to organize the farewell of the dead Va- queiro. In this process, public attention is directed as much toward the surviving relatives as toward the dead person. The group, with its continual presence and help in the house of the deceased, super- vises the smallest details so that the Vaqueiro's last trip will be made with dignity, according to local values.

As part of this dignity, the laying out of the deceased acquires special importance. Clothes, in general, are important social indi- cators for Vaqueiros. In the past, only the wealthy were dressed up for burial, but now even the poorest aspire to reach a certain level. Today there is not so much competition among the houses; rather, there is a desire *not* to stand out in any way. One of the Vaqueiros' favorite sayings is: "Neither raise yourself up because you are rich nor lower yourself because you are poor." When Vaqueiros leave the *braña* to visit people in another *braña* or an *aldea* to attend fairs or shrine fiestas, to shop in neighboring towns, or to go to the city, they always wear their best clothes. Leaving the house to emigrate or to be married involves taking along considerable luggage. In the weddings of yore, the bride's cortege included, among other things, a pack animal if she were going to another *braña*, or a cart if the terrain permitted, with the clothes and linens her family had given her displayed to advantage. As the burial trip is the ultimate one, one thus sees why the dead must go impeccably dressed. If the house of the dead person is very poor, the Vaqueiros are tolerant about the presentation of the body, but this is not the case if they note any kind of avarice or selfishness on the part of the family of the deceased, if they might have able to improve the final appearance of the dead person, even at some sacrifice. In this situation, the Vaqueiro is a severe judge of those who should fulfill their obligations to the departed. This is true not only in regard to dress. Those at the wake are also concerned that the dead be kept company while in the house, that neighbors and family should bid the dead farewell, that there is no stinting on the coffin or other funeral paraphernalia, and finally, that the dead have a worthy resting place in the cemetery. The Vaqueiros' principal weapon is verbal criticism, which can tarnish the good name of the house.

While all are vigilant that the final send-off be done right and with dignity, all contribute to this process their help and knowledge. Specialists come forward during the funeral proceedings and provide their skills for any dead person in the *braña*. These include, or included, those of both sexes who lay out bodies, the prayer leader, the man who divides up the bread, the cooks who used to prepare the funeral banquets, and the amateur carpenters who made the coffins. Other less specialized helpers do other necessary work in the house of mourning, such as taking care of the farm animals, mowing the meadows, or milking the cows; still others spread the news of the death, go with family members to take care of religious and civil formalities, console the most bereaved, and keep the body company. The burial is a precise indicator of who belongs to the group, as the *aldeanos* often point out. Those who remain close their ranks in order to say farewell to one of their own. The different levels and kinds of relationship—friends, neighbors, and relatives—are strengthened and renewed at these times as at no other.

The wake is the most intimate of the funeral gatherings. Neighbors from the *braña*, especially those who live nearby, will be present in addition to immediate family members, especially those who live in the same *braña*. Attendance at the wake, then, is required of those people who have maintained a day-to-day level of contact, those who share work and live together, companions in fiestas and evenings spent together inside. Although this kind of intimacy also produces friction and tension, nevertheless these are the people who are the first to arrive in urgent situations like the birth of a cow and death.

The funeral and burial draw the widest audience, those who maintain the most public level of relationship in the little universe that surrounds the *braña*, including less intimate friends and neighbors, relatives who live far away, people from the immediate parish and from surrounding parishes, and *aldeano* acquaintances. Such a group, then, is comprised of occasional acquaintances, the kind one would see on a market day, relatives whom one would see maybe once a year at the killing of a pig or in times of crisis, old male companions or female friends who married out into another *braña*. As if to mark more precisely the different levels of relationship, the funeral procession can be joined at different points along the route—the most intimate at the house, the less intimate along way, and the least intimate at the church. With very rare exceptions, the *aldeanos* choose this last option. The norms for attending a funeral permit one to modify or affirm one's place in the different social alliances. The number of those attending signifies the memory of the deceased among the living, the status or reputation of the family, and the importance of the house.

The traditional methods of conveying the cadaver from the house to the parish church mark a climax of solidarity. It demands everyone's effort, both physical and emotional. The sons, who entered the house thanks to their progenitor, remove their parent from the house. The law of nature, the succession of generations, is fulfilled as some depart and others arrive. Outside the house, however, the procession once again becomes the business of the group—the neighbors and relatives with whom one has shared one's life in the *braña*. This ritual journey, interrupted from time according to the symbolic geography of the *camino sacramental*, suggests an attempt to delay the final departure of the dead Vaqueiro. The responses and the generous contribution of alms that accompanies them, make the trip longer.

The largest gathering forms at the parish church. Very often all of the houses of the parish and those of neighboring parishes are represented by at least one member. The last good-bye in the cemetery and the symbolic handful of holy dirt demonstrate that all are burying the dead together. Once the serious task that has brought people together is over, those present turn to lively interaction. Many Vaqueiros, especially the men, see each other only at funerals. Funerals provide the people with an enriched fund of local news. The gossip they share on these occasions is savored afterwards.

The dead person goes accompanied by prayers and alms generously offered by those attending. The alms end with the burial, but not the prayers, which continue in the *novena*. The *novena* reestablishes the original neighborhood nucleus with which the funeral process began. As at the wake, in the *novena* the people of the *braña* gather together for prayer in the house of the deceased. They help to relieve the sorrow of the survivors, allowing them to reintegrate themselves in the world of the living. All try to reestablish the order that was sharply interrupted by death.

As if in payment for all the help and solidarity they receive the people of the house of the deceased offer their neighbors, relatives, and friends a generous amount of food. Offerings of food and drink appear continually throughout the life cycle of the Vaqueiros. The newborn's first emergence from the house is accompanied by a piece of bread, the "bread of tears" [*pan del choro*], which is given to the first person encountered. Another sweet bread, *la bolla*, is a present from a godmother to her goddaughter on Easter. The mother who has recently given birth receives different foods as presents. The saints are offered food as well; a piglet to Saint Anthony, corn to the parish church, the best calf to the Virgen del Acebo. Banquets have a central importance in baptism and marriage, too. Help in agricultural work, transhumant journeys, and attendance at shrines, fairs, and fiestas are accompanied by conspicuous picnicking. Hospitality to friends and visitors takes the form of repeated offers of food and drink. Commensality is a constant in the social interaction of the Vaqueiro.

Vaqueiro funeral banquets must be understood in this context. First, the meal serves as an exquisitely refined form of social labeling. Although the house usually restricts itself to frugal and simple fare, when guests are present, the meal is very ample in quantity and quality. All of the houses reserve something from the last pig slaughtering for these special events, even though it condemns everyday meals to monotony. Given the presence of guests in the house of the deceased, the funeral process becomes one of these public situations calling for ample hospitality. As with clothes, one should not do worse than anyone else, no matter how badly off one is. Second, the meal is a form of thanks. Any labor that is not paid for in money always calls for an invitation to an exceptional meal. This also happens when there is some kind of moral debt, whether because of the granting of a special favor, a loan without interest, or the simplification of some bureaucratic procedure. Inviting those who attend a funeral to partake of food and drink is an attempt to respond to the altruistic attitude of those who left their own work in order to do that of their neighbors and to accompany them in their bereavement. Note that the outside specialists—the priest, sexton, and grave-digger—are usually paid in cash while the Vaqueiros who attend the funerals, as well as the various funeral specialists in the *braña*, are invited to eat and drink. Commensalism is an expression of a reciprocal relation while payment in money supposes an economic transaction with a professional.

The traditional meal may also be seen as a response to the local human ecology. Due to the distances, the lack of roads, the dispersed habitat, and the traditional route, a funeral in the *braña* may involve a trip of several hours, complicated by the strain on those who carry the coffin. There are no stores or taverns in the *brañas* to relieve the thirst and hunger of the tired participants. Family members who have come substantial distances also have to eat [*hacer por la vida*]. The people of the house of the deceased are obliged to attend to all of them. The funeral meals, then, satisfy the biological needs of the living.

Yet they are not only for this purpose. A woman told me, "They served the big meal before the body left, when the body was in the house." I asked her, "In order to feed the people, those who came from outside?" She replied, "No, it was a religious ceremony, a custom then. They said they did this because it had an effect [*efecto*] on the deceased." Hence the meal is also an offering to the deceased, a sacrifice to the dead. When a Vaqueiro dies, people from his or her house go to the stable and sacrifice one or more "lesser animals" [*ganado menudo*] (as compared to the more highly valued cows). The offerings of these animal substitutes should be carried over the same route as the deceased; a death among the humans is matched by a death among the animals. The animal, a metonymic sign for the person giving the sacrifice, is the bridge that joins the living and the dead, an efficacious intermediary between humans and the divinity. With the sacrifice of the animal, the forces of dispersion and disintegration that surround death melt away; the destructive impulses, conflicts, and tensions in the family and the group are transferred to the animal and thereby tamed by this ritual violence.

The ingestion of the victim not only increases the vital forces of the participants but symbolizes the unity of the group and the perpetuation of life. This act of communion with the dead and simultaneous cognitive separation of the dead from the living may be seen more clearly once animal sacrifices are suppressed in favor of the Eucharistic sacrifice of bread and wine, or more simply, the *car-*

ito. The fact that participation is obligatory, that a specialist controls the ritualized distribution, and that the sacrifice may be substituted by a mass, all validate the designation of this event in the popular category of "religious ceremony." I will speak later of the relation between the living and the dead, but I want to emphasize that due to the segregation of the Vaqueiro community, commensality has played a fundamental role for the Vaqueiros. The fact that the people of the *braña* have retained this kind of custom, the need for their own kind of liturgy parallel to the orthodox ceremony, despite the criticisms it has evoked and the inconveniences it has caused, shows that this tradition fills the very important function of ratifying, as on no other occasion, the feeling of the group in the face of outside antagonism.

Finally, the meal and its preparation help to distract the attention of the deceased's family members from the painful fact of the death. Meal after meal, intricately involved in the repaying of those attending the funeral, keep them busy in the most critical hours of mourning with conversation and company. The food ritual, marking successively and specifically the different steps of the funeral process and even the postburial *novena,* eases the transition to life without the deceased.

The norms regulating attendance at the funeral proceedings and those for carrying the coffin show the special relevance of the institution of the house. It is not surprising that it is the death of the *amo,* the one who controls the family economy, that occasions the greatest attendance. The *amo* is also the one who married at home [*el casado en casa*], who formed the family, contributing to the maintenance and the renovation of this small enterprise. Those who die before contributing to the future of the house have their coffins carried by their age group; those who have contributed permanently to the house by marrying, however, are carried out by members of the house. Nevertheless, the house has an obligation to all who were born in it. Even though some of its members have to emigrate or marry outside the house because of the rules of inheritance, the house repairs this injustice in death by holding funerals for those who are absent.

Throughout the funeral process, the house is the basis for relationships and identification. On a general level of communication, representation at these ceremonies does not require a specific person but rather an anonymous member of the house, just as in the popular conception the identity of the deceased derives from his or her ascription to a particular house. For the same reason, the neighborhood or location in situations of death is as important a factor as kinship for those who live outside the house. There is solidarity between the houses in these situations in spite of the inevitable competitiveness of day-to-day relations.

The funeral of someone surrounded by family at home is very different from that of the person who has neither house nor family. The following is the case of a poor woman who was a beggar. She was given a funeral like that of others, but the attitudes it provoked were different.

And those who die without relatives. . . . Here an old woman died who had no relatives. She had a little house at X, then she sold it or I don't know what happened, they took it away from her. Then she was a servant in the house of L in M and did things around there. She died in P's stable. She had come begging . . . she wasn't a normal woman. And she had some wine (laughs), it was at the wedding of A from El V, I think, and she had drunk something and smoked too, smoked a lot. When they knew that there was a wedding or something like that they would come and be given things. Tobacco, too, because they always gave out tobacco on those days. And she ate a lot, and then she felt sick and lay down in that stable, and was there a day or so, and then she died there. We went to pray for her, at least. And the arrangements had to be made, the *celador* and two others had to do it. And they made her a coffin with some boards and painted it, so it was like the ones you buy. People here made it, as she had no relatives, and those of C, who were somewhat neighbors, when she had the house in X. We went up to the hayloft, one or two from each house, and three from some, from all the houses. The priest came up the day they took her down to N; no one else did. People from the village took her down, a funeral like any other. I didn't go, I was a kid, but one from each house must have gone, and from other villages. After this woman died, the lice all left her, you could see them walk all over her, and they left all together, she had so many, when she died and got cold. The women who dressed her a little here said they all left her. They dressed her, of course, changed her some, put on other clothes. She would have had something, and if not they would have put on some clothes of a woman from here. I remember when we went to pray there that I had not seen any other [dead person]. . . . I must have heard that other people had died in the village, but she was the first I had seen. Furthermore, since the woman was totally impoverished, with lice, and then, of course, it was not sad—an old woman who wasn't related to anybody—when one went to the stable, it was like a day for playing, with everybody laughing. They said that the little horses [lice] were going up your legs, or someone else's, and so on.

One's connection to the house does not end with death. The dead today have as their final home an edifice, a pantheon, which is the perpetual property of the house and very clearly bears its name. In their visits to the cemetery on All Saints Day, the Vaqueiros await the prayers of the priest for the dead proudly mounting guard in front of their respective property. The purchase of niches is today much more than a fashion or a convenience. When a Vaqueiro buys a niche, he is buying a piece of land in the *aldea,* a territory to which he has rights as a dwelling for his dead. The eagerness to have a place for after death, in the "good" section of the cemetery, correlates with the desire and preoccupation to improve the place of the living. House and niche have parallel values.

The graveyard is not the only holy place where humans are buried. The house also has its *sancta sanctorum.* It is said that when a woman gives birth, the placenta is buried underneath the *llabanas,* the stones in the fireplace, at the focal point, underneath the hearth. This is the place for the "Christian things" that do not go to the cemetery. Similar animal products are placed outside the house.

Yes, yes, before it was like that, they lifted up a stone, but inside the house, and they dug a little and there they buried the placentas. So that the dogs wouldn't get them outside, because dogs, when they smell something, dig and get it out, and we didn't want the dogs to get them, as it is Christian stuff. Those of cows, no, they were not buried in the house. They're thrown outside, up higher than the house, we carried them up there with a shovel, yes, but we didn't bury them.

Dead animals are buried in the meadows and fields of the house, but always with the precaution of placing them "higher" so that the house will go higher as well. The structural integrity of the house is endangered when one of its elements dies.

All that dies—underground. Put them well under so they don't come out. And do it higher up. Those of C had their calf die last year, and they buried it at the high point of their land, above the house. And this year, too, another died, and that one, too, they buried high up. They say it has to be higher, that if it is buried below that what remains also goes down. It is so the goods of the house go up, go forward, so they do not get lost. And the hens, they should not be thrown downhill. Always up from the level of the house.

The obligations of the house to its dead do not end with the funeral or burial. The interaction of the living and the dead continues. A year after the death there is a "second funeral," and the people of the *braña* gather for a new banquet. I will speak of this in my next chapter.

PART THREE

THE
AFTERLIFE

Introduction:
The Second Funeral

In 1915 an Asturian scholar wrote, "The funeral banquet is always celebrated, for otherwise the Vaqueiros believe, the dead come back to ask for a second funeral" (Acevedo y Huelves 1915).[1] This "second funeral," now known as the "first anniversary" [*cabo de año*], is a Vaqueiro ritual whose most notable feature is the consumption of food and drink. Anniversaries evoke in people's minds such words as "meal," "eating one's fill" [*fartura de comida*], and "banquet" as well as detailed descriptions of menus. These rituals are organized by household members on the first anniversary of the death of one of the household adults. Although these banquets do not always take place on the exact anniversary of the death, they are distinguished from funeral banquets proper by the passage of a substantial amount of time after the death. Nevertheless, both rituals have much in common. In 1975, all Vaqueiro adults had been present at least one *cabo de año*, and all had participated actively in subsequent variants in which bread and wine were consumed instead of a complete meal. Such anniversary celebrations continue today. The following description of the first anniversary feast is based on people's memories; the description of the bread and wine derivative is based on my own presence and participation.

The first anniversary begins a day before the ritual with the slaughtering of several rams or sheep, a calf, or even a cow. At nightfall, the cooks of the *braña*, male or female, begin to prepare the food for the next day. The first anniversary feast is attended by numerous guests and is remembered as Pantagruelian.

247

The first anniversary is exactly one year later. When we gave it here the house was full; people were here in the living area, the old kitchen, and the shed, all of them full of tables, and served as at a wedding, a huge meal at noon and supper as well. There were more than one hundred persons. More! The entire village, as is the custom, and the relatives. Everyone from the village brings a cup and a spoon so there will be enough. There is soup, rice, stew, steak, and cakes. Huge kettles! Sheep and rams were killed for it. So much meat! And bread and wine. A real feast.

After the meal the prayers begin. The first anniversary is also considered a "service" [función], "religious service," part of "the religion that each person holds," and so on. The prayers consist of a series of Our Fathers.

It was for all of the dead. First for the main one, who was the last to die, and then for all those who had passed on from the house, with an Our Father for each. And then they prayed for the dead of the house of the person who needs it most, and then they would say, "For the souls of the dead of each of those who are present here." And then for the entire village and for the animals. Someone would know how to pray; R, may she rest in peace, was always the one who prayed.

People commonly compare these prayers with the mass and the specialist in prayers [arrezos] with the priest. The following episode is recounted so that people would not forget the sacred obligations of the first anniversary while enjoying the profane aspect of the meal.

In one of them I understand that the people were eating and drinking, and the deceased did not find the anniversary they were giving him acceptable. And later a poor man came and they gave him food, too, and I believe he said some pray-ers, and the dead man, the one they gave the anniversary for, said, "The one who got me out of the pains [of the other world] was the person you gave food to afterwards, not the first ones." Because these anniversaries are as though you are giving a mass. Oh yes, dear, don't think it's only to eat! After eating the prayers start, and someone came who prayed.

This little story shows the attention and preference that should be given to the poor at the first anniversaries, which are sometimes referred to as "having a service for the poor," "an effective act of charity," or more simply, "alms." The mere announcement of a first anniversary attracted many beggars from the parish and those nearby, who, without a formal invitation, were welcomed amiably. The leftover food was given to the most needy. But it was not only the beggars who were hungry; everyone was poor.

They served food to the whole village. This was the mass they gave. Now they give masses to the priest and do not have the anniversaries they had before. They said that those anniversaries were more effective because they served food to many poor people, were more effective than giving it to the priest, for the priest was already well off and the people in those days were hungry. People were on the lookout for an anniversary where they could eat their fill of stews and meat, because they were dying of hunger. When the children heard that there would be an anniversary so they could go and eat—
Oy Dios!

It may seem strange that poor people should give a banquet that they claimed "involved a frightful expense, more than a wedding," that people should come in large numbers, and that this should be considered a good thing. In this sense, the Vaqueiros assert that the first anniversary was "a faith that existed in the house," "a morality [moral] of the village and the families." Faith and powerful moral reasons were indeed involved in the first anniversaries, for the dead themselves demanded them.

It was done for all the dead of the house. It was done when there was a loss in the house, when one of the household died, when a cow died after running in circles in a meadow, or when there was some accident or disaster in the house. Especially when there were losses of animals. And when there were losses in the house, because those who were in the other world needed something, when the dead, the deceased, needed something.

The first anniversaries that the dead had willed, or that they asked for, had to be fulfilled. The living were reminded of their obligations by a misfortune, a series of losses, and a recent death, sufficient motives, when taken together, for a first anniversary. Sometimes the dead were more explicit in their messages [avisos], appearing in dreams or at work to their relatives or neighbors. In some stories, the family protests the expense and refuses to listen, complaining that "there is no meat." In these cases, the dead person replies cynically, "Don't worry, I'll get it for you very soon." Shortly thereafter, a cow, the "best one," will break a leg. Many first anniversaries have been given for this reason, organized rapidly so the meat will not go bad. But many times it is the neighbors who are hungry and "hear" messages. Those who do not believe the dead pay dearly.

> One time that [dead] man of P was in need of something. A neighbor was watering a meadow—the dead man didn't appear to the people of his own house because they wouldn't have been able to take it—and [the dead man] said, "*Fulano, fulano,* are you here in the meadows?" "Yes, I am here watering it; you have come to water it, too, right?" "Yes. Listen, tell those of my house to kill a cow they call La Paloma and give an anniversary. And what is left over, for something always is, they should give to the poor, and if they don't do this, that they'll take what's coming to them." "Sure, I'll tell them." And he went and told them, and they said, "This is just a story this man has made up because he wants us to give an anniversary. This comes from people who want to eat. These are just fabrications." They paid no attention. The best cow, La Paloma, was killed right before their eyes. And they had to do it just as the neighbor had told them; after that [the dead man] never appeared to them again.

In the mid-1950s, the practice of celebrating first anniversaries with the slaughtering of animals and the consumption of meat was discontinued. The Vaqueiros explain its demise in various ways. One is that "people only went for the fun of it, to stuff themselves and to drink." In other words, they got happy on the wine and the banquet ended up as a fiesta, as happened in the following case, one of the last traditional first anniversaries.

> We gave a first anniversary here, and in the evening, when the people were good and happy, they began to dance. Naturally, people came from other villages, and they were more interested in dancing than weeping. Everybody ate well and drank what they wanted. Furthermore, [the death] was a year before, and who was sad by then? Whoever had been sad was a little sad, and whoever hadn't been wasn't sad at all. And since there were more people for dancing than for a funeral . . . the young people wanted to dance; those who didn't played cards. By then people had no more grief.

Due to this festive behavior, which was virtually the inevitable conclusion of all anniversaries, the feast came under criticism from priests and *aldeanos.* But Vaqueiros offer an additional explanation for why the custom has declined.

THE AFTERLIFE

Now that everyone is well fed, they don't give the first anniversary because there is no longer hunger in the houses.

Just as now a mass is said and the priest prays, so before they said it was more effective to have a service for the poor than to have the priest pray. And now things have changed. The priest prays, and it's cheaper.

Well, they got rid of that; the priests couldn't stand it. They said that all that was spent on food should be spent in masses, because that way instead of the people eating it, they [the priests] would.

The practice of holding first anniversaries did not disappear completely; instead it was gradually transformed. Since one of the drawbacks was the excessive cost, the meat and the slaughter of animals was eliminated, and the banquet was reduced to the symbolic consumption of bread and wine in the *aldea*. Today, after holding religious services in the church, Vaqueiros still gather in a tavern where they have their "anniversary." For awhile, the morning consumption of bread and wine in the *aldea* coexisted with a subsequent dinner banquet for neighbors and relatives in the *braña*. Here an *aldeano* describes a recent Vaqueiro first anniversary in the *aldea:*

When they have a mass said, above all on the first anniversary of a death, they inform relatives as if it were the funeral. And, of course, many people come. They fill this dining room and the kitchen. They have it up here because they want to be by themselves. They ask for white wine, red wine (heated with sugar in the winter), and bread. And they eat bread and drink wine until none is left. Then they have coffee. And then they pray for the dead of the house and the obligations of all present. The family, neighbors, and closest friends from other villages come. And it comes out rather expensive. Then they go downstairs and invite each other to drinks, chat for awhile, and leave.

While the traditional first anniversaries were usually only held after the death of an *amo*, those of bread and wine are more frequent since they are held for every deceased person. The expense, although less than in the past, is still considerable. At one of the last anniversaries I attended, thirty-eight Vaqueiros consumed thirty-five pounds of bread and thirteen liters of wine, in addition to coffee and other drinks. This was a second anniversary of a death and hence was not as well attended as a first anniversary would have been. The custom is dying out under the same kind of criticism as the feasts, but since the ceremony of bread and wine is on a much smaller scale, people are more willing to tolerate it.

Vaqueiros appear to have welcomed the pious traditional custom of willing edible alms to the poor on the funeral day. Indeed, they adapted it so that relatives and neighbors were among the principal guests. The funeral banquet on the first anniversary acquired greater importance and favor in people's minds than the banquets on the funeral day. While in the *aldea* only those better off would give edible alms to the poor at their funerals, all who died in the *braña* would expect the poor to be fed for their first anniversaries. All of the houses obeyed the sacred commandment to feed the hungry, that is, themselves and those with whom they live.

The first anniversary gathers the *braña* together in commensality. Even those who cannot attend in person because they are invalids or are sick are brought a serving [*la prueba*]. Although living together is difficult, and there are neighbors with whom one is not on speaking terms, on this day they are invited, and they accept the invitations. Problems with relatives, over disputed inheritances for example, are also laid aside on this occasion. Rich and poor alike share the same table and the same food. On this day there are no distances between people. The first anniversary transcends the envy and resentments that comprise daily life, the passions and miseries of social life. Meals are shared with friends; shared meals create friendship.

Prayers are shared generously during the first anniversary as well. The first prayers are directed to the deceased of the household that organizes the celebration and to all of those who passed on from the house. The second round of prayers will recall the most needy dead out of the total anonymous dead of all present. Finally, prayers are said for the entire village, including the cattle. The ritual solidarity of those present encompasses all those who are absent.

The ritual focuses on two different communities, that of the living and that of the dead. Each is offered a different compensation: food for the living, prayers for the dead. But the interaction between the two worlds does not necessarily go smoothly. The dead are the ones who demand the ritual, who present themselves to the living, who punish selfishness, who "provide" the meat for the first anniversary, and who direct and control the ritual so that its distinctive phases, sacred and profane, are enacted properly and in turn. The relation and communication of living and dead is effected by the dead by means of messages, dreams, losses, misfortunes, and more deaths. The "principal" dead person is the most important, and the most dangerous, since he or she was the last one to die. This person serves as spokesperson for those who have passed on, as the liaison between the two communities.

Those who have died do not automatically join the world of the dead. For months they cannot resign themselves to leave the world of the living: they lurk around the houses in which they lived, shriek and make noise in the attic, intrude in the life of their family and that of their neighbors, and appear in the meadows, at the door of the house, and on the paths. Their behavior is anomalous and aggressive because they "are in need," "they cannot rest," "they are in a bad place," or "in pain." The first anniversaries placate or bring serenity to these dead who still participate in the world of the living as well as to those who have already forgotten it.

The dead behave exactly the opposite of the ways they were expected to behave in life. Note that those who suffer most from the expense of an anniversary are the dead's closest family, those who live in the same house, those with whom the dead formed a unit for work and pleasure. An anniversary is not given for all members of the house. Children and youths are excluded from the ritual because they do not need it. But the adults, the oldest ones, the *amos*, those who hold the reins of the family economy, are those who offer it and who demand it. The dead person, who in life competed with siblings and neighbors for the benefit of the house, is the one who in death wastes its goods, exhausts the family savings, and produces debts. The people who in life were the "slaves" of the cattle, in death sacrifice the best cow for the neighbors. The person who was selfish, who had lawsuits and disputes with other houses, now generously invites the entire community without exceptions. The inevitable competition of daily life is thus ritually redeemed in death.

The first anniversary is the second funeral, the popular funeral ceremony of the *braña* for Vaqueiros who have passed away. Death can occur in an unexpected way, suddenly and always brutal. The first funeral is precipitous, hurried, too sudden. There must be time for one to become accustomed to the change, to the transition from the community of the living to the community of the dead. The funeral is an official ceremony with rules set by and interference from outside: the priest goes up to the *braña* for the body, and he bears the entire burden of the ritual, praying and leading the ceremony. The Vaqueiros themselves must go down to the *aldea*, accompanying the body to its final home in foreign and hostile territory.

The anniversaries have their own specialists; the man handy at dividing the bread correctly among those present, the man who slaughters the animals, the knowledgeable person who directs the prayers. The "mass" of the Vaqueiros contains the same symbolic elements as the "other" mass: sacrifice, communion, communication with the other world, prayer, and alms. Those who have the right and the duty to send off those who have gone are the ones who shared their life, with whom the dead lived and worked, the congregation formed by the Vaqueiro community. While a funeral is the farewell to a dead individual, the first anniversary is a collective offering to the souls of all the dead. Through the prayers, the particular dead person makes a final departure from the *braña* in order to join the collectivity of the dead. The passage of time eases this necessary transition, which coincides with the end of mourning.

Then the fiesta begins. After death, life goes on; and so the young people dance while the older people talk and play cards. People drink and sing. The atmosphere of the entire *braña* is festive in the evening, once peace has been made with the dead and with the living as well. The anniversary contains components of tragedy and comedy, tears and laughter, feast and prayer, sorrow and joy, funeral and fiesta. As ambivalent as life itself, these rituals teach that getting along well and generosity to all are more important than the accumulation of wealth and egotism. At least during the anniversary, ill will is mixed with wine and swallowed with bread and meat in the communal meal.

The anniversaries of bread and wine persist in spite of criticism. The Vaqueiros choose the most insulated locale of the tavern in the *aldea*, separated from the mockery of the *aldeanos*, to eat and pray. The old sacrifices have been reduced to their minimal symbolic expression: a piece of bread and a glass of wine that all consume in communion with their own kind, both present and absent. These rites have not disappeared because they strengthen the collective identity, an identity very necessary to a marginal group. The anniversary invites observers to reflect and meditate; the struggle of interests between the house and the community, between "me" and "us" has no meaning in the face of the great tragedy of death.

It is the dead who provide this lesson. But who are they? What are they like? Why do they behave this way? The following pages attempt to answer these questions.

　　　　　　　　　　　　　　　　　　　　THE AFTERLIFE

5
The Spirits

Death and human misfortune are not always unforeseeable or unexpected. In many cases the death of a Vaqueiro or a serious accident may be preceded by certain signs or warnings, which, received
by animals or by humans, presage these unhappy events. The most
important of these negative signs is the appearance of the "spirit"
of the sick or dying person to her or his relatives, or to neighbors,
while the person is still alive. Death, in this sense, begins before
dying. Similarly, after death, the spirits of the deceased continue to
participate and interfere in the world of the living. Clinical death,
therefore, does not mean the automatic disappearance of a Vaqueiro. The transition from living to dead is a complex process for
the people of the *braña*. Let us look first at the spirits of the living.[1]

THE SPIRITS OF THE LIVING

A spirit is identified by the way it presents itself. People know that
a spirit is present because of the unexplainable fear it produces, a
sensation of terror without apparent cause. This fear is generally
accompanied by darkness, for although there are daytime apparitions, the spirits usually prefer to circulate at night. Another condition is temporal proximity to death or an accident. The Vaqueiros
assert that "when the spirits are about is when people are ready to
go." But these beings also can be perceived directly by the senses,
the eyes and especially the ears. The spirits can produce a wide
range of sounds, including shouts, cries, wailing, weeping, or
moaning. People often define spirits as "things that make noise."

255

Perhaps it is because so many of these manifestations take the form of sounds that it is said that the spirits are "invisible."

Ah! You want to know about what we call spirits, eh? At the time of [the death of] my mother nothing was heard, but almost, almost—it was strange, because when they hear something they would say, "Hey, Fulano is going to die, or somebody is going to die." Yes, at night, when someone dies, something is about, yes. It is like a shadow that sighs, or something is about, yes. It is invisible. If someone is seen to be dying, to be very sick, before they do, things are heard around here, like sighs or wails.

Vaqueiros like to illustrate their theories about spirits using their own experiences and those of others. In some cases, spirits emit comprehensible sounds or mutter a few cryptic words that acquire their true meaning only after the person is dead. The following case is typical in that spirits tend to communicate with the people who know the dying person well.

I have very little hearing. But I heard this. A mailman died near La F. I don't know if he threw himself in the river or fell in. He had always brought the mail to my house, saying, "Eh!" One day when I heard "Eh!" I answered, "Come in, whoever it is!" Cripes! No one came in, and I took fear. A few days later I heard that he had died. I had heard it clearly. No one else in my house was still in the kitchen; they were all in bed. I was alone, listening to the news. I just about recognized the voice. Not for sure. But after he died I said, "Of course! It was he!" He had come to the door so often and said the same thing. I heard it very clearly, but nothing else. I have heard a number of them.

Sometimes these voices sound like they come from persons alive and real, without the intervention of spirits. But this is not the case when there are rapid and unexpected changes in the direction of the voices, which seem to switch about with considerable speed.

Another time I was on my way to La C at night, and I heard some moans on a lower path about one hundred meters away. And I thought it was someone joking, so I began to moan as well. Him lower down and me higher up, until I got near the house where I was going to play cards. And suddenly, just like that, the moans switched to a mountain we call the C! The woman, who later died, lived there. That got me scared, and I banged on the door, pum, pum, "Open the

THE AFTERLIFE

door!" And they came out and listened, and no one else heard it. It couldn't have been a person because I wasn't afraid at all until it changed location. It changed all of a sudden. I don't know; the only thing I know is that the next day they took the woman to Oviedo, and the following day she died.

In addition to lamentations and verbal expressions, spirits betray their presence by strange noises or the use of instruments. The dying person may be far from the *braña*, but it seems as though part of the person comes to the longtime habitat, does familiar work, visits the house, and goes over well-known paths. For the ethereal spirits, distances are unimportant.

Like that day in C house. I was closing the door to the balcony and I heard a plas, plas, like three knocks in the kitchen, and it sounded like the big hook fell down, and at the same time the keys of the door rang as if there were two or three of them together in the door to the living area. I heard it very clearly. R died that day two hours after this happened. I was so frightened I could hardly speak. A chill! Something that grabbed me! I took the lantern, even though the lights were all lit, with a fear that wouldn't go away, looking behind me, afraid that the lights would go out, totally terrified. I looked in the kitchen to see if anyone was hiding there, saw that nobody was, that the hooks were all in place, and was even more frightened. And I left the house, going down the stairs backwards, with a fright that didn't leave me until I got on the path, a fear that someone was going to grab me. The next day in the morning in L they said that R had died in Madrid. She had died at noon, and this had happened at ten or eleven o'clock in the morning. I didn't know she had died. At the time I didn't think about it, I was just frightened. But I realized it when I went to bed that night: "I wonder if it is R." Then it was as though someone was pulling on my hair. I got all cold and all nervous, trembling. I never said anything. When I looked around the living area, I thought that someone was trying to scare me, and I wondered who it was.

In addition to making itself known by sounds, the spirit can sometimes be seen. Those who are going to die appear to their relatives and acquaintances in fields, meadows, paths, or at the door of the house. These are the places the person normally frequents, but his or her presence at the moment of the apparition is anomalous and impossible. These apparitions, since they include the person who is going to die, are referred to as "visibles." But they cannot be touched. The spirit is not the same as the person but somewhat "like" the person.

It's not a shadow. It is something visible. They say that there is nothing, but there *is* something. Something there is because . . . there are people who have seen it. I don't know, dear! I don't know what it can be. They are visible things that are seen [*son visibles que se ven*].

The spirit is something that appears. I think that if you go to touch it you don't feel anything. It is a representation, a thing, I don't know. They are white screens [*pantallas*] that represent things. The spirit would be like a person. Look, for example, I die tomorrow, and today, since I was here, you see me as I am, the spirit.

Cases of spirits with human faces are remembered in some detail, since they prove beyond a doubt the truth of the belief. People's accounts dwell on the clothing worn by the apparitions, sometimes identical to the clothes in which the dead person will be laid out. In the following case, two neighbors witnessed the apparition:

One day early in the morning I was standing in the path, talking with one of P's sisters, who was in a hayloft at the top of the ladder. And we saw A's mother go by on the upper path, as if on her way to C house, as if wrapped up in a mantle. She just barely appeared above the wall and then was gone. We both saw her. "Where is María of A going so early?" "She must be going to C house; I don't know." But it was clear that it was she, and that she was going uphill. And at nightfall P's sister and I were talking again after having shut up the animals, and María's daughter, may she rest in peace, came by on the way to get some things for her at the store. And she stopped and the three of us talked for awhile. "Well, I have to go because I have to buy some bread and other things for my mother who is sick." "How long has she been ill?" "Well, she's been in bed now quite a few days without getting up." I said, "What? We saw her go by here this morning." She said, "No, that's impossible, unless it is her spirit; no, it's impossible." In a few days she died.

Visions of weddings and funerals are quite common. Both ceremonies, in spite of their obvious differences, can signify misfortune, according to the context. For example, if a wedding appears in a dream it is, by inversion, a metaphor for death, for it is assumed that the dream represents the opposite of reality. By the same token, a funeral in dreams represents good news. Yet the vision of a funeral, as opposed to a dream, always presages the proximity of death. Unfortunately, most of the visions consist of weddings in dreams and funerals when awake. When people are half-awake, they see both. Some of the visions of funerals are not simply of abstract, symbolic funerals but the funerals of specific persons.

And my mother said that another time, when we were building the house, and we were all little and there weren't enough beds for all of us, she was sleeping in the *parreiro*. The *parreiro* was something used long ago to store hay. She said she didn't know if she was dreaming, but that it's possible she wasn't. That she first heard what seemed to be a wedding, with people going by on burros and shooting off rockets, and then she heard what seemed to be people talking together, the sound of conversations, "run, run, run," as if a funeral procession was passing there, near the house. All the noises, the little bell, the priest as if he were singing the funeral, everything. She said, "I felt like I was petrified with fear." A neighbor woman's mother, J, who had been very ill, died the next morning.

My brother-in-law from B said that one night he went to the mill and at a turn in the path he saw people, horses, and everything; there was an air so hot that it went past his face like this, and then he saw a gleaming coffin and a dead man in it, carried by four men from the village, and all the people went by. And the next day or so a villager died, and he was carried away by the same four men!

In addition to this kind of personification, the spirits show their presence by the way they affect the environment. This is seen, in particular, in the abnormal movement of trees. Spirits can also change into birds or lights.

Once when M from C came from courting, he doesn't like to talk about it, but it seemed to him that down the hill from X the trees seemed to be falling one after another. And about a year or so later a worker was killed on the hillside there. He was going down the path calmly and saw all the trees coming down on him.

And then there is the case of S, who died in the war, and before that they saw him here, and when they got close to him he changed into a bird, the black one.

My brother, a day or two before my grandmother died, was coming from a neighbor's house. She was born here, later went to Madrid, and a day or two before she died a phantom turned up on the path, a white thing. He was a little frightened, and the phantom lit up two lights. He took off through a field and got home by a shortcut. Two days later the news came that she had died in Madrid.

All of the above cases of sounds and apparitions presage death; all end with the statement that someone indeed died, whether a person who lived in, previously lived in, or who had simply passed through the *braña* or the adjacent landscape. Although occasionally a considerable time passes between the vision and the death, even several years, more frequently the interval between announcement and death is a matter of days or hours. Serious accidents or injuries are also foretold in these visions. One hears the cries of the injured or the laments of the family. In the case of death as well, whether natural or accidental, instead of sounds or visions of the spirit of the person who will die, a person may hear the laments and cries of family members or neighbors. Thus the premonition of death at times explains certain behavior that would go unnoticed in other contexts.

One time my mother went to get something in the *corredor* beneath the house, as she had done hundreds of times. And she heard squeaks and cries and came back to the house in a fright. They were voices she knew, dear. Well, the next day it was María who cried in the same place. The cart got away from them, and those were squeaks she heard the day before.

One of my aunts was killed, drowned, when she was sixteen, in the mountains. Her mother, my grandmother rest in peace, went out to call her, "Lula, Lula." People gathering chestnuts heard the cries in the morning, heard her calling Lula before she died. The day before she drowned they heard [her mother] call her.

THE SPIRITS OF THE DEAD

The spirits also appear after death. This is less common, and some Vaqueiros question the reality of these appearances, although all believe in the premonitions. Yet everyone can cite examples that appear to confirm the phenomenon, and some have had personal experiences. These stories are much like those above.

X, three or four years ago, he must of had cancer; he died in his house. He was abandoned, girlie. Why didn't they take

THE AFTERLIFE

him to the hospital? He would let out long sighs while he was slowly dying. We would pass by, below the house, and hear him lament, girlie. "Ay . . . !" After he died, two boys were going by here, and there, in the lower part of his house, they said they saw something black go by them, and they took a fright such that they almost died. It was something with a black swatch, no, not like a bird, like a person.

I have heard about it, but I have never seen anything. Now old M, he said he saw a woman, and he's not the kind of person who lies. He said he saw a woman named L, whom I knew, after she was dead, and he said he saw her go down the path that goes up to C from the river in a grove of trees. She had a rope in her hand; she was going for firewood. And he took a good look at her, and he said she was completely dressed, with a kerchief of herbs on her head, an apron of *muletón*, and a green jacket. He said she was dressed just as usual and was going down there with a rope in her hand.

In the two foregoing cases, the content of these visions is essentially the same as those of the visions of people before they die. But others are quite different. Many of the spirits that return after death come to seek help from living. These spirits are said to "need something," usually masses or prayers. Note the fact that the message, transmitted through an intermediary, is directed to a family or a house. The obligations of a house do not end with a funeral. The members who survive have to solve the problems of those who have passed on.

And they say that the spirit is about before a person dies. And not afterwards. But then they say that some people needed things and came back, and told people brave enough to listen to tell the family of a certain house that they needed masses or things like that.

And there are [spirits] who ask that a mass or two be said for them; then they don't come back anymore. Here we say that when spirits come, or there is some strange noise, it's that some dead family members are in need. We have the custom of giving a mass or alms to the saints or whatever to get rid of it. Because, of course, I get frightened. I say to myself, "My God, what does it need? Someone needs something, and who is it?" That's when you don't know who it is, of course. You know it's someone from the house. No, it wouldn't go to another house, just to sit down. When something comes we say, "Maybe it's so-and-so, the last one who died, for example, who needs something." You don't know who it is. I give the masses, and it is said, "Let them be for the person most in need of this house or family."

Some spirits tell their family members what it is they need. The two cases that follow happened long ago; they include dialogues between the living and the dead. The spirits that speak are usually the most veteran of the dead.

One time the dead mother of my grandmother spoke with my grandmother. It was some time after her death. This was in S [braña]. She went to her daughter, my grandmother, and said, "Juana, Juana, don't be afraid." And my grandmother said, "Who are you?" "I am your mother, your mother, don't be afraid." And she said, "Ay, mother, speak with me awhile mother. I want to see you." And then her mother said, "I can't, dear, I have to go. I'm in a hurry. Give a mass to a so-and-so [a saint]." This was the spirit talking. And the daughter said, "Ay mother, come here." And she then replied, "I can't talk to you anymore. I can't say anything else." I don't think she said anything else. The daughter said she couldn't see anything, and had the mass said.

They say about M, the grandfather of R, that he never lied. Once when he was in Madrid—in Madrid they don't believe in apparitions [visibles]—long ago, he's dead now, they didn't have as many cars as they do now, and he made his living carting in Madrid with mules. Anyway, he was in his stable and he said a brightness came in front of him, like a circle, and came into the stable, and he heard one of his sisters who was already dead speak. "Brother"—yes, I think that's what she said—"Don't be afraid, for I am your sister. You must pray six stations that I need." Six stations—I wouldn't know how to pray them, but you who have studied would know. It would be like saying the rosary. And she said, "Because I need them." And he knew how to pray them, and he knelt down right there in the stable—six stations would be six Our Fathers and Hail Marys and Salves or . . . I heard him tell me this many times. That he knelt down right there in the stable and prayed them. And before he was finished his sister went away, brightness and all, and he never saw her again.

The spirits are not always as polite and considerate as in the two above cases in which they humbly ask for prayers. More often, the spirits show a certain aggressiveness, especially those not long dead. Although in the above cases the spirits of the dead speak, on most occasions they are very vague; often they are totally mute and communicate their desires symbolically. At times this communication occurs by means of pain and distress, fear, or restlessness among the surviving family members.

Ay Dios! My father, may he be in heaven, what he didn't suffer from those things . . . I think it was my mother, you know. After my mother died, my father and I would be together, and I didn't feel anything. He said that he felt something, like a pneumatic drill, that came down to pierce him when he was in bed, time and again. He felt something that trapped and weighed upon him, and I felt nothing. And he changed bedrooms, and it was the same, he felt the same thing.

Many times when we were in bed after mother died, you could hear someone walking in the attic, as if the boards were moving, and at the same time someone was dropping grain and . . . it wasn't mice; it was like this, "pum, pum . . ." We all heard it. "Listen, there's noise in the attic." "Hush," M would say, "don't frighten us." And finally H said that we had to give another mass and see if it went away.

Another common method for the spirits to communicate with the living is by way of accidents and bad luck. When there is a string of losses, the cows abort or the calves die, a good cow breaks a leg, the harvests are lost, or when there is a series of accidents in any one house, whether of humans or animals, the dead are thought to be responsible. In such cases it is said that "the dead eat the living." To cut short their feasting they must be given the spiritual "food" that they need, whether masses, prayers, alms, or traditional anniversary feasts. Consider, for example, the following case of a spirit returning after a year to demand the sacrifice of animals.

I'm going to tell you something else. Right here in F [*braña*], and this is the pure truth, during the war at least two brothers died. And one of the brothers came back to speak in the kitchen to a sister—and this isn't just a story, she told me herself. "Sister, give me an anniversary, for I need it." "And sister replied, "How can we do it for you since there is no meat?" This would have been in the war years when times were bad. And he told her that he would get the meat. And it's true, as the sister tells it, he did get it. When the cows of the house went to the mountains one of them dislocated a hip, and they used it for the anniversary. Otherwise, of course, they wouldn't have killed a cow.

People say that when you don't give an offering to the church "the dead eat the living," because if you do not give to those who have passed on, there are losses of cattle. You have to give in case they need it. They give plenty of warnings. I myself have seen here substantial losses and other things, but if you give them masses and other things they go away. They say that if you give money for a mass and the priest says it, it is for the dead.

In addition to the regular need for masses and alms, the dead also return to avenge in death the neglect they suffered in life. It is not uncommon for the elderly to blackmail their relatives with the threat of future visitations in order to get better treatment. By the same token, people believe that paying scrupulous attention to a sick person and providing a generous send-off for a corpse can prevent these reprisals.

If you do not give a mass they say, "Listen, if you don't give me a mass when I die, I'll come and burn the house down." They say that the spirit comes. How many times my grandfather would say that if we didn't have the funeral the way he wanted it he would come and burn the house. But he didn't come back. The soul, the spirit can return, but the spirit does not burn the house; if it returns, only the soul does, what can come back of the rest? These are things that they say used to happen, that it would burn down the house, or . . . when things happen in the house, they say, "Listen, it must be because we didn't give a mass for the dead." There must be something to it.

If the losses and accidents continue in spite of masses and alms, then there is another possible explanation: the dead may have made promises that they forgot, or did not want to or were not able to fulfill when they were alive. Debts, whether to humans or to the divine, can bring fatal consequences if not repaid generously. The promises of the dead must be fulfilled by the living, whether by immediate family members or those who live in the house where the dead person lived. Often these dead, patient but inexorable, wait their turn before informing the living of their needs. In the meantime they have no rest.

In X house here, a sister married into Y house. And when her parents died, they ordered her brother to give her a calf. And he didn't do it, and almost every year he lost a calf, and one fell down the mountain. And that year he gave one to his sister. He sent her to the stable and said, "Listen, Z, go to the stable and pick the one you like the best." And then it all stopped.

X said that my grandmother came, who was dead. And he said that she came to talk to him to tell the people of the house to give an anniversary for her, for she had promised it. And that those of the house said that they had already given one, and she said, "No, that was for some who were ahead in line, who needed it more."

Since those who have passed on are usually not very explicit about their desires and problems, and promises must be fulfilled according to how they were made, when recurring losses or accidents occur, people must have the message that comes from beyond translated into terms they can understand. They ask persons who have the gift to attract the dead and communicate with them. There are three kinds of people like this in the region. The first is the most numerous group: those who receive occasional visits from a dead person of their own family or of their neighbors who inform them of their needs. These are likely people known to be brave [gente de valor], although they may not think of themselves that way. Their contact with the other world is very sporadic, perhaps a couple of times in an entire life. There are others who have more frequent contact with the dead, who may have amassed a small collection of visions, although they may not always be able to have visions on demand. These, too, are local people, and it is said that they "speak with the dead"; now they are quite rare. Finally, there are those who can communicate with the dead at will. These people are considered true professionals. They are called spiritists [esperitistas] and animas [souls]. They operate on a regional basis. People come to them from distant townships to learn about any deceased person. According to some local beliefs, they have this exceptional power because they were born at noon on the Day of the Dead. The woman who speaks below, a local specialist, recognizes a little sorrowfully that although she has a certain degree of power because she was born in November, she does not have enough to be a spiritist because she was not born on November 1.

Don't you see that I was born in the month of All Saints and All the Dead, which is the same month. I was born in the middle of the month, and I am in relation with God and the Virgin, thanks be to God. If I had been born on the Day of the Dead at twelve noon, then I would be a spiritist. Then the dead would come to talk to me, and I would know if they needed a promise or if they needed anything. No, I don't talk with them; most times, when someone is going to die, I see something visible, but it seems I have little ear [*oído*] for seeing them [sic]. They don't come up to me, and they don't talk to me . . . sometimes they talk to me, but they don't come up to me because I'm not strong enough for . . . I have a weak heart.

The following excerpts are about persons of the intermediate category, those who have a certain amount of contact with the dead on certain occasions. The second quote shows how these local specialists work. Note that they interpret and participate in the demands of the dead.

There is something to it. Once there was a [temporary and local] teacher, who was very holy. A teacher! And he would get up before dawn and go outside because he said that sometimes something would come to talk with him, and he would go out so he could talk with them . . . the dead, I think, were the ones who came.

In X there used to be The Crow. He was already gone before my time, but I know where he lived. He came here to L house and told grandfather that he had talked with the dead and that they needed I don't know how many masses. And grandfather paid no attention. And The Crow said to my mother, "Your father-in-law didn't pay attention, but it's me they are putting pressure on." Meaning that from the other world they were pressuring him so they would be given masses. And my grandfather gave the masses, because he got scared.

The above case is typical of the efforts of local specialists to solve the problems of friends or neighbors. When there is no local specialist, or when their efforts are unsuccessful, the Vaqueiro will go to one of the regional professionals, where the relation is similar if more formal. One of the most famous of the old-time spiritists was known as the *ánima* of Sampol (Concejo de Boal). She received many visits from people of the region. Two of these consultations are described below. Notice the characteristics attributed to *ánimas*.

Not all spirits can be seen, because sometimes they keep on moving. There was something of this in my house, and I'll tell you about it. When I was a little child there was a leaf, like a leaf of corn that would go through the house, in the main room, under the beds. It was one of those things connected with spirits, because the old folks who died needed things. It was around for a long time. And there was an *ánima* over in Sampol, a village bordering on Galicia, and everyone would go to that *ánima* there. An *ánima* was something living, but like an animal; it was said to be held together by bandages and nothing else. And my father and the women went together, and the *ánima* said to him, "So, what do you want?" "I have come prepared to give what is necessary for the dead of the house"—because things were going around the main room. And she called him back in and said, "Well, your grandfather just left here very happy because you got him out of purgatory." I don't remember now just how many stations she ordered to be prayed in the house. And you know the reason for all this? For a curse, "I swear the sea of God" [*Jura el mar de Dios*], and it was true, for my father had often heard him say it. And that [dead] man had gone to speak to her. And I don't know how many masses had to be given and stations prayed in the house, and then nothing more was heard in the house. She was an *ánima*; she spoke with the dead. This was why they were in need, and they were going around in the house, because of this curse. I was surprised that she knew about the curse, this "I swear the sea of God." It seems that the sea is holy [*bendito*], and you can't swear. . . . Other times you lose cattle, or so they say. There were always losses; calves dying. . . . I was really surprised by that . . . for they say that when one goes one does not return, yet the spirits . . . because it was true, my great-grandfather did swear that curse, for my father remembered that he did it all the time.

When things go wrong it's because the dead need something. Because the dead offered something and they forgot to deliver it. My dead husband, too, may he be at rest, one went to an *ánima* called Sampol, and so did my sister-in-law, E's wife, who also had many losses, like us. My sister-in-law went because my father had a dispute with some neighbors, for I was still in the house then. I was a girl, and he offered a mass and didn't give it. The *ánima* told her that he had had this dispute with the people of the village and that he offered a mass and didn't give it. Because he loaned a thousand pesetas to somebody and then the person didn't want to repay it, and it was a member of the village, and my father had his married son in the house and the daughter-in-law, and my father didn't want them to find out about it. And he did what he could so they wouldn't find out. And this *ánima* uncovered the whole thing. And he had offered this mass and didn't give it. And afterwards they gave it. And look, she told us that we had to give many masses and that a man had also died having offered for a mule he had lost. And he found the mule but he didn't give the mass. That is the worst thing there is, because no matter what he offered it for, for the dead, to help them get out. And my father came out all night because they settled things afterwards, but he hadn't given the mass; he forgot.

It is significant that animals, especially cattle, are the objects of the wrath of the dead. Losses, accidents, and diseases of cattle are signs of the dead's needs and warnings of the obligations of the living and those who preceded them.

ANIMALS AND SPIRITS

Four kinds of animals as well as human beings are receptive to premonitions of death—dogs, foxes [*raposas*], horses, mules, and burros [*caballerías*], and especially cows, who are said to "sense death" [*sienten la mortandad*]. When the Vaqueiro has doubts about the cause of fears or visions, he watches the cattle, because the cattle "know" when there is a death nearby.

I understand that they sense things, that they hear things . . . the cows know. Look what happened when F died—they [the cows] didn't want to go by there on the path, neither those of C nor those of O. They started to get skittish and look around and get a little . . . crazy. They get that way when people are going to die. The cows sense death.

Cattle are thought to be perspicacious by nature; they are thought to "smell" death and experience this presentment fearfully, just as humans do. The same is true of dogs and foxes. A sudden shift in the behavior of these animals means a warning of imminent change in the physical world, like snow, or the social world, the death of humans.

The other day my cows got scared in the meadow. These cows sense things as well as people do, by smell. I was coming with them there above X, and they were walking very calmly. Then one began to raise her head and stop, and stare, startled, looking down the path. What did I know! I said to myself, "Something's going to happen; they sense something, either snow or death." And they ran back to end of the meadow. "Well, I'll leave them for now." But in a few days . . . this was three days before the woman died. Cows sense it in advance; that I have observed. They have an amazing sense of smell, huh?

Even now, if someone dies around here, or gets sick in a house, the cows sense it. I've seen this myself. Dogs, too. When my father died, one of the mongrel dogs, a devil of a dog that used to be around these houses, on that day he went to the corral to bark. That dog sensed if somebody was dying. A man in M always had dogs and bitches, and they would go to the mountain there to bark when somebody died in B. They have a sense of smell like cows . . .

And another thing, the fox senses these things a lot, because it begins to howl a lot, and I think it, too, figures these things out. They begin to look toward the houses and run without stopping. I believe they sense a person there . . . dead, no, not dead, dying.

These animals not only "sense" death among humans; they also "see" spirits directly. Cows especially are thought to enter into direct contact with the supernatural world.

We don't see anything, but the animals see the spirit of a person. When they sense that someone is sick or is going to die, the animals begin to complain loudly, like a dog when he barks. And then, if the cows are on a path and the sick person goes by some days before, they begin to sniff and buck. They see the spirit and we don't. The animals see it, even though they're animals. Remember when X's cows didn't want to go past him? Praise be to God, dear, it was because they sensed it, that their master was going to die.

Cattle do not have presentiments about all humans. They cannot detect the death of small children, for instance, because, it is said, infants do not go in the stable so the animals have not known them. Children apparently have no spirits or, if they do, the spirits do not show themselves. But the cattle readily perceive the spirits of adults, even those who visit the braña infrequently. So it seems that social experience is a key factor in the definition of spirits. The cows appear to take into consideration bonds of friendship and neighborhood, for their senses of smell and sight permit them to recognize the spirits of the dying and the dead over long distances.

No, they don't hear children. . . . Anyway, children don't get around much, and there are some who are born and don't get out of the house, and the cattle aren't afraid of them. The old folks are heard more; if an old person dies, the cattle get scared. Once my mother was going beneath the hazelnut tree of C house with three cows. And the last one shied and seemed almost glued to the ground next to the hazelnut tree of C house. And that afternoon word came that X, of C house, had jumped from a fifth-floor window in Madrid. So you see, cattle sense things and so do people.

Other animals have come to symbolize death. Their presence near a house means that someone is about to pass away. They are commonly known as "animals of fear" or "animals of the night." Among the former are crows and magpies [*pegas*], and among the latter, owls. These animals are frequently associated with spirits. A vision of one or more of these birds has the same connotations as a vision of human spirits. For example, if two crows kiss, it means that a human couple is broken up by the death of one of its members.

Some days before my grandmother died the crows could be heard. There were two in a tree in a meadow. They say that when someone is going to die the crows make this noise, "cua, cua, cua, trrrr . . . ," and that it undoes a marriage; when two crows put their bills together, a marriage is undone.

It appears that the animals of death sense and are attracted by the "fever" of humans; where there are crows and magpies, death is near. Some times they even produce, and not only presage, sickness and misfortune.

There in my wife's village a crow began to caw—"caw, caw." And a man went out and began to throw stones at it to scare it off. Well, that man just keeled over. They had to go and pick him up. He didn't die, but for many months he was laid up with a bad leg, and he still limps. I don't know whether the matter of death was involved, maybe so. When the magpies are around, they say that death is around, too. But the case of that man is true. I saw him with his legs in bad shape. He was sick for a long time with bad legs until he went to [the hospital in] Oviedo. That's true; it's not a story.

It is best not to intervene with these forces of death. An encounter with these birds alone and at night provokes a fear similar to a vision of spirits and the same reaction—flight. The following story was related in the context of a conversation about spirits in relation to other examples of visions and appearances. My informant considered it the same kind of situation.

Another day I was coming from F, from the dance. And when I crossed the river I sat down against an oak tree and fell asleep. But as soon as I fell asleep a big barn owl came to rest on the branch above me, and cried, "OOO." A screech! The owl flies at night, and maybe it had come with me. I didn't know if it is bad luck or not; the truth is, I woke up with a great fear to see it in front of me. I didn't waste any time getting up [to the *braña*].

The animals of the night—the owls—appear in the dark like spirits. The sounds they emit, and those of the spirits, are called by the same name, *glaios* [translated here as squeaks or screeches], and evoke similar fears and worries in humans. The animals of fear—the crows—are black birds; supernatural visitors sometimes appear as birds of this color. The magpie [*pega*] is an exception to the prevailing color symbolism: its breast is white while the rest of its plumage is the color of the night. Perhaps for this reason, this bird produces a certain ambivalence in those who see it.

The magpies can bring happiness just as well as sadness. They say that when a *pega* sings it might bring a letter from the family; other times it might be the reverse. When R's husband died, they say a magpie went right into the main room. It must have sensed it.

Wolves and bears, two other animals held to be accursed, produce even more fear. The wolf is still a fairly common presence in the region, and almost all Vaqueiros have encountered one at least once. The bear is much scarcer and has only been seen occasionally by transhumant Vaqueiros in remote sections of the high mountains. The fear both animals evoke has stereotypic features, especially when they are seen at night.

I am not afraid . . . except of wolves. They are savage; you have to be afraid of them. I saw one once during the day, but not at night. . . . If you see one at night, your face gets all cold and you can't talk and your hair stands up on end; it's not fear, it's terror that enters the brain. Your face gets frozen and your hair . . . that's the truth.

Even daytime sightings of wolves provoke paralysis of the body and some of its faculties, in addition to fear for the livestock.

Well, one day I was with the sheep; I was with another woman on a hillside. And I saw that the sheep were acting scared, running towards us. We said, "What's wrong with them? What's happening?" I couldn't figure out what to do. I got a case of nerves and I couldn't do anything. But the other woman began to whistle at it. We didn't see it; it was among the sheep, and we weren't close enough. I couldn't do anything; I was scared. They say that when you see a wolf you go mute, that you get . . . I don't know, but anyway, you can't talk. The sheep kept running, but the wolf stood still in the middle of the path when she whistled. Then it went back the way it had come, looking over its shoulder at the sheep. It didn't have a chance to catch them, although it was in there among them. Then it went into a pine grove, and we didn't see it again. The wolf gets people scared. You get a kind of terror [*pavor*] when you see it. I realized that I couldn't whistle, even though it was in the daytime, in the afternoon, and I was with the other woman. I got kind of scared. They say you get so scared your clothes fall off your body and your hair stands up on end.

Seeing wolves during the day does not provoke as much fear as seeing them at night. It also depends who sees whom first. The worst is when the wolf sees the human first. Compare the following cases:

One time I had to go to Oviedo—X was in the hospital— so I left here around three in the morning. I was alone, at night, and when I got to some boulders, I heard something growl as it came along the path. It was a wolf. I shined the flashlight on it, and saw its eyes about as far away as that place. Zooks! When I saw it, I shit in the milk, what a fear got into me! But even so, I let out some yells and took off after it. Ay, dear! it seemed that all my clothes were falling off my body. Ay, dear! But I came out of it and started running. . . . I was really scared.

Look at what happened to F. It was a weekday, and we had sent him to cut *hartos*. But instead of coming home he went to the tavern, and left the *pala* and the scythe among the pine trees. On his way home it was already dark, and he got so scared he couldn't talk and he couldn't walk. And he began to tread very slowly and listen carefully to see if he heard anything, and he heard nothing. He said he didn't dare to go pick up the scythe he had left. He couldn't shout.

THE AFTERLIFE

In this last narrative the appearance of a sudden and inexplicable fear is due to wolves. Yet the same fear could have been due to spirits. Since these fears are quite similar, I ask about the possibility that spirits were involved.

No, not spirits . . . it was more likely wolves. You don't know. It's likely that wolves were nearby, and even if you don't see them, they see you. He could not move, and for awhile he could barely move, from the fear that got into him.

I have gotten afraid at night from wolves, because your clothes get loose; it seems that they separate from the entire body. With the spirits it's the same, yes, it's the same fear, they say it's the same.

Because of this similarity, sometimes one is unsure about what has caused fears and noises. In the two following cases, both hypotheses are considered:

Look, when I was a youth we would take our grain to be ground at the mill of a relative on the river at C. And I had a load, and to keep it on, a staff. And I felt something, like an attack from the rear, and fear, great fear! It was dark then, near a chapel in C. And I remembered the spirits they talk about. But the next day, I am pretty sure, I went back after the other load, which was flour for bread, and there near the chapel—there was snow on the ground—there were a lot of wolf tracks. That's what happens to the body; it starts to tremble and your wool stands on end, man. And the next day the same thing happened. I felt them; it seemed that they drew me on with their eyes, two wolves, until I crossed the creek. Then I didn't see them anymore. I got cold all over, but I wasn't frightened. I did go very carefully at night, without making much noise, in case there was something to be frightened of, but I didn't get scared.

Something happened to me, too. It was a year ago this coming November. I went to P that day and I came back down at nightfall. And a little above here, in a village called O, where I'd been very, very often, a fear began to get into me, like a coldness in the body. There came a moment when my clothes came off of me, and I was [as if] without clothes, frozen, cold. I kept on going. Until my legs got stuck and I couldn't keep on any longer. It was on a slope near some chestnut trees, and it was already a little dark. It seemed that something was pulling me back. By then I . . . I was hardly feeling anything at all. There was a house nearby, the last one of the village, and I called the man who lived there, and he came out—he was our friend—he said, "It's the wolves, the wolves. They came after me once, and your clothes came off you; it means that the wolves are near you." He picked up a pitchfork and went up with me to the end of the forestry road, to the entrance of A . . . and no, it wasn't wolves. You see, I got the idea in my head that my mother had died that night. I went up to my house, and my mother was as well as ever. So I came here, and the next day, at dawn, someone from F came and said, "Damian (a man with an ugly black face who's dead now) sends word for you to come and see him." I said, "But is he very sick?" He said, "Yes, very sick; you may never see him again." So that same day I took a horse and went to see him, in the afternoon. The man was in bed, and he asked for tobacco and smoked a Goya. That was eight at night. At ten he was dead. I heard he sort of fell asleep on his side and never woke up. This man was very well known in this house. He always sat there where you are sitting and ate, a very good friend. He would stop here a lot on his way to see the doctor in P. It was his shadow that got me scared. This is true. This is true; it's not a story. This is very true; it happened to me and it is certain.

The only difference between wolves and spirits is that one can verify the presence of the former. It is not usually possible to confirm the presence of a spirit at the time, although a subsequent death may confirm it. Nevertheless, when the wolves are "felt" but not seen, the two situations are quite similar.

While people prefer to see wolves before they are seen by wolves, they would rather be seen first by bears, for it seems that bears do not like to be surprised. The mutual fear that humans and bears inspire in each other can be seen in the following conversation among three men (A, B, and C) and myself (D). I cite it at some length because it expresses the common wisdom on the subject in a spontaneous and entertaining way.

A: All beasts get afraid, try to escape, go away when they have somewhere to go. The bear does, too, at the sound of the human voice at least. But, for example, you get scared, you get totally scared by it. Take me, I could die of fright. The wolf is very suspicious; when the wolf sees a dead animal, it won't touch it, right?
B: It's true, I saw seven together. No more than seven. They

were fighting and clawing each other. It was during the day, and I wasn't afraid.

A: Shit in the milk! They scare you, even in the daytime. As soon as you see them it frightens you some, *hombre,* that is a savage beast.

B: And in the old days when they would go to the high pastures, you'd see them all the time. They would travel at night . . . if you were out at night you might see them. They are always in the high mountains. I don't know why. And they would kill livestock. That's for sure. How many cows have gone up to the high mountains that never came back? There are cows that are brave and defend themselves from the wolf. But generally when cows see them they scare, run, and get attacked. Burros, too; they know they are defeated when it happens at night. But not during the day.

A: They say that if the wolf sees you and you don't see the wolf, you feel more frightened than if you see the wolf first: if you see it first, they say, you don't get frightened. But if a wolf sees me first and I don't see it, I can't talk. I get cold, shivers, your clothes pull away from you; it seems like it grabs you from behind. You don't know what the fear comes from— when it's at night.

B: And with the bear it's the opposite. If it sees you first it goes away; if you see it first it gets scared and attacks.

D: How does one know if they are wolves and not spirits?

C: There are no spirits, María.

A: Spirits you don't see, and everyone is convinced they exist; they exist.

C: Spirits are very different from wolves.

A: Because you can see them.

B: Because a wolf is like a dog. Of wolves I'm not afraid, of spirits I am.

D: But if you can't see them, how do you know it is them?

A: Well, if you get scared, you suspect that it is a wolf. That is, if you don't see anything, or hear anything strange, and you are afraid and you don't know why. . . . Wolves, at night, when a man carries a light, will not come close. But I would bet that if you don't see it, you get more scared because you don't know what it is. It can be something in your body that tells you, "They're here" . . . or . . .

B: And from the spirit comes this fear, this thing. A terror that seizes a man. Unless you have special valor, it scares you, something you can't see, that takes you by surprise that way . . . it's something sudden that . . . that scares you.

D: Does the wolf sense death?
A: No, we don't know. They . . . how do we know what they sense? They are wild beasts.

Wolves and bears, then, like spirits, are feared for the danger and the surprise that their appearance produces. During the day the danger is concrete: the wild animal could attack the cattle. At night the fear is much more abstract, such that it becomes easily fused with fear caused by the spirits. This would seem to indicate that the contact and proximity of wild animals with humans is accompanied by the same symptoms as the interaction between the living and the dead.

THE BELIEF

When I began my fieldwork among the Vaqueiros, a woman in whose house I staying asked me whether I was afraid to walk on the paths at night. When I said I wasn't, she was surprised, and she was quick to tell her relatives and neighbors about my "valor." I, surprised at her surprise and at the minor commotion this caused, asked without obtaining a clear answer about the sources for the "fears" at night. That weekend we went to a Saturday-night dance in a nearby *braña*, a half-hour walk away. My hostess and I were accompanied by a dozen people, among them several girls and their chaperones, usually their mothers. After about three hours at the dance, I was somewhat tired, and remembering that I wanted to get up early the next morning, I suggested to my landlady that the two of us go back. The woman made some excuses but finally, when I was going to go back alone, she decided to accompany me. Gripping my arm tightly, she went the entire distance with considerable trepidation, constantly looking behind her and to the side, and answering me in monosyllables. The next morning, while I was with her in the meadow as the cattle grazed, I tape-recorded my first cases of spirits, together with the following commentary.

> Yesterday I came . . . think of that, I came back thinking about those things. It's what I am most afraid of! Yes, I was thinking about it, but I didn't say anything to you because I thought, "She probably doesn't believe in this." But I was dying of fright. I thought I heard something behind us. Like the boy they took to Oviedo [to the hospital]. [She calls to a cow] Asturiana . . . ! One day last year we talked to the priest about it, and he said, "There are no such spirits or such things; this is something that only you believe in." He said it was something that we imagined, that all of this is something

THE AFTERLIFE

we think up, because nothing like this really exists. But I think they must exist. They say these things only show themselves to a person who has valor. To a person without it, they don't show themselves. So it will never show itself to me, because I have no more valor than a hen. They say things like that. And I am afraid. People do hear things. I never heard anything, except for what I've told you, but there are people . . . because my mother did not lie. I think they hear things more in these villages than in the outside world. . . . People would talk about it in Madrid, there are so many people there. . . . When somebody dies like that, they can't go out in the street, no. But when I begin to look behind me, it seems to me I feel some fear. I begin to look behind me and even though they say it's bad to look behind you, that you see spirits, and I don't know, but I can't help looking back. And you say that you are never afraid at night. That was what I was most afraid of, but I didn't say anything to you.

It was because of this moving confession that I started to study fear and the spirits, that I acquired a rudimentary vocabulary that enabled me to begin to ask questions on the subject and to begin to find my way into the world of the supernatural beings of the people of the *braña*. I no longer tried to get people to go out alone with me at night. But, more important, my landlady's words showed how much Vaqueiros and others believed in spirits.

My landlady's initial caution turned out to be typical of the Vaqueiro attitude toward outsiders in this matter. Some Vaqueiros act skeptical with outsiders, denying the reality of the spirits. This skepticism does not usually last very long, since conversations often draw out experiences involving the skeptics themselves or their families. There are several examples of this kind of contradiction above. Also, it is not unusual to get a flat denial in response to a direct question about belief in spirits while in more relaxed conversation the same person will recount a number of personal episodes of noises or visions. It is noteworthy also that the word *dicen* [they say] is frequently used to refer to opinions about spirits. The vagueness and impersonality of this term allows a speaker to avoid personal commitment in situations of uncertainty. It is not used, however, when the speakers narrate their own experiences. And finally, in the face of outside skepticism, it is common for people to deny one part of the belief while accepting the rest, as with the assertion, for instance, that the spirits appear before a death occurs but not afterwards. In my opinion, this emphasis on the before and the denial of the after takes place because outside critics deny the reality of spirits of the dead and affirm the irreversibility of death, but they say nothing about the spirits of the living, since this belief is not even known on the outside. For the outside world, the word "spirit" or "ghost" connotes exclusively things connected with the dead. Here are some Vaqueiro statements on the matter. Observe the contradictions in the comments.

> After we die it is rare that someone can return. . . . Some-
> times they come back, but a mass is said for them and that
> fixes it.

> About after death, nothing was ever heard; what you ask
> about is before. Before death there is something. No, it's true
> there are things, I believe it. After people die they say this
> doesn't happen, but before they say that they speak, that's
> what they say. I have only heard about it. I don't know if there
> is something, or if it is true, or anything. I believe there is
> something; I believe that something exists. But then I haven't
> heard anything, either of [spirits of] the living or of the dead,
> nor do I want to [ni falta].

This last phrase is frequently repeated. When Vaqueiros express doubts about the reality of spirits, many nevertheless verbally knock on wood, as it were, adding a desire or an invocation that they not receive this kind of visit. At the same time, they tend to associate the specific belief with some reference to a supreme being, for example, a reference to a powerful hand ["hay una mano poderosa"].

The Vaqueiros are also aware of the subjective nature of spirit apparitions. Some remark, for example, on the intangibility of spirits and the fact that only some people see them, which they attribute to the mental nature of the belief and the individual's level of "valor".

> They say that there are shadows. They say that there is an
> aire, an aire that . . . well, that is the spirit, something that
> shows itself. I believe that if you tried to touch it, you
> wouldn't feel anything. It is a representation of something.
> Maybe we imagine these things; I wouldn't be surprised. I
> didn't see anything after death.

> They say that it is an aire, a shadow. . . . What's more,
> when two people are together, only one sees it. The other
> doesn't see anything. They say that it shows itself to people
> who have the valor to see it, but not to those who don't. I pre-
> fer to see a wolf.

THE AFTERLIFE

Other Vaqueiros claim that spirits may be just a dream. Some even suggest that the visionary's own blood can cause the vision. Here the word blood connotes fear.

Because those who say that things appear to them, its because they are in bed, sleeping. And it is a dream, when the person is on their mind.

But the blood must produce this to people. One's own body. Because it's enough for one to see a light, and the light is seen; of course, no one has the valor, but if someone went to catch it, he wouldn't catch anything, because nothing is there. Have you ever heard of it appearing to a drunk? In La E they tried to scare a drunk and said, "Ay!. . . I am a soul in pain. . . ." And the drunk said, "You are in pain? Drink wine like me and you'll see how it goes away!."

For many Vaqueiros, the belief in spirits is not a dogma to which they cling blindly but a matter for argument and criticism, albeit in a selective way. Any conversation about spirits will elicit negative as well as positive examples. The negative examples show how certain individuals make use of their neighbors' fears to get what they want, generally economic gain. One frequent topic, for example, is how people pretend they are spirits of the dead.

On the subject of fears, you can't believe everything you hear. What exists after death is hard to know about, because no one came back from there except for the guy who fooled someone whose father had died. The father would have been an old man like me when he died, and he left a son. And someone went and climbed up on the roof of the house, which was sod and a hole for the smoke. The son was in bed, and he heard something and said, "Who goes there?" And the guy said, "I am your father." And then he continued, "I died owing a cow to Pichu and you have to take it to him, and have an anniversary and kill so many rams." And the son said, "Anything else?" "No, nothing else." So the next day the son got up and went with the cow to Pichu's house. And Pichu played dumb, "Where are you going with her?" "Well, I'm going to put her in the corral. Didn't my father owe her to you?" "Yes, I hadn't gotten around to telling you." And he put the cow in. It was Pichu who went up on the roof. These people believed that the dead came back. There are those who say that hell is here. This is an abuse; there is no forgiveness for this. Out of fear, just in case, if there is a spirit, whether it is the blood, or. . . .

These stories evoke the listeners' pity for the victims and a total rejection of the con men, along with a reference to divine chastisement. The stories all have the same form and content; only the persons involved, what the "dead" ask for, and other aspects vary. They tend to be old tales, designed to remind Vaqueiros not to be too gullible. Today people don't consider themselves capable of repeating such a feat "out of fear, just in case." At most, people play practical jokes to show up those who boast about their bravery.

Here in the old days there was a book that attracted the dead when it was read. One man said he wasn't afraid, in B [braña]. They told him to go outside the house, and they read from the book, and asked him, "Are you afraid?" "No." "Are you afraid?" "No, not at all." And the third time, "Are you. . ." "Open the door or I'll knock it down!" (laugh) But this could have been a trick on him. They asked him, "Who did you see coming?" "So-and-so with his hat over his eyes." Someone in on it with them in disguise.

Sometimes Vaqueiros even doubt the specialists, either because of their lack of efficiency or because of an alleged abuse of power.

I think The Crow [a specialist] told my grandfather one time that he had to give I don't know how many masses for the dead. And my grandfather went down to see the priest. And the priest said, "I don't know, but these masses smell of The Crow." What do you know about that! There were those who said that the priest would give something to The Crow so that folks would go to order masses. Who knows? He would say that he had spoken with the dead.

There are other cases as well in which people consider the participation of spirits to have been dubious, for instance, a situation in which there no fear is produced at all. While some incidents are suspect, people are certain that others have natural causes, for example, that something that fell on one's shoulder was a dead branch or that a strange noise was produced by an animal. These incidents reflect a need to verify the origin of the situation, even among informants who nevertheless have recounted to me perfectly typical incidents of encounters with spirits.

There can be no doubt, then, about the strength of the belief. It might be supposed that the constancy and retention of these ways of thinking stem from a cultural pattern imprinted on the individual born in the braña, with certain ways of perceiving, thinking, and believing. By the same token, people with other cultural predispositions would have difficulty seeing or hearing spirits. But this is not the case of one immigrant to the district, a man from another Spanish province who entered the group through his marriage to a Vaqueiro woman. Although his attitudes, worldview, and knowledge differ significantly from those of his neighbors (for example, he is quite devout and religious), in the matter of spirits his acculturation has been effective.

When I came here they said that you saw this, spirits and all, and I said, "This is nonsense. The things they hear are noises and silly things." But when P of C [braña] was sick I went to give him some shots. And one day I was coming back home late from C, and what should happen, a good ways before getting here, but a bird comes along, "Cheeoo, cheeoo, cheeoo." I said, "Can it be that this bird is coming along singing these nice things to me? In any case, I'm going on." I said, "Well, maybe it's something I'm carrying that's making the noise." I stopped and no, the noise continued. And when there were more noises I said, "All right, as soon as I find a stone I'll throw it at the bird." Indeed, a little farther on I found a stone, I threw it in the brush, and the thing came at me! I felt the air from it, and it brushed my face. Until then I hadn't been afraid, but then I was really afraid! And the bird didn't leave me until I got to the first house in the braña. I came in a horrible panic. And some of the people here asked me, "Didn't you pray?" And I said, "I was so frightened I didn't remember to pray."

This was not the only thing that happened to him. He related the following incident, very similar in content to those described by Vaqueiros acculturated from birth.

Listen, I'll tell you something else that happened to me. Once, when I was in the house, I had to go out. I think it was to the stable, and as I was going out I heard something that sounded like a stone that was loose and was being moved by a cat or something. I went "Fsst!" to scare the cat to see if . . . and I thought, "What is it?" and the noise kept on. "The cat didn't run away, it's not afraid. All right, if the cat's not going to go, I will." To get over into the meadow there is a stile, or something high like that. But I never had any trouble with that. I can still get over it now, and then I was sprier, I was newer. So I went to climb [the stile] after the cat, and as soon as I put my foot on it, I slipped and fell over backwards! It was strange! Because I wasn't afraid, like now I am not afraid, when I went out. But it was something sudden—I put my foot on it and went over backwards, and got such a fright that I went back in my house. And how was I going to go out and take care of the cows, since in that house you had to go outside to get down to the stable. And I said, "Well now, what do I do?" I had a horrible fear, as never before. "How can I have this fear if I've never had it? But I do." And I didn't say anything about this to my wife, just, "You have to go down with me." And I made some excuses that I had to do this and that. And she went down with me, we took care of the cattle, and then we ate. And after that I stayed in the kitchen, without going out into the main room; I didn't even dare to do that. That was too much! I had to wait to go out until she went out to go to bed. Fear, I felt nothing but fear. Later, after awhile, I told my wife. I said, "This happened to me. I didn't tell you so as not to frighten you." And those days an uncle of my wife had died, in France. I don't know if it was the same day, or close to it. And she said, "Of course! My uncle, once when the stones had fallen down, fixed the wall there, maybe it was that." Because she then told me what had happened to her. "That day, I also sensed that they came in, as if they opened the stable and put the saddlebags of the burro next to the big baskets [maniegos] there, because he always did that when he came."

Although this episode is typical and contains the essential ingredients and cultural assumptions (fear, the proximity of a death, etc.) the narrator's explanation of the phenomenon differs significantly from those of the rest of the group. He attempts to adapt the belief to the religious dogma to which he had greater exposure, whether because of his own inclinations or his cultural environment.

For this reason I think this can happen, since it happened to me. When I was in the city I didn't observe any of these episodes. And that is why I thought they were fears that got into you for any old thing you heard, like your own jacket that made you afraid thinking it was a strange noise from the other world. And, of course, for this reason. . . . Some will say that the person who is afraid doesn't see anything, but all of us have fear. Some of us more, some less. I myself was coming here from C by the mountains, snowing and dark, almost at night, and a man said he had seen wolves, and I didn't get afraid. But other times this fear gets into you that is inexplicable. Of course, if we believe in God, we believe in the spirit. But I previously thought that, apart from believing in God,

THE AFTERLIFE

these were things not of the spirits, but things that were scraping, any old things. Like the guy who hung his umbrella on the back of his collar and then said that someone was grabbing him from behind, things like that. These things [of spirits], I think they have to happen before a person dies, by logic. But I think that after we die the soul lives on. I think that the soul and the spirit are two different things . . . no, the soul and the spirit might be the same, I don't know. I don't think the soul is the blood, nor that the soul is the heart or anything. Spiritism exists but is not authorized by the Church, because it can be used to find things out for bad purposes. There are some who say that their mothers or fathers appear to them; I don't say it is a lie, because I believe the spirit exists; it could be true. About warnings, many times I think they are not simply that someone is going to die, but rather are warnings to a person who doesn't believe in order to make him a believer.

This man's experience indicates the difficulty of isolating oneself from the cultural environment of the group as well as the importance, or need, of using common symbols of a group with which one identifies, although their interpretation may vary. And vice versa, the people of the *aldeas*, although they live quite close to the Vaqueiros, try to deny the similarities in their beliefs and emphasize the differences.[2]

Finally I want to show the extent to which the belief in spirits continues. The criticism of the *aldeanos* and the different professionals in the area make the Vaqueiros cautious with people from the outside. Some have even raised doubts and objections in regard to the reality of the phenomenon. Yet when someone is going to die, it is very rare that either people or animals do not "sense" something. All of the cases people mention in this chapter occurred in the somewhat distant past. Yet in 1972 I was able to record a case within seconds of a vision, and I could witness the real terror of the person who had seen it, and the surprise and concern of his relatives and neighbors.

One winter night I was in a warm kitchen in a *braña* house talking with five people: my two hosts, a woman of sixty-five (A) and her daughter of forty (B), and a neighboring family composed of a man about fifty (C), his son (D) and his daughter-in-law (E), aged twenty-four and twenty-three, respectively. Our conversation was about spirits. Some of them told me of incidents in their village that had happened to them or others. C was a little skeptical, maintaining emphatically that after death there were no spirits. The conversation turned to other things, and at one point C went out, presumably to urinate. At that time B was working in the next room. A couple of minutes later, C burst into the kitchen, slamming the door behind him, pale and panting. With a trembling voice, he told what had happened. I captured his words on my tape recorder, which had been on during the previous conversation. Note the surprise and fear of the others as well.

A: What's wrong?

B: [from the other room] Who left the door open?

C: Wait . . . [out of breath]

D & E: But what happened?

C: Nothing . . . I went by . . .

B: [enters] What happened outside?

[Some laugh nervously]

E: You're joking, huh? You're joking!

D: [Very serious] No.

C: I shit on . . .

D: It's no joke.

B: I shit in the milk, he came in and left the door open near me, but flying, eh? . . . Look, what . . .

[All speak quickly]

E: Leave him, he saw something, he really saw something.

C: I didn't see anything. But I felt . . . there in the path, something growling, coming at me. . . . I didn't see anything [nervous, swallowing his words].

D: And what was it?

C: *Coño!* I don't know! I didn't see anything!

E: But didn't B see it?

C: B was inside, *coño!* I shit in the whore milk! It seemed to me it was coming, a black thing, I don't know if it went into the loft or to . . . I was already afraid, I had already gone in like a flash! B was inside . . .

[All speak very quickly, conjecturing]

D: I saw he had gotten afraid.

E: I thought he wanted to make a . . .

C: Yes, make a . . . Balls!

B: Know what it was? The shadows of the hazelnut bushes, that's all.

C: What hazelnut bushes or shadows? There's not any light!

E: And what did you hear? What did you hear?

C: *Coño,* I heard something come at me, something black, by the path, and I entered like a flash. A fear got into me . . . !

[Everyone speaks at once again, very nervously]

C: I didn't close the door or anything. I just came in. When I saw it come near me . . . I said, "I'm not waiting around!"

E: I thought it was to scare us.

All: No, no, it wasn't, no it wasn't, no.

A: I thought it was B who went out with a light and scared him.

C: There wasn't any light! I don't know what it was. I only felt something come by the path . . . and if the door had been locked, watch out!

[All laugh nervously]

A: It's better if we don't talk about this . . . [fearfully]

B: I got scared when I saw him come in, to see him . . .

C: I don't have fear now, not now.

A: This means someone is going to die.

C: It might have been someone who years ago came by here, God knows who!

A: This, this could have happened because you said that there aren't any spirits.

C: No, I said that after death there aren't any but before death, yes.

D: Yes, that's what he said.

A: [To me, since the next day we were going to the high mountains in my car] I don't know. Tomorrow María, you'll have to drive slowly . . .

6
The Saints

The journey of the dead to their final destination is just as complicated as the transition from life to death. Here I will explore the
habitat of the spirits and the interrelations of the dead with the
saints in Vaqueiro cosmology.

THE SOUL AND ITS DESTINATION

Vaqueiros were perplexed when I asked them to explain the notion
of a "spirit." Some vaguely related the spirit to the concept of the
soul [alma]:

> The spirit is like the soul, the soul that can be sensed.
> The spirit that goes about is the soul of the person that goes
> about at that time . . . and attracts . . . or I don't know what it
> is. When one is going to die . . . if it's not the soul, what could
> it be? How could the spirit go around just like that? The spirit
> is this—that you get afraid or see a shadow at that moment.

But although the word soul [alma] is used frequently, it does
not always connote spirituality. There is no general consensus on
the matter, but there is a tendency to associate alma with a concrete physical substance—blood.

> Blood is the alma. A person who's going to die is out of
> blood. And blood, they say, is the alma; that's what I under-
> stand. The alma is the blood. And when you die the blood
> ends, the soul ends.

286

Well, the *alma* . . . is the blood. I think it's the blood. And afterwards, as soon as we die, there is neither *alma* nor blood; it's all over. I don't know much about this. And the spirit is when things are heard at night, things that scare you.

Alma also connotes valor and daring, as can be seen in the following lines, which take the figurative meaning of the word literally. Note the connection with blood in this context.

Soul is valor and daring. "Look what *alma* he showed. *Coño*, he would have stabbed you or shot you or anything." Blood comes to an end because we dissipate ourselves and it gradually runs out. It doesn't help to put blood in us, because the blood they put in us quickly curdles. And we can't do anything about it, for our other organs stop working—our other machinery. *Alma* is valor; it's like putting yourself among a bunch of dead people, or something like that. When they say, "Look what *alma* that guy has," it would be when someone does harm, beats someone up, or is violent.

Alma also means breath and life. Death, in this context, means the end of *alma*. "They say that the *alma* is the last sigh, that a person sighs and dies on you. They say when a person dies the *alma* is the sigh given out." These three meanings underline the vital, concrete, and material aspect of the *alma* to which most Vaqueiros point. Nevertheless, a few Vaqueiros refer to other more spiritual meanings of *alma* that derive from religious beliefs.

The *alma* . . . what is the *alma?* Here we say that there is only one *alma*, which is the blood. But in religious terms they say that there is another kind of *alma*. The part about the blood is what we say here, but few [outside] people know this.

The same kind of problems, contradictions, doubts, vagueness, and uncertainty about the notion of *alma* are to be found in the Vaqueiros' idea of the "other world," which they often refer to using the dichotomy "good place"/"bad place."

I also heard that they come back after they die. They say that when they die and have done for them what they need, that they go to the good place, and from then on they are all right. You know, people say that when those of us who are bad die, they go to the bad place, and those who are good go to the good place; well, that's what I mean. That's what they say; I don't know if it's true or not. I. . . since I was never there. . . .

The other world is associated with two closely related sets of dichotomies: above/below and sky [*cielo*]/earth. Bodies first go to the earth, and then, it is held, go to heaven [*cielo*].[1]

They say we go to heaven, at least many people say so. I don't know if it's true. I don't know if we go to heaven or to the earth . . . first of all we go to the earth. Now there are niches, the people don't go—the priest doesn't want to put people in the ground; he'll have his reasons. But before people died and—I carried a lot of them to the cemetery and put them five feet underground and covered them up. Many people say now that people don't go to heaven, I don't know.

Don't you see that they say "the soul goes to heaven"? I don't know, I don't have an opinion; it's what I heard the old folks say. They say that the other world is when you die and go into the earth. Now they use niches, but when you go to another world it means you go into the ground; you are no longer in this one: you are in this one, but we are above and they are below. You go into the hole.

Heaven is vaguely associated with the atmosphere.

I believe that up here no one knows what is down there. It would be very hard for anyone to know. The [seasonal] teacher of A, who is very religious, they said to him, "All right, *hombre*, you who know so much, is heaven up or down?" And he said that he didn't know. He said that it is probably up. He said, "*Hombre*, up above there is no end. From here on up there is infinity." I think that if they put a platform up there, if they went higher they wouldn't find anything. I don't know, there is something in the atmosphere up there; there's probably the atmosphere. If you went up, you would get to the atmosphere, but you wouldn't find an earthly being or anything else, not at all. That's something I don't know, where heaven is. God knows where it is, because there are so many kilometers that God knows what's there. Even the people who have studied it don't know. Maybe there is no heaven—and all we see is the blue.

In fact, I think this is something we don't know. I think heaven is an immensity beyond what we can see. It is like the end of the earth; what are you going to see? Where is the end of the earth? Since the earth, they say, is round, you walk around and around and you end up in the same place.

Given this interest in the physical location of heaven, the Vaqueiros are somewhat perplexed about space exploration.

THE AFTERLIFE

At death, I don't know dear, some of us go to one place, and some to another. Those who are bad will go to one place and the good . . . to another. But as no one came back . . . the old folks would say that no one comes back. And then they were saying that they wanted to bring the moon down. Is that over now? They were saying they wanted to lower the moon from the sky, that men were going up to the sky. Have they stopped talking about that? That was awhile ago—they were fighting to go up, but they wouldn't have gotten there; they said they wanted to throw it down.

The soul goes to heaven . . . that means when one dies one neither talks nor things like that; the soul, if there is one, has to go to heaven. Heaven is what is up above. I don't know for sure, I never went up there. You know, they say they went up there, that there is another world, and they saw it. You know about the satellites that went to heaven; they say they saw it. Well, is that true? Could be.

The orthodox doctrine of heaven, purgatory, and hell has little importance in the *braña*. People make some references to heaven, but very few to hell and even fewer to purgatory. The good place and the bad place is not equivalent to the dichotomy heaven/hell, since, as we have seen, from the bad place one can move to the good place by means of prayers or masses. The definition of hell, in reply to my specific question, is quite different.

In hell, they say, we burn. I don't know anything else. We know the word; people use the expression "Go to hell."

Hell is devils. [Laughs] He who has bad thoughts would go to hell and he who has good thoughts to heaven. X says that in the infernos the fires are lit with oak. [Laughs] That's what they say, but it's not true. How can there be infernos? Where are they? What room are they shut up in?

Well, heaven and hell are the same. Hell I believe is the here and now.

At times the orthodox doctrine is known through contact with the world beyond the *braña*, or is based on the Vaqueiro's understanding of metaphors for the other world.

Purgatory is for those who have less punishment; purgatory is less severe than hell. Hell was bad, it burned you. Haven't you seen it in circus sideshows? Branches with fire. I saw it in sideshows when I was little. You had to pay to enter hell. Hell was worse; it was for those who were punished more. And heaven was for the good people, of course, and purgatory for those in between. Everything is above; didn't you know that Saint Peter held the keys to heaven?

One doesn't know. Here nobody wants to go to hell. I have a book that says the train of hell is worse than that of heaven, that there are two trains. Purgatory would be something you have to suffer, if it is so.

Although the Vaqueiros are unclear about just where and what the other world is, they know how one is assigned to the good and the bad places. It depends on how one acts when alive. The moral reward or penalty the places connote is evident.

And some go to heaven and others go to hell, or so they say. They say that he who is in the grace of God goes to heaven, and he who doesn't die in God's grace goes to hell. This means that those who were more peaceable, with the soul clean, who didn't kill anybody, would go to heaven. They would be more peaceable than those who went to hell. To hell would go a person who killed or robbed somebody. It's a place where they say the bad are boiled in a cauldron of fire. I often heard it said when I was a child. That he who was bad they boiled there on the fire, and the good people went up to heaven to enjoy God. I heard this, but I don't know if it is true.

Cosmological questions about the soul and its destination cause much perplexity in the Vaqueiros. Very few reply assuredly, and those who do employ the impersonal "they say" [dicen] to answer these questions. In most cases, they refer me to the knowledge of these matters held by educated persons, and especially to the priest, who is thought to make a living by these beliefs.

Of course, one does not know; if one were certain . . . it's not known. Some say that there is another world, others no. Some say there's no such thing as a soul. Let's see, you never talked with someone who has studied? a priest? Do they believe it, or not? They have to defend their bread, right? Like us. I'm sure some priests don't believe a lot of the things they say. But they have to protect their livelihood; they have to talk that way and set an example, sure, or else. . . .

He who thinks wrong will go to hell, and he who thinks right will go to heaven. Sure, they write that and argue it, but somebody just invented it. I think the person who thought it up put it in a book and the others studied it and got it in their heads. And any person who studies can invent something like that, or something a lot better.

These quotes reflect a critical and skeptical attitude toward an essential part of the official religious cosmology. The doubts and vagueness previously quoted on the subject of the soul and its destination show how little these beliefs have affected the people of the *braña*. Their indifference on this matter is in marked contrast to their interest in spirits and apparitions. One might think that the Vaqueiros have no systematic ideas about the other world, but that would be mistaken.

THE PEOPLE OF THE OTHER WORLD

Most of the Vaqueiros' religious practices and beliefs are centered on a hybrid Saint Anthony, the Santa of El Acebo, and the *Ánimas*. The people of the *braña* pay an elaborate attention to these figures.

The people of the *aldea* consider devotion to Saint Anthony especially characteristic of Vaqueiros. The *aldeanos* often criticize the religious behavior of the people of the *braña*—their lack of attendance at mass and their lack of participation when they do attend—but they make an exception in regard to the Vaqueiros' devotion to Saint Anthony. Vaqueiros do observe strictly the "holy day" in honor of Saint Anthony (June 13) by attending mass and refraining from hard or unusual work. This does not mean they do no work at all, since the cattle cannot distinguish which days are holy and at the very least have to be fed. Indeed, the presence of cattle helps to explain the difference in beliefs between *aldeanos* and Vaqueiros. The cult of Saint Anthony has a markedly functional side. The Vaqueiros' devotion to this saint, who specializes in protecting animals, is a cultural response to the way of life, interests, and values of herdsmen. It is difficult for the *aldeanos* to understand because they are predominantly farmers. The moments in which the people of the *braña* invoke the saint and make him promises are very numerous: these moments always have to do with situations involving farm animals, especially cattle.

When a cow is taken to a bull, he who has faith may say, "I will pray an Our Father to Saint Anthony so that the cow gets pregnant." We do this because we have more faith in him, in regard to cows. This is something we heard the old folks do. Anything that comes up, we say, "To Saint Anthony." When a cow coughs you always say, "Saint Anthony."

We have a lot of devotion to him, and when a cow spins around or breaks a leg, we say "Saint Anthony help her." And alms are offered and deposited in the box to Saint Anthony in X church.

The kind of offering varies according to the gravity of the problem. A very frequent as well as very critical problem is the birthing of calves. This always occasions some kind of promise of money. The promise is not just verbal. The promised coins are placed next to the frame of the stable door so that the saint will pay attention and not forget.

Yes, I would give a mass for the promises of the house, whether for family members or even for cattle, as when a cow is dying, or you see that the cattle aren't producing, or you see it in danger, so that it produces. And you have to keep the promises, because if you don't, it's worse. My own mother, when a cow is in labor, would take two *duros* and put them there. "This is for Saint Anthony or the *Ánimas*, if things turn out right." And then she says, "Hey, in the door there I left two *duros* wrapped up for that cow. They have to be given to the priest." And they would get lost if they weren't tied up above the stable door in something like a little handkerchief on the door frame, or nailed to the door. And it is an offering, a promise so the cow will give birth all right.

When the animal is in danger or dying, whether from complications of labor or from any accident, the promise is likely to be a mass to the saint, which is ordered from the parish priest.

Well, those are beliefs. Then listen to this, about a mass I offered the other day when I was with the animals in the pastures. A cow got onto a very steep incline, very dangerous, and it couldn't help itself, and if it began to fall it would be killed. You see the danger, you could see the harm it could do, and so you commend it. And the cow maybe had to get out on its knees but it got out all right even though it couldn't do it upright. And when the cow saw it was in a fix, and couldn't go in any direction, it turned around on its knees, because it knew that if it didn't it would fall down. And furthermore, it came straight back up; if it had gone to either side it would have fallen. And when it got to a place where it could handle itself, it jumped out at once. This cow is worth twelve thousand *duros,* and in a situation like that some men might try pulling it, others not, but most of us make an offering to Saint Anthony. And it works, I believe it does. They say you have to believe in it.

Although Saint Anthony is in charge of the welfare of farm animals, especially cows, he is best known for finding lost objects. In the *braña* this means he finds lost animals and provides information about persons or animals outside the region. The prayer, used by prayer people or *entendidos* serves to "pray" [*arrezar*] the animals and thereby assure the protection of the saint in case of loss or sickness.

They never taught me how to pray over the sheep. You might go to the hills and lose maybe half the flock. And you would come and someone would say, "So-and-so knows the prayer." And she would go off a little ways where no one could see her and pray. "No problem, child, you can go to bed, for the sheep are all right." And you would go home and they would say, "What? You didn't bring the sheep?" And you would say, "No, but so-and-so said they were all right." And you would sleep peacefully.

Saint Anthony appears to do the same work as a Vaqueiro. He watches over the birth of calves; he checks on lost animals; and he cares for animals when they are sick. The people of the *braña* can relax because the saint is a "shepherd" who, together with his dog, guards the animals.

They say that when the animals stay out, the wolves and foxes eat them. They say that as soon as this woman says the prayer of the animals, that Saint Anthony starts to guard them, Saint Anthony agrees to watch over them, and no one touches them because they are prayed for. The little dog of Saint Anthony, they refer to that, too. I don't know about it.

But the supernatural shepherd, like his mortal colleagues, demands a fee for his services, whether in masses, alms, prayers, and even an annual *lacón* [the lower part of the foreleg of the pig]. The saints "eat" too. Some "earn" more than others.

It's a custom. Here always every year a *lacón*, as soon as it is salted, is taken down to mass and offered so that the pigs of the coming year will be good, a *lacón* for Saint Anthony and the *Ánimas*. The Day of Saint Anthony there are *lacones* at the door of the church to be auctioned off, and what is made is spent on Saint Anthony. The saints don't eat much but . . . Saint Anthony is one of the ones that makes the most.

The *lacones* may be taken down to the church any Sunday, but the auction is formally organized after the high mass on Saint Anthony's Day. On the esplanade of the church, the majordomo shows the *lacón* to everyone, holding it over his head, and begins the auction with the words, "How much is this *lacón* worth?"

We've offered *lacones* many times. If a pig got sick, we would offer a *lacón* to Saint Anthony here. From here in my farmyard I heard a man from X—the one who hung himself—shouting, "So much has been offered for the *lacones* of Saint Anthony; they're worth that much and more. Let's go folks, they're good for you and good to you!" People would shout their offers, as much as they could afford. We, me and my deceased wife, have given many *lacones*.

Although in theory Saint Anthony responds to the prayers of the Vaqueiros everywhere, various images of the saint throughout the area provide models for what he looks like. All the parish churches have a Saint Anthony image, and in the only *braña* where I have been that has a chapel, Saint Anthony has prominent place. This multiplicity of images suggests to the people of the *braña* that there are various Saint Anthonys, including one somewhat unorthodox female Santa Antón.[2]

Saint Anthony is . . . didn't you see him up there in the chapel? He has a moustache and a beard, and a little dog next to him. He must live in the chapel here, but this is not the only Saint Anthony, because there are many.

That Saint Anthony is here, down from C. And over near N [*aldea*] is another. And in L [*braña*] is celebrated Santa Antón, in January and September.

An offering box for alms is placed beside the images of Saint Anthony in the churches. Substantial alms are given on many of the occasions noted above. The mental ease of the Vaqueiros is in the hands of the saint. Perhaps that is why some Vaqueiros entrust him to distribute their alms among the other saints.

Yes, I put all my alms in the box for Saint Anthony, and I say, "Let the saints divide it up," so I don't have to divide it up among all of them myself. I put several *duros* in there just the other day.

The main rival of Saint Anthony is the Virgin or Santa of El Acebo.[3] Unlike Anthony, she receives devotion in only one spot, the shrine that bears her name. Located at the summit of the Acebo Mountains, it takes two hours to get there on mountain paths from the town of Cangas de Narcea, about ten kilometers away. The site has summer pastures where Vaqueiro herdsmen would go with their flocks; in the winter it is covered with snow. It seems that the Virgin is named after the mountain range in which her shrine is located, *los Acebales*. According to legend, the Virgin appeared to herdsmen on an *acebo* [holly] tree. This legend is kept alive in the traditional iconography of the image. The figure rests on a column that imitates the trunk of the holly tree. Also, there used to be a large holly behind the shrine that would shelter pilgrims.[4]

In 1575, when the first miracle for which documentation exists took place, there was only a poor hut dedicated to the Virgin, with an image and a wooden cross, supposedly built by shepherds and cattle herdsmen. This first miracle involved a paralyzed woman, María de Noceda, who was cured when she was attending mass. In thanks, she lived for several years at the hermitage, taking the name María Santos, and pilgrimages began to increase. Local tradition holds that there was another, more important miracle before; that a herdsman in the mountains, looking for a cow lost in the fog, found the hermitage and in it a mass attended by a number of unknown persons. They handed him a lighted candle, and when the service was over, they mysteriously disappeared. The candle supposedly worked many miracles for women in childbirth and persons who were dying, cases for which the Vaqueiros especially turn to the Virgin of El Acebo today. Until 1575, only herdsmen visited the chapel. The main church was built at the end of the sixteenth century. With some modifications, it is the same church that still stands there today. The circumstances of its construction also have stimulated the local imagination. The people of the *braña* tell the story with a touch of skepticism.

They wanted to make the chapel lower down because it would be closer to where people lived, and they got everything ready, but the next morning the timbers were higher up, and in the place where the Santa appeared, next to a holly tree. And then they said, "This happened because the Santa. . . ." Something else happened, too. They say that a man stayed to watch the timbers another night, to see if it was an accomplice of the priest, or someone else, and at dawn the man was with the wood higher up, and he didn't know how he got there.

They were going to build the chapel below or at the middle of the mountain. So they had everything there. But suddenly, one night everything went up, above, at the top. It happened three times. . . . Well, I don't think the Santa walked so far . . . if she did not walk in those days more than she does now. . . . Who knows! We have a lot of faith to her.

Although this legend is common for mountain shrines in the north of Spain, from Asturias to the Basque country, it has special significance for the Vaqueiros. In choosing between the mountain and the valley, the Virgin chose the former, the habitat of the Vaqueiros. Since Vaqueiros do not usually have churches or chapels in the brañas, the Santina of El Acebo, by her choice, becomes their patron and symbol. Furthermore, the environment in which the shrine is located is the same kind as that used by long-distance transhumant Vaqueiros. Its proximity to the traditional high-mountain pastures has helped to convert a visit to the Santa into a regular feature of these trips. The times at which the shrine is opened and closed for the year coincide with the arrival and departure of the cattle. It should not be forgotten that transhumancy has been a constant characteristic of Vaqueiro life and has helped form the identity of the Vaqueiros as a social group.

The interrelation of the Santa and the cattle can be seen from the kinds of offerings the faithful dedicate to her. The Feast of the Virgin, September 8, has traditionally been considered the "day of promises" of visits and money as opposed to September 12, which was dedicated to "offerings" in kind. Now this distinction has been blurred, since most offerings in kind are paid in their equivalent in money, on the advice of the chaplain of the shrine, who indicates the evolution and status of these substantial donations.

> The fiesta of the eighth is that of the promises; after the eighth is the fiesta of the offerings when the Vaqueiros used to leave animals. They used to bring cows or sheep, very many of them, and I was here for the time of the lambs and the goats. The first year I came here [1961], they brought a calf from one of the higher, Vaqueiro brañas. At that time I was new and it was a little awkward, and I told them to figure out what the animal was worth and give it in money. In the old days there had been a lot of it; on their way to the upper pasture they would pass by here. The auction took place in the yard, and I was the auctioneer. The offerings consisted of cattle, lambs, butter, and milk. Now they bring an occasional chicken.

At least as long ago as 1681, the earliest date for which complete accounts exist for the shrine, these offerings were substantial. In that year they were worth 322 reals.[5] It has been traditional for Vaqueiros to offer the ramu, a holly branch from which butter and bread were hung. Some branches even bore silver coins. The donors

THE AFTERLIFE

would place the offering on the main altar, accompanied by the sounds of the *pandeiro* [drum] and lovely traditional songs.[6] The shrine chaplain describes other offerings:

They also leave about a hundred kilos in all—wheat, oats, grain. . . . They may also leave fatback and, until recently, oil. And they still leave candles that last eight days. Another custom is that when they are sick they offer their weight in wax. Have you noticed how much wax they use up? In the old days Vaqueiros used to come back from Madrid with wax, and they weighed themselves in wax.

The Vaqueiros also bring wax candles, which are lit in such large numbers as to be dangerous. What the shrine historian A. Colunga reported for 1925 still applies today.

The faithful flight to present their offerings, whether masses or wax, and those who bring a candle want to see it burn all the way down. With so many people it is a constant danger. Some people, either because they carry many candles or in order to have their hands free for their prayers, stick the candles in the ground, or lean against something, causing many accidents, which without the constant favor of heaven could be disastrous.

The votive offerings the faithful leave on a side altar are also made of wax. They represent dozens of figures—among them heads, limbs, and human bodies—as well as miniature animals— pigs, mules, and especially cows and calves. Another kind of votive offering is clothing: usually either a cap or uniform from military service, or the shroud [*embolubre*] used by some sick people who have recovered after the doctor has given up on them. In thanks and to fulfill a promise made on the brink of death, the "wrapped ones" [*embolubraos*], as they are called, go to the shrine of El Acebo carrying a "wrapping" or shroud that recalls the old-fashioned winding cloth. It is a simple short cape with a hood made of a dark color for adults and a lighter color for children, and tied around the neck with ribbons. The promise is fulfilled by wearing the *embolubre* when climbing up to the shrine. After entering, praying, and visiting the Virgin [*pasar por la Santa*], the wrapping is left on a side altar as a votive offering. The *embolubraos* are believed to be dead people who are "resurrected" and "shrouded," according to the priest of the shrine. Both kinds of clothing thus refer to sorrowful separations. While that of the *mili* is reversible, some youths take advantage of the occasion to emigrate making the separation definitive, as is, of course, death. Youths leave their uniform at the shrine when they come back home, and the *embolubraos* offer the shroud once they have left the world of shadows.

Most of the offerings today are given in cash. The pilgrims not only bring their own alms, but also those of their neighbors and relatives, paying scrupulous attention to deliver exactly what was given to them. Although they refer at times to the cartloads of money collected at the shrine, these references, and the fact that the Santa "makes a lot of money" and "is rich," are for the people of the *braña* evidence of the Santa's spiritual power, an incentive for their faith, and a cause for pride and generosity. For this reason, the masses at El Acebo are more expensive than elsewhere and are considered more effective. Many of these masses are offered for the dead of the house; others are promises that the dead made when they were alive. The shrine chaplain speaks in the second quote:

> Sometimes we also give a mass to the Virgin of El Acebo; yes, they're more expensive. They say that the Virgin of El Acebo is the most miraculous saint around here.

> The Vaqueiros come here many times to offer masses for their dead. They have a lot of devotion to their dead. It is not so much due to warnings from them as dreams. Also a man will have made a promise to the Virgin and say to his children, "I hope you'll keep it." And maybe five or six years will pass and these children will come back, saying, "No, it's that my father told me to do this, and I dreamed of him." They start to think, "I hope my father isn't in bad straits."

Certain promises require the supplicant to be physically present at the shrine, whether to visit the image or to participate in one of the rituals, such as carrying one of the *andas* [handles of the image-litter] in procession, or walking barefoot or on one's knees from the point at which one first sees the shrine. In cases of serious illness or danger of death, whether the case is for humans or animals, a promise is made at the same time as a human specialist is consulted.

> Yes, I have gone to El Acebo. It's a very famous place around here, extremely so. An immense number of people go there. I don't know if it's true or not, but they say the priest makes so much he can retire right away. I went twice, once when I was old, once as a boy. You go for a promise that you made that has to be fulfilled there; when you are sick, or with animal, or relative, or friend, then you might offer to visit the shrine or have a mass said. I went for a promise; as you can see, I am not a disbeliever. Just recently? No. This time I was

so bad off I couldn't think at all because if I had thought of it, I would have done it.

Well, they went with [a sick child] to doctors and healers and to visit all the places, to Acebo and Villaorín. Villaorín is over near Luarca, and they say it is a very miraculous Santa, yes, like the Virgin of Acebo and other places. They went to all of the Santas. I don't remember them all.

Now as in the past, the Santa of El Acebo takes care of difficult childbirths. Animal births, however, are the business of Saint Anthony.

We often turn to the Virgin of El Acebo. When my daughter-in-law began to give birth, I offered to visit the Santa. I always felt she was miraculous for that. For the cows we always apply to Saint Anthony; to El Acebo for the births of cows, no, for women, yes.

The visit to the shrine involves not only donation but also acquisition—the acquisition of objects that have been blessed and protect one from various misfortunes. On the feast day of the Virgin, a couple of men inside the shrine touch objects that people hand them to the mantle of the image. Outside in the procession, people can touch the mantle with their objects themselves. Men often have their berets blessed in this way, and women their scarves or other items of clothing. It is better if these objects do not have to be washed, because washing is thought to remove part of the blessing. They also "pass" to the Santa ribbons of various colors, which they will later tie around the wrists or necks of children, and *roscas*, doughnut-shaped breads, that are consumed after the blessing or taken back home. The passage of the Virgin leaves its little miracle on these products. For example, in the case of bread:

If you pass a bread, for example, to the Santa, it does not go bad; it stays as if it were made that day—a little harder, but it doesn't go bad. Something must happen to it, because the other ones do go bad.

In addition, many Vaqueiros touch the Virgin with cowbells and the medallions that they hang from cow collars. These talismans are thought to protect the cattle from the danger of the high pastures. Another source of protection for animals thought to be in danger are the "eight-day candles," which are lit in the shrine and then taken home to bless the cows. This custom is current not only among the transhumant but also among sedentary Vaqueiros. The stands and booths that surround the shrine are well supplied with objects for ritual use and animal protection (ribbons, scapulars, candles, medals, etc.), and the sellers provide ample information derived from their long experience, they say, of many years at the shrine. One of the things you can buy is a *domina*, used by the Vaqueiros as follows:

> They call them *dominas*, I think—they put things in them to put on the cows. I don't know what they put in them; they buy them at El Acebo. It is something put in a tiny pouch, I don't know what it is, they say it is good, it is put around the necks of the cows. Uy! My husband believed a lot in her; he would touch the cowbells to the Santa.

In fact, these pouches, called *evangelios* elsewhere in the north of Spain, are supposed to contain clippings of the Gospels.[7] But even objects designed for other uses find a protective purpose for cattle in the *braña*. For example, the common tablet, for sale at El Acebo, containing a religious image and the inscription "I will bless this house," is often placed over the stable door. Crosses made of holly wood are nailed up on the stable to protect the animals from "evil eyes." This bush is considered holy because of its relation with the Santa. In the shrine the Vaqueiros ask for wax, incense, and holy water for their houses and their stables, when Christians or animals are ill.

Even those Vaqueiros who believe the least go to the shrine to "visit" the Santa and leave her alms when they return from the high pastures, whether on the day of the fiesta or any other day in the summer. In these visits they also settle up old promises made during illnesses, misfortunes, or difficult childbirths. It is the visit to the image, always with lighted candles in hand, that is the most frequent contact, more frequent and more preferred than attendance at mass or other official shrine services. The day of the fiesta, the esplanade of the shrine is crowded with people, and all take part in the procession. The music of the *gaitas* [small bagpipes] is punctuated by the deafening explosion of fireworks. Shortly after, the area around the shrine is dotted with groups of neighbors, picnicking. Then the music and dancing begins. At nightfall the Vaqueiros go off on their mounts to their *brañas*.[8]

Together with Saint Anthony and the Santa of El Acebo, the *Ánimas* complete the basic pantheon of the Vaqueiros. In local usage, it is common to refer to these three helpers at once. The *Ánimas*[9] receive the same kind of offerings as the other two main divinities—the fruits of the earth that are taken to El Acebo or the *lacón* of Saint Anthony—with whom they have a special competition.

We have faith in Saint Anthony, as with the Santa of El Acebo or the *lacón* of the *Ánimas*.

To get a good calf from a cow, you have to commend her to Saint Anthony or the *Ánimas*, or to all the dead of the house. When we make offerings, they are to Saint Antonín the Blessed, which is the one we have here, and to the Santina of El Acebo.

Lacones go to the *Ánimas*, the day of the *Ánimas*. Actually the *lacón* is taken down whenever possible, but it is offered to the *Ánimas*. To Saint Anthony, too. It is taken down to mass. You offer a *lacón* so the pigs of the following year will be good, a *lacón* for the *Ánimas*. And sometimes people even take wool down to the priest, and ears of corn, this in F and C [*brañas*] on the Day of the Dead. At X house they still take corn down so they'll have a better harvest the next year.

Lacones are not the only things offered to the *Ánimas*. Accounts with the dead, as with the saints, are more commonly settled with religious services. Masses or alms may be substituted for these offerings in kind. Note in this context that prayers are often directed to the particular *Ánimas* or dead of the family or house. During the year, any misfortune or loss means a warning from those who have passed away, that they need masses or alms.

We give maybe four or five masses a year. Maybe two on the Day of the Dead or the Saints. They are given because when something bad happens we say, "Let's give a mass for whoever needs it most." When we sold that cow, we had already offered to give a mass. Sometimes I offer something when piglets are born, an alms maybe, without saying how much, maybe five, maybe twenty *duros*. And the masses are given for those who need them most, or people from the family or house who have passed on.

As with Saint Anthony, Vaqueiros try to involve the *Ánimas* in the protection of animals by giving them alms. They leave money in a highly visible spot so the *Ánimas* will notice it.

Up above the door, now almost no one does it, but before we did, we would put some money, to give to them later in the church. It wasn't put there to remind us, because we would remember anyway; it was just a custom. When we had sheep or lesser animals that were missing, we would put some coins on the windowsill and give them to the saints, for the *Ánimas*. When the cows gave birth we always gave a mass, and still do; I just recently gave one. I offered it for the soul of the house most in need, and the priest says it when he can.

Debts to the living are repaid to individuals, but debts to the dead are sometimes paid in the church to the collectivity of the *Ánimas*, which seems to serve as a clearinghouse for those who have passed away. Unpaid debts may cause the dead to take revenge on cattle.

I don't know [what the bad place is]. What I do know is that they say it is bad to owe something to anyone when you die, whether money or whatever. My father once needed some money, not much, two pesetas maybe, I don't know for what. And then the person died who gave them to him, and I don't know what bad thing happened to him, but he felt remorse and went and gave it to the church. And whatever it was that was happening to him stopped. I don't know what it was; I think he said it was something with the *Ánimas*.

Each house is responsible for its portion of *Ánimas*. In church, masses that have been ordered are announced, "For the obligations of X house of Y [*braña*]." These obligations refer to the dead of the house. Masses to *Ánimas* are of two kinds—those referred to as "with people," which name specific dead, especially on an anniversary, and those "without people," which are directed to all the dead, particularly those who need it most.

The masses with people are like anniversaries, funerals, and those without people are those given to the priest to say when he wants. We give a lot of them. For example, each time that a cow gives birth we say a mass, afterwards, for the *Ánimas*. Some go and give it for a particular day, and tell the people of the village and attend. To that kind of mass [without people], no, I don't go. We always give one on All Saints Day. On that day a lot of people go down.

Masses and alms for the *Ánimas* of the dead are effective throughout the year, but masses and alms given on All Saints Day in particular, here celebrated as the Day of the Dead, are believed to have a special effect.

On the Day of the Dead one attends mass, the services and things that the priest normally does. And the masses are normally given, and alms. They used to say that an alms given on that day was worth a hundred.

According to local opinion, this holy day was invented recently in order to placate the dead, who otherwise would be prowling around the houses at night, complaining. The feast day is a way to keep them at arm's length from the world of the living.

> I don't know if [the dead] come or not. That's why they set the Day of the Dead, in order to give masses and things so they don't come back. That's why you go to church, to give things. You go to light a candle, or give money, and you cooperate there with the dead.

> It turns out this Day of the Dead was set up less than a hundred years ago. Before that it didn't exist. And they said they would come in the house complaining at night, and they said that those who were in the cemetery needed something, and that's when they set up the Day of the Dead.

The morning of the Day of the Dead is spent fixing up the graves. The Vaqueiros go en masse to the cemetery, where they weed around the gravestones and clean the niches or stones. They always bring some kind of present—now a wreath of natural or plastic flowers, in the distant past other kinds of offering, whether directly to the graves or indirectly by way of the church.

> Yes, I've heard that they took meals to the graves on the Day of the Dead. And you know until recently they took ears of corn to the church, ears and stalks, for the priest to sell and use the money for responses or whatever.

After the religious services, the Vaqueiros go to the cemetery and stand in front of the graves or niches belonging to their house. The priest gives a blessing and prays before each group of niches. The Vaqueiros think that the presence of living members of each house is essential to obtain greater attention for their dead. When their turn comes, they pray and respond to the prayers of the priest while handing generous contributions to the altar boys. After finishing the round of responses, the priest gives a general blessing to the graves from the center of the cemetery and retires. This ritual, then, is at once a collective remembrance of the dead and a remembrance of particular groups of the dead because responses are said for each house. These responses are yet another way in which the centrality and significance of the house in Vaqueiro culture is expressed. The living members of the house thus explicitly ally themselves with their dead, once a year in the full light of day. There are certain similarities here with the traditional anniversaries. Indeed Vaqueiros prepare on the evening of this day an offering of food and drink for the dead, a kind of spartan version of the anniversary banquet.

> Look, you'd take a cup very full of water. And you put it here, and nobody drinks it or spills it. Because the *Ánimas* have to come at night to drink it. And we would put the bread and the knife for them to cut it with; and in the old days they were loaves made in the house or bought. And the next morning we would look to see if they had eaten anything. My sister would say to me, "Look, it seems there's not so much water, right?" And I would say, "No, it's just the same." Here it's still done, if I remember to do it. If I go to bed without remembering, I don't. They did it in all the houses. And some years, if we didn't have bread—because we were out of it or we couldn't get it, as in the years after the war—we would say: "Oy! the Day of the Dead and there's no bread to leave out." And we would leave the cup of water, but not the bread. They said the dead came out at night, and if they didn't find it you could hear them complaining at night in the house. These would be the dead of the house, those who had died, a grandmother, or a son, or a brother, or whatever.

These attentions to the dead in some cases extended over the whole year.

> Always water, my mother would say to us. Many times she would have us go out for water at night. "The house must not be left without water. Otherwise if the *Ánimas* come to drink and there isn't any, they go away weeping." In those days you had to go out for water. She meant the dead of the house . . . the *Ánimas* . . . drank the water and felt satisfied.

The cult of the *Ánimas* also finds expression on Maundy Thursday in the "matins candles" [*velas de las tinieblas*]. The candles would be lit the morning of Thursday of Holy Week in the church and left burning until the next day at ten in the morning. The Vaqueiros refer to this day as a "holy day" and observe it by refraining from hard work in the fields. They attend church with two candles, now purchased in the *aldea*, one to be left in the church and one to take home. In the past these typically were sent by relatives in Madrid, the emigrants in this way collaborating in the homage to the dead. These holy candles, then, had two uses; those left in the church, were to provide light for the dead; those taken home were to bless the animals and to ward off the dangers of storms.

It used to be the custom here always to take and light a lot of candles on Maundy Thursday, candles painted with entwined colors, very pretty, that came from Madrid. . . . They were left twenty-four hours before the altar . . . for the *tinieblas* and then, as they were very big, they were taken home. Someone would pick them up the next morning, when the holy day was over. Other people would say *"Ay Dios!* to provide light for the dead who are there we'll let it burn all the way down."

One goes down to the church on Maundy Thursday with the candles of the dead, they say of the *tinieblas*. And then, when they pray over them and all, they say that they are good to light on the days when there are thunderstorms. My husband also would drip some wax from holy candles on the head of each cow, from a candle of Maundy Thursday. They said it was so they wouldn't get lost or be hit by lighting, because up there it thunders a lot.

While Saint Anthony, the Santa of El Acebo, and the *Ánimas* monopolize much of the local religious attention, there are other saints, male and female, that receive a lesser local cult,[10] or in some cases, the devotions of single individuals. The people of the *braña* traditionally observe certain days by not working, even though they no longer evince special fervor for the saint of the feast involved. One of these is the Ascension, here described with an animal metaphor.

That holy day in May, the Ascension; we say that it is important, because we say that on that day the hens can't even move their eggs. Of course, they do move them. But by that we mean it is a sin, that you can't sew or wash or. . . . No, we really don't sew or wash.

On this day, negative miracles, divine punishments resulting from violations of the work taboo, occur as well as positive miracles recalling the small miracles of El Acebo. The idea of sin is expressed through the physical defects of domestic animals, victims of divine wrath.

Old folks, the oldest in the village, said that when [the next day] they creamed the milk that they had gathered that day, and made butter from the cream, that the butter would last a year or two and not go bad, because it was made with milk from that day. Since this day is a full holy day, if, for example, you sift flour to make bread, the next animal born in the house will be born making the same [sifting] motion with its legs or wings. If a hen is incubating eggs, the chickens will hatch with their wings moving that way.

On Ascension day, if you sow anything, for example, squash, and you have a hen that is incubating some eggs, the chickens will hatch their wings twisted, just like the leaves of the squash plant. That happened to a woman here, and from then on her hens didn't hatch good chickens. Many died, and others had twisted wings.

Some of the lesser saints with local devotion are images with which the Vaqueiros have a kind of neighborly relation, like the patron saints of the parishes or those that inhabit nearby churches and chapels.

Hombre, I have devotion to some saints as much as others, but since we have the Virgin of Mount Carmel here in N [parish church], I always go and give her something when I go down, and pray an Our Father or a Hail Mary.

For the same reason, when one changes one's customary path or moves from one place to another, one has less contact with the old "placed" images, and eventually one's devotion to them diminishes.

Sometimes we made promises also to the Virgin of the *Angustias*, because we often went down to the mill. Now, since one goes by auto, one doesn't go by the chapel of the *Angustias*. Whenever we would go to the mill, we would drop a coin in the offering box of the Virgin. Before, we might say, "Ay! a sheep is missing; I hope the wolf doesn't get it; offer a coin to the Virgin of the *Angustias* and remember to give in the day you go by there, eh?" And the sheep would turn up.

Other saints transcend their specific locality and receive the religious attention of various parishes or an entire township. They are offered identical promises as the major saints, and their usefulness is quite similar. San Francisquín, for example, is a colleague of Saint Anthony.

There are others, like San Francisquín of Folgueira. Have you heard of him? Many have great faith in him, too. He's very important for the animals. X's wife here offered a *lacón* to San Francisquín, and some others did, too. And some have offered themselves to visit the saint; he's very miraculous also.

If San Francisquín is a second Saint Anthony, the Santa of El Acebo has a cohort of "sisters" that is far more numerous. There is a local theory that there are three sisters who occupy mountains and high places. They communicate by ringing their bells. Who exactly the three sisters are is disputed, however, and people tend to include the one to whom they are most devoted.

Well, consider this. Here we have some *santas* nearby, like that of El Acebo, Colobreiro, and Belén. It is said that these three are sisters, from the same father and mother. Yes, they are sisters, they look alike, and they say they look alike, and I have seen them and they do look alike. They are all three on high points, all three high up.

They say there are three that are sisters and that they can hear each other's bells. One must be *los Dolores* of Paredes, that of Belén, and another that of El Acebo. Of course, they're very far apart and can't hear the ringing of the bells. Listen, they may be sisters, but I heard that that of Paredes was also a sister. Yes, look, here a lot of us commend ourselves to *los Dolores*. Some offer to go every year they can, on September eighth at Paredes, the same day as at Colobreiro and El Acebo. I have a lot of faith in the Virgin of *los Dolores*, and whenever something happens to me, I offer a lot, and to the Virgin of El Acebo, too.

In accordance with the sexual division of labor, the male saints are charged principally with the care of animals while the female saints are more likely to be assigned childbirths. In order to get to certain specific *santas*, trips have to be made, something unnecessary in the case of Saint Anthony, whose images are always nearby. Women may go to female saints to fulfill promises they have made concerning themselves, their daughters, or daughter-in-laws.

Well, yes, I have a lot of devotion to the Virgin of El Acebo, and to the Virgin of *los Dolores* as well. I commended A [her daughter-in-law] so she would give birth successfully; the day she had her first pains [*dolores*] I commended her to the Virgin of *los Dolores*.

This woman's husband, who was present during the conversation, suggested ironically that this kind of trip had a profane as well as a religious purpose. These trips, usually made by large groups of women on the feast day of the *santa*, include a dance, providing an entertaining day of vacation and diversion. The wife (W) protests her husband's one-sided interpretation and emphasizes the ritual aspect.

H: Look María, you know the main reason why women would offer to visit that *santa?* In order to get away and go together and have a nice day.
W: At the fiesta.
H: But at times without any devotion at all, in order to have a nice time. "Oh no, I am offered to . . . ," and often it is a lie, an excuse to go off with the others.
W: Oh no! I didn't just go; I offered her when I saw she had pains.

There are still other female saints whose places of residence are not known to the Vaqueiros. They often are individual devotions, like this one.

And the Virgen del Camino,[11] I never knew where this Virgin was. I was always devoted to the Virgen del Camino, like when I gave birth to the children, or a thunderbolt that scared us a lot. "Ay, Virgen del Camino! Ay, Virgen del Camino, deliver us from misfortune!"

A very similar lack of spatial specificity surrounds the figure of God. It appears to be more difficult to imagine this divinity because it is difficult to locate him, although some people associate him with the cross. Theoretically, God appears to derive his existence by way of the printed page—his definition in the catechism—and this is something many adults have forgotten. Doubts about God's identity, which do not appear in relation to the saints at all, are expressed, for example, in this commentary.

God would be . . . Did you see Saint Anthony up there with a moustache and beard? He would be something . . . they say that God made Christ and all those that are on the cross . . . I don't know. Well, that's why I say that he's on the cross, he is something, I don't know how that could be, if one only knew what he was . . . I don't know what they are. But he who does not see . . . we have to see him so we all know and then can say, "Yes, God exists, we saw him and he's like this and that." Since we don't see him, we can't say what he's like. They say that God is all powerful and other words I don't remember; how do I know what he's like? One thing is for sure; we ought to know a lot of things, we should have studied more.

Invocations of God are frequent and everyday, but they take the form of linguistic clichés like "if God wants it," "God help us," and so on. This frequency of invocation is not matched by a cult or active devotion. There are few specific named versions of God or

Christ, and the few that exist have been converted locally into "saints" like San Salvador, the patron saint of the parish church. One exception is the sign of the cross, which is used very often in relation to cattle, somewhat less in regard to humans, as a protection against evil. If when one leaves the house a ritual gesture like a cross is necessary to avoid evil, these precautions are multiplied in regard to transhumant cattle, since the trip is longer, the safeguards fewer, and the dangers greater. Transhumant Vaqueiros use a great number of little rituals to protect the cattle, most involving the cross. For them it is not only a gesture, but a practice that they mark on the hide of the animals. The widow of a transhumant Vaqueiro says:

> Yes, my husband, may he rest in peace, bought at the pharmacy Zotal, or something like that, some black stuff with which he makes a cross like this, which left a good mark on the hide [of the cow], and it would stay there all summer, on the right shank and the left foreleg, an arm and a leg making a cross.

It appears that God interferes little in human affairs, perhaps because of a lack of specialization, since Saint Anthony takes care of the cattle, the *santas* take care of health, and the *Ánimas* specialize in giving warnings. The local idea of God is expressed through an image of force. God is equivalent to a "power," "something that dominates us," and especially "a strong hand," the phrase used most frequently. Even when people are uncertain about particular aspects of the religion, everyone agrees on this supreme "power," even the most skeptical.

> I've heard about that [heaven and hell], but I don't know if it's true or not. But I do believe that there is something that has power over us.

> We know where we go [after death], to the earth. *Hombre,* I'm not one of those who say there isn't a power. I have never seen it, but it must exist. I am convinced that there is a powerful hand; I don't know what it is or what it isn't.

> God is . . . an infinite man; I once knew it, the right words. My grandmother said that there is a powerful hand, and yes, I believe it.

Although God is a "lesser" saint in terms of cult and usefulness, he is considered to occupy a very important place in the divine hierarchy. He is responsible for life itself.

They say that the soul is the blood, that when the blood ends we die. What do we know what there is in the other world? Also, others say that there is no God. There has to be a God; how could there not be one? If there was no God, things wouldn't be born that are born in the world. A baby is made, only because a man goes with a woman, and it comes out with eyes and limbs and all. If there were no God. . . . There must be a God, *hombre.* I believe it. But that is something, something we don't know for sure, but that *visibles* circulate, yes, that's sure.

God is also responsible for death and human destiny. When I asked the question, "What is a powerful hand?" People replied, "the fate of each of us." Fate or lot [*suerte*] includes the kind of death one will have, and the final reparation for the injustices of life. More concretely, God is likened to a tribunal.

You must know that the rich person has gotten that way by a thousand dirty ways, pushing the poor around. They all die badly. That's why they say, "There's no God, but let's behave well, just in case." Because if there is no God, there is certainly a court that judges us and has power over us, which is just the same.

In addition to the moral enforcement implied here, God has a third task, which is the responsibility for social order and human civilization. "They say that God exists, God exists, I don't say he doesn't. He probably does, he does, there has to be one; if not we'd all be savages." Indeed, religion itself appears to be an essential axis in the classification of beings, for humans are "Christians" in opposition to the animal world. (The following statement, voiced often, puts it succinctly: "We, the Christians, have the same pieces as the pigs.") Religion consists of the strict observance of moral rights and rules and the ethical values of society; if one does not help one's neighbors, one at least should not harm them.

I was never one for those tricks [in selling cattle]. I was very religious. I never did anyone out of a penny. Look, there are those who will sell an animal and say, "You said so much, buy it and hand it over," but I never did that; I never even took a glass of wine from someone. I was without any self-interest and told the truth. I always liked to be straight [*lo legal siempre me gustó*].

About those things [jokes about sick people], I never heard any. Those aren't joking matters, because they say that the best religion is not to meddle with anybody.

THE INTERMEDIARIES OF THIS WORLD

People do not always deal with the saints directly. There are two kinds of religious intermediaries available to the Vaqueiros—the official, clerical ones and the unofficial, lay ones. The official intermediary with whom the Vaqueiros are least acquainted is the "Pope of Rome." I was able to obtain only a few descriptions of this somewhat distant figure, who nevertheless seems to epitomize certain characteristics of the clerical class for the Vaqueiros. Perhaps most notorious is their association of political and religious power. Another aspect is the importance of "study" and the wisdom that characterizes this kind of person. It is very significant that knowledge about and interest in the Pope comes from the local prayer people [*rezadores*]. Here a prayer woman interprets an attack on the Pope in Colombia:

Paul VI is a man of much saintliness. He knows sixteen languages—there is no man in the province who knows as many as he—sixteen languages! That John XXIII knew fourteen languages. And he [Paul VI] wanted there to be peace in the world; poor guy, he was right, everybody wants peace. And he went to say an outdoor mass in some country asking for holy peace. And in the country he went to there was a guerrilla, who was very bad; in that country they didn't want peace. And when he found out that Paul was going to say mass, that bum got dressed up as a priest and went up to Paul, who was there in good faith, and attacked him with blows and kicks. Luckily Paul had guards, and the boys who were there that day came and protected him; otherwise he would have been killed, and we'd have war in Spain again. Look you, for three days I was so upset I couldn't take anything but water. *Ay Dios!* If war comes to Spain again . . . now that we are rich and the stores have everything. And they made that bum a prisoner. They did right, because he wanted war in Spain. And Franco was so upset they had to put a towel with ice in it on his head, like it was a hat, because he had a stroke, poor thing. But he got better, thanks be to God, for he brought Spain all the way up. See how he sent roads and water and light. And look, I am a poor old lady, but I have this [electric] light, and *Ay Dios!* weren't we suffering in the dark with our little gas lanterns? Now with him we have had thirty-five years of peace, and we are well off; but some like him and others don't.

If God is considered a power or a court, it is not strange that his most important representative on earth, the Pope, should be referred to the same way. By the same token, all political power has certain "religious" features. The Vaqueiros' association of Franco and the Pope would be due to the fact that they both have (or had) power. Both theoretically kept the peace, provided prosperity, and maintained the order of the society. This association was reinforced by the way the Vaqueiros understood the Spanish Civil War. War itself supposes an attempt to defeat those who are in charge, a subversion of the order of society which, as we have seen, is attributed to God himself. The Pope is thought to be an intermediary with God because of his "studies." A person who speaks fourteen or sixteen languages can speak with many different kinds of interlocutors, including celestial beings.

The closest official intermediary with the saints is the parish priest. On a local level, the priests are probably the most "studied," along with the other professionals—doctors, veterinarians, and teachers. And in the smaller parishes that lack these other professionals, he may be the only authority. The priests traditionally took responsibility for communication with the outside world; the transactions of bureaucracy in profane matters as well as sacred ones, and the greeting of illustrious visitors—political and governmental. If God is the being responsible for order in the world, the priest attempts to maintain this order. But while the priest has great power in decision-making in the *aldea*, in the *braña*, in spite of his recognized authority, he has very little control, because he is physically separated from the dispersed habitat of the *brañas*.

People today make a strict distinction between old and new priests, which reflects the changes produced by the Second Vatican Council in the relations between priests and parishioners (see Luque 1976). The behavior of some new priests has changed drastically in relation to traditional rituals. I knew one priest who had forbidden offerings in kind in the churches, who had burned wax votive offerings and removed the images of saints, leaving only a crucifix in order, he said, to "modernize" the church. Since the word "procession" seemed old-fashioned to him, he substituted the word "walk" [or march, *marcha*] and used a powerful megaphone, unnecessary given the sparse attendance. People refer to acts like these, which are somewhat aggressive, by saying, "these aren't priests," or "these priests are getting rid of religion," and so on. But

THE AFTERLIFE

perhaps the greatest offensive has been against local beliefs. These priests tend to be in favor of "progress" and "rationality," which either means that they show little interest in the ideas and beliefs of their parishioners or else they openly dismiss them.

But I think it's the priests who are doing away with it [religion]. Because I heard that in X a woman wanted to give twenty *duros* to the priest to see if God would see fit to have her cows deliver well. And he said, "Since you're giving it so the cows will deliver well, keep it and give it to the veterinarian. Because if you give me twenty *duros* and I say a mass, it won't make any difference." And they don't leave any saints in the church, just Christ and that's all.

The old priests tended to pressure their parishioners to attend Sunday mass. Although for *aldeanos* this was not a great sacrifice except at harvest time because the churches were nearby, for the Vaqueiros it was quite a problem. Except for certain fixed occasions, the feasts of some saints, Vaqueiro attendance at mass is quite sparse, in part due to the time required to reach the parish church. The Vaqueiros order a lot of masses dedicated to the dead. But ordering masses is not just a way to compensate for not being able to attend mass easily; it is an essential ingredient of Vaqueiro religion.

Masses, yes, a lot are given. I think here in the high villages we give more. Because we cannot go so often to mass at X [parish church] as they [*aldeanos*] can. It is our religion.

This point of view did not, of course, coincide with that of the old priests, who insisted on church attendance as the mark of religiosity. The new priests are more tolerant in this respect, and less interested in formal behavior. I have often heard them counsel from the pulpit their parishioners to attend church when they felt like it and not just to fulfill obligations. The new priests have been more useful in practical ways, too. On many occasions they have taken on the job of getting the civil authorities to provide running water, electricity, and other improvements to the *brañas*. The people of the *brañas* are very grateful and refer to the most active priests with praise. These activities have helped to reinforce the Vaqueiros' image of priests not only as religious figures but as political intermediaries. At times people try to attend mass as a way to thank the priest, as deference, rather than for a specific religious purpose.

But today, because the rules seem to have changed, the Vaqueiros do not know how to behave. Some innovations that at first seem positive, like not charging for certain services in the church, are criticized by the Vaqueiros, given their practice of strictly fulfilling transactions with the divine by way of the church. In other words, the young priests and the Vaqueiros seem to be using different languages. At times this is literally so, for many of the sermons the young priests deliver are not understood by their Vaqueiro audiences. Yet nobody doubts the learning of these priests. The Vaqueiros consider themselves ignorant folk who do not understand the mysteries of life and death, of God and why things happen as they do. They are used to having people who have studied teach them what is real and impose "truth" on them, and so the Vaqueiros commonly refer anyone who asks them spiritual questions to one of these authority figures: priests, teachers, or doctors.

Of the various moral rules the priest used to enforce, the Vaqueiros considered the first commandment very important. Blasphemy, the expression of anger against the divinity, is repressed by a constant cultural pressure. Vaqueiros think there is civilian punishment (due, according to local opinion, to the "authorities") for blasphemy, which is considered to be subversion of God. Two men answer my question as to whether they are religious in this way:

> [A lame man:] Of course, not to blaspheme; like some who blaspheme against God. I never did. You know when I got most angry? It would be at times like when I would reach for a scythe [to cut grass] for the cattle, and have to sit down on the ground and not able to get up; I would have to get on my knees, with my staff and the scythe; that's when I would get most angry. But as for praying, I never prayed much.

> I'll tell you the truth, and I don't go much to church, I know myself. Many companions tell me, "Bah, you are like a saint." I say, "No, I don't swear, I live just the same without swearing; everyone knows what he does." I, if I get my blood boiling, I let it out some other way. And fulfilling my obligations. Because what I say is, I don't go much to church, but I do what I have to do.

The priest, because of his studies, knows the prayers with which to contact the bureaucracy and the divine. In this aspect, the clerical intermediaries serve as models for the lay intermediaries, the prayer people of the area, who are generally women. In each *braña* there has been at least one person specialized in this task. As I have already referred to some of these specialists, I will deal here with their religious status and character in relation to the priest.

More than opposition, I would say that the local intermediary has a complementary relation with the priest. The prayer woman is usually someone known in the Vaqueiro community for her reli-

THE AFTERLIFE

giosity. It is not unusual that she goes to mass more often than her neighbors, that she prays a lot, and that she works to maintain moral standards. It is often said that she is a saint, or that she is very saintly [usa mucho la santidad]. One prayer woman is described thus: "She was very religious, very saintly; she was always keeping men and children and everyone in line or she would go up with [her neighbor's] cows, and praying, always praying."

Like the parish priest, the prayer women learn prayers and rituals from books they own and read with avidity.

X is religious, yes. She prays a lot and has many scapulars and medals. Now she is sick in bed, but she left me a note with the candles I'm supposed to buy, and what has to be donated [as alms, in the church]. She has many church books, old books, and she reads them a lot, and she has one of these things of Saint Anthony.

But there are differences. While the priesthood is considered a profession, the woman knowledgeable in prayer practices for the pleasure of it [por gusto], whenever friends or neighbors ask her or whenever a collective prayer has to be organized. Her services are never paid for in cash, unlike the priest's, although sometimes, if the prayer woman is very poor, she may be given a small gift in kind. Often the prayer people are considered to have a something extra, a special gift in addition to their pleasure in and capacity for prayer—this is known as "the hand" [la mano]. To "have the hand" [tener mano] means not only to attempt to cure, divine, or communicate with the unknown, but also to be effective at it. The hand, together with the knowledge of the prayer to Saint Anthony, makes divination possible:

She had some hand. When she tried to guess, she guessed right. Because when my husband, who was so dedicated to the cows, went to the high pastures with them and took one of the bells and touched it to the Virgin of El Acebo, she knew it. One day I asked her. I said we had the cows in the mountains and how were they doing, and she said, "Well, look girl, they went down to a village called L, and three of them are there, and for the thunder and all they have a bell that they touched to El Acebo, and within the sound of that bell lightning bolts don't fall." She already knew that they had touched it to El Acebo.

The hand, according to local opinion, is not so much a mysterious ingredient as it is a trait or a personal skill with which one is born, together with dedication [afán] and interest for the activity in question. In order to have the hand as a prayer woman it is essential to have a good memory, for if one makes a mistake when reciting a prayer, or forgets something, the prayer will be ineffectual. One also must know a variety of prayers and be familiar with all things religious. On the other hand, "being saintly" and "using saintliness" implies that the prayer woman shares some qualities of the saints; the terms are used more metaphorically than literally. For the power to cure, divine, and bring peace to the dead are divine, not human traits. Just as the spiritists communicate with and transmit the needs of the spirits because they are halfway between life and death, the prayer woman communicates with the saints through prayer and transmits something of the saints' power. Those who "have the hand" not only have a great facility in speaking with the saints; they also become the human instruments of divine beings. Divine beings are characterized by their power, and since the prayer woman "uses" this power effectively, she is therefore "saintly" in some way.

Furthermore, the prayer women are the depositaries of cultural tradition, since they know the old prayers; they are responsible for passing on this local knowledge, by way of the house, to qualified descendants. They do not merely transmit this knowledge; they also continually revise it, picking out significant items from the official ritual and creating new uses for them, in accord with new needs and the local vision of the cosmos. However, women learned in prayers attribute to themselves a modest role; they see themselves as students or helpers of the priest, the ultimate religious authority. For example, the prayer people often knew the old prayers, the official catechism, to an extent that would surprise the priests.

And we went to be tested to see who knew more doctrine. And I knew the old catechism, which was very long, as well as the Our Father, all of it. The day I went to be tested for my marriage, well, the priest had a girl to do the cleaning, but it wasn't like now, that some of them have women there, but it's true that she was young, and she knew us. And she listened behind the kitchen door—she told me later—and she was amazed because he had never asked anyone so much; it was because I knew it all—and then the *señor* priest gave me a piece of cake and said, "Because you knew the catechism so well, I give you this piece of cake."

In the *brañas* these women fill a gap in the same way that midwives and healers make do in the absence of a doctor. But they do more; their traditional wisdom competes to some extent with the official wisdom. In this respect they have an advantage over the priest, for they choose aspects of religious belief that have a particular meaning for the group, and they use language that all share. They know what is needed. One should not forget that official religious instruction had a limited impact on the *brañas*. The only times the priest checked on what was learned was in preparation for certain rituals, like first communion or marriage, and then only rote memory of the catechism was accorded importance. In the *aldea*, religious indoctrination has been more continuous and persistent because of the presence of the priest; in the *braña* a parallel system of beliefs has developed with its own specialists. Today Vaqueiro children who want to receive first communion go to the church daily to receive religious instruction. There are also religion classes in the schools, and there are more and better teachers. But when today's Vaqueiro adults were young, seasonal teachers were the only source of religious education. They taught the children catechism along with a rudimentary knowledge of arithmetic, reading, and writing. These teachers were also considered religious specialists because they had "studied" (although the seasonal teacher had not usually had formal studies). They often served as spokespeople or intermediaries with the outside world.

The Vaqueiros' lack of formal religious learning had no impact on devotions and local practices based on Vaqueiro religious traditions, which were much more spontaneous and meaningful to the people. A woman recalls below the poetic and imaginative customs she devised as a child, when she cared for the sheep alone in the hills. These practices included a miniature infantile anniversary:

I would be alone and didn't know how to pass the time. And butterflies that were about at that time of year, there were a lot of little blue ones that we said were "cows of God." And they would settle and I would bring them flowers so they could eat. And I would catch them and hold them, but don't worry, I wouldn't hurt them, and I gave them flowers so they would eat and they liked it. I passed the time that way. And another thing. On a rock I put fatback, and sausage, and I filled up the whole rock, every day putting out a little piece. And I would say, "This is for Saint Anthony and the *Ánimas*, so they'll help me to care for the sheep." Every day I had this obsession. And one day my friend was with me, a neighbor girl, and I didn't say anything about this, nothing to anyone, and she was with me and I started running. "Where are you going?" "I'm off to the animals." I ran to the rock, put it down and ran off again. [Laughs] And the best of what they gave me for a lunch I would leave. I had this crazy idea that

The Saints   317

Saint Anthony and the *Ánimas* ate it. I know, of course, they didn't eat it; it would still be there; anyway I had the custom of leaving it there for them every day.

Most Vaqueiros cared for the "lesser" animals (sheep) when they were children, and this is one of the reasons for their spotty and abbreviated formal educations. Vaqueiros have religious beliefs "in their own way." I did not meet a single Vaqueiro, no matter how skeptical, who did not believe in the "powerful hand" and the saints—this despite the fact that many had doubts about or did not believe in certain aspects of the official religion. Vaqueiros may talk among themselves about "people who don't believe," but the persons are rarely specified. In any case, disbelief is not considered something bad. I was able to gather the following testimony about specific persons, now dead, who denied the effectiveness of certain religious practices.

One time my older brother came from Madrid—he was someone who really didn't believe—because he had lung trouble, and we all went to meet him. And my grandmother said—she had a rosary and everything—you know what they're like, now you don't see them but before they were common: "Well now, I'm going to pray the rosary in peace and in the grace of God." My sister went to let the horse loose, and when she let it go, it slipped and fell and slid off a precipice and was killed. And my brother said to my grandmother, "Now pray, pray, and a lot of good your prayers did, huh? You praying and the horse getting killed.

As old X said, I don't know if you knew him. His wife asked him to take boughs to be blessed. He said to her, "Did those of last year do all right?" She said yes. "Well you can leave this year's in the house. Because I forgot last year's in Y's stable, and then I brought them back home." [Laughter] See, instead of him taking them down to the church to be blessed, it's as if I took them to the stable and left them there, and then picked them up and said they had been blessed so I wouldn't have to take them down.

These two cases are exceptional, since speaking or acting against heaven in this way is considered foolhardy. When faced with the supernatural world, the Vaqueiros consider themselves "cowards" and "weak." Consider the analogy they use to explain this feeling.

The *braña* people—we are from the *braña*—are generally backwards; not backwards, exactly, but a little cowardly.

THE AFTERLIFE

More credulous in religion than those of the *aldea*. More cowardly, feeling weaker. Say, for example, if you go to Madrid, and you have to speak to someone who seems to be more important than you, more intelligent or with more money, you speak to that person with a little bit of fear, because one has to treat those people with more . . . I don't know how to explain it.

The Vaqueiros use the same word, "cowardly" [*cobarde*, here almost timorous], to describe how they feel when they attend mass in the parish church, not only in relation to the priest but also to the other parishioners, the *aldeanos*. Let us look once more at the interaction of the two groups, here as regards religious matters. As we have seen, the *aldeanos* frequently criticize the religious behavior of their Vaqueiro neighbors: their infrequent church attendance and their ignorance of the liturgy. The parish church has been a typical backdrop for supposedly humorous jokes and anecdotes about Vaqueiros.

There was a Vaqueiro who had never gone to mass. And his mother wanted him to go. "I won't go, mother, I won't go to mass, because I don't know how to go in, because I never went down there." "Look, you go down there, and just do what everyone else does. Go, and when you enter the church you have to take holy water, and you'll do what the others do." So the man went down and went to enter the church, and saw others take holy water to cross themselves and put his hand in the font and felt only water there. "Eh," he said, "all the meat's gone, only the soup is left." [Laughs] And he continued, and since his mother told him to do what the others did, he knelt down by a woman who was kneeling. And he saw that the sexton was lifting the chasuble to the priest, as they used to do. And he did the same with the woman next to him, raising her skirts! The woman, of course, started to scream, and all hell broke loose.

The parish church has also been a source of discrimination against the Vaqueiros, as we saw in regard to funerals. Formal discrimination in the church ended as well after a number of "revolutions" of the following nature, some of whom had famous protagonists, like a valiant woman of a rich house in the *braña* at the beginning of the century.

It was old C, the grandmother of the C here now. In the old days they treated us Vaqueiros like gypsies. Here in P [*aldea*] in the church there used to be a bar, and the Vaqueiros couldn't be in front of it, always behind it. And one time this C, the one who is so fat in the photograph, went ahead and crossed it; she pulled out the bar. Well, she wouldn't have pulled it out, but she didn't pay any attention to it. She went on past it, and so did the others, and from that day on the Vaqueiros sat with the *aldeanos*.

In the eyes of the Vaqueiros, the priest pertains to the *aldea* where he lives; sometimes he shares the myths and prejudices of the *aldeanos* toward their mountain neighbors. It is also significant that in the past the tensions and disputes between *aldeanos* and Vaqueiros took place in the parish church, where the priest often tolerated the actions and attitudes of the *aldeanos*. The Vaqueiros were second-class parishioners because of their seating in the church, because they were not allowed to participate in certain ceremonies, and also because of their own self-isolation and lack of knowledge of official ritual. Today one notes a subtle tension that increases when the Vaqueiros do not attend church as a group, as they usually do, but alone. In the words of the people of the *braña*, in the church they feel "cowardly" and very sensitive.

Well, the people here are a little more cowardly than the *aldeanos*. In the church, for example, they [*aldeanos*] are more at home than those of the *braña*, perhaps because we go there less, or for whatever reason. Another thing, the women of X [*aldea*] have their own kneelers, and those of the *braña* go to benches and kneel there. Because one time a *braña* woman went to kneel on one of the kneelers, and a woman from X came and took it away from her. It's happened occasionally.

In the face of God, the Vaqueiros feel like "cowards" with "fear" and "weakness"; they feel the same way in the parish church, which is the turf of the *aldeanos*, and are very hurt by the small incidents that the *aldeanos* have substituted for the open antagonism of earlier times. God is an important personage whom one must approach with the same humility and meekness as one would approach an important person in the city—the best simile at hand—who is intelligent, rich, and powerful. For such contacts the Vaqueiro is almost always represented by someone who has studied, who knows manners, etiquette, and protocol, and who "has seen the world." The people of the *braña* have their own saints and their own specialists in order to get in touch with this eminent "personality."

Conclusion: The Long Way of the Dead

The Vaqueiro transition from living to dead is not instantaneous but rather is a gradual and complex process. The notion of the spirit expresses the belief that one part of a Vaqueiro dies while he or she is still alive, and that another part continues to live after he or she is dead. The intuition and anticipation of death is joined with the remembrance of the dead in the last good-bye to the human being. Learning to be dead, like learning to be alive, is a question of time and culture.

The spirits that appear before a person dies often emit pitiful sounds: they weep, cry out, wail, and mourn. Given the context in which a spirit appears, it may seem to be sad and complain about abandoning life. This "shadow" of the sick or dying person in effect duplicates his or her own laments in different places, notifying people of the imminent departure. So the sighs are not just sighs of pain or sorrow; they are also an effort to attract the attention of the living. This is done by various means. Least common is the verbal discourse of human beings, for although the spirit will occasionally mutter some name or interjection, its language is so vague as to be almost unrecognizable. More frequently it uses signs that serve to reveal its presence, like moving objects with which it was once identified, or disturbing and provoking fear in people. Thus the spirits often appear to be speechless.

There are also spirits that, by making sounds or appearing in certain habitual places, seem to try to deny death. These spirits stick to their work or daily tasks, dress in their everyday clothes, occupy the places they have always frequented, and attempt by this

321

behavior to convey a sense of continuity that is inappropriate to their condition. Even those who present themselves in human form and with a serene aspect are characterized by their muteness, even if the message they transmit by their presence is sufficiently clear. But not all spirits show this studied indifference. Indeed most are characterized by their aggressiveness. Spirits scare their relatives, bother and worry their friends and neighbors, menace their acquaintances, and spook people on the roads and paths, all without apparent motive.

Some kinds of apparitions, nevertheless, give us an idea of the significance of these spirit activities for the living. I refer in particular to those apparitions related to the representation of death in the abstract, a funeral or a wedding in a dream, as well as those related to a concrete death, the funeral of someone specific or a spirit wearing burial clothes. Here the announcement and the premonition of death could not be more explicit. But the premonition extends to any human misfortune, including nonfatal accidents. In this way symbols turn up isolated from their context to foretell future situations of grief; only later do they acquire a specific meaning. The spirit is only one of these symbols; note that the people refer to it as "a thing," "something that shows itself," "a representation," "like a person," or "as if it were a person," and not the person itself. The spirit symbolizes the dose of death included in life. That is why, by means of the spirit, death begins in life.

Life does not end with death either. After death the sounds continue, and so do the apparitions of the spirits. Some do the work that the dead person did when he or she was alive, absorbed in the same tasks as the living and indifferent to death; others are menacing, restless, and bewail their fate, their death. In this phase, they not only lament but try to communicate with the living by various means. In contrast to the spirits before death, most of whom were mute, some of the spirits after death speak for themselves; others speak through intermediaries. Almost all produce fear or nervousness, losses and misfortunes, and all share a common objective; to make their needs clear to those still living. Unlike the spirits of the living whose medium of expression is their message, the spirits of the dead seek from the living very concrete help. In order to make their state of need known, they provoke a string of losses and accidents. Their preferred victims seem to be domestic animals. Spirits of the recent dead demand anniversaries about a year after death; those longer gone ask for masses and prayers. The spirits who have been dead the longest are the most polite and well-mannered; they try not to scare the immediate family members they talk to, and they gently calm them so they will not be afraid. (They are not excessively loquacious, however; if the living try to prolong conversation, they say they are in a hurry.)

The spirits of the dead work their will as both judges and victims. They are judges because they punish the selfishness of the living when they do not answer the petitions and fulfill the promises that the dead made when alive. After death, the spirits avenge mistreatment they received when they were alive and sick or aged. In all of these cases, the spirit enforces a moral standard. The message is that, although it may be difficult, one has to protect and care for the weak, be just in dividing inheritances, be generous with those who remain, and at the same time honor those who have passed away.

The spirits of the dead are also victims, because at times their aggressive behavior is due to their peremptory need for help. The spirits "are badly off," "have no rest," "are in a bad spot." If being in a "bad spot" implies prowling around the house and the paths, pacing the stable or the attic, and the *braña* and the world of the living in general, "rest" is achieved locally when the dead person definitively departs for the proper place for spirits, the world of the dead. Various circumstances impede this final trip. Let us look more closely at the requests of the spirits. The anniversaries are close to human needs; masses and prayers are closer to divine needs, for they are shared with God and the saints. The spirits are said not to rest precisely because of old debts either to humans or to the divine—that is, to their relatives and neighbors, who are the beneficiaries of the anniversaries, and to the saints, the beneficiaries of promises. Debts both of omission (the unfulfilled promise) and commission (a blasphemy, for example) must be corrected. Although the motive is evident, it does not seem that the punishment fits the crime. Forgetting some prayers seems a minor cause for a number of deaths in a stable; blasphemy should not trigger a series of losses. And it does not seem right that the dead, should make their innocent and even ignorant descendants suffer for their own faults. What do such abuses mean?

Let us note that promises, although they may be for insignificant gifts or alms, are made to the saints in order to achieve significant ends; the health of the animals, the successful delivery of a calf, the recovery of a lost animal, or the recuperation of human health. From this perspective, what the supplicant offers does not bear comparison with what the divine receives. There is an implication that humans must maintain a strict observance in their agreements with the saints. In effect, what is established is a contract.

Similar transactions take place between the living and the

dead. The spirits address themselves either directly or indirectly to their family members. It is inconceivable that a spirit, without a house of its own, would turn up to ask something from the neighbors. The dead thus appear to recognize and observe the bonds of kinship. This does not mean that the dead and the living always belong to the same lineage, for the house might have passed into the hands of a nonlineal relative. In such a case, the spirit still will enter the house with total freedom. In the popular usage, saying that an "old grandmother" from the house returned for some reason might refer more generally to an "old woman" and not necessarily to a particular ancestor. In the same way, the demands of the dead are not directed to specific individuals or specific family roles, but rather to the members of the house as a whole, although the *amo* of the house has a particular responsibility for fulfilling them. It is membership in the house then, whether by blood or affinity, that unites the living and the dead. The obligations and rights to the house do not end with death; inheritance of the house not only supposes material objects, but also the entirety of its dead. In addition to the obligation to maintain, enlarge, and transmit the house to future generations, there are also certain ritual obligations to the ancestors. "Obligations" [*obligaciones*] is precisely what the masses celebrated in the church for the dead of the house are called. The eternal rest of the dead is everyone's responsibility, more specifically the responsibility of those with whom one has lived and shared one's existence. This contract between the living and the dead thus serves to emphasize the dependence of each Vaqueiro on the others, including those who have passed on and those who have yet to be born. The fact that if one does not fulfill a promise while alive, one will fulfill it in death, come what may, implies a moral lesson. One must attempt to fulfill not only the promises of the dead but also one's own promises, so that they will not fall due on one's successors. One is reminded that the living of today are the dead of tomorrow. The necessity and obligation of fulfilling the promises of the dead under fear of the sanctions of the other world strengthens the trustworthiness of human transactions. In the *braña* all debts, to the saints or to the living, are purely verbal.

Although the members of a house are the only people directly responsible for its dead, the entire community participates in communicating with the dead. For instance, local intermediaries generously place their specialty at the disposition of their neighbors and friends, in spite of the risks involved. When it is not possible to acquire the information by other means, these persons help to attract the dead, learn their needs, and transmit messages to living family members, in this way helping to stop the losses and misfortunes of others. Such specialists range in ability from those who receive occasional and spontaneous visits from the spirits to the spiritists, or *ánimas*, who display a great facility and familiarity in this kind of communication. There is a continuum of relations between the world of the living and the world of the dead: the specialists, who might be termed amateurs, are those closer to life; the *ánimas*, perhaps, are the most interesting and special of these intermediaries. Let us review their principal features. Date of birth is an important criterion for a spiritist, implying that their power is at least in part inherent. Note that optimal date of birth is in fact the day formally dedicated to the dead. This suggests an initial ambivalence: the intermediaries with the dead begin to live on the Day of the Dead.

Second, all spiritists are religious and compel the communication with the spirits by prayers not known to all. The spiritist spends a certain amount of time—from a few minutes to a day—reciting various religious formulae that form a bridge with the other world. One must have a certain amount of learning and a certain disposition to become a spiritist: one must have a personal interest in learning the prayers, a good memory, time for study. Certain teachers, generally temporary ones, had these attributes; in addition, they were often responsible for teaching catechism in the area. It is interesting to note that the replies of the dead—their requests for masses and prayers—are related to the form of the questions posed, also through prayer. Thus, religion is a necessity for the intermediary. The ambivalence here is that prayer does not only help one communicate with the dead, but also with God and the saints.

A third characteristic of spiritists is that they are generally old and maintain a particular kind of relation with the spirits. Contact with the other world is dangerous, and the risk increases with age. Thus, while the first appearances from the other world tend to be sporadic, over the years they become almost continual. The incursions, usually impersonal at the start of a career, become intimate and interdependent in old age, leading to an authentic struggle between spirit and spiritist. Two different models turn up in the local descriptions: the Crow, whom the spirits put "pressure on" [*aprietan*], and the more serene attitude of the *ánima* of Sampol, whose degree of control of the other world and acceptance of her role are considerable. These figures have one foot in life and the other in death; both feet will end up together but one is never certain where.[12] For this reason, one goes to these people with both mistrust and respect, and with a contribution, whether in money or in kind, in order to predispose them in favor of the living.

Conclusion: The Long Way of the Dead   325

Finally, we note an ambiguity in the local definition of *ánima*. People say she is "a living *thing*," "like an animal"; they also claim that she lives without eating, that her body is "only held together by bandages," and that she remains immobile in her bed. Such remarks reflect the ambiguity that surrounds the role; the *ánima* is not considered human but a thing that lives. Animals are alive but not human, but she is not really an animal either. *Ánimas* comprise another unhuman category of being. The *ánima* does not eat like other humans, stays immobile, and her corporeal substance, barely held together by bandages, slides away into other forms of being. In other words, the *ánima* is neither human nor animal, neither dead nor alive, or is all of these things at once. The metonymic association *ánima/animal* is not accidental; it may shed some light on the nature of this intermediary. Let us then look at the world of the animals that have relations with the dead.

The four animals that catch the advance notices of death form a fairly heterogeneous group; at first glance, cows, horselike animals, dogs, and foxes have little in common. Three of these categories are domestic; the fourth, the fox, is not. The domestic animals can be distinguished internally in terms of relative productivity, the cow offering the maximum contrast with the unproductive fox. The cow is the key animal of the *braña*, around which the life and economy of the inhabitants revolve. The Vaqueiros make their principal, often their only, income from the sale of milk and calves. Cows are used for work, transport, and as a source of fertilizer. The same positions hold in regard to the right to space within the house. The cow has an important place there, as the stable generally occupies the ground floor of the house, immediately beneath the living quarters of the humans.[13] The Vaqueiros' interest in improving and modernizing the quarters of these animals, often in preference to those of the humans, attests to their importance in the house.

The physical proximity of the cows and their masters is reproduced in other ways. For example, on an intellectual level, the cow serves as a kind of model or metaphor. Local ideas about the Vaqueiro woman's beauty, behavior, work, maternal feeling, intelligence, and values in general acquire their meaning in reference to cows. On an affective level, the love and attention for cows, especially in their crisis of birth and death, reproduce that among humans. The games Vaqueiro children play, for example, revolve around cows, and this is an example of an important kind of socialization.[14] One can appreciate the influence of the cattle on the life of their masters on a cognitive level as well. Cows, like children, are surrounded with amulets, objects that have been blessed, and prayers, which place them under divine protection. Finally, cows are individualized by being named, and each wears a distinctive bell that permits it to be identified audibly among all of the herds of the *braña*.

Horses and mules are used almost exclusively for labor and transportation. Because bovine animals also serve these functions, horses and mules are not indispensable although still useful. Now they are being replaced by automobiles and tractors. The stable for horses or mules is not accorded the same attention or care as that of cattle. Indeed they do not have designated quarters in the house. They might occupy a space meant for pigs, an old cow barn, or a loft divided off from the rooms. When these animals are not needed, they often are let loose near the *braña* or in the mountains until they are needed again. Horses and mules have much more distant relations with humans than cows do. For instance, they do not have proper names, other than "the mule" or the "jack," nor do they have a substantial place in the lives of their masters. The Vaqueiros lament their loss, of course, but this is primarily because of the economic value of these animals.

The dog is useful only in guarding the house, or in hunting, an activity almost nonexistent in the *braña*. There were more dogs in the *brañas* in the past when there were goats and sheep to herd and protect from the wolves. Now the few remaining dogs are semivagabond, wandering around the houses on the lookout for garbage and scraps, especially at the time of slaughtering. Dogs are marginalized in the house in keeping with their lack of utility. They are not even useful as models for socialization. In the *braña* dogs do not serve as playmates for children; they play with a small *xato* or calf instead. Nor is the dog compared with humans as a means or metaphor for understanding human identity. The only commentary that people make about it is that it is "like a wolf," albeit domestic.

The fox not only has no domestic function; it is positively harmful to the household, as it invades the domestic space to abduct or kill hens, or other fowl or minor livestock. The fox enters the house only surreptitiously. It is always unwelcome because it strikes at the goods of the house. As it is part of the wild world, its intrusion is a violation of human space. The fox occupies the other end of the spectrum from the cow: it is not only an unfriendly being but even an enemy. The mutual dependence of humans and cows contrasts with the opposition and struggles of humans and foxes. Although the fox pertains to the wild world, it is not a perfect representative. Locally considered a kind of rascal, the fox is a sly thief that takes advantage of the least human lapse to get what it wants. It will not attack or confront humans directly, although misbehaving children sometimes are threatened with phrases like "if you are bad the fox will come after you," "the fox will eat you," and so on. Since the fox "eats" small household animals, the metaphor is pertinent in the case of children.

The partial wildness of the fox contrasts with the perfect wildness of two other animals, the bear and particularly the wolf, which is called a beast [fiera] or savage beast. While the fox steals and kills small animals marginal to the household economy, the wolf and the bear threaten the household directly by attacking the most important animals of the stable: the sheep, calves, cows, and mules, that is, the most domestic animals. Indeed, the danger is thought to extend to humans themselves, since the wolf is said to kill people. It is said that the bear will "charge" humans. Given these serious risks, such animals are not treated lightly, unlike the fox, who sometimes is depicted as a figure of fun. The fox may kill a hen, but physical danger to humans or the death of a good cow, the fruit of the greatest efforts and preoccupations of the Vaqueiros, is a wholly different order of danger. These wild animals are considered amoral, the anarchic slaves an instinctual appetite that leads them to attack humans and their property indiscriminately and wantonly. The conduct of these "accursed" animals even among themselves (they fight and claw each other) is described by the Vaqueiros as chaotic, without ethical rules or ordered relations. The wild world is thus in dramatic contrast with the domestic world, which the cow neatly symbolizes—an animal who knows her masters, obeys them docilely, and contributes in many different ways to the honor and prosperity of the house.

But even in those cases where the wolf and the bear respect the physical integrity of people and animals, they attack their psychological integrity by means of fear. The uniformity and unanimity of local descriptions of the fear produced by contact with these animals is significant.[15] Here are some of the stereotypical symptoms of reactions to wolves: "the face gets cold and cold," "the clothes go off the body," "the body feels it," "they make you tremble," "my speech was cut off," "it makes your hair stand on end," "I couldn't move," "it seemed that something drew me on, the light in the eyes of the two wolves," "then they grabbed me from behind," "by then I hardly felt anything," and so on. In summary, contact with wolves leaves humans cold or frozen, white, without clothes, speechless, immobile, and without feeling; these symptoms, which suggest a cadaver, could not be more precise.

Fear of the wolf is expressed in identical terms as fear of the spirits. I excerpt the following phrases from cases of spirits: "I had such a fear that I could hardly talk," "a cold," "a thing that grabbed me," "it seemed like they were pulling your hairs," "a coldness in the body and a nervousness that I couldn't bear, trembling," and so on. Furthermore, the fear produced by wild beasts is the same as that caused by a hypothetical incursion into the cemetery, the house of the dead.

> You can get the fear from anything. If a person travels alone by night fear may enter him/her. Right now if you were outside you would be afraid. The wolf causes fear from the idea you have that it may eat you. [You can get] fear from the wolves or from someone or something that scares you. Don't you know what is felt if you are traveling by night and I scare you, what would you feel? Something in the body so that it seems as though you undress and someone grabs you. That is fear; if you don't know what it is, a fear gets into you that you can't bear. If you go alone to the cemetery at dusk, a fear enters you that almost knocks you out. Since you know the person is buried, and as we have this thing about spirits and what we see and hear, and [although] those who are dead don't do anything to you, they say they are out and about in the cemetery, and I say, "Well . . . for those who go to the cemetery, their world is there, the skeletons. . . ." Ugh! I don't want to think about it.

The fear of wolves is worse when they are not seen than when they are and reaches its climax at night. These two characteristics, invisibility and nocturnalness, are so typical of fear of the spirits that people consider both spirits and wolves as the possible source of their fears, and even confuse the two. In fact, invisibility seems to be subsumed in the night, for there is no way to see wolves in the dark, thus the concrete association wolf/spirit is reduced to the terms "fear" and "night." The same words turn up in the other two groups of animals that symbolize death; those of fear and those of the night. Nocturnalness is an evident characteristic of the barn owl, the "animal of the night." The animals of fear are characterized mainly by their color—black, the symbol of the night. Magpies, significantly, are considered ambivalent, bringing both happiness and sadness and having both black and white feathers. This symbolism pertains to other living things as well, for example, moths: a black moth is supposed to bring bad news while a white moth brings good news. The dove, as opposed to the crow, brings good luck.

The association of spirits and wild animals, and birds of fear or the night, shows that they have many features in common. As the spirits do, these animals signify death and appear preceding it (at the smell of "fever"). Their behavior signifies the opposite of what it would mean in humans: the "couple" relation of two crows that kiss means the end of a human couple by the death of one of its members; A meeting with crows, as with wild animals or spirits, can mean accidents or physical injury. Crows are similar to spirits in other ways—their calls [*glaios*], their sudden and menacing appearance, and the fact that spirits, too, often appear as black. Finally, we note that the "animals" of fear and the night are actually birds. Many spirits appear to Vaqueiros as birds, or change from human form into birds of the same color. Certain aspects of the spirits, like the speed at which they move around or the sounds they make, reveal an etherealness whose metaphorical expression is the flight of birds. The spirits, in the local idiom, would be "like" black birds at night.

Both beasts and spirits attack cattle. The wolf will eat calves and the dead will avenge themselves on the most vulnerable animals of the stable, the cows (and, to a lesser extent, horses). People who when alive cared so much for the cattle, as spirits use cattle as a way to strike out at the supposed neglect of their relatives. Possessively, the spirits try to steal the cattle and take them away to the world of the dead. Perhaps out of nostalgia, they try to "eat the living," choosing as their victims the choicest cows in a herd. The behavior of the cattle when they sense "visions" of spirits—their fear and lack of control—is an animal duplicate of human fear, for they "sense" death and its coming just as humans do. Like their masters, they seem to realize the tremendous change that the death of humans signifies. In spite of what might appear to be an instinctive reaction to death (Vaqueiros refer to their sense of smell), the fact that they do not see the spirits of children but do see the spirits of those far away implies that the visions cows have, like those humans have, are profoundly social. With cows as with humans, what counts for a spirit is the experience of an entire life, not a partial one, the time necessary to ratify the bonds and alliances that make life in society possible.

Note that the powers attributed to cattle are shared by a group of humans, the spiritists. The spiritists speak with the spirits that the cows supposedly see. Both, thus, have special powers in their role as intermediaries. The spiritists mediate between the world of the living and the world of the dead, and for this reason have bivalent characters, elements of both worlds. Cows mediate between the animal world and that of humans, for although they are animals, they have certain human characteristics. Clearly the connection between the two worlds is the process of domestication, for the cow is born wild [*brava*] and pertains to nature until over time it is made cultural [*noble*].[16] The cow is the best example of the most complete domestication. Observe that the other animals that serve as intermediaries (from horses to foxes) show progressively less of this attribute. Their contraries and opposites dwell in the wild world, the world of fear and night, and include the spirits themselves. I have represented this association of animals and death in figure 6. In this diagram, the pure categories are at the extremes while those closest to the vertical center line are most ambiguous. The horizontal line represents the three possibilities of human existence discussed in this chapter—living humans, spiritists, and spirits. The diagram reveals some other mental configurations that surround the idea of spirits by their association with animals of the Vaqueiro environment. The equivalent of domesticity in animals is the process of socialization in humans; this process supposes an ordered society, the observance of social norms, and the adherence to ethical values. These values have disappeared in the spirits and have been replaced by the anarchy and amorality of the state of nature. One could say, then, that the dead are wild. The similarity of birds and spirits in contrast to earthbound creatures indicates the distancing of these creatures from domestic life and the earthly world. The spirit seems to fly. Birds and spirits mediate between sky and earth, between beings of this world and the other world.

In these pages I have emphasized the features of the majority of the spirits, especially the most recent ones, but not of all spirits. The oldest ones appear to have their own, different rules, a calmer attitude and demands that do not involve the health of the cattle. It

WHITE BIRDS			BIRDS OF FEAR AND NIGHT		
dove white moths	magpies	black moths	crows and owls		
humans spiritists	*ánimas*	spirits of the living	spirits of the dead		
cows horses and mules	dogs	foxes	bears	wolves	
DOMESTIC BEINGS			SAVAGE BEASTS		

FIGURE 6 PROCESS OF DOMESTICATION

is a long way to heaven; the spirit has not finished it's journey. The profundity and richness of meaning to be found in these beliefs make sense only in context. The use of animals as models for different modes of existence can be ascribed in part to the effect of the environment, to a way of life intimately linked with cattle.

As we have seen, the attitude of the Vaqueiros is neither magical nor dogmatic. They evince differing degrees of adherence or skepticism to the belief in spirits, although all recognize their importance. No Vaqueiro demonstrates absolute denial or total certainty; individual attitudes run the gamut between these two extremes. Contradictions, uncertainty, an acknowledgement of the vagueness and impersonality of the evidence or the subjective nature of the phenomenon, the partial or selective denial of visions, and the classification of the phenomenon as a mental matter show that the belief is subject to criticism and discussion on the part of those who hold it. The Vaqueiros' honesty and concern for proof is clear from their spontaneous presentation of negative examples, whether concrete proofs of falsification or convincing doubts, alongside positive and convincing examples. In spite of this rationalism, the belief not only persists, it is even adopted by outsiders who take up the Vaqueiro way of life without a childhood acculturation. In other words, it seems that the fact of sharing a social life supposes the acceptance of common symbols, although the interpretation of these symbols may vary (see Fernández 1965).

Compared to the relative consistency and consensus of the Vaqueiros' on the belief in spirits, there are certain cosmological issues about which they are quite insecure and confused. The concept of the *alma* is one of these slippery and uncertain matters. The Vaqueiros emphasize the vital, concrete, and material aspects of the *alma*, and appear to ignore the spiritual connotations of the word, or at the best reduce them to mere articles of faith and religious dogma. It is precisely the dichotomy of *alma*/body that provokes perplexity in the Vaqueiros and elicits many of their doubts, vaguenesses, and inconsistencies. It seems that the Vaqueiros are more willing to accept the idea of a spirit as a symbol of a person who has died than the idea of a human being divided into the antagonistic and Manichean parts of body and soul. The symbol serves to express the integrity of the person. Furthermore, while the notion of spirit is a part of the experience of the living and is produced by the living as an expression of the intuition and anticipation of death on the one hand, and as the memory of and a reminder of the dead on the other, *alma* is a very abstract and distant term that defines the dead per se, without relation to those who are still alive. Perhaps the Vaqueiros show so little interest in this idea because it touches them so little. The dead exist in the memory and the experience of the living.

An identical uncertainty appears in relation to the habitat of the dead. The Vaqueiro cosmology of the "other world" is very unsystematic, and it would appear that they have not paid much attention to the matter.[17] They seem to be less interested in the way the dead live than in the particular way the dead interact with the living, that is, the way the dead affect the living and vice versa, since spirits depend on their relatives to get from the "bad" to the "good" place (a matter that *is* clear and explicit). Just as the concrete and material aspects of the soul are emphasized, so when the destination of the dead is raised, Vaqueiros talk about the physical location of bodies—previously the earth, now niches. The dichotomies up/down, and sky/earth show the Vaqueiros' difficulty in combining cosmological dogma with their own sensory experience. Here the distinction *alma*/body again appears disassociated and disassociating; the body is undoubtedly taken underground while the soul hypothetically goes to heaven, which is vaguely associated with the "atmosphere." This interest in fixing the actual location of heaven in the sky is assumed to be at the root of the space flights and the lunar landing, which have clearly had an impact on local perceptions.

If heaven is associated with the "upper atmosphere," albeit vaguely, hell does not have a spatial location at all. The Vaqueiros associate the "bad place" with the misfortunes of life and the hard struggle for survival. The cosmology of hell is considered a kind of children's story, and a symbol of the condition of permanent misfortune. One goes to the good or the bad place, depending on one's behavior while alive. Yet these places are more like theoretical concepts than precise ecological designations, for no one can assign specific individuals to them with any certainty. The good and bad places are not exact equivalents of heaven or hell; rather they seem to comprise an intermediate stage with variations only in a greater or less tranquillity. The dead come back because they have not finished leaving; they have to be helped along in their transition.

When pressed on these matters, Vaqueiros will refer to persons who have "studied," especially to the priest, who lives for and from this knowledge. They also refer to certain books, like the catechism; to specific pictoral versions, like the circus sideshows; or to linguistic clichés or formulaic prayers that mention the matter about which they have been asked. These attempts to treat cosmological issues in concrete terms, and the absence of a coherent explanation, show that the Vaqueiros lack curiosity in these matters. Indeed, one might think that they regard the sky/heaven as an empty place. But this is not so. Let us consider the "saints."

Saint Anthony is the saint most characteristic of the *braña* and the figure the Vaqueiros invoke the most. His specialty is the care of the *braña* animals, and his position relative to them is like that of God relative to humans. The Vaqueiros, like many Spaniards, say *"Jesús!"* when a "Christian" sneezes; when a cow coughs, they say *"San Antonio!"* Saint Anthony is responsible for a key aspect of the economy of the *casa*, the care of animals. The invocations, promises, and offerings the saint receives demonstrate his specialization in these tasks. The saint will not only watch over the birth of a calf or the sickness of a cow, but also will care for lost animals, protect them from predators, and help to locate them. The saints' tasks thus reflect those of the Vaqueiros themselves, especially the male Vaqueiros. Saint Anthony thus becomes a supernatural shepherd who, together with his dog, helps out when the Vaqueiros have looked for their animals in vain or when they begin to lose hope. The saints appear to be very much like the people who venerate them.

In addition to giving alms or prayers to the saint, the Vaqueiros give more substantial offerings: a *lacón*, wool, chickens, and even pigs. All of these offerings function metonymically. Saint Anthony receives the *lacón* (part of the foreleg of the pig) in exchange for the pig's health; wool stands for sheep; chickens and even pigs, small animals, for the health of cows and calves, large animals. These offerings signify the terms of a contract. The saint is offered symbolic compensation for the life and health of the animals. Saint Anthony is known from the many images in the local churches. This plurality of depictions ratifies his status as a domestic saint, the saint of the ecological base, a familiar and everyday deity who takes responsibility for problems arising from the administration of the house and the periodic crises of the animals that belong to it.

While Saint Anthony is an everyday and domestic saint, the Santa of El Acebo, who is turned to less frequently, covers a broader geographical area. This is clear from the association of her shrine with long-distance transhumancy. Local tradition attributes the first miracle of this *santa* to a situation frequent among transhumant Vaqueiros—that of a herdsman searching for a cow in the dense fog of the mountain pasture. Other details of the story have similar parallels in Vaqueiro beliefs: the Vaqueiros would consider the group of unknown persons who disappear mysteriously to be spirits; the candle they give the shepherd is considered just as miraculous today as in the past and is used frequently by the Vaqueiros. Even the circumstances of the construction of the shrine, in spite of the fact that it is a legend common in the north of Spain,[18] has a very specific meaning for the Vaqueiros. It is that the *santa* chose to dwell in the place most appropriate to the cattle herders, their particular transhumant habitat.

The kind of offerings the Vaqueiros make to the *santa* also are related to their way of life. In addition to the donations they give to most saints—alms, masses, and prayers—they bring more and more varied offerings in kind, including the traditional fruit of the earth (whole or processed corn, wheat, bread, rye, or oil); animal products (butter, fatback, or milk); small animals like chickens, lambs, and kids; and also larger animals, calves, cows, and even pairs of oxen. Note that while the Vaqueiros ask Saint Anthony for the health of these animals, the animals themselves are offered to the *santa*. If, as we have seen, the offering is a metonymic symbol for what one hopes to receive, offering these animals would signify the request for something much more important for the Vaqueiro.

Some of the products, like wheat, rye, or wax are offered in a very specific quantity—the weight of the person making the offer, scrupulously measured. Here the meaning is obvious: the product stands for the person. In the same way, the Vaqueiros offer wax reproductions of body parts (arms, heads, legs, breasts and so on) that have been cured, either full sized or reduced. And the articles of clothing offered—the military uniform, the *embolubre* or shroud—suppose a victory over life-threatening situations, which one way or another mean a separation from the *braña*. All of these offerings show the specialization of the Santa of El Acebo in matters pertaining to illness, the danger of death, and the loss of human members of the household. While Saint Anthony takes responsibility for the health and well-being of the animals in the small and diffuse dangers of everyday life, the *santa* is kept for critical occasions like death. But she is not used only for animals, but also for something much more important—the health of humans. Thus the only commensurate compensation at times is the sacrifice of the beings closest to humans, cows. The Vaqueiros, who frequently go to the shrine to ask for the health of the animals, leaving wax votive offerings or other, smaller live animals, do not hesitate to offer their best cow when their own health or that of another member of the house is at stake. These are the most extreme situations, as one might deduce from the magnitude of the offering. This type of offering is made only when other sacrifices, which may include penitential pilgrimages barefoot or on one's knees, are not considered important enough for what is being sought. The importance of the Santa of El Acebo in human affairs can be seen not only in relation to death but also in relation to life, especially fertility. Just as Saint Anthony helps at the birth of calves, so the *santa* helps at the birth of humans. This division of labor at a metaphysical level reproduces that between men and woman in the *braña:* men help the cows to give birth while women help other women in labor and childbirth.

In addition to visiting the shrine of the *santa* with specific requests for help or in fulfillment of promises, the Vaqueiros find it useful as a source of holy objects that will enable them to prevent various misfortunes. They bring material objects to the shrine—money, animals, produce—and in exchange receive spiritual things—talismans and blessings through their contact with the image. The contact with the divinity makes these objects sacred. By means of these objects, the house, stable, children, and cows can share in the blessing. Any sudden crises, or the traditional crisis like the departure of transhumant cattle, that of youths for military service, that of adults for their final journey, and the creation of a new life will be accompanied by supernatural assistance. The shrine of the *santa* has become the focus of religious attention for an ample hinterland of western Asturias, not just for the Vaqueiros, because the health of humans is a common issue.

The *Ánimas* are just as popular as Saint Anthony and the santa of El Acebo for the Vaqueiros, and they are offered similar presents. The significance of these offerings follows the same metonymic logic noted above: the ham hock, including the hoof, stands for the pig; some ears of corn represent the harvest; and wool stands for the sheep. The *Ánimas* are often invoked for the same reasons as Saint Anthony—at the births of cows and pigs, or the loss or death of an animal. But these promises frequently are made immediately after some sign of misfortune. For example, one or more masses will be offered immediately after the death of a cow. This seems to indicate that the function of the *Ánimas* is to provide warnings or signs of a possible future series of misfortunes. It seems, in other words, that they are responsible for reminding the living of the ritual obligations due to the saints, and for punishing the neglect and omissions of Christians in this matter.

Let us consider more specifically the *Ánimas'* role as intermediaries. The dead and the *Ánimas* in many respects appear to be interchangeable in local perception, as the reader may have noted from the Vaqueiros' own comments. The boundary between the two concepts seems very vague when considering the masses that each receives. In theory, masses directed to the recent dead suppose the attendance of relatives. These are the masses known as "masses with people," in which the priest mentions the dead person for whom the mass is said. The masses for the *Ánimas* do not require the attendance of relatives; like the masses given to the other saints, they are "masses without people," and are said in an anonymous fashion. But this distinction is not always made in practice. Certain masses may be ordered for the soul of a specific person but not attended by relatives; other masses may be dedicated "to the person most in need who has passed away from the house or the family" without specifying the name. Many masses to the *Ánimas* or the dead, then, have a certain ambiguity as to whether the spiritual sacrifice is meant for individuals or groups. This ambiguity is often expressed through the dichotomy church/ house. Some rituals that take place on the Day of the Dead show the particularization of the dead by means of the institution of the house. In the cemetery, for instance, several members of the same house clean and adorn the graves or niches, respond to the prayers the priest says in front of them, and bring certain presents—flowers, alms, and prayers—for those who have passed on.

It seems the dead respond to the visits the living make to the cemetery. Although the *Ánimas* may visit their old house to quench their thirst any time during the year, the Night of the Dead appears to be an obligatory date for them to stop by and have a simple meal, a piece of bread and a little water. This custom suggests the permanence of the needs of the dead of a given house and their continuing dependence on the house, an expression of the biological and cultural continuity between the living and the dead. The insignificance of this minimal culinary effort contrasts sharply with the Pantagruelian anniversaries and the spirits' traditional demands for meat. Further, the way these spartan meals are offered indicates that they are offered more as a deferential courtesy than as an obligation that the Vaqueiros meet under threat. Observe that if the *Ánimas* do not find these presents, they do not get angry; they simply complain piteously or even "go off crying." If, on the contrary, they do receive the meal, they "go away satisfied," merely because they have had some water. In other words, it seems as if these nostalgic *Ánimas* had lost their right to visit the house, or at least their power to make the living fulfill the old demands for real banquets.

In fact, local opinion has it that the Day of the Dead was invented in recent times so that people could remove the dead from the house, thereby preventing the dead from bothering the living with their visits and nocturnal noises. But where do the dead go? The church seems to be the place for communication with and depiction of the *Ánimas*. There they have their offering box, like the other saints. The living often repay their debts to a dead Vaqueiro there. The church commemorates the Day of the *Ánimas*—the Faithful Dead—with attention and solemnity similar to that of the other saints. This ritual in the church emphasizes the common and collective nature of the dead as a whole, and helps to explain the local understanding that an alms on this day "is worth a hundred." This holy day is an attempt to center attention on the dead. At the same time it shows the desire of the Vaqueiros to keep their interactions with those who have passed on within controllable limits and in a certain order. They locate this order in the church and its adjacent cemetery. The dead appear to offer a certain resistance to their removal from their old homes, as if life were still attractive for them and household ties very important. To prevent their return, one must go to church at least one day a year to establish a formal, periodic contact. By means of the annual visit to the cemetery, the masses, alms, and offerings given in the church, the living confront the dead in the light of day and force them into a new role. The living "collaborate" with the dead, ensuring that they are converted definitively into saints by means of the anonymous category of *Ánimas*.[19]

Observe that all of the characteristics of this feast day—its designation as "holy," the Vaqueiros' attendance at mass, their abstinence from work, the auctioning of hamhocks, and so on—show a ritual comportment toward the *Ánimas* identical to that toward other saints.[20] And vice versa, the dead over time become *Ánimas*, lose their aggressive nature and begin to act like Saint Anthony or the Virgin of El Acebo. Hence they cure the cows that, as spirits, they previously had tried to take away with them; they help out at the birthing of the same animals that they previously made miscarry; they find the animal that was lost; and they make harvests rich that at other times were so sparse. But all of these benefits, which aid in the success and prosperity of the house, are not something that they bestow gratis. The help of the *Ánimas* is conditioned by the generous payment of promises that characterizes relations with the divinity. Promises are remembered with great care and they are scrupulously paid. The preoccupation and the fear of not fulfilling what was offered is understandable for two reasons. While all supernatural beings take vengeance for unfulfilled promises, the dead and the *Ánimas* in particular take responsibility for enforcing the punishments that the house deserves on such occasions. This vengeance will often center on the most valuable animals, the best or most fertile cows. For if Saint Anthony is a shepherd-saint, one must not forget that the *Ánimas* were once Vaqueiros, and as such they know all about cows and what they are worth to their owners. That is, they know how to choose their vic-

THE AFTERLIFE

tims. The *Ánimas'* punitive behavior is very similar to that of the spirits, but the critical difference is that while the spirits still show a strong dependence on the living to get to the "good place"—lurking around the house and the *braña,* sacrificing animals for themselves, and demanding meat and anniversaries—the *Ánimas* have already gotten to this "place" and are no longer as dependent on the living. Rather, the house is dependent on the *Ánimas.* With the recent dead there are still debts and pending accounts, but with the *Ánimas* and the saints there is a strict and reasonable contract. While spirits demand bloody offerings, the saints request masses, prayers, and alms. Where is the boundary between one form and the other? Perhaps when spirits begin to fly? or when they become tamed?

As time passes, the dead begin to look and act like saints, or, more properly, like *Ánimas.* So the Vaqueiros are perpetually in contact with a continuum of spiritual beings, ranging from those below, that is, the spirits who insist on remaining around the house, to those "up above," the *Ánimas* who have already settled in the good place together with the saints. The spirits below were once human beings and continue to look like them. The metaphors used to describe them—shadows, airs, screens—express the idea that they are blurry copies of the living. For the same reason, the Vaqueiros speak of spirits in more concrete and anthropomorphic terms than they do when referring to God or the *Ánimas.* Furthermore, the spirits have feelings similar to those they had when they were alive. That is why it is those most recently dead who wreak their vengeance most violently, especially on their own relatives. Reparation is made according to sacrifices whose prices are set according to the offense of the living but generally involve animals. When the Vaqueiros sacrifice animals, they sacrifice part of themselves; they hand over what is most like humans, living creatures, the most valuable things they own. The animal is not being punished in the place of the person but represents that person. When someone in the *braña* dies, all the Vaqueiros die a little—the cow for the person, one life for another.[21]

The transition from dead to *Ánima* is added by the masses, prayers, alms, and offerings in kind given by the family members. It is illuminated, literally, by the candle that is lit on Maundy Thursday, like those of the Santa of El Acebo. On this day, the anniversary of a specific death, that of Christ, the candles in the church substitute for the bread and water that the Vaqueiros leave in the house; their purpose is to light up the *tinieblas,* the darkness the dead must traverse to become *Ánimas.* Recall that the spirits are "like" black birds of the night; the candles "give light" in death to begin the trip and leave the earthly world and the living in peace. The dead and the smoke from the candles follow an identical path toward the "good place," the sky/heaven, like the birds who have their natural environment there. But bad things like storms, also come from the sky, and are repelled by the same candles, which communicate between the earth and the sky. The church is no more than the office of the saints; their habitat is accessible only by the ethereal medium traversed by birds and smoke.

The saints are more just and benevolent than the spirits although they can be dangerous as well. Through sacrifices, the Vaqueiros try to get the saints to listen to their requests and accept their reparation, thus preventing additional misfortunes. While the spirits demand mostly blood offerings, the anniversaries, the saints usually will accept masses, orations, and offerings without blood. It could be said, then, that the saints, including the *Ánimas*, have achieved a certain distance from humans. Rather than being interested in specific vengeance, they seek to maintain their alliances with communities in general, the main expression of which is attendance at mass. The spirits are linked to the house, to families and households; in contrast, the saints have jurisdiction and influence over the Vaqueiro group in general. The tie of divinity and the house is thus produced by way of the spirits, that of divinity and the group by way of the *Ánimas* and the saints.

The circulation of the spirits stops when they turn into *Ánimas*, for sanctity is characterized by the lack of movement. The saints are "objects of contemplation . . . the essence of serene stability and the endpoint of movement."[22] During the feast of the Ascension, an exemplary "holy day," this immobility even includes hens, "who cannot move their legs." The metaphor suggests an extraordinary violation of the laws of nature whose fundamental characteristic is permanent activity. For the cows have to be milked every day and the fields ploughed at the proper time, just as the hens lay their eggs. On the "holy days," the Vaqueiro should approach this ideal of immobility represented by the saints as much as possible—by doing only the most indispensable tasks. If the quietude of the day is not respected, because of ambition or egotism, the wrath of the saints will be visited on the objects of the Vaqueiros' attentions. Animals born with defects, said to reproduce and betray the movements of the prohibited work, are common. Animals, the principal subjects in the interaction of the saints and humans, whether they serve as the beneficiaries of promises or the coin in which promises are paid, thus are marked negatively on these sacred days, which suggests a violation of divine law. These laws further specify obligatory attendance at mass, purely contemplative activity for the Vaqueiros that doubles as an opportunity for meeting and socializing with relatives and friends merely for pleasure. In the last analysis, these "holy days" suppose a distribution of time as well as a cultural organization of work and leisure. Some days are dedicated to the relations of humans and saints, others to material activities in the Vaqueiro environment.

Space is also organized. The saints divide up the territory and maintain a neighborly relation with the Vaqueiros from their fixed locations in the churches and chapels of the area. This relation implies mutual rights and duties between the nearby images, patron saints, both male and female, and their human neighbors. Comings and goings from the *braña*, economic activities, and fiestas involve stopping at and visiting the scared geographic enclaves; in addition, at certain times, they involve purposeful pilgrimages (particularly by women), which are demonstrations of deference and respect. The variety of saints makes possible a series of requests for help in situations of danger, according to the jurisdiction of the image, beginning with those closest and ending with those farthest away, if the situation does not improve. There is a logic to the distribution of saints: the male saints, who aid in the care and health of the animals, must live within a certain proximity, as the veterinarian does, the *santas*, female saints, who aid in problems of human health, parallel the human doctors, ranging from the local ones to the most famous ones of the province.

The variety of saints is explained locally by a curious kind of kinship. The Vaqueiros, like other Asturians, tend to "sanctify," that is, make saints out of, images that are really the Virgin Mary (as with the Santa of El Acebo), and explain their similitude and multiplicity by making them "sisters." These sisters communicate with one another by the sound of their chapel bells, at the same time symbolically expressing their jurisdiction over a given geographical area. All men learn how to care for cows, but the women are in charge of the health of the members of the house. Since Vaqueiro medicine is transmitted from mothers to daughters, the *santas*, who are also healers (some with more "hand" than others), have had to learn how to cure from their "family." The importance of territory, professions, aptitudes, neighbors, and kinship are all reproduced in the supernatural scheme.

In spite of the uncertainty as to what God looks like, the Vaqueiros place him at the apex of the divine hierarchy, above the male and female saints. God's practical usefulness is very diffuse and is concretized only in the sign of the cross, the most common way of blessing cattle. The sign of the cross works the same way as the prayer to Saint Anthony and the cowbells touched to the image of El Acebo. Yet the sign of the cross is used mainly for humans beings and indeed is precisely the symbol that distinguishes "Christians," the word used to differentiate humans from animals and to signify the relation of persons with God.

Vaqueiros emphasize God's "power." God is "something that controls," especially "a powerful hand." This last concept includes not only the possession of power but also its exercise, since for humans the hand is the main instrument of the will. God's power makes him the lord of life and death, responsible for "the things that are born in the world" and each person's fate. Furthermore, God uses his power actively and coercively, since he is "a court who judges and rules us." Like any judge, God has his laws, which he imposes on people. If it weren't for God, the Vaqueiros would be "savages," for God is also responsible for human order and society, and it is he who makes people into "civilized" beings. Indeed, for the Vaqueiros, "to be religious" means adhering strictly to ethical rules and moral values. "What's right," the "best religion," is "not to do anything to anyone" and even "to help everyone." It could be said, then, that God, through religion, provides humans with the set of laws by which society is constructed; in other words, God is the origin of culture.

Thus to be on good terms with God, one must be on good terms with other people and subordinate individual passions and interests to the moral order of the society, since this order is God's law. Over time, good conduct will be rewarded and bad conduct punished. The Vaqueiros believe that the misfortunes that befall them originate in specific behavioral errors and can be avoided only by maintaining correct behavior with God, the saints, and humans. Because God is the source of pleasure and pain, he brings death and misfortune as well as life. He punishes as well as blesses the human being who, like God, has a dual nature.[23] For the Vaqueiros, God appears to be very distant; perhaps he is too busy directing the earth and the heavens. In a certain sense, this is an advantage for the Vaqueiros, since they do not want God to busy himself too much with them as he is the ultimate source of sickness and death. When Vaqueiros are dying with great pain, God is asked to "remember" them; when God pays attention to humans, it is often to judge or chastise them. For other purposes, the Vaqueiros get along quite well with the saints to whom God has delegated his power. The saints are much more accessible in their celestial habitat by means of churches. In comparison to the saints, God has little practical use, is not clearly visualized, and does not specialize. His power and jurisdiction are considered to exceed the boundaries of the group, for he is the creator of all things and beings in the world.

But not everyone is a "Christian," and this attribute is not conferred at birth. One could even say that persons share many of the features of animals: they "have the same organs as the pig," for instance. Aside from the ethnocentric definition of human as "Christian" that implicitly denies the humanity of believers in other religions,[24] Christianity is acquired gradually by the process of socialization. Just as the cow becomes "blessed" through the process of domestication, God domesticates people and places them under His blessing. The benediction of God supposes a contract with humans/Christians: God will provide them with health and prosperity as long as they maintain order in society and fulfill social norms and ethical principles. God will punish severely, those who violate the contract and do not submit to the divine yoke, just as the herdsmen punish their unruly [*bravo*] cattle.

In contrast, the savage world is characterized by anarchy and the absence of ethical norms and orderly relations. Wolves and other beasts kill, rob, infect, and cause misfortunes to humans and their domestic animals. Wild beasts are immoral; they let themselves be ruled by their instincts and passions, and they cause damage indiscriminately. Yet the recent dead evince a similar amoral conduct: they either do not recognize the domestic animals they dedicated so much care to while alive, or else they move them excessively and possessively after death. Nor do they respect family ties, for they prefer to attack their own household and relatives, to spook their own children, neighbors, and friends without any consideration for social alliances. The attitude of the anonymous and distant collectivity of the dead known as the *Ánimas* is very different. The *Ánimas* are allies of the divine and are considered to be like saints. They respect human norms and the contract that humans have with the divine. One could say they are the "civilized" dead. By contrast, the recent dead make dangerous attempts to hold on to this world and have not had enough time to adapt to the other. They have not become tame like the *Ánimas;* they are, thus, the "wild" dead.

The essential criteria that define the different categories of existence are wildness and domesticity. The cow is obviously the model from which these criteria are derived, because the cow is born wild and gradually becomes domesticated. Death is a situation that destroys all of this effort, that wipes out every trace of domestication. Yet it is only a passing phase, a transition to a final destination and a new order—that of the saints. This suggests that one must train for sainthood after death, for sainthood requires an apprenticeship, a period of domestication and consolidation. The relation of persons with God is based on the model of human relations. The *amo* is responsible for the *casa* and its human and animal members; God is the *amo* of the house of heaven and of humans, and he, too, has the task of domesticating divine beings. From the category animal to human and finally to saint, one notes a progression that could be conceived as a continuum of successive transformations, a never-ending interrelation between nature and culture, humanity and divinity, that defines the human being.

Epilogue:
Between Beasts and Saints

THE CULTURAL PROCESS OF DEATH

In this research I have tried to analyze the cultural process of death, to follow the long and complex itinerary of the deceased. Now I will summarize my findings in relation to the ecological, social, and symbolic contexts of the Vaqueiro's world.

The importance of the ecological base can be seen most clearly in the Vaqueiros' notion of sickness, through the assignment of good and evil to various aspects of the Vaqueiro environment. This is particularly true for animals, to which Vaqueiros pay elaborate and minute attention. Vaqueiro notions of illness are cultural classifications of adversity in general. The specific etiologies reveal to us how their world is experienced and understood. By means of animal and other metaphors related to the environment, the Vaqueiro universe is represented symbolically in vertical and horizontal ways. In the aspect of symbolic curing, the situation of disorder that constitutes the sickness is enunciated by procedures that activate basic cultural meanings. The Vaqueiros create models of disorder that relocate the sufferings of the sick person in external images and events. The animals and their association with the other worlds allows for restructuring of personal experience on a cosmic, symbolic plane.

The human body, too, is an analogy for the universe. Therapies having to do with the body tend to emphasize the same ideas of equilibrium and balance as the therapies applied to the universe. For sickness dislocates the relationship of men and earth, the Va-

345

queiros and their physical and social environment. Imbalances and the interference of animals are also found in the sickness produced by interaction with other human beings, like the sicknesses of envy. These sicknesses are clearly social, and their treatment involves applied attempts to restore the equilibrium of the social group. Sickness, therefore, does not stem from a single source but rather from a variety of contexts, from the inevitable interaction with the environment, with humans, with the divine, with the interior of the human being, and with the world outside the *brañas*. The causes of illness can be natural, social, and supernatural.

The animal world appears once more in relation to the spirits. In regard to the animals associated with death, the same horizontal distinction can be made as with the animals associated with sickness, that is, the distinction between domestic and wild. The spirits are associated with wild beasts, especially appearing during the night, and with night birds or black-feathered in a vertical association, that of the "animals of fear and of the night." Here there seems to be no trace of the reptiles and burrowers from the ground that were associated with sickness. But it should be noted that Vaqueiro bodies are put underground after death as the placenta is after birth.

All of these animals serve as metaphors whose distinctive features define the kind of existence led by the spirits. This classification of the animal world is made from the point of view of humans and thus is naturally adapted to human needs. In this case the classification responds to intellectual rather than economic needs. The animals are symbols of categories of existence, physical and metaphysical ones. These categories can be set in relation to their zoological counterparts shown in figure 7.

Being dead involves an apprenticeship, a period of domestication in which a new order of existence is learned. These beliefs and associations acquire meaning from the particular context in which they emerge, the influence of the environment, and a way of life intimately related to cattle. But they are also related to the ambivalence of living human beings: like humans, the spirits are *between* the beasts and the divine. I emphasize *between*, because I believe it would be wrong to overlook the ambiguity that has turned up time and again in this study in regard to a number of different matters (for instance, in the specialists, in regard to the classification blessed/accursed, in the animals, the witches, and the spirits). A binary system suppresses the gradations, the qualitative and analogical ways of thinking in the real world.

Research on death is a useful way of getting at the social struc-

Heavenly level	God	Saints	*Ánimas*	Storms	Eagles
Level of air	White birds Deer	Swallows	Magpies		Animals of fear and night
Earthly level	Christians	Spiritists	*ánimas* Spirits		Witches
	Cows and domestic animals		Dogs/foxes		Wild beasts
Underground	Placenta	Cadavers	*Encanta*/serpent		Animals of sickness

FIGURE 7 COSMOLOGY OF DEATH

ture of a human group. In the case of the Vaqueiros, the various rituals of death, from the most basic level of the house to the widest context of several parishes, clearly indicate the different levels of social organization; the different gradations of kinship, neighborhood, and friendship; and the mutual rights and obligations involved in each. But more than this, these rituals are dynamic, serve as social intensifiers inasmuch as they renew social and family ties, create and recreate the bonds of relation and interaction. Many others, including Malinowski, have acknowledged the importance of death for the definition and demarcation of social groups. But most have placed their emphasis on the effect of death on society. I have placed my emphasis on the cultural side of the process, on ideas, beliefs, and attitudes more than on social structure or economy. These latter aspects are important and I have noted them, but I have subordinated them to the cultural concepts to a certain extent. In this respect, my study is different from most others on the same subject.

I feel that classic ethnography has given excessive weight to ritual seen from a formal point of view and from "outside." As I suggested in my introduction, part of the reason for this might simply have been the difficulty of communicating well in non-European languages, hence prioritizing observation over communication. The best study of death shares this drawback. Hertz analyzed the three components of the system of beliefs and practices that surrounded death, and showed the relation among them. He looked at the body, soul, and the survivors in the three phases of the rite of passage. But the main protagonists, those who die, are barely mentioned; when they are it is only as bodies, not as minds or persons. His model has been developed further in recent studies, but they have maintained practically the same structure.[1]

In my research I have tried to fill this gap, a gap noted by others (Fabian 1973; Palgi and Abramovitch 1984). Death is a legitimate subject in its own right. I have tried to find out not only the impact of death on the survivors but also the cultural baggage with which the Vaqueiros confront their own deaths and how they learn to die. This approach, then, attempts to understand contents as well as forms and to emphasize the point of view of the actor. The fact that I have studied a culture where death was discussed easily and frequently, and where suicide was deemed acceptable under certain conditions, made the task considerably easier than it would have been elsewhere.

Perhaps the reader will agree by now that the process of death is broader than has been traditionally conceived. The relation of death with pain, age, and suffering seems to be critical for understanding the death process coherently. Where the boundaries of this process lie must be determined for a given culture. Death is no simple and obvious fact; it is a complex mass of beliefs, emotions, and activities that differ from one society to another are added to the organic event. Sickness and suicide are as integral to the process of death as mortuary ritual and the conditions of afterlife.

Death cannot be separated from its social context. It primarily affects the house in which it occurs, but certain deaths have more important social meaning than others, especially those of the old *amos*. Their deaths signify a relay of generations, the transmission of property, the periodic crisis critical for the survival of the institution and the human beings that people it. The permanence of the house requires that the old *amo* be considered a usufructuary, one link in an immortal chain. The ideology of the house affects the different personalities of those who live there, whether that of the father who should be in charge or those of other members who must be silent and obey. The natural death of the old *amo*, attended by a well-chosen heir with a family, is evidence of success in worldly terms, a guarantee of continuity.

Conversely, violent death, particularly suicide due to domestic problems, points up the negative aspects of the Vaqueiro way of passing houses. The house solves some problems but creates others that, in extreme cases and with certain kinds of people, are resolved in suicide. It is impossible, of course, to predict which individuals will commit suicide, but it is not at all difficult to figure out what kinds of people are most likely to do it. Most vulnerable to suicide, aside from the *amos* who find it impossible to fulfill their roles adequately, are the women and those who do not inherit. They are locally characterized as "defenseless" within the system of houses.

Studying natural death without considering violent death, or vice versa, would be partial and insufficient. The former shows how the house is organized, the relation of the individual to the collectivity, the structural norms, the ordinary procedures, and the ordered relations; the latter identifies problems in human relations, structural tensions, flaws in communication, and endemic family conflicts. The two kinds of death provide different perspectives on the institution of the house. Yet one frequently finds these ways of dying examined in isolation, providing an excessively dark and negative or unnaturally idyllic and happy view of the community studied, the one permeated by violence and aggressivity, the other by solidarity and mutual aid. One wants to ask, "Does everybody die this way?"

The house is not isolated in its sorrow but is supported by the wider Vaqueiro community. At a certain point, death becomes a collective affair, both in requiring a house to live up to its responsibilities and in supplying it with its due. First the sick person, then the dead person, becomes the center of the community. Significantly, the attentions are similar (a visit and presents) for those who are born and those who are dying. Elaborate interchanges are organized between those of the house, those from the *braña*, and those from the outside. The doors of the house are open (and so is its pantry) more or less according to the different degrees of social interaction and geographical proximity. In the funeral process all levels of social relation are present and explicitly distinguished.

This collective organization can be seen in the group of specialists who appear to make the arrangements after death (those who shroud, pray, cook, cut the bread, make the coffin). Their help is evidence not only of solidarity but also of necessity, for there are no commercial alternatives in the *brañas*. In addition to these specialists, there are other, less visible helpers—those who cut the dead person's hay or carry the body down the mountainside. In addition to the specialists who appear at death, there are those who came before (nurse-practitioners and midwives, healers and bonesetters, prayer persons and diviners) and those who come after (spirits and *ánimas*, and again prayer persons and diviners). All comprise a generous response to precise ecological conditions, but they are much more: links between nature and the Vaqueiros, the sick and the healthy, the living and the dead, and the saints and humans.

The house continues to have fundamental value after death. The dead belong to the house as do the emigrants. When a house is inherited, all of its dead come along with it. Eternal rest, the payment of pending debts, and the immobility of the dead are transacted by means of the house. The continuity of the relation between the living and the dead is a result of their mutual dependence as well as their mutual identity: what remains of the dead in us and what the dead have taken away that is ours.

The social context is just one aspect of the process of death. The ideological aspect—how it is defined, evaluated, and predicted—helps us to understand it in different ways. A natural death is considered to be the human equivalent of death in nature, hence the frequent comparisons of this kind of death with the state of meadows in winter, with old cows, and especially with birds, metaphors for the environment that point to the lack of violence or rupture in this kind of dying. The old Vaqueiros who die naturally do so without illness. They die from old age, when their blood, the sap of their life, wears out. They disappear without causing trouble for the survivors, even helping out with small tasks, "defending themselves until the very end."

An unfortunate death is one in which the natural process is interrupted by external causes or human agents. Death by suicide is perhaps the least "natural" and most "cultural" way of death: it implies a social cause in the majority of the cases, such as legal or familial problems, or a physical cause, such as disease, which has grave social consequences—pain and suffering for the severely ill and for those who care for them. Suicide shows up the Vaqueiros' lack of defenses, which, for whatever reason, have led them to interrupt the normal process of life.

For me the most interesting aspect of death lies in its cultural definition: the Vaqueiros do not automatically disappear at physical death but continue on a long passage that began in life with the physical, social, legal, and intellectual decline of the Vaqueiro, or, in local terms, with the loss of *gracia*. Different persons lose *gracia* in different ways: some lose it gently and slowly (those who die natural deaths), others lose it swiftly and sharply (those who die violent deaths). Loss of *gracia* has physical causes (the change of speed of the blood) and social concomitants (changes of diet and a reduction in activity, work, and responsibility). A consequence of this process is the handing over of control in the house. This transfer of legal responsibility is repeated in the social sphere by a reduction of social activity and the gradual restriction of the radius of interaction from the region of the *braña* to the house. Finally, as the intellectual faculties decline, people can lose their awareness of life and death.

The factors that contribute to the maintenance of *gracia* are good health, ("a good stomach"), interest in work and activity, economic independence, the intensity of family and friendship relations, acceptable mental health, and so on. Obversely, a painful and chronic illness, personal insecurity, becoming a burden on others, and not being able to take care of oneself all lead to *aburrimiento*, lack of interest in living, or to *arrepentimiento*, the express renunciation of life. Life is *gracia*, a pleasure in things, activity, and a struggle; *aburrimiento* means tiredness, impotence, and passivity. With *aburrimiento*, death is preferable to life.

One learns how to die just as one learns how to live. The child born in the *braña* stays in the house at first, only gradually venturing out to get involved in social relations beyond the family and outside the *braña*. In death this process is reversed; there is a gradual disengagement from social life, from fiestas and entertainment, from relations with friends and neighbors, and from work and eating. *Gracia*, as Pitt-Rivers (1989) suggests, is a gift from the gods, but so, too, is *desgracia*, misfortune. From this point of view, suicide is not the strange, aberrant, unnatural act it is usually considered to be, but rather a decision that any Vaqueiro might come to in certain circumstances, the end result of a coherent process.

Indeed, it might be said that some Vaqueiros, although physically alive, are socially and cognitively dead when they have lost their *gracia*. The loss of *gracia* is not just a psychological state but also a cultural category imposed on the individual with given symptoms. This is precisely what the belief in the spirits of the living implies. A spirit is evidence of the existence of death in life or the continuance of life after death. The spirit of the living is the cultural self that has died, divorced from the physical self that is still alive. In other words, people can begin to belong to the world of the dead before clinical death. It is possible that many of the suicides, those who are "accelerating" their deaths, belong to this class of the living dead when they lose their grace.

There is plenty of behavioral evidence for the duality of spirits. Spirits do not, as is frequently supposed, come in one uniform model; rather, they come in many types, and these types change, ranging from animals to divine beings. Anthropological literature may portray spirits as aggressive (one wants to ask, are all of them so?) or may emphasize their nature as judges and benefactors. These oversimplifications may be due to a synchronic approach that leaves out the different kinds of spirits (both living and dead), the different "ages" of the spirits (the recent, the longer gone) that change over time, and their various situations (they may be in good or bad places).

After a process of domestication, thanks to the light of the candles that family members provide to illuminate its trip, the spirit metamorphoses from a night bird into a day bird, a symbol of the divine. At the end of this long journal, the spirits become *Ánimas;* they become immobile and command a cult from the living like that of the saints. We find the same fluctuation in the continuum of specialists who talk with the dead and the saints—from spiritists to the shamanlike *ánimas* to the prayer persons. These intermediaries try to maintain a difficult equilibrium between the *braña* and the outside, and between this world and other worlds.

As I have shown, the Vaqueiros express their perceptions of the different categories of existence by means of metaphorical associations with the animals around them. From the living person to saint, from' the *amo* of the house to the *amo* of the sky or heaven, there is a series of transitions, an elaborate gradient of the different possibilities of being. Perhaps the most interesting aspect of this vision of the cosmos is that there is no quantum leap, no sharp division between the living and the dead, between human beings and divine beings. Ethnographic descriptions of other peoples remark on similarities between the humans and God, how we resemble those we venerate. The Vaqueiros, with their belief in spirits and *Ánimas,* extend this similarity farther. For them, divine beings are human beings, too. I wonder whether we have a general tendency to reify unnecessarily the boundaries of popular categories, perhaps overconditioned by the traditional subdivisions of the discipline and our penchant for closed mental compartments. Where does religion begin and social structure end? Are the *Ánimas* supernatural beings or the distant kin of the Vaqueiros? What are the similarities and differences between apparitions of saints and apparitions of neighbors? This last question itself merits another study. Such a study might well be informed by the Vaqueiro notion that holiness is not an absolute but rather a relative state, a state that presupposes an apprenticeship, a period of domestication like the apprenticeship necessary in the life of society for the living and in the afterlife for the dead.

VAQUEIROS AS "DIFFERENT"

The careful study of death among the Vaqueiros—taking death in its widest sense, as the Vaqueiros themselves do, as a long process that begins before and ends long after physical death—has led to a complex portrait of a sophisticated cosmology, one quite at variance with what is known about most Spaniards.[2] This difference is confirmed by the aura of oddness that surrounds the Vaqueiros, as well as the fact that for three centuries the *aldeanos* and other speculating outsiders have posited mysterious origins for the Vaqueiros. If, as seems clear in the introduction, the Vaqueiro are simply Asturians who practiced transhumancy, then there are a pair of legitimate alternatives to explain the source of their ideas. For instance, it could be that their highly coherent cosmological views, their notions of spirits, their attitudes toward and values for animals, are an archaic survival of ideas that were once common throughout alpine or even the wider Indo-European culture, and that they survived among the Vaqueiros, as among other isolated groups, because of the Vaqueiros' lack of contact with official culture centers, because of the remote location of the brañas and because of the difficulty in instructing and catechizing people in a transhumant culture.

Another possible explanation is that, because of this same ecological isolation, the Vaqueiros gradually invented their cosmology, adapting ideas from the wider culture, like that of souls in purgatory and saints, to fit their own special needs, untroubled and "uncorrected" by teachers, priests, or inquisitions. In this view, their culture, rather than a survival, represents a kind of creative involution, a progressive bricolage and elaboration of ideas with an end product as fresh and singular as that of the miller Menocchio in Carlo Ginzburg's The Cheese and the Worms (1980).

I can only raise these questions here, for surprisingly little is known about European rural cosmologies. Stepping back from this work and reading or rereading what others have done, I find little material with which to compare it. Few studies of contemporary European peasant communities examine local meanings of words critically rather than assume that the meanings are those of the wider society, for this kind of cosmographic material. Exceptions must be made for the work of Carmelo Lisón on Galicia and of José Miguel de Barandiarán on Euskadi (Lisón 1971b, 1979; Barandiarán 1972–83). Both have found and described for their zones (significantly, of dispersed settlement patterns) quite eccentric cosmological notions. Other kind of habitats in Spain have been studied, some quite close geographically to the Vaqueiros, but taken at face value the cosmology of their peoples seems to be far more orthodox and unsurprising.[3] It should be noted that in these latter cases the settlements are larger and more nucleated, more accessible and less dispersed. They are thus more susceptible to control from ideological centers of church and state. Studies of cultures that are transhumant like the Vaqueiros, in Spain and elsewhere, have focused on different problems (for instance, Tax Freeman 1979). An exception is Le Roy Ladurie's historical study of Pyrenean shepherds,

Montaillou, which showed a freedom for speculation among transhumant pastoralists that may also play a part in the Vaqueiros' "differentness" (Le Roy Ladurie 1978).

One way of getting at this issue would be through historical research on cosmologies and worldviews in medieval and early modern Europe. This field is now quite a fertile one, considering the work not only of Ginzburg (1966, 1989) and Le Roy Ladurie (1978), but also Jacques Le Goff (1981), Jean-Claude Schmitt (1976, 1982, 1983), Natalie Zemon Davis (1983), Alan MacFarlane (1978), Ottavia Niccoli (1990), David Sabean (1984), Gabor Klaniczay (1990), and W. Christian (1981a, 1981b), as well as others who are not disposed to take for granted an orthodox worldview in the peoples they study.[4] As more research is done, it will be interesting to see the extent to which Vaqueiro notions turn up elsewhere. Many of them obviously do: the notions about the evil eyes and envy exist throughout the Mediterranean culture area; so do many of the curing prayers and rituals, the concept of grace, the feast days from the Roman Church calendar, the solstice rituals; the belief in and use of professional healers both of scientific medicine and the parallel herbal cures, and so on. All of the Vaqueiro system is not invented, that is for sure. While it is certain that Vaqueiros hold elements of their cosmology in common with other European groups, present or historical, it is hard not to think that there are original touches as well. This would be particularly true for the cosmological matters keyed to particular animals and plants of the Vaqueiro ecology, which have led to cultural configurations that could not exist outside the Cantabrian subalpine zone, at least with this specific content. And the mix, the combination of native and external cultural categories and understandings, is perforce an original one.

I have consciously resisted referring to or using others' work on a similar theme while preparing this study. Instead I have tried to be rigorous in my use of Vaqueiro words and explanations, and have tried to draw the general Vaqueiro notions out inductively, aware of the likelihood that similar words and acts in other cultures can have meanings that are subtly or radically different. In this sense, I have approached my material with a self-imposed set of blinders. I have presented, in their own words, and then with my glosses, the way the Vaqueiros experience death, and what this reveals about the way they see this world and other worlds.

I would venture to say that in all cultures the study of death and the ideas that surround it will reveal the central themes of the culture: the origin and destiny of humans, the relations of humans and nature, the configuration of the universe, and the nature of society. These matters are inextricably connected to how death is defined and when it is considered opportune. Finally, I have tried to demonstrate that the study of suicide cannot be undertaken in isolation but must be considered in the general context of ideas on the nature of death, human personality, and beliefs in nonhuman powers. The anthropological study of suicide should begin with an understanding of the cultural valuation of different ways of dying, the conditions under which suicides take place, and the reasons why suicide is more or less acceptable in popular perception. The relation of cultural values to the structure of the forces that affect the suicide is critical to understanding the event (La Fontaine 1975). An analysis of suicide should make clear cultural perceptions about when it is worth the trouble to live and when it is worth the trouble to die.

NOTES

INTRODUCTION

1. For Schneidman and Farberow (1960), the social and psychopathological levels coincide in the concept of the self. Hendin (1964) explains suicide in terms of psychosocial determinism. Robins et al. (1959) considers it a communicative process. For J. D. Douglas (1973), it is best studied in the context of situated meanings. For suicide in Spain, see also Estruch, and Cardús 1981.

2. Riley (1968) pointed out that in 1965 the bibliography on death and bereavement in the social sciences did not exceed four hundred entries. Kalish (1965) and Palgi and Abramovitch (1984, 385) say the same thing.

3. Bloch and Parry point out that Hertz (1960 [1907–9]) was an exception because of "his central preoccupations with the social construction of emotion and with the relationship between the biological individual and the social collectivity." Hertz studied mortuary ritual to show "how these rituals organise and orchestrate private emotions" (1982, 5.3).

4. Psychologists like Nagy (1948) have shown that attitudes about and reactions to death are learned rather than instinctive.

5. Other alternatives exist, as this study shows.

6. In his paper, Goodenough treats terminal illness, death, and a funeral in Truk as a continuum. He describes the impact of the process on society and the way that society deals with sickness and death, but he also focuses on the behavior and values of the dying person as an active participant in the process.

7. Goody (1962, 13) has shown that institutions centered on death-funeral ceremonies, cults of the dead, ancestor worship, and beliefs in the afterlife were core interests of the first anthropologists, but that interest in these topics declined with evolution. There may be a certain revival of interest underway. More recent work includes Bartel 1973; D Lester 1974; Blauner 1977; Fabian 1973; Huntington and Metcalf 1979; Humphreys and King 1981; Danforth 1982; Badone 1989.

8. Danforth analyzes Hertz's classic theme of "second burial ritual." Bloch and Parry's collection deals with the symbolism of sexuality and fertility in mortuary rituals from a sociological perspective.

9. See a classic definition of ideology in Fried 1959, 404.

10. On death in other regions of Spain, see Gonzalez Hernández 1990 and Bethencourt 1985 for the Canary Islands; Gondar Portasany 1989, 1991 and Lisón 1990 for Galicia. For Portugal, see Pina-Cabral 1986. For death in Europe, see the special issue of *Anthropological Quarterly* (Taylor 1989).

11. These are the most important Vaqueiro *concejos*, although the

Vaqueiro area includes the following *concejos* as well: Navia, Villayón, Allande, Cudillero, Pravia, Salas, Belmonte de Miranda, Somiedo, and Teverga.

12. J. Uría Riu's volume, which I cite repeatedly in this chapter, contains a collection of articles published from 1924 to 1968 on historical and ethnographic aspects of the Vaqueiros. It is by far the best work on the subject. Unless otherwise noted, the sources for the historical material in the following pages may be found in this book, 98–124.

13. This discrimination still existed in at least one *aldea* in 1955, according to my Vaqueiro informants.

14. On discrimination in general, see Acevedo y Huelves 1915, 115. Present-day Vaqueiros do not remember being served with glasses.

15. I have also written about Vaqueiro margination in Cátedra 1972b, 1977, 1978b, and 1989a.

16. According to W. A. Christian, Jr., who has studied this process historically in Christian 1976.

17. For a more complete account, see Cátedra and Sanmartin 1979, 6–40. See also Cátedra 1979, 1984, and 1989a.

18. The high summer pastures have not always been located in the township of Cangas de Narcea, but Puerto de Cangas is a generic name given to long-distance transhumance by many of the Vaqueiros in the zone I studied. See Cátedra 1977 for more about transhumant zones, the causes of the maintenance or disappearance of the phenomenon, and its social effects. S. Tax Freeman (1979) dedicates much of her study to transhumance among the Pasiegos, who make even more moves than the Vaqueiros but in a more limited orbit.

19. Exactly fifty-eight houses of the zone I studied in 1972. Of this number, forty-one houses are from *brañas* that are almost totally transhumant.

20. I discuss this subject in a later chapter. For comparative material on houses in Galicia, see Lisón 1979; in Asturias, see Valdés del Toro 1976.

21. Often the siblings do not request the *legítima,* especially when they are well settled elsewhere, and thus they have a certain moral right to return to the house, generally in the summer. In any case, even when the siblings demand the *legítima,* it is not always given. There are ways to make it seem that the third has evaporated by means of fake sales that benefit the heir. Having to pay the *legítima* can be a serious burden on these small, marginal enterprises.

22. Aristébano is part of the parish of Paredes (Luarca) as governmental unit, although it is part of the parish of Naraval (Tineo) as a religious unit.

23. I collected this information directly from the inhabitants.

24. The people of Silvallana almost all go to Las Tabiernas, those of Relloso to Bustellán, and those of Adrado to Bustellán and Los Corros. Some of the people from Pena, Monterizo, and Aristébano go to Las Tabiernas and Los Corros; some from Escardén and Barreiro go to Las Tabiernas and Bustellán; part of Candanedo goes to Bustellán. I have done

fieldwork in the three brañas de alzada, in most of the above home brañas, in three other sedentary brañas (Leiriella, Busmourisco, and Busindre), and also in the aldeas of the parish of Villatresmil.

25. Instituto Nacional de Estadística 1973. Some of these counts may have been made secondhand (in the towns and without checking the data), since there is contradictory information that comes from not knowing about the custom of transhumance as well as some obvious errors. The brañas de alzada traditionally have not been counted as inhabited places. See Acevedo y Huelves 1915, 80.

26. See Cátedra 1971 and 1972a. Both works were done under the direction of Carmelo Lisón.

27. I read Mitford 1963; Waugh 1948; Lifton and Olson 1974; Stannard 1975; Sudnow 1967; Warner 1959.

28. Wilson has raised important questions about the representativeness and evaluation of ethnographic evidence.

29. On experimental ethnography, see Marcus and Cushman 1982; Clifford and Marcus 1986; Marcus and Fisher 1986. Among other experimental authors, apart from the pioneering work of Bateson 1958; Levi-Strauss 1974 (1955); and Bohannan (Bowen 1954), see the works of Geertz 1973; Balandier 1957; Maybury-Lewis 1965; Chagnon 1968, 1974; Rabinow 1977; Dwyer 1982; Crapanzano 1980; Rosaldo 1980, 1989; Schiefflin 1976; and Favret-Saada 1980. See also Cátedra 1991a and 1991b for my reflections on methodology.

30. Originally in Spanish: "lo poético—el juego verbal de varios tipos y el lenguaje indirecto de alusión metafórica y metonímica—surge en seguida en el ámbito rural."

CHAPTER 1: SICKNESS AND THE VAQUEIRO COSMOLOGY

1. Early drafts of this chapter were published (Cátedra 1986a, 1986c).

2. The cult of this image is discussed in the final chapter.

3. On Easter Saturday in some aldeas farmers sprinkled their fields with holy water shaken from laurel branches to protect against insects and other pests, pronouncing this prayer:

Fuera sapo, fuera rato,	Get out toad, get out mouse,
fuera toda comición	get out all pests
que ahí te va el agua bendita	for here is holy water for you
y el ramo de la pasión.	and the passion branch.

It is common for Vaqueiros to sprinkle holy water on cattle.

4. In other versions of this formula, collected by Uría Riu in 1912 and 1917 respectively, the accursed animal is a culebra or serpentona. As for the deer or doe, it is referred to as bendita and not de Dios, as it was in the version I gathered. According to Uría Riu, the reference to the deer proves the antiquity of the prayer, since this animal had disappeared from the Asturian mountains by the seventeenth century. See "Algunas supersticiones y leyendas relativas a los animales entre los Vaqueiros de Alzada" (Uría Riu 1976).

5. In the versions collected by Uría Riu, the references to heights are,

respectively, the arrival at *aquel lindo cuento* and *pasar la lombatina*. As for the horn, in his first version it is a *bocina;* the second contains no reference to the instrument. According to Uría Riu, *la bocina, bugaro,* or *bugare* appears in other legends as a way to call for help when thefts of cattle or other aggressions occur. Today Vaqueiros consider conch shells blessed and blow them to ward off storms, calling them sea snails [*caracoles del mar*]. The place where the serpent retreats also varies. In Uría Riu's first version, it goes *por debajo del tronco barronco, raiz de fresno infeliz* and in the second *por debajo del tronco barronco, raiz de San Feliz* (my emphasis). Note the association of a saint with the serpent and the underground. Saints, as we will see, are ambiguously valued.

6. A note in the death registers from the parish of the informant who is speaking indicates that in 1873 a Vaqueiro girl died from a snake bite. There is no mention of death from a lizard bite.

7. One finds the idea in the following riddle from the region, the answer to which is the lizard [*lagarto*]:

> En el campo se crió — It grew up in the country
> verde como la esperanza — as green as hope
> de los hombres es amigo — to men it is a friend
> y a las mujeres espanta. — and women it frightens.

8. I have written at greater length on this matter (Cátedra 1979).

9. The cow and the ox are eaten only on ritual occasions, which I will describe below. Under normal circumstances, one might buy beef from a butcher, but one would not slaughter and eat one's own cattle. An exception among domestic animals is the mule. The mule is accursed because it is sterile. This anomaly within the animal world is of special importance to the Vaqueiros, taking into account the high value they attach to fertility. See Cátedra 1981.

10. This belief is embodied in popular folklore in a verse known throughout Spain:

> En el Monte Calvario — On Mount Calvary
> las golondrinas — the swallows
> le quitaron a Cristo — removed from Christ
> dos mil espinas. — two thousand thorns.

People in the *aldeas* of other regions of Asturias believe it is a sin to harm these birds, but among Vaqueiros I have not encountered this category stated explicitly.

11. This aspect also appears in a folk song:

> Dicen que las golondrinas — They say that swallows
> nacen con pechuga blanca — are born with a white breast
> también la Virgen María — so, too, the Virgin Mary
> fue concebida sin mancha. — was conceived without a stain.

12. Lévi-Strauss and Evans-Pritchard have both treated this subject, the first in his analysis of totemism and the second in his studies of Nuer

religion. Mary Douglas (1970 [1966]) and James Fernández (1986) have also made important contributions.

13. See Uria Riu (note 4 above), who collected these two variations in 1915 and 1917, respectively:

Aguila bendita
que en el cielo estás escrita
con papel y agua bendita
deja lo que llevas
que non es tuyo nin mio
es de Dios que lo crió.

Aguila maldita
que en el cielo estás escrita
en el mar y en las arenas
en el cielo y en las estrellas
deja la prenda que llevas
que nin es tuya nin es mia
es del dueño que la crió
que bien caro le costó.

Uria Riu considered the second version the most complete and archaic because of the adjective *maldito* applied to the eagle, something he considered more "logical."

14. The Vaqueiros have used the first two therapies most extensively, along with the prayer of the storm [*truena*]. The other two are used more in the *aldeas*, since there are neither churches nor priests in the *brañas*.

15. This prayer seems to be a paraphrase of a Latin version, according to Lisón. See his "Sobre antropología cognitiva; el arresponsador gallego" (Lisón 1974).

16. I will discuss this saint at greater length in the final chapter.

17. Note the moral values, ethical content, and sexual symbolism in the associations of serpent/woman, greed/courage, and so on. It is significant that this kind of story, quite common in rural Spain, takes place on the Night of Saint John. It seems clear that cyclical changes, like the vernal equinox, stimulate in people dependent on nature a fascination that evokes legends. In this context, fertility is an essential ingredient. Lisón has written a fine article on the rituals of Saint John, "Variaciones en fuego ritual" (Lisón 1971a).

18. I have written more about the power of water for fecundity in Cátedra 1979, esp. 55–57. I discuss the ambiguity of woman in this chapter.

19. This also includes the "serpent's stone" [*la piedra de la culebra*], which is supposed to be made by the snake and cures its bites. The following popular riddle refers to the snake's curative power:

Soy larga, lisa y redonda   I am long, smooth and round
y me miran con horror.   and they look at me with horror.
Mi camisa quita males.   My shirt will cure sickness.
adivina este primor.   Figure this one out.

20. This version was collected by Manuel Fernández Garcia (1954, 405). It is for curing the *cuxio*. The two last lines are: "*Se sos de vilano, ande nun faigas daño. /Se sos de can, al monte a tsadrar.*"

21. I have developed this idea in Cátedra 1981.

22. Following Diamond cited in Radin 1972 (1956), the separation of good and evil into approaches is a result of "civilization." An intransigent view of existence eventually developed. Ambivalence, on the other

hand, is common in the myths and rituals of the so-called "primitives," the trickster being a prime example.

23. The lungs are considered key organs because of the high frequency of diseases of the thorax in the past. According to the parish registers, thoracic diseases were the major cause of death.

24. I discuss envy more extensively in Cátedra 1976a. For comparative material, see the classic work by Foster 1972 and the recent Gilmore 1987.

25. As we will see, the woman generally enters the house by marriage. Her position is difficult and insecure until she bears children, who legitimate her presence there. If her husband dies, her children will receive the inheritance, and as their mother she will have a place in the house. She may then marry a brother of the deceased. But if she is widowed without children, she will have to return to the house where she was born, because her parents-in-law will "prefer" another son. It is thus the children that unite a woman to the house.

26. Some details vary according to the *entendida*, but the form and content of the ritual has a basic consistency. The one I have cited above is the most elaborate.

27. An attitude, after all, not uncommon in Western society. This has meant, however, that medicine in our society has not advanced as it should. Once the remedy for a specific ailment has been discovered, the search for its cause and its relation with other diseases are neglected.

28. Physical strength is an economic imperative. Men and women have to have good health in order to harvest hay, transport soil that has fallen down the steepest slopes back up to the top (done until recently and sometimes still practiced), or make the long transhumant journeys on foot. No son who has a physical defect is preferred in inheritance.

29. On dirt and pollution as anomaly, and cleanliness as order in our lives, see the classic work by Mary Douglas 1970 (1966).

30. Children are at least the most striking victims of infections. Infant mortality was very high in the past. The mortality rate for the province as a whole was 25.35 deaths per 1,000 inhabitants in 1900, and 8.43 per 1,000 in 1954 (Instituto Nacional de Estadística 1960). The rate for the Vaqueiros would be much higher, since they live in one of the most isolated zones of the province.

31. In other words, I am not excluding other interpretations. One would fall into a kind of medical reductionism if one accepted the evil eye *only* as contagion. M. Douglas (1970 [1966], 41–44) refers to it. This kind of explanation by doctors is very common in Spain.

32. The brazier represents the traditional *tchar*, the central hearth, still found in the poorest houses and the site of many rituals. On the symbolism of fire, see Lisón "Variaciones fuego ritual" (1971a).

33. In the period of *mocedad*, envy focuses on the choice of a mate. Young men and women "envy" the mates of others and try to take their place. They also envy the popularity of the most fortunate. The period of courtship, which is rather different from that in most other parts of Spain, is not a tacit engagement for marriage or something that supposes

any formal agreement. Nor is it monogamous or monandrous. Men and women have various friends, at times simultaneously, and courtship is considered a kind of game by both. But the game can get out of hand and become risky. The level of expectation and risk is not always easy to calculate. Individuals may find themselves rejected without alternatives as well as publicly humiliated (since the affairs of the youths are closely followed by the community, providing it with a major source of entertainment). There is also the influence of the parents, in favor of the house and dowry transactions. Envy continues to exist in the new house between man and woman over the division of benefits and duties. The woman gets the worst of it.

34. These *lutches* took place at dances, spinning circles, and other nocturnal gatherings. Single men and women wrestle together, striking above all at the genitals. Sometimes the winner would end the battle by undressing the loser. Married couples would fight in the hayfield, ending the struggle in the hayloft making love. In its most ritual form, in the high meadows, men and women would struggle in the solitude of the mountains while herding. Now struggles between the sexes are rare. According to Lisón (personal communication) they also take place in parts of rural Galicia.

35. Edmund Leach, in his interesting essay "Virgin Birth" (1969), refers to Mary's function as an intermediary and her anomaly as both virgin and mother.

36. During her menstrual period, the woman is not considered capable of acting as a mother, working, or engaging in any social or sexual relation. At these times, the woman is totally "feminine," that is, "accursed."

37. The ritual is employed more frequently to unbewitch cows that have been "eyed."

38. On other occasions a beret, another masculine symbol, is used, so the woman will expel the placenta after giving birth.

39. A few drops of menstrual blood are a powerful drug if put into a young man's coffee. The operation known as *echar el pauto*, makes the *empautado* crazy for the woman whose blood bewitched him. With luck, she will be able to marry him, but an excessive dose will kill a man. This shows the Vaqueiros' preoccupation with the boundaries of the body, its entrances and exits, and their preoccupation with the boundaries of the group, the fear evoked when its survival is threatened. The theory of the human body as a model for the society is elaborated by Mauss (1936) and M. Douglas (1970 [1966]).

40. According to men, the ultimate definition of a witch is "a woman who doesn't have hair around her genitals." This trait is much feared by the men of the *braña*, who consider it sufficient cause for the annulment of a marriage. For the Vaqueiros, what sexually attracts and excites a man is the woman's pubic hair. Since a witch does not have this hair, when she attacks a man, she is really "raping" him.

41. For the purpose of this argument I have emphasized the negative aspects of Vaqueiros womanhood. Yet there are women who have been

preferred and others who actively administer households. Many women circumvent and manipulate the system. I have always been surprised by the relative liberty, equality with men, and importance of the women of the *braña* (and probably in almost all of the north of the peninsula) in comparison with other parts of Spain. Perhaps this is due to their greater economic importance in farm work. [I would second this note as being applicable to the neighboring province of Santander—Trans.]

42. These registers are from the parish of Naraval (Tineo, Asturias). I have catalogued information on over a thousand deaths from these records, which include much information on sickness. I hope to use the information in future work. The scarcity of medical diagnoses in the registers suggests that formal medical help was very rare in the Vaqueiro zone. According to Tolivar Faes (1976, 19, 197, 232), the first doctors began practicing in the Western part of the province in 1878 and 1884, although there were *cirujanos* at the end of the eighteenth century. Even today, doctors are very unevenly distributed throughout the region.

43. These categories commonly appear in the death registers.

44. According to Tolivar Faes (1976), of the forty-two doctors in the *concejo* of Luarca, at least twenty-five of them stayed no more than three years in the town. Doctors in the *aldeas* must be even more transient, given their lack of amenities and isolation.

45. I refer here to only one aspect of these specialists, their economic position. Lisón (1974, 21–50) has studied these people, their anomalous position, and their ritual use. His analysis, esp. 25–31, is generally valid for the *entendidos* of the *braña*.

46. The *entendidas* of envy that I know of, a dozen or so, are all women.

47. By this the informant means that the father did not make a living from his ritual specialty; in other words, he belonged to a rich house.

48. I discuss the matter more fully in Cátedra 1976b.

CHAPTER 3: VIOLENT DEATH

1. Other authors have advanced figures similar to Soto Vázquez's first estimate. Feo Parrondo (1980), using the census and the lists of residents for 1970, arrives at the figure of 6,448 Vaqueiros. Given these figures, the suicide rates given by Soto Vázquez ought to be doubled.

2. These labels, of very dubious value, are typical of most official statistics. Jack D. Douglas (1973 [1967]) has shown the serious theoretical and methodological errors in their use.

3. There is a discrepancy between my total of these statistics, 160 suicides, and that of Soto Vázquez, 168.

4. It is very difficult to establish the date of a suicide, since some cases become atemporal models in the local perception.

5. My impression was corroborated by my reading of some of the judicial dossiers when doing my fieldwork.

6. It is very probable that this wasn't the only war-related suicide. Soto Vázquez remarks on seven suicides that took place in 1941, some of

which might have had similar motives. According to his information, "fear of legal persecution" accounted for a total of four Vaqueiro and *aldeano* suicides (Soto Vázquez 1965).

7. Very often a situation of leviration exists in which the dead man's brother cohabits with the widow without marrying her. As a widow, her son will not have to do military service.

8. In the first case, they were perplexed because single mothers are not stigmatized socially, especially if the woman comes from a poor house. In such a case, a child may mean a peaceful old age. In the region, the phrase "have a family" is used for the birth of a child in or out of wedlock, showing the greater importance accorded to maternity than to the legal status of the mother. It is not uncommon for the mother to marry after her child is born, and she may not necessarily marry the father of the child. Other expressions that refer in particular to the child of a single woman all stress a natural and ingenuous origin: "child of God," "child of the world," and "child of friendship."

The people were perplexed in the second case because the suicide was connected to a crime. Crime is uncommon in the *braña*, and passionate behavior is even less common. Sexual affairs, even between married persons, are gossiped about with relish in the *braña*, but they almost never have the dramatic consequences of this case.

Compared to the high number of suicides discussed in local conversations, the other form of violent death, murder, represents an insignificant proportion. Aside from a case that took place in Madrid (case 21), I heard of only two murders and one attempted murder in the area. I discuss murder in relation to suicide in Cátedra 1984.

9. I have written on this subject (Cátedra 1979, 57–77).

INTRODUCTION TO PART THREE

1. The meaning is somehow ambivalent because the dead ask for *un segundo entierro*. *Entierro* means both funeral and burial.

CHAPTER 5: THE SPIRITS

1. I have written a few pages on the matter (Cátedra 1987).

2. The people of the *aldeas* have similar notions about spirits, for example, about the "lights of M mountains," an ingrained belief with a different form but similar assumptions and content. Aldeanos tend to give "scientific" explanations for such mysteries.

CHAPTER 6: THE SAINTS; AND CONCLUSION

1. Perhaps, in part, because the Spanish word *cielo* means both heaven and sky, the Vaqueiros combine the two.

2. According to W. Christian (personal communication), Vaqueiros apparently do not distinguish clearly between Saint Anthony of Padua, whose feast date is June 13 and who is usually shown holding the child

Jesus, and Saint Anthony the Abbot, often called San Antón, whose feast date is in January and who is portrayed with a beard and accompanied by a piglet (the little dog). It is Anthony the Abbot who is known throughout Spain as the patron saint of farm animals; Anthony of Padua is considered a finder of lost objects. As is true of other herding communities in the north of Spain, most Vaqueiros have combined the two saints in one.

3. I have written on Saint Anthony and the Santa del Acebo in Cátedra 1979.

4. It appears they used it as a relic. I have taken this information from Colunga 1925.

5. At the beginning of this century, it was customary to have a "blessing of the cattle," especially for the Vaqueiros who came to the shrine with cattle. On the Sunday after September 8, the priest prayed with a hysop and blessed the cattle at the shrine, concluding the rite with these words, "May the Virgin protect the cattle and increase them." See Acevedo y Huelves 1915, 55.

6. This custom is described in verses still remembered today.

A la Virgin del Acebu,	To the Virgin of El Acebo
este ramu chi intrigamus	this bough we present here
pa que nos guarde las vacas	so she'll protect our cows
que nus crien bonus xatus.	and they'll raise us good calves.
En la braña de Acebal	In the *braña* of Acebal
aunque no se cueche un grano	even if nothing is harvested
a la Virgen del Acebo	for the Virgin of El Acebo
nunca le faltará un ramu.	a bough will never be lacking.

7. The name *domina* may be a corruption of the word *nomina,* supposedly powerful sacred inscriptions or scraps of writing repeatedly condemned in manuals of "superstitions and spells" like those of Pedro de Ciruelo (1530) and Martin de Castañega (1529). As late as 1966, *evangelios* sewn by nuns were being sold at the shrine of Las Caldas in Santander (Christian, personal communication).

8. The Vaqueiros are not the only visitors to the shrine, but the chaplain estimates that Vaqueiros comprise two-thirds of the visitors. In 1961, twelve hundred mules, the traditional Vaqueiro mode of transport, were counted. Now most Vaqueiros travel to the shrine by automobile. For an analysis of Asturian religious festivals, see Fernández and Fernández 1976.

9. The word *ánimas* normally would be translated as souls in Purgatory, but given the idiosyncratic beliefs of the Vaqueiros, I have thought it best to leave this word in Spanish and not prejudge precisely what the Vaqueiros mean by it.

10. Some of them are probably old devotions. Christian (1972b, chap. 2) shows how there are fads and fashions among the saints.

11. The Virgen del Camino is the patron saint of the region of León. Her shrine attracts many pilgrims from Asturias [Trans.]

12. The *ánima* of Sampol, according to an Asturian author (Cabal

1972, 491), was not only a medium but also a witch, due to an alleged accident at baptism. One finds other spiritists coming under the same suspicion.

13. In the past, cows occupied the same floor as humans in some houses. This still holds true for some of the dwellings in the transhumant *braña*.

14. I have written on these aspects in Cátedra 1981.

15. Lisón (1974) has written on the fear of wolves in nearby Galicia.

16. I refer to these categories *brava/noble* applied both to humans and cows in Cátedra 1981.

17. Kopytoff (1971), commenting on Fortes (1965), remarks that Africans evince a similar lack of elaboration and interest in the cosmography of the other world. The Nuer, following Evans-Pritchard 1956, also seem little interested in the matter.

18. Christian (1981a, 91) says: "The legend motif of the return of the image to the country site, rejecting the parish church may be an echo or a metaphor for what was in some sense a liberation of devotion from parish control—or, put another way, the resistance of local religion to the growing claims of the church. It may also have been an expression of the implicit tension between the intensely social life-style of these urban-type villagers and their agricultural and pastoral vocation. In this sense it was a statement of peasant or rural 'otherness.' Although Christian is writing about New Castile, his words apply quite well to the case of the Vaqueiros vis-à-vis the *aldeanos*.

19. This analysis of the transition of the dead to *Ánima* is in accord with the theory of Kopytoff 1971, who has demonstrated that the dichotomy living/dead has been reified excessively by anthropologists when it is more appropriate to consider it a continuum.

20. This identity is reinforced by the fact that the day of the remembrance of the dead (November 2) is celebrated in the area under study on November 1, the Feast of All Saints. The proximity of the two dates facilitates the similarity of the two devotions.

21. I follow here the classic work of Evans-Pritchard (1956).

22. Or better, "beyond movement," according to Fernández (1976, 149) whose phrase I cite.

23. The dual nature of God may help to explain why the devil is not an important figure for the Vaqueiros. Evil is represented in a unitary way in this kind of divine trickster, and diffusely in human beings (the idea of the witch) and the environment (accursed beings and things).

24. This is probably an ancient category, which helps to justify the rejection of Spaniards of other faiths, Jews and Muslims, in the sixteenth century and certain racist attitudes toward the Indians of the New World.

EPILOGUE

1. Danforth 1982 and Huntington and Metcalf 1979 follow the same model, although with more details and more sophistication.

2. I have been influenced by Christian on this particular theme.

3. See Christian 1972b or Douglass 1969. The best work on the role of centers of power in the diffusion of modes of comportment in Europe is Elias 1978. Elias has written a beautiful book on the loneliness of the dying (1985).

4. Another interesting line of research is Verdier 1979. On the history of death, see Aries 1977 and Vovelle 1974. On the history of ghosts, see Finucane 1984. A new perspective on violence, in this case in the Basque country, is Zulaika 1988. On pastoralists on the same region, see Ott 1981. On Asturias, Renate L. Fernandes 1990.

BIBLIOGRAPHY

Acevedo y Huelves, B.
  1893   *Los Vaqueiros de Alzada en Asturias.* Oviedo: Diputación Provincial.
  1915   *Los Vaqueiros de Alzada en Asturias.* 2d ed. Oviedo: Diputación Provincial.
Arensberg, C. M.
  1963   The old world peoples: The place of European cultures in world ethonography. *Anthropological Quarterly* 36: 75–99.
Aries, P.
  1977   *L'homme devant la mort.* Paris: Editions du Seuil.
Badone, E.
  1989   *The appointed hour: death, worldview, and social change in Brittany.* Berkeley: University of California Press.
Balandier, G.
  1957   *L'Afrique ambiguë.* Paris: Plon.
Balikci, A.
  1960   Suicidal behavior among the Netsilik Eskimos. Northern Coordination and Research Centre, Ottawa.
  1970   *The Netsilik Eskimo.* New York: Natural History Press.
Baragaño, R.
  1977   *Los Vaqueiros de Alzada.* Salinas, Asturias: Ayalga Ed.
Barandiarán, J. M.
  1972– *Obras completas.* 20 vols. Bilbao: Gran Enciclopedia Vasca.
  83
Bartel, B.
  1973   A multivariate analysis of European death ritual. *Ethnología Europea* 7:111–28.
Bateson, G.
  1958   *Naven.* Stanford, Calif.: Stanford University Press.
  1972   *Steps to an ecology of mind.* New York: Ballantine Books.
Bendann, E.
  1930   *Death customs.* London: Dowsons.
Benedict, R.
  1959   *Patterns of culture.* Boston: Sentry.
  (1934)
Bethencourt, A. J.
  1985   *Costumbres populares canarias de nacimiento, matrimonio y muerte.* Santa Cruz de Tenerife: Aula de Cultura de Tenerife.
Blauner, R.
  1977   Death and social structure. In *Passing,* ed. C. O. Jackson, 174–209. London: Greenwood.

Bloch, M., and J. Parry, eds.
1982   *Death and the regeneration of life.* Cambridge: Cambridge University Press.
Bohannan, P., ed.
1967   *African homicide and suicide.* New York: Atheneum.
Bowen, E. S. (pseud. Bohannan, L.)
1954   *Return to laughter.* New York: Harper & Row.
Breed, W.
1963   Occupational mobility and suicide among white males. *American Sociological Review* 28:179–88.
Burns, R. K.
1963   The circum-Alpine culture area: A preliminary view. *Anthropological Quarterly* 36:131–55.
Cabal, C.
1972   *La mitología Asturiana.* Oviedo: Instituto de Estudios Asturianos.
Caro Baroja, J.
1946   *Los pueblos de España. Ensayo de etnología.* Barcelona: Barna.
1973   *Los pueblos del norte de la península ibérica.* 2d ed. San Sebastián: Txertoa.
Cátedra, M.
1971   *Estudio antropológico social de una comunidad. Los Vaqueiros de Alzada, Asturias.* Tesis de Licenciatura, Facultad de Filosofía y Letras, Universidad Complutense de Madrid. Unpublished.
1972a *Estudio antropológico social de los Vaqueiros de Alzada del occidente de Asturias (España).* Tesis Doctoral, Facultad de Filosofía y Letras, Universidad Complutense de Madrid. Unpublished.
1972b Notas sobre un pueblo marginado: Los Vaqueiros de Alzada (ecología de braña y aldea). *Revista de Estudios Sociales* 6:139–64.
1976a Notas sobre la envidia: Los ojos malos entre los Vaqueiros de Alzada. In *Temas de antropologia española.* ed. M. Cátedra et al. 9–48. Madrid: Akal.
1976b Que es ser Vaqueiro de Alzada. *Expresiones actuales de la cultura del pueblo,* 155–82. Vol. XLI Anales de Moral Social y Económica, Madrid: Centro de Estudios Sociales del Valle de los Caídos.
1977   Transhumancia: Las dos vidas del Vaqueiro de Alzada. *Revista de Estudios Sociales* 19:119–36.
1978a El segundo entierro. Vivos y muertos en las brañas vaqueiras. *Historia 16,* 3:41–48.
1978b Notes on the history of Spanish Anthropology. *History of Anthropology Newsletter* 5, no. 1: 10–15.
1979   Vacas y vaqueiros. Modos de vida y cultura en las brañas asturianas. In *Vaqueiros y pescadores. Dos modos de vida,* M. Cátedra and R. Sanmartin, 9–93. Madrid: Akal.

1981　Las vacas son también buenas para pensar. *Revista de Estudios Agro-Sociales* 116:221–54.

1984　*Death as a cultural process. The Vaqueiros de Alzada (Spain).* Ann Arbor, Mich.: University Microfilms International.

1986a　Bendito y maldito: categorías de clasificación en el universo vaqueiro. *Los Cuadernos del Norte* (Oviedo) 7, no.35: 70–85.

1986b　Mito e historia de los vaqueiros de alzada. *Analisis e investigaciones culturales* 26:11–28.

1986c　El cuerpo es un sistema. *Jano* 30, no. 717: 8–24.

1987　Entre bêtes et saints. Esprits des vivants et esprits des morts chez les vaqueiros de alzada. *Études Rurales* 105/106: 65–78

1988　*La muerte y otros mundos.* Madrid and Gijón: Jucar Universidad.

1989a　*La vida y el mundo del vaqueiro de alzada* Madrid: CIS-Siglo XXI.

1989b　"La gracia y la desgracia" in *Homenaje andaluz a Julian Pitt-Rivers*, special issue of *El folklore andaluz* 3, ser. 2, 69–78. Sevilla: Fundación Machado.

1990a　Especialistas de la curación: La integración tradicional de la modernidad. In *Actas do II Coloquio de Antropoloxía* 49–70. Santiago de Compostela: Museo do Pobo Galego.

1990b　"Algo fuera de su sitio': El origen de las enfermedades entre los vaqueiros de alzada. In *Los espacios rurales cantábricos y su evolución,* comp. Garcia Merino et al., 58–68. Cantabria:Servicio de Publicaciones, Asamblea Regional de Cantabria, Universidad de Cantabria.

1991a　Técnicas cualitativas en antropología urbana. In *Malestar cultural y conflicto en la sociedad madrileña,* 81–99. Comunidad de Madrid,Serie Documentos 2. Imprenta de la Comunidad de Madrid.

1991b　*Los españoles vistos por los antropólogos.* M. Cátedra (Ed.) Madrid and Gijón: Jucar Universidad. (Introducción. Los españoles y los antropólogos. In *Los españoles vistos por los antropólogos,* 9–23. Desde una fresca distancia. ¿Porqué no estudiamos a los norteamericanos? In *Los españoles vistos por los antropólogos,* 231–70.)

Chagnon, N.
1968　*Yanomamo: The fierce people.* New York: Holt, Rinehart and Winston.

1974　*Studying the Yanomamo.* New York: Holt, Rinehart and Winston.

Christian, W. A., Jr.
1972a　*Trovas y comparsas del Alto Nansa.* Publicaciones del Instituto de Etnografía y Folklore Hoyos Sainz. Santander: Instituto Cultural de Cantabria.

1972b　*Person and God in a Spanish valley.* New York: Academic Press.

1976   De los santos a María: Panorama de las devociones a santuarios
españoles desde el principio de la edad media hasta nuestros
dias. In *Temas de antropología española,* ed. M. Cátedra et al.,
49–105. Madrid: Akal.

1981a   *Local religion in sixteenth-century Spain.* Princeton, N.J.:
Princeton University Press.

1981b   *Apparitions in late medieval and renaissance Spain.* Princeton, N.J.: Princeton University Press.

Clifford, J., and G. E. Marcus, eds.

1986   *Writing culture: The poetics and politics of ethnography.*
Berkeley: University of California Press.

Colunga, A.

1925   *Historia del santuario de Ntra. Sra. del Acebo,* 2d ed. Sala-
manca: n.p.

Crapanzano, V.

1980   *Tuhami: Portrait of a Moroccan.* Chicago: University of Chicago Press.

Danforth, L. M.

1982   *The death rituals of rural Greece.* Princeton, N.J.: Princeton
University Press.

Davis, N. Z.

1983   *The return of Martin Guerre.* Cambridge, Mass.: Harvard University Press.

Devereux, G.

1931   *Mohave ethnopsychiatry and suicide.* Washington, D.C.: U.S.
Government Printing Office.

Douglas, J. D.

1973   *The social meanings of suicide.* Princeton, N.J.: Princeton Uni-
(1967)   versity Press.

Douglas, M.

1970   *Purity and danger.* London: Penguin.
(1966)

1970   *Natural symbols.* New York: Pantheon.

Douglass, W. A.

1969   *Death in Murelaga. Funerary ritual in a Spanish Basque village.* Seattle: University of Washington Press.

Durkheim, E.

1951   *Suicide: A study in sociology.* Glencoe, Ill.: Free Press.
(1987)

Dwyer, K.

1982   *Moroccan dialogues.* Baltimore: Johns Hopkins University
Press.

Elias, N.

1978   *The civilizing process.* New York: Urizen.

1985   *The loneliness of the dying.* Oxford: Blackwell.

Estruch, J., & S. Cardús.

1981   *Plegar de viure; un estudi sobre els suicides.* Barcelona: Editions 62.

Evans-Pritchard, E. E.
  1937 *Witchcraft, oracles and magic among the Azande.* Oxford:
        Clarendon Press.
  1956 *Nuer Religion.* Oxford and London: Oxford University Press.
Fabian, J.
  1973 How others die. Reflections on the anthropology of death. In
        Death in American Experience, ed. A. Mack, 171–201. New
        York: Schocken.
Favret-Saada, J.
  1980 *Deadly words: Witchcraft in the Bocage.* London: Cambridge
        University Press.
Feo Parrondo, F.
  1980 Los Vaqueiros de Alzada en el occidente asturiano. *Estudios
        Geográficos* 160:303–19.
Fernández, J. W.
  1965 Symbolic consensus in a Fang reformative cult. *American An-
        thropologist* 67:902–29.
  1976 La poesía en moción: siendo desplazado por diversiones, por
        burlas y por la muerte en el país asturiano. In M. Cátedra et al.,
        Temas de antropología española. ed. C. Lisón, 131–57. Madrid:
        Akal.
  1982 *Bwiti: An ethnography of the religious imagination in Africa.*
        Princeton, N.J.: Princeton University Press.
  1986 *Persuasions and performances: The play of tropes in culture.*
        Bloomington: Indiana University Press.
Fernández, J. W., and Fernández, R. L.
  1976 El escenario de la romería asturiana. *Expresiones Actuales de
        la Cultura del Pueblo,* 231–61. Vol. XLI Análes de Moral So-
        cial y Económica. Madrid: Centro de Estudios Sociales del
        Valle de los Caídos.
Fernández, R. L.
  1990 *A Simple Matter of Salt.* Berkeley: University of California
        Press.
Fernández García, M.
  1954 Notas folklóricas del cuarto de los valles. *Boletin del IDEA*
        8:23.
Finucane, R. C.
  1984 *Appearances of the dead. A cultural history of ghosts.* Buffalo,
        N.Y.: Prometheus Books.
Fortes, M.
  1965 Some reflections on ancestor worship. In *African systems of
        thought,* ed. Fortes and G. Dieterlen. London: Oxford Univer-
        sity Press.
Foster, G. M.
  1972 "The anatomy of envy: A study in symbolic behavior." *Current
        Anthropology* 13:165–202.
Frazer, J. G.
  1913– *The fear of death in primitive people.* London: Macmillan.

1924
Freud, S.
1959a Mourning and melancholia. *Collected papers,* 4:152–70. New
(1917) York: Basic Books.
1959b The psychogenesis of a case of homosexuality in a woman.
(1917) *Collected papers,* 2:203–31. New York: Basic Books.
Fried, M. H.
1959 *Readings in anthropology.* New York: Thomas Y. Crowell.
Geertz, C.
1960 *The religion of Java.* Glencoe, Ill.: Free Press.
1973 *The interpretation of cultures.* New York: Basic Books.
1984 *Works and lives. The anthropologist as Author.* Stanford,
Calif.: Stanford University Press.
Gilmore, D.
1987 *Aggression and community: paradoxes of Andalusian culture.*
New Haven, Conn.: Yale University Press.
Ginzburg, C.
1966 *I Benandanti.* Torino: Einaudi.
1980 *The cheese and the worms: The cosmos of a sixteenth-century
miller.* Trans. J. and A. Tedeschi. Baltimore: John Hopkins University Press.
1989 *Storia notturna; una decifrazione del sabba* Torino: Einandi.
Gluckman, M.
1937 Mortuary customs and the belief in survival after death among
the south-eastern Bantu. *Bantu Studies* 11:117–36.
Gondar Portasany, M.
1989 *Romeiros do Alén. Antropoloxía da morte en Galicia.* Vigo:
Edicións Xerais.
1991 *Mulleres de mortos.* Vigo: Edicións Xerais.
Gonzalez Hernández, M.
1990 *La muerte en Canarias en el siglo XVIII.* La Laguna: Centro de
Cultura Popular.
Goodenough, W.
1970 *Description and comparison in cultural anthropology.* Chicago: Aldine.
1975 A terminal illness in truck. Working paper, University of Pennsylvania.
Goody, J.
1962 *Death, property and the ancestors: A study of mortuary customs of the LoDagaa of West Africa.* Stanford, Calif.: Stanford
University Press.
Gorer, G.
1965 *Death, grief, and mourning in contemporary Britain.* London:
Cresset Press.
Gough, E. K.
1958 Cult of the dead among the Nayars. *Journal of American Folklore* 71: 446–78.

Halbwachs, M.
   1930   *Les causes du suicide.* Paris: Alcan.
Hendin, H.
   1964   *Suicide and Scandinavia: A psychoanalytic study of culture and character.* New York: Grune.
Hertz, R.
   1960   *Death and the right hand.* Glencoe, Ill.: Free Press. (1907–9)
Honigmann, J. J.
   1964   Survival of a cultural focus. In *Explorations in Cultural Anthropology,* ed. W. H. Goodenough, 277–92. New York: McGraw-Hill.
S. C. Humphreys and H. King
   1981   *Mortality and immortality: The anthropology and archaeology of death.* London: Academic Press.
Huntington, R., & P. Metcalf.
   1979   *Celebrations of death.* Cambridge: Cambridge University Press.
Iga, M.
   1961   Cultural factors in suicide of Japanese youth with focus on personality. *Sociology and Social Research* 46:75–90.
Instituto Nacional de Estadística
   1960   *Reseña estadística de la provincia de Oviedo.* Madrid.
   1973   *Nomenclator de las ciudades, villas, lugares, aldeas, y demás entidades de población: Provincia de Oviedo.* Madrid: Censo de la Población de España de 1970.
Jackson, D. D.
   1957   Theories of suicide. In *Clues to suicides,* ed. E. S. Shneidman and L. Farberow, 11–21. New York: McGraw-Hill.
Kalish, R. A.
   1965   Death and bereavement: A bibliography. *Journal of Human Relations* 13:118–41.
Kaplan, A.
   1984   Philosophy of science in anthropology. *Annual Review of Anthropology* 13:31–38.
Kenny, M.
   1963   The Atlantic fringe. *Anthropological Quarterly* 36:100–130.
Klaniczay, G.
   1990   *The uses of supernatural power: The transformation of popular religion in medieval and early modern Europe.* Princeton, N.J.: Princeton University Press.
Kopytoff, I.
   1971   Ancestors as elders in Africa. *Africa,* 41:129–42.
La Fontaine, J.
   1975   Anthropology. In *A handbook for the study of suicide.* ed. S. Perlin, 77–91. New York and London: Oxford University Press.
Leach, E.
   1969   Virgin birth. *Genesis as myth.* London: Grossman.

1979   *Cultura y comunicación.* Madrid: Siglo XXI.
Le Goff, J.
1981   *La Naissance du purgatoire.* Paris: Gallimard.
Le Roy Ladurie, E.
1978   *Montaillou: The promised land of error.* Trans. B. Bray. New York: George Braziller.
Lester, D.
1974   A cross-national study of suicide and homicide. *Behavior Science Research* 4:303–18.
Levi-Strauss, C.
1963   *Totemism.* Trans. R. Needham. Boston: Beacon Press.
1966   *The savage mind.* Chicago: University of Chicago Press.
1974   *Tristes tropiques.* Trans. J. and D. Weightman. New York: Ath-
(1955) eneum.
Lienhardt, G.
1961   *Divinity and experience. The religion of the Dinka.* Oxford: Clarendon Press.
1962   The situation of death: An aspect of Anuak philosophy. *Anthropological Quarterly* 35:74–85.
Lifton, R. J. and E. Olson
1974   *Living and dying.* New York: Praeger.
Lisón, C.
1966   *Belmonte de los caballeros.* Oxford: Oxford University Press.
1971a   *Antropología social de España.* Madrid: Siglo XXI.
1971b   *Antropología cultural de Galicia.* Madrid: Siglo XXI.
1973   *Ensayos de antropología social.* Madrid: Ayuso.
1974   *Perfiles simbólico-morales de la cultura gallega.* Madrid: Akal.
1979   *Brujería, estructura social y simbolísmo en Galicia.* Madrid: Akal.
1990   *Endemoniados en Galicia hoy.* Madrid: Akal.
Luque, E.
1976   La crisis de las expresiones populares en el culto religioso: Examen de un caso andaluz. *Expresiones actuales de la cultura del pueblo,* 87–113. Vol. XLI Análes de Moral Social y Económica. Madrid: Centro de Estudios Sociales del Valle de los Caidos.
MacFarlane, A.
1978   *The origins of English individualism.* Oxford: Basil Blackwell.
Madoz, P.
1847   *Diccionario geográfico-estadístico-histórico de España y sus posesiones de ultramar.* 16 vols. Madrid.
Malinowski, B.
1954   *Magic, science and religion.* New York: Doubleday.
(1925)
Maloney, C., ed.
1976   *The evil eye.* New York: Columbia University Press.

Marcus, G., and D. Cushman
  1982   Ethnographies as texts. *Annual Review of Anthropology*
         11:25–69.
Marcus, G., and M. Fisher
  1986   *Anthropology as a cultural critique.* Chicago: University of
         Chicago Press.
Mauss, M.
  1936   Les techniques du corps. *Journal de la Psychologie* 32.
Maybury-Lewis, D.
  1965   *The Savage and the innocent.* Cleveland: World Publishing Co.
Mead, M.
  1939   *From the South Seas: Studies of adolescence and sex in primi-
         tive societies.* New York: William Morrow & Co.
Mandelbaum, D. G.
  1965   Social uses of funeral rites. In *The meaning of death,* ed. H.
         Feifel, 189–217. New York: McGraw-Hill.
Mitford, J.
  1963   *The American way of death.* New York: Fawcett.
Nagy, M.
  1948   The child's theories concerning death. *Journal of Genetic Psy-
         chology* 73:3–27.
Niccoli, O.
  1990   *Prophecy and people in Renaissance Italy.* Trans. L. G. Coch-
         rane. Princeton, N.J.: Princeton University Press.
Ott, S.
  1981   *The circle of mountains: A Basque sheepherding community.*
         Oxford: Oxford University Press.
Palgi, P. and H. Abramovitch
  1984   Death: A cross-cultural perspective. *Annual Review of Anthro-
         pology* 13:385–417.
Parsons, T.
  1963   Death in American society: A brief working paper. *American
         Behavioral Scientist* 6:61–65.
Pina-Cabral, J.
  1986   *Sons of Adam, daughters of Eve.* Oxford: Clarendom Press.
Pitt-Rivers, J.
  1989   Postscript to honor and grace: The place of grace in anthropol-
         ogy. Unpublished ms.
Rabinow, P.
  1977   *Reflections on field work in Morocco.* Berkeley: University of
         California Press.
Radcliffe-Brown, A. R.
  1948   *The Andaman islanders.* Glencoe, Ill.: Free Press.
Radin, P.
  1972   *The trickster.* New York: Schocken.
  (1956)
Reina, R.
  1966   *The law of the saints.* Indianapolis: Bobbs Merrill.

Riley, J. W.
   1968   Death and bereavement. *International Encyclopedia of the Social Sciences* 4:19–26.
Robins, E. et al.
   1959   The communication of suicidal intent: A study of 134 consecutive cases of successful suicide. *American Journal of Psychiatry* 115:724–73.
Rosaldo, R.
   1980   *Ilongot headhunting 1883–1974: A study in society and history.* Stanford, Calif.: Stanford University Press.
   1989   *Culture and truth: The remaking of social analysis.* Boston: Beacon Press.
Rosenblatt, P. C., R. Walsh, and A. Jackson.
   1976   *Grief and mourning in cross-cultural perspective.* New Haven, Conn.: Human Relation Area Field Press.
Sabean, D. W.
   1984   *Power in the blood, popular culture and village discourse in early modern Germany.* Cambridge: Cambridge University Press.
Schmitt, J. C.
   1976   "Suicide in middle ages." *Annales ESC* 31, no. 1: 3–28.
   1982   Les reverants dans lá société féodale. *Le Temps de la Reflexión* 3:285–306.
   1983   *The holy greyhound: Grunefort, healer of children since the thirteenth century.* Cambridge: Cambridge University Press.
Schiefflin, E. L.
   1976   *The sorrow of the lonely and the burning of the dancers.* New York: St. Martin's Press.
Seremetakis, C. N.
   1991   *The last word: Women, death, and divination in* Inner Mani. Chicago: University of Chicago Press.
Shneidman, E. S. and N. L. Farberow
   1960   A socio-psychological investigation of suicide. In *Perspectives in Personality Research*, ed. H. P. David and J. C. Brengelmann. New York: Springer.
Smith, A. D.
   1973   *The concept of social change.* London: Routledge & Kegan.
Soto Vázquez, R.
   1965   El suicidio entre los Vaqueiros de Alzada asturianos. *Boletín del IDEA*, 54–55: 167–82 and 69–88.
Spencer, H.
   1896   *The principles of sociology.* New York: Appleton.
Spooner, B.
   1976   Anthropology and the evil eye. In *The evil eye*, ed. C. Maloney, 279–85. New York: Columbia University Press.
Stannard, D. E. (ed.)
   1975   *Death in America.* Philadelphia: University of Pennsylvania Press.

Sudnow, D.
   1967   *Passing on: The social organization of dying.* Englewood Cliffs,
          N.J.: Prentice-Hall
Tax Freeman, S.
   1979   *The Pasiegos: Spaniards in no man's land.* Chicago: University
          of Chicago Press.
Taylor, L. (ed.)
   1989   The uses of death in Europe. *Anthropological Quarterly* 62,
          no. 4.
Tolivar Faes, J.
   1976   *Historia de la medicina en Asturias.* Salinas, Asturias: Ayalga.
          Ed.
Tylor, E. B.
   1920   *Primitive culture.* New York: Putmans.
   (1871)
Uría Riu, J.
   1976   *Los Vaqueiros de Alzada y otros estudios (De caza y etnogra-*
          fía). Oviedo: Biblioteca Popular Asturiana.
Valdés del Toro, R.
   1976   Ecología y trabajo, fiestas y dieta en un concejo del occidente
          astur. In M. Cátedra et al., *Temas de antropología española,* ed.
          C. Lisón. Madrid: Akal.
Van Gennep, A.
   1960   *The rites of passage.* London: Routledge and Kegan Paul.
   (1909)
Verdier, Y.
   1979   *Façons de dire, façons de faire: La laveuse, la couturiere, la*
          cuisiniere. Paris: Gallimard.
Vovelle, M.
   1974   *Mourir autrefois.* Paris: Gallimard.
Warner, W. L.
   1959   *The living and the dead: A study of the symbolic life of the*
          Americans. New Haven, Conn.: Yale University Press.
Waugh, E.
   1948   *The loved one.* Boston: Little, Brown.
Wilson, G.
   1939   Nyakyusa conventions of burial. *Bantu Studies* 13:1–31.
Wilson, M.
   1954   Nyakyusa ritual and symbolism. *American Anthropologist*
          56:228–41.
   1957   *Rituals of kinship among the Nyakyusa.* Oxford: Oxford Uni-
          versity Press.
Zilboorg, G.
   1936   Suicide among civilized and primitive races. *American Journal*
          of Psychiatry 92:1347–69.
Zulaika, J.
   1988   *Basque violence: Metaphor and sacrament.* Reno and Las Ve-
          gas: University of Nevada Press.

INDEX

Goiter: blessing for, 48
Gold: blessing, 49
Good death, 350; kinds of death, 193; lack of suffering, 119, 125. *See also* Happy death
Good place, 333; soul's destination, 287–91
Goody, J.: death study in African cultures, 4
Gorer, G.: death study among British, 4
Gracia: end of life, 196, 350–51; loss by elderly, 138–41
Grave: burial customs, 225–35; Day of the Dead, 303–4
Grave digger: postburial food, 224–25

Halbwachs, Maurice: cultural aspects of suicide, 2
"Hand, the" *("la mano"):* healing power, 104–15, 315–16
Hanging: suicide method, 157, 166–72, 191
Happy death *(muerte feliz),* 119; lack of awareness, 152
Harmful animal, 39
Healing: specialists, 82–116
Health care: specialists, 82–116
Heart: illness associated with, 59, 65
Heaven *(cielo):* soul, 288–91
Hell, 333; soul, 289–91
Herbs: blessed plants, 47–48
Heredeiro: inheritance, 130–32
Herni (herniadura): illness, 56
Hertz, R.: death study, 347–48
Holly. *See* Acebo
Holy water: the blessed, 32–33
Horse, 327; premonition of death, 268
Hospitals: Vaqueiros as patients, 89
House *(casa):* cultural definition, 15; death, 348–50; dying at home, 128; inheritance, 187–89; suicide motives,

172–82; transmission after death, 194–96
House, the (tomb): See *Casa, la*
Huesera (ossuary): burial customs, 226

Icema (eczema): illness, 63
Idelfonso, Saint: prayers for, 47
Illness: animals, 31–67; body as system, 56–67; cosmic disruption, 56; environment, 31–67; envy, 67–82; specialists, 82–113; suicide motive, 170–72
Incense: the blessed, 32–33
Inheritance (genetics): suicide cause, 187–89, 201
Inheritance (law): death, 15–16, 348; natural death, 128–38; peace in old age, 194–96; suicide, 174–81

Jesus: mules as the accursed, 32; swallow as the blessed, 40; wounds, 47–48
John, Saint: blessed days, 48–51; night of, 361n.17
Justicia, la: See Law, the

Lacón: offering to *Ánimas,* 301; offering to Saint Anthony, 293–94
La Espina (parish, Spain): discrimination against Vaqueiros, 10
Language: local voice, 27
Las Tabiernas *(braña):* study of, 19
Last rites. *See* Extreme Unction
Law, the *(la justicia):* suicide inquiries, 167–68; suicide motives, 198
Legitima: inheritance, 16, 358n.21
Le Roy, Ladurie E.: transhumance study, 353–54
Lice: illness, 74